$\mathfrak{Seraph}$ of the $\mathfrak{End}$

—VAMPIRE REIGN—

1

STORY BY **Takaya Kagami**
ART BY **Yamato Yamamoto**
STORYBOARDS BY **Daisuke Furuya**

Seraph of the End
VAMPIRE REIGN

1

CONTENTS

CHAPTER 1
The World of Blood Legacy 003

CHAPTER 2
Humanity After the Fall 079

CHAPTER 3
The Demon in Your Heart 147

CHAPTER 1 The World of Blood Legacy

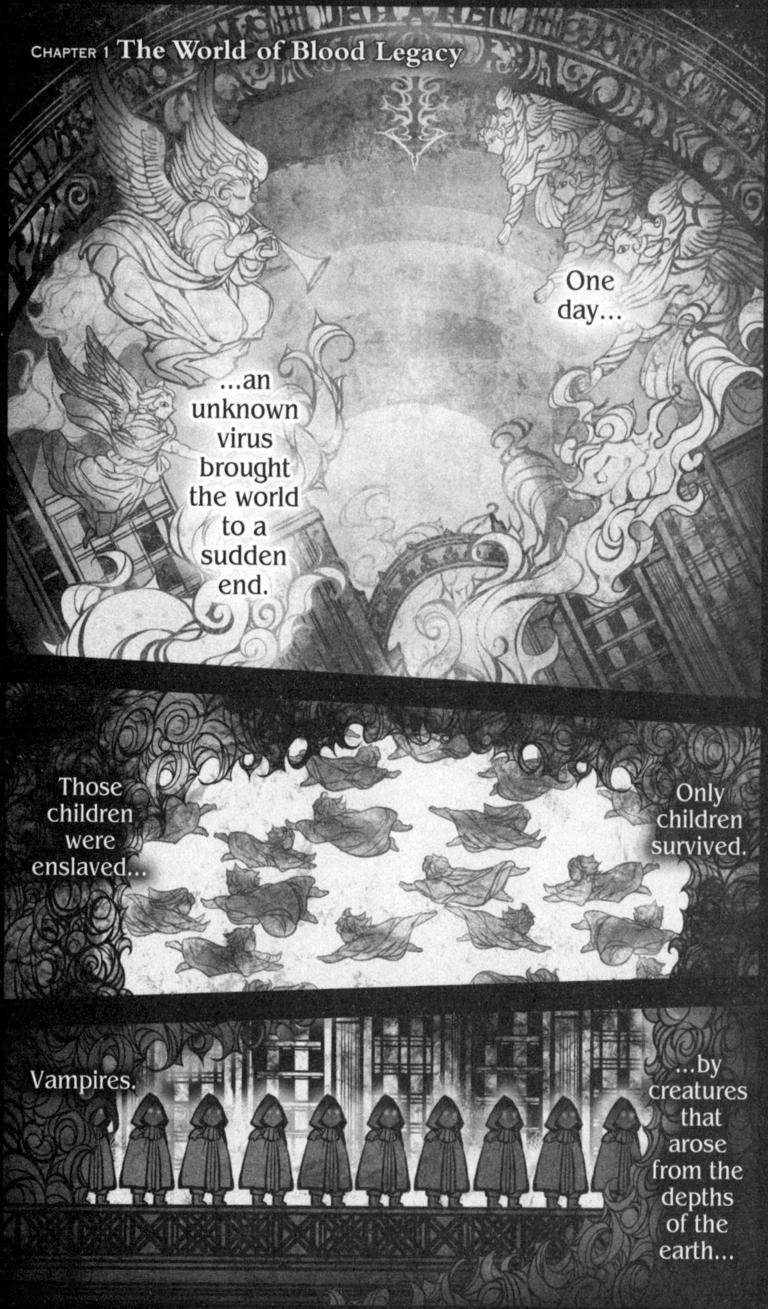
One day...
...an unknown virus brought the world to a sudden end.
Only children survived.
Those children were enslaved...
...by creatures that arose from the depths of the earth...
Vampires.

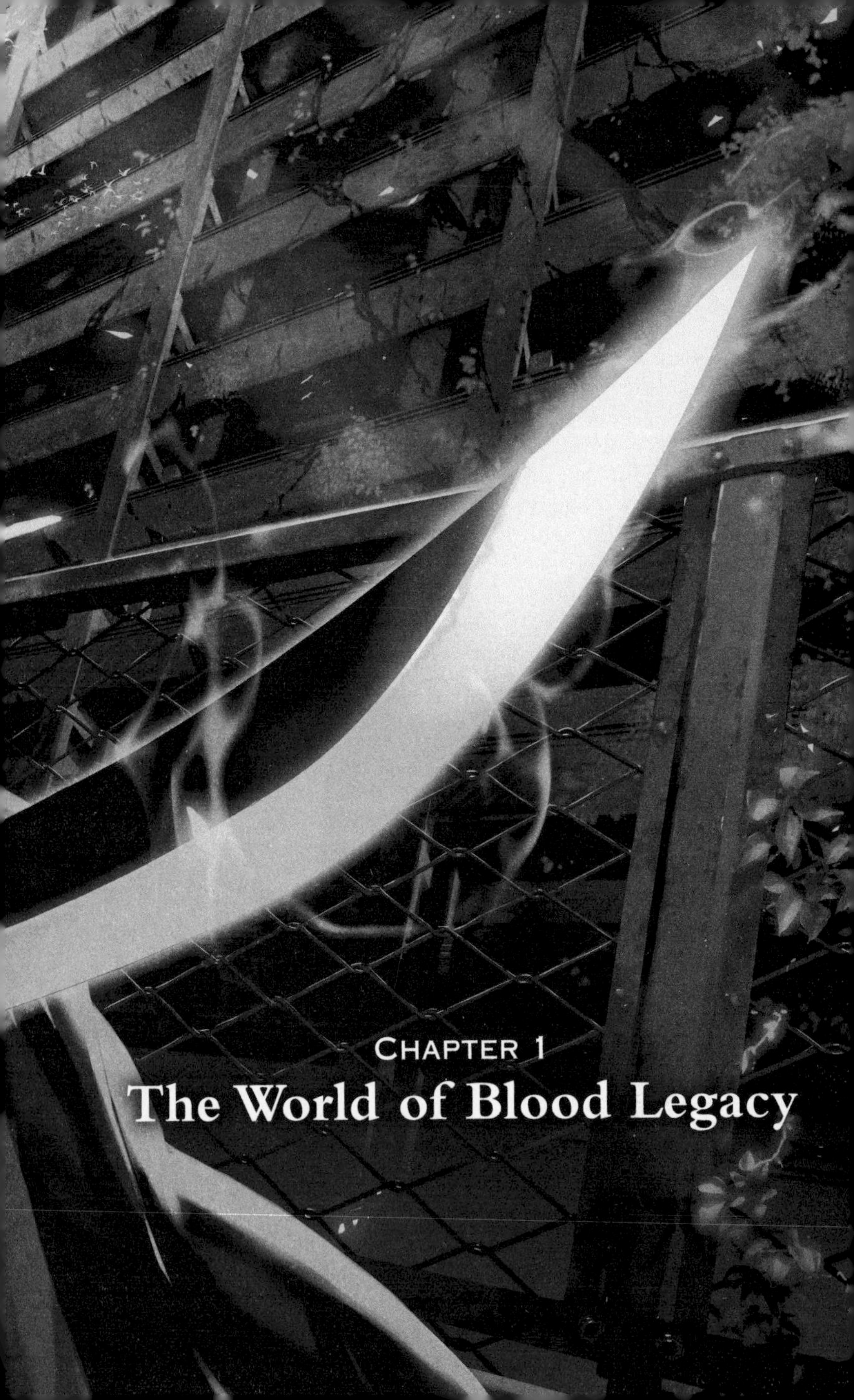

Chapter 1

The World of Blood Legacy

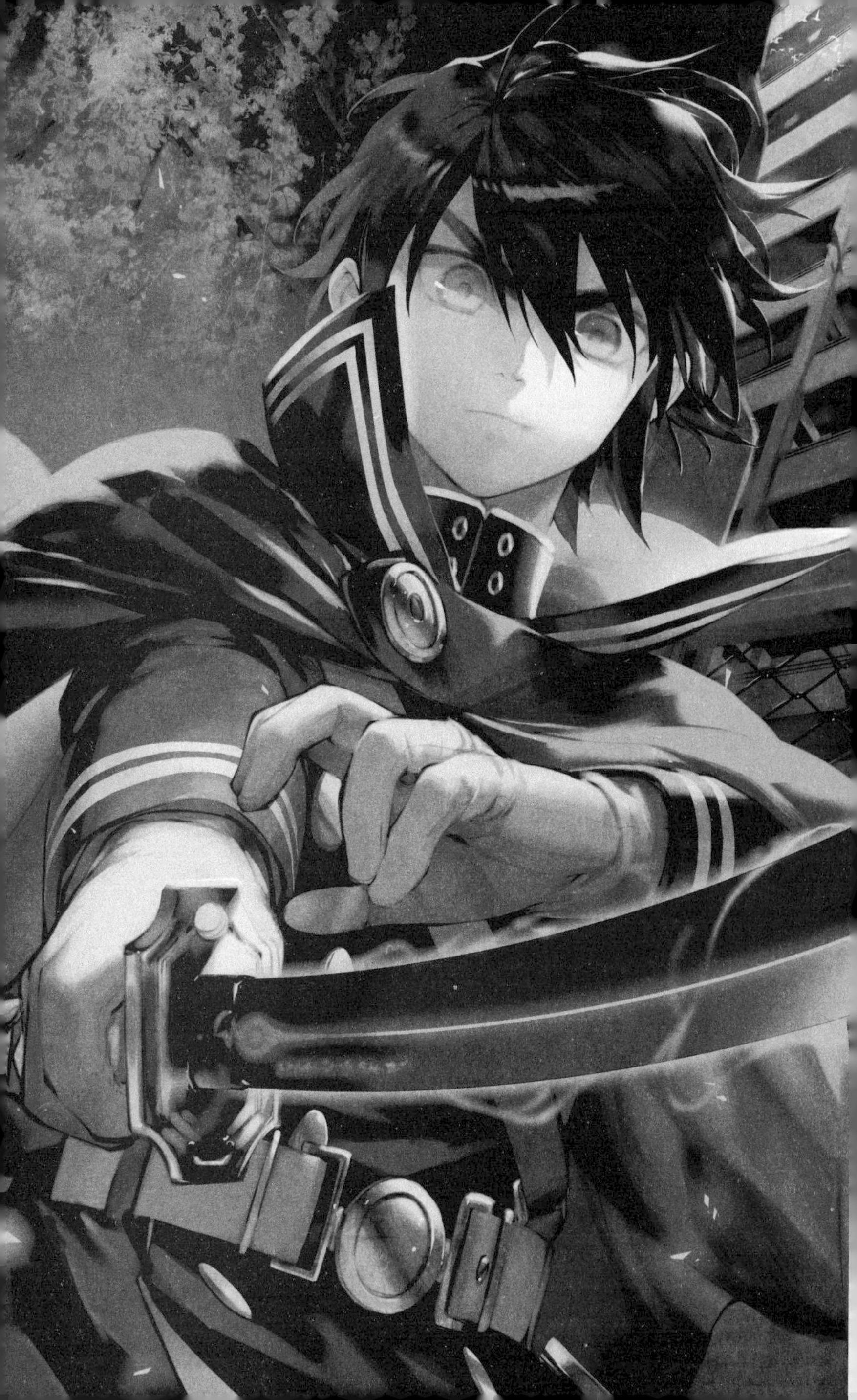

Seraph of the End
VAMPIRE REIGN

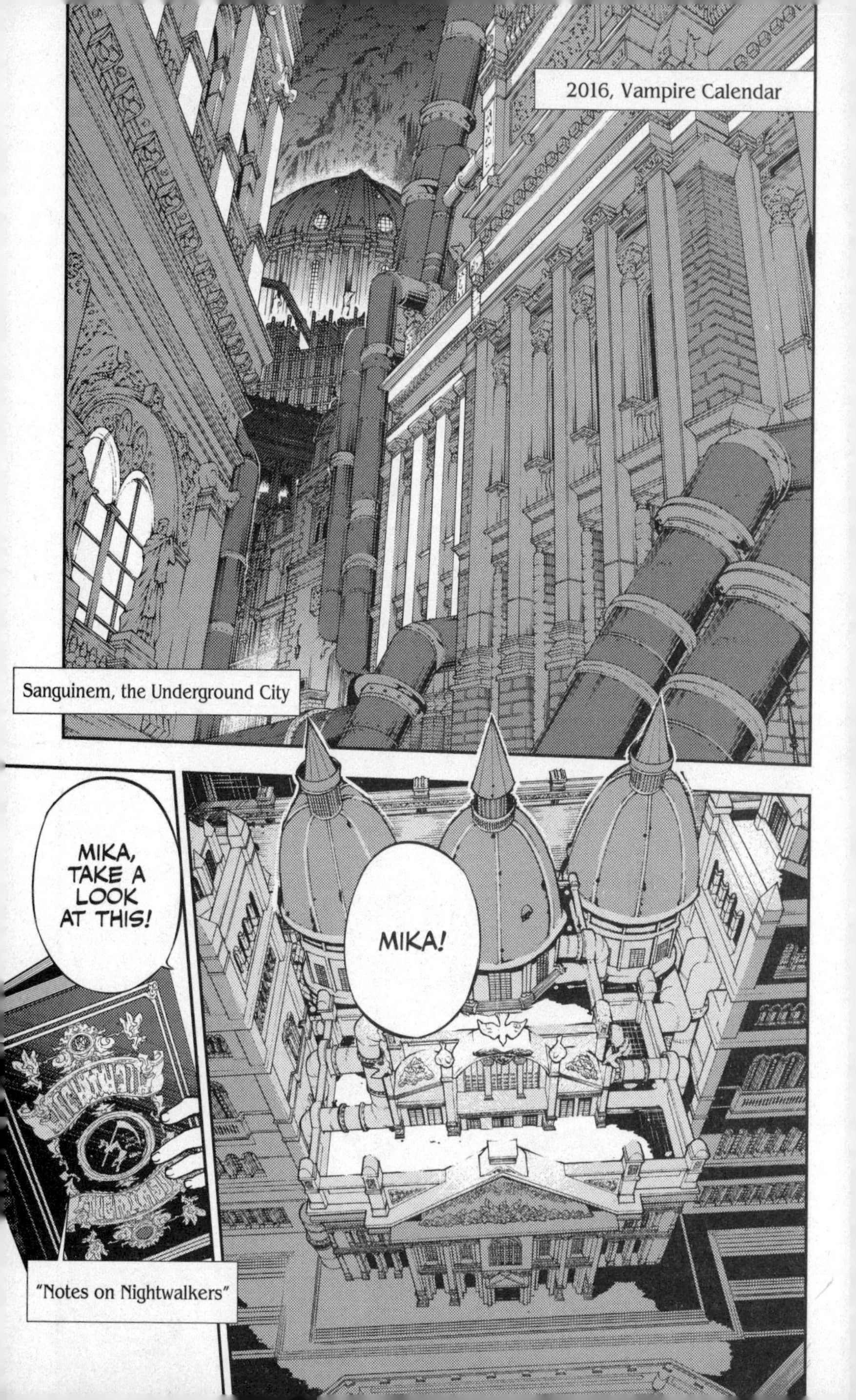
2016, Vampire Calendar
Sanguinem, the Underground City
MIKA!
MIKA, TAKE A LOOK AT THIS!
"Notes on Nightwalkers"

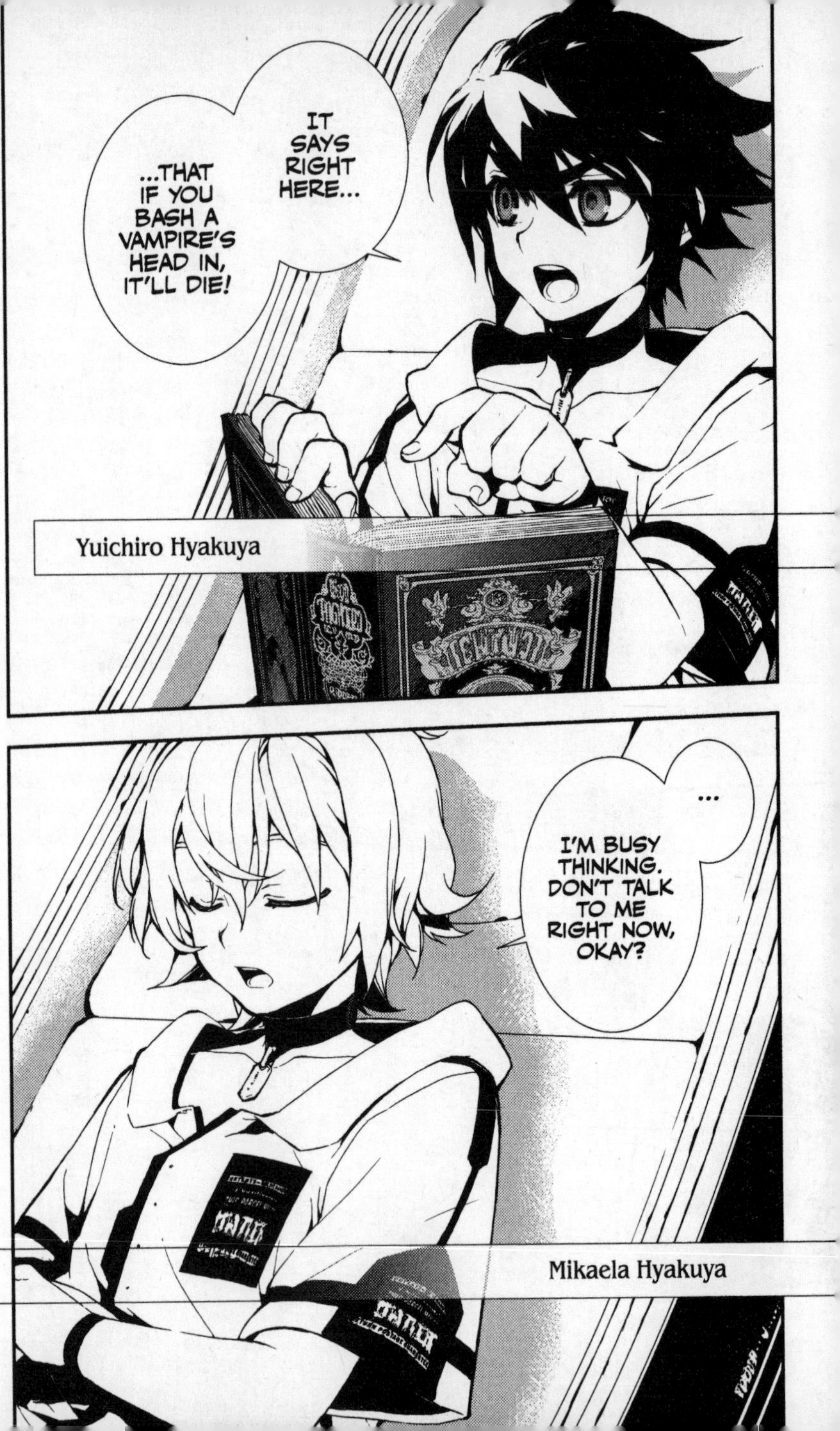
IT SAYS RIGHT HERE...
...THAT IF YOU BASH A VAMPIRE'S HEAD IN, IT'LL DIE!
Yuichiro Hyakuya
...
I'M BUSY THINKING. DON'T TALK TO ME RIGHT NOW, OKAY?
Mikaela Hyakuya

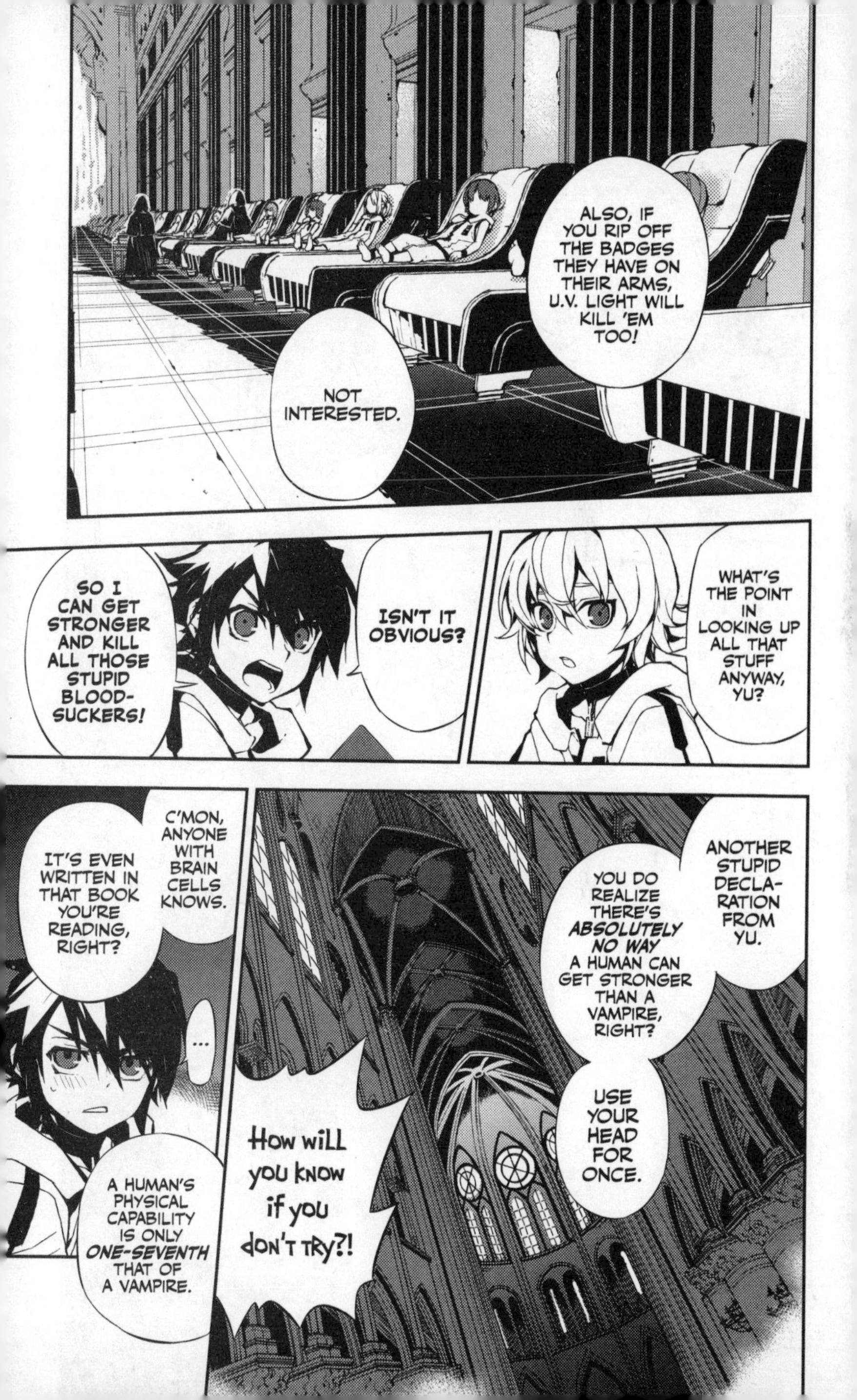
ALSO, IF YOU RIP OFF THE BADGES THEY HAVE ON THEIR ARMS, U.V. LIGHT WILL KILL 'EM TOO!
NOT INTERESTED.
WHAT'S THE POINT IN LOOKING UP ALL THAT STUFF ANYWAY, YU?
ISN'T IT OBVIOUS?
SO I CAN GET STRONGER AND KILL ALL THOSE STUPID BLOOD-SUCKERS!
ANOTHER STUPID DECLA-RATION FROM YU.
YOU DO REALIZE THERE'S *ABSOLUTELY NO WAY* A HUMAN CAN GET STRONGER THAN A VAMPIRE, RIGHT?
USE YOUR HEAD FOR ONCE.
How will you know if you don't try?!
C'MON, ANYONE WITH BRAIN CELLS KNOWS.
IT'S EVEN WRITTEN IN THAT BOOK YOU'RE READING, RIGHT?
...
A HUMAN'S PHYSICAL CAPABILITY IS ONLY *ONE-SEVENTH* THAT OF A VAMPIRE.

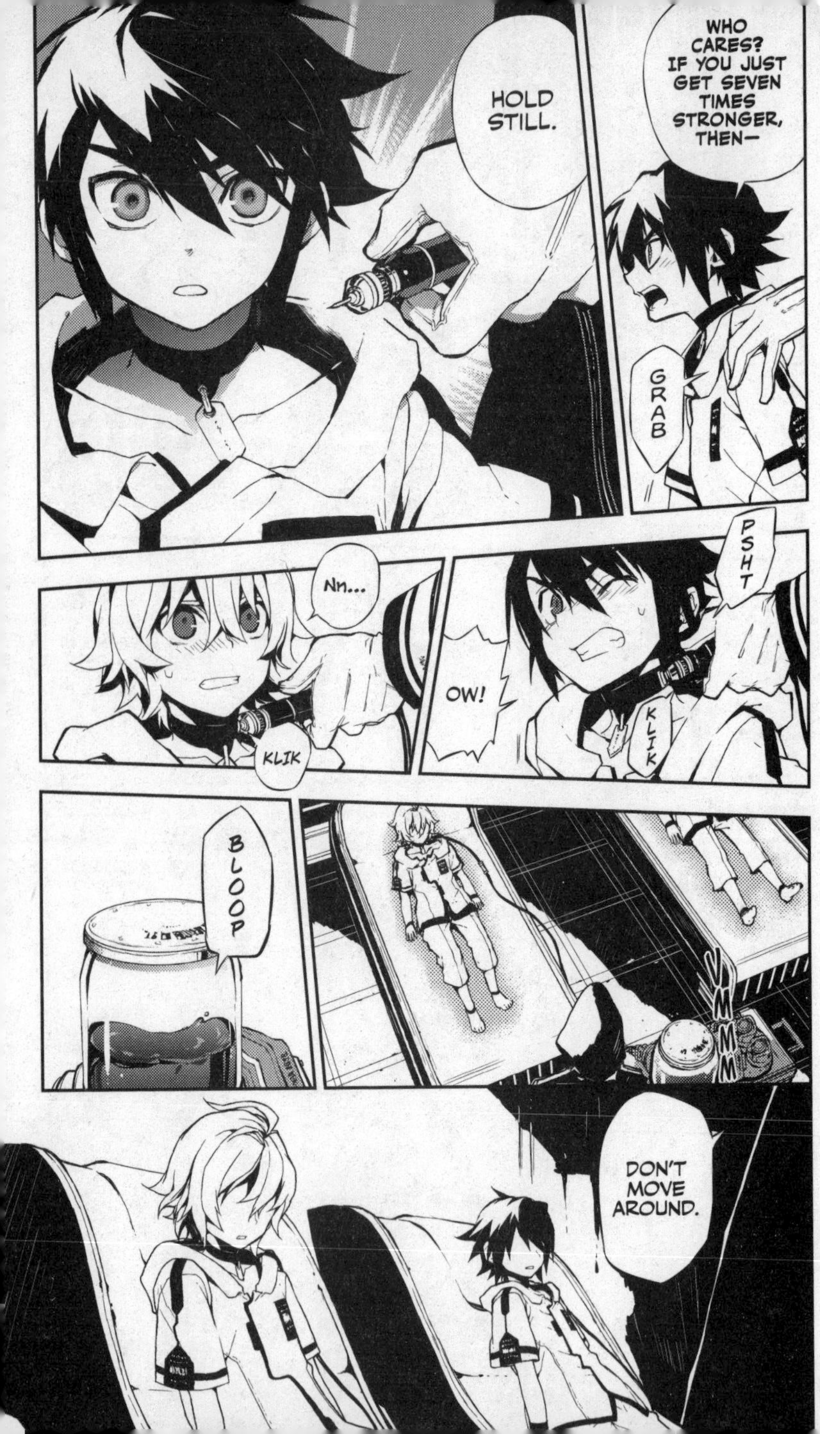
WHO CARES? IF YOU JUST GET SEVEN TIMES STRONGER, THEN—
GRAB
HOLD STILL.
PSHT
OW!
KLIK
Nn...
KLIK
VMMMM
BLOOP
DON'T MOVE AROUND.

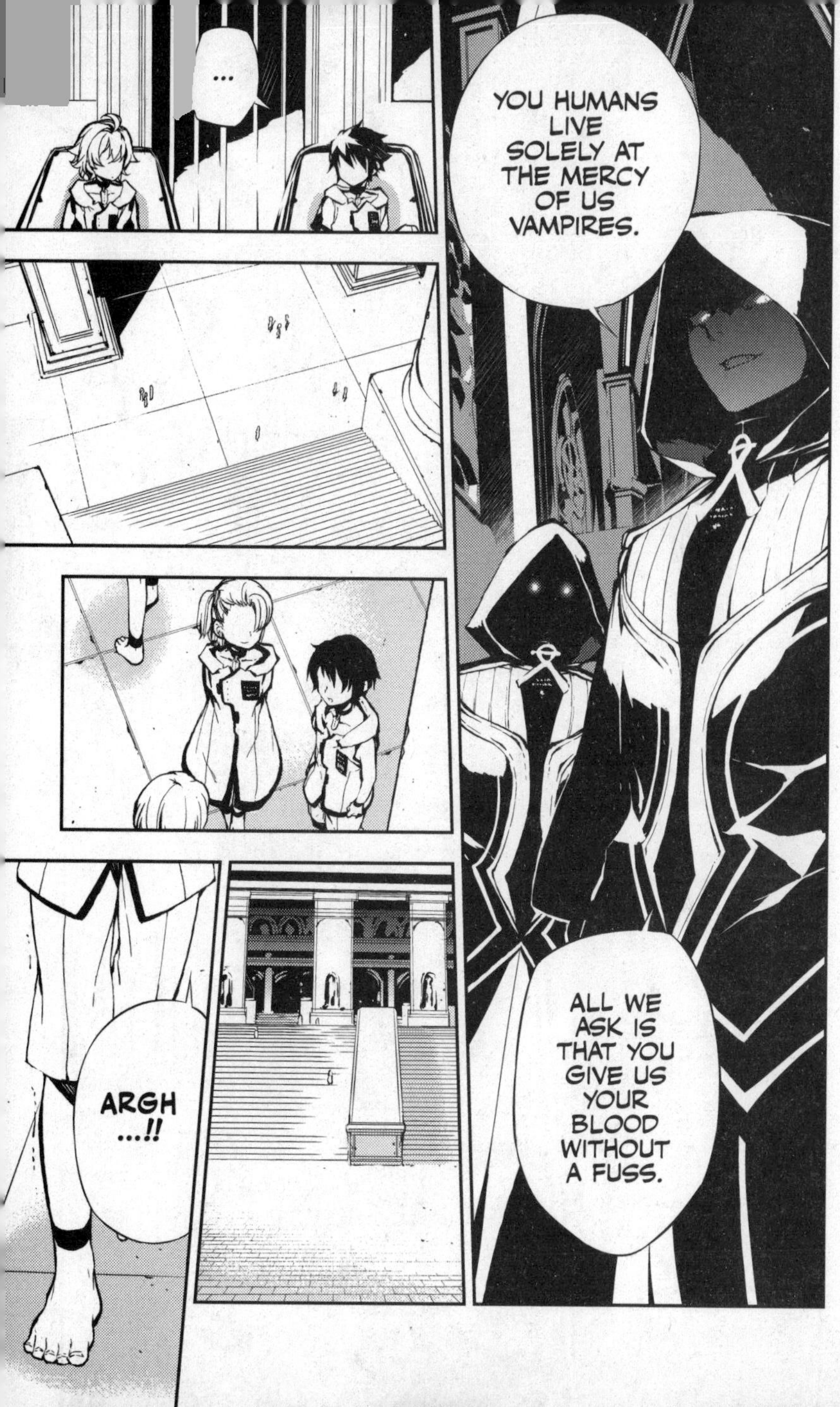
YOU HUMANS LIVE SOLELY AT THE MERCY OF US VAMPIRES.
ALL WE ASK IS THAT YOU GIVE US YOUR BLOOD WITHOUT A FUSS.
...
ARGH ...!!

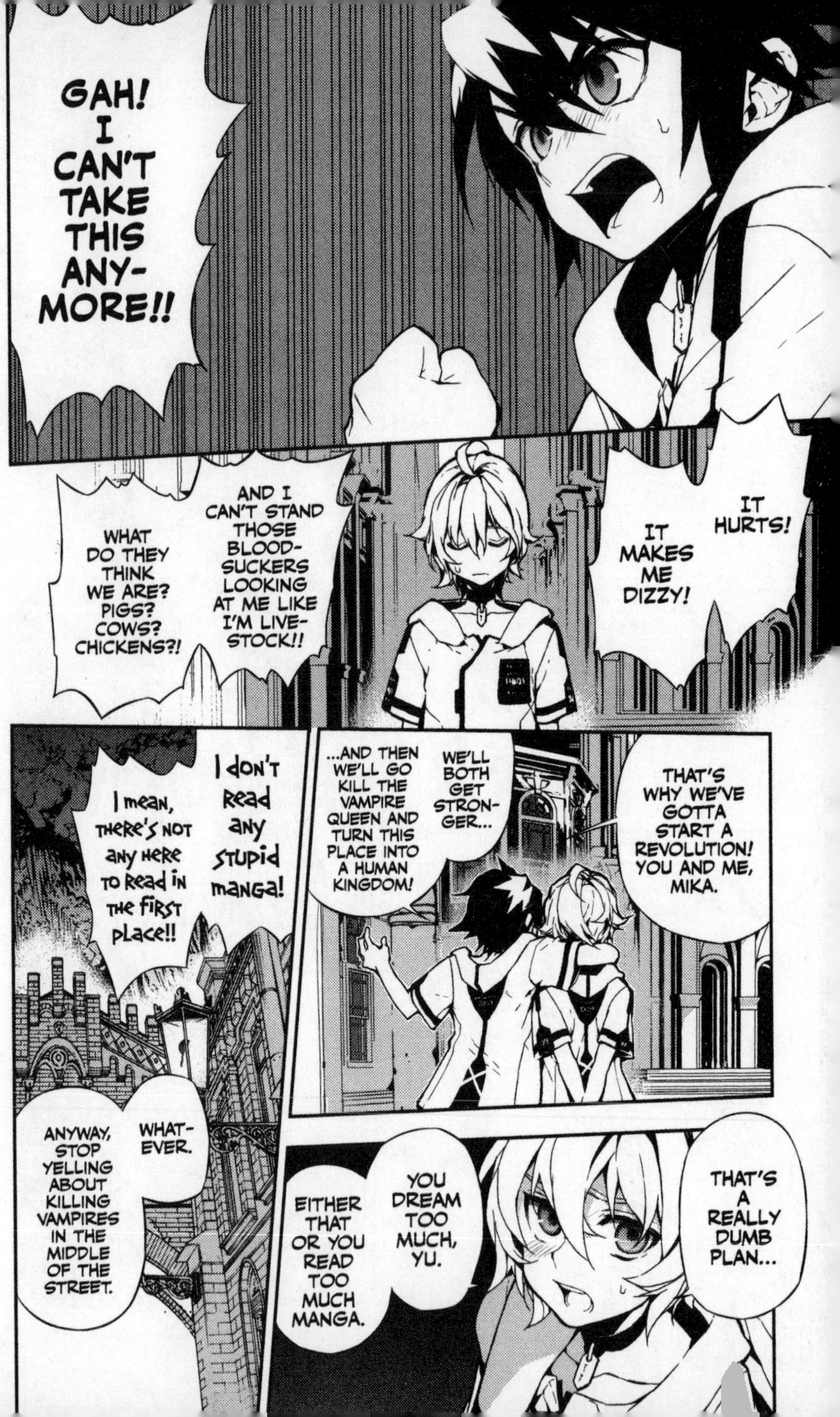
GAH! I CAN'T TAKE THIS ANY-MORE!!
IT HURTS!
IT MAKES ME DIZZY!
AND I CAN'T STAND THOSE BLOOD-SUCKERS LOOKING AT ME LIKE I'M LIVE-STOCK!!
WHAT DO THEY THINK WE ARE? PIGS? COWS? CHICKENS?!
THAT'S WHY WE'VE GOTTA START A REVOLUTION! YOU AND ME, MIKA.
WE'LL BOTH GET STRONGER...
...AND THEN WE'LL GO KILL THE VAMPIRE QUEEN AND TURN THIS PLACE INTO A HUMAN KINGDOM!
THAT'S A REALLY DUMB PLAN...
YOU DREAM TOO MUCH, YU.
EITHER THAT OR YOU READ TOO MUCH MANGA.
I don't read any stupid manga!
I mean, there's not any here to read in the first place!!
WHAT-EVER.
ANYWAY, STOP YELLING ABOUT KILLING VAMPIRES IN THE MIDDLE OF THE STREET.

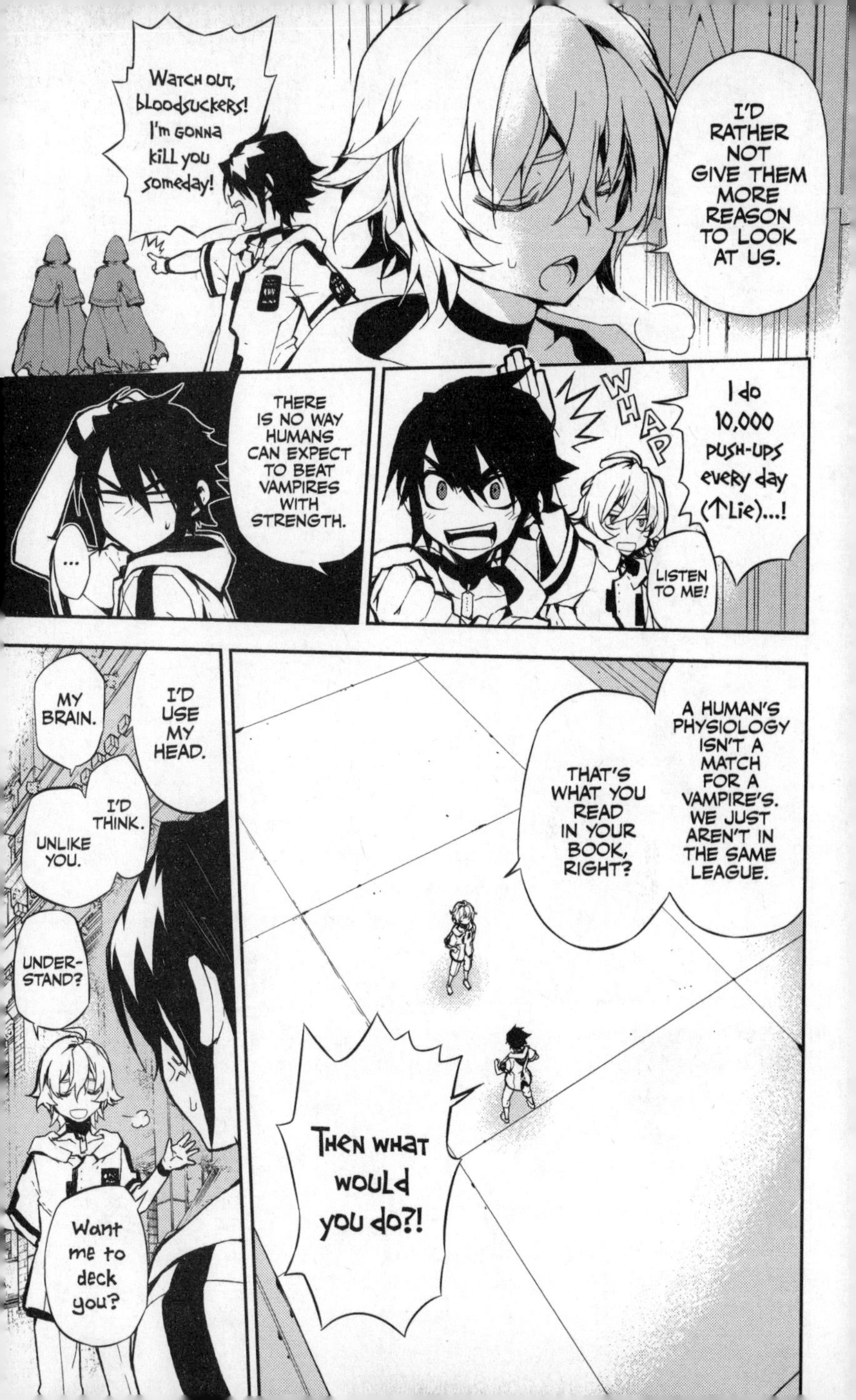
I'D RATHER NOT GIVE THEM MORE REASON TO LOOK AT US.
Watch out, bloodsuckers! I'm gonna kill you someday!
I do 10,000 push-ups every day (↑Lie)...!
WHAP
LISTEN TO ME!
THERE IS NO WAY HUMANS CAN EXPECT TO BEAT VAMPIRES WITH STRENGTH.
...
A HUMAN'S PHYSIOLOGY ISN'T A MATCH FOR A VAMPIRE'S. WE JUST AREN'T IN THE SAME LEAGUE.
THAT'S WHAT YOU READ IN YOUR BOOK, RIGHT?
Then what would you do?!
I'D USE MY HEAD.
MY BRAIN.
I'D THINK.
UNLIKE YOU.
UNDER-STAND?
Want me to deck you?

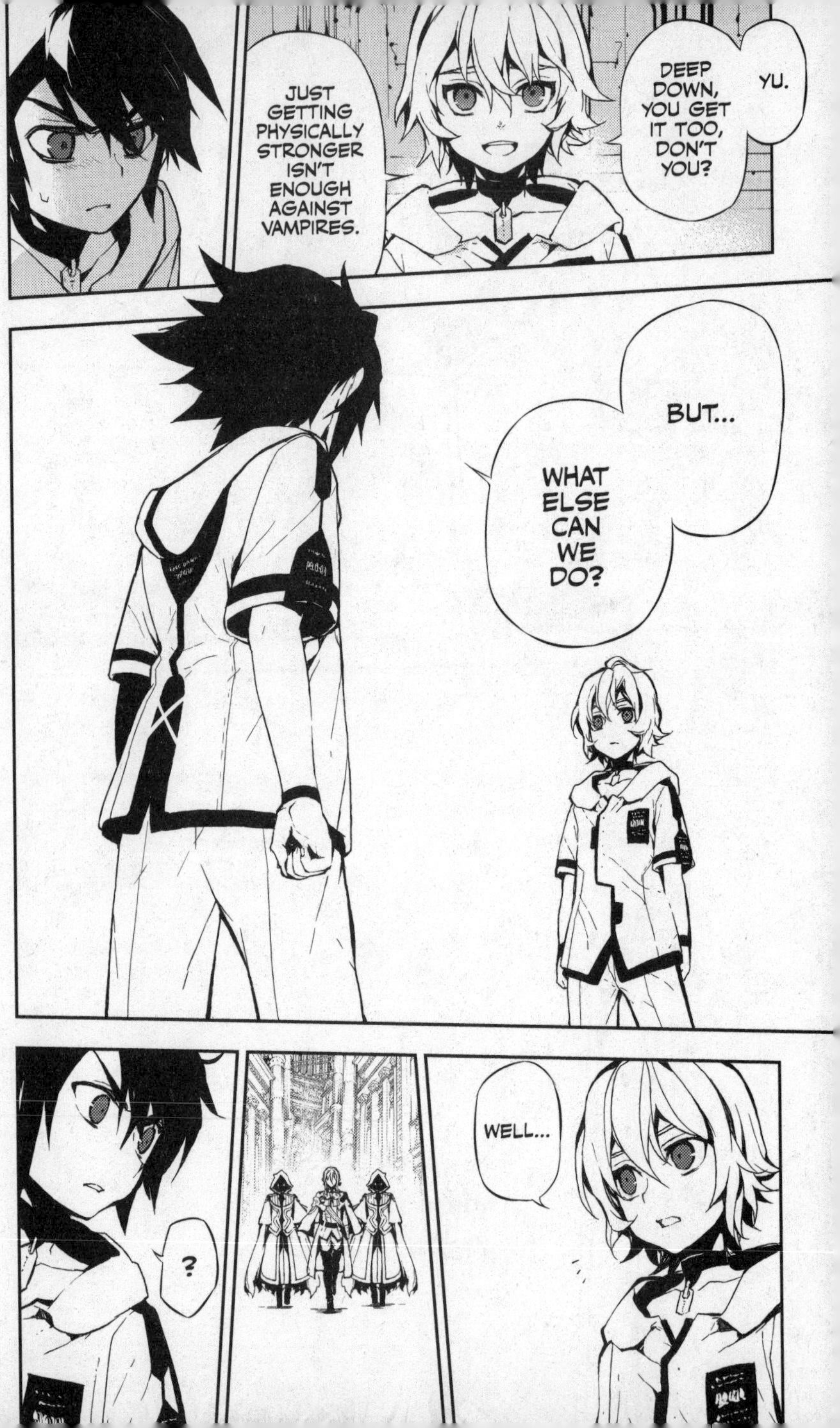
YU.
DEEP DOWN, YOU GET IT TOO, DON'T YOU?
JUST GETTING PHYSICALLY STRONGER ISN'T ENOUGH AGAINST VAMPIRES.
BUT...
WHAT ELSE CAN WE DO?
WELL...
?

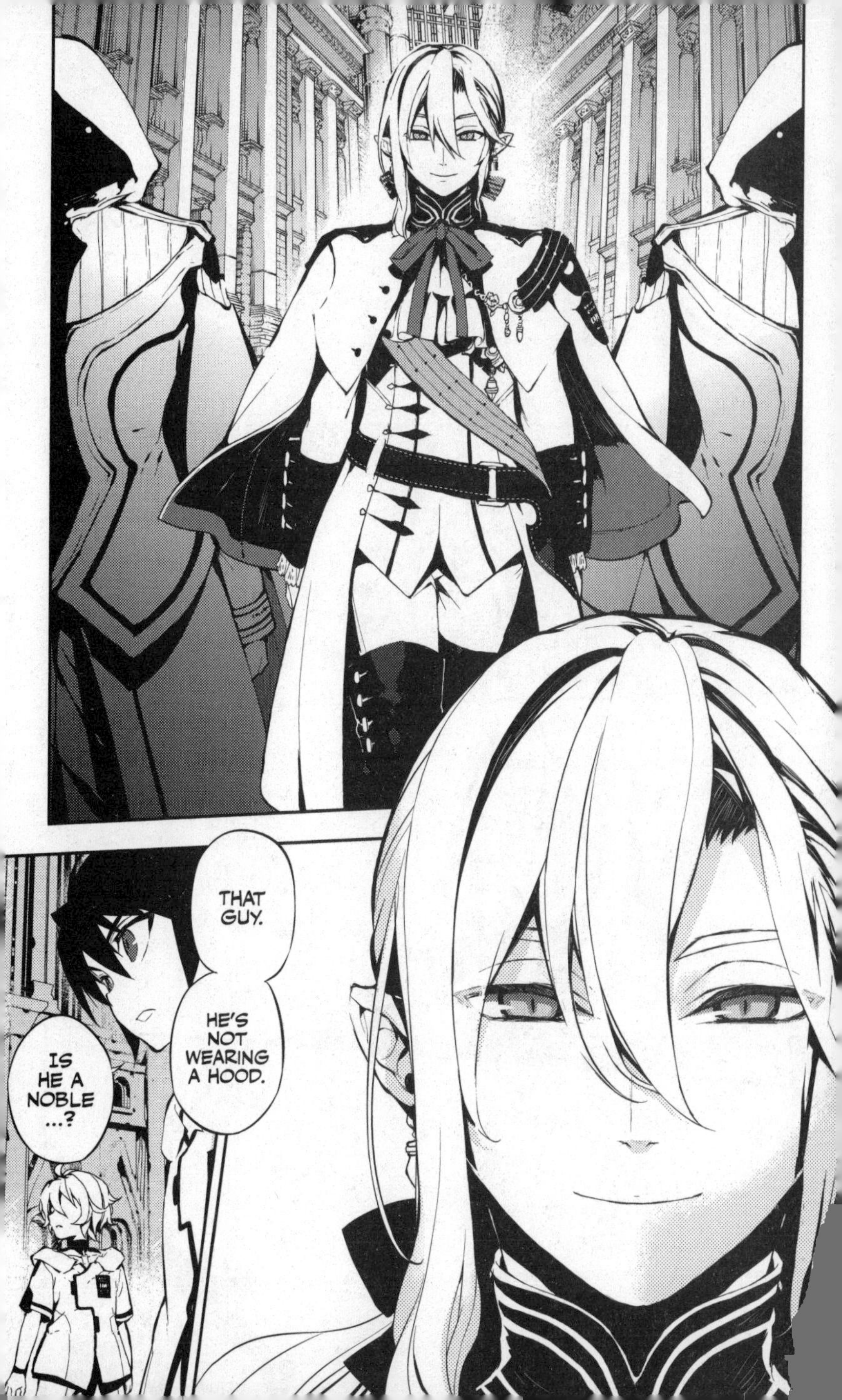
THAT GUY.
HE'S NOT WEARING A HOOD.
IS HE A NOBLE ...?

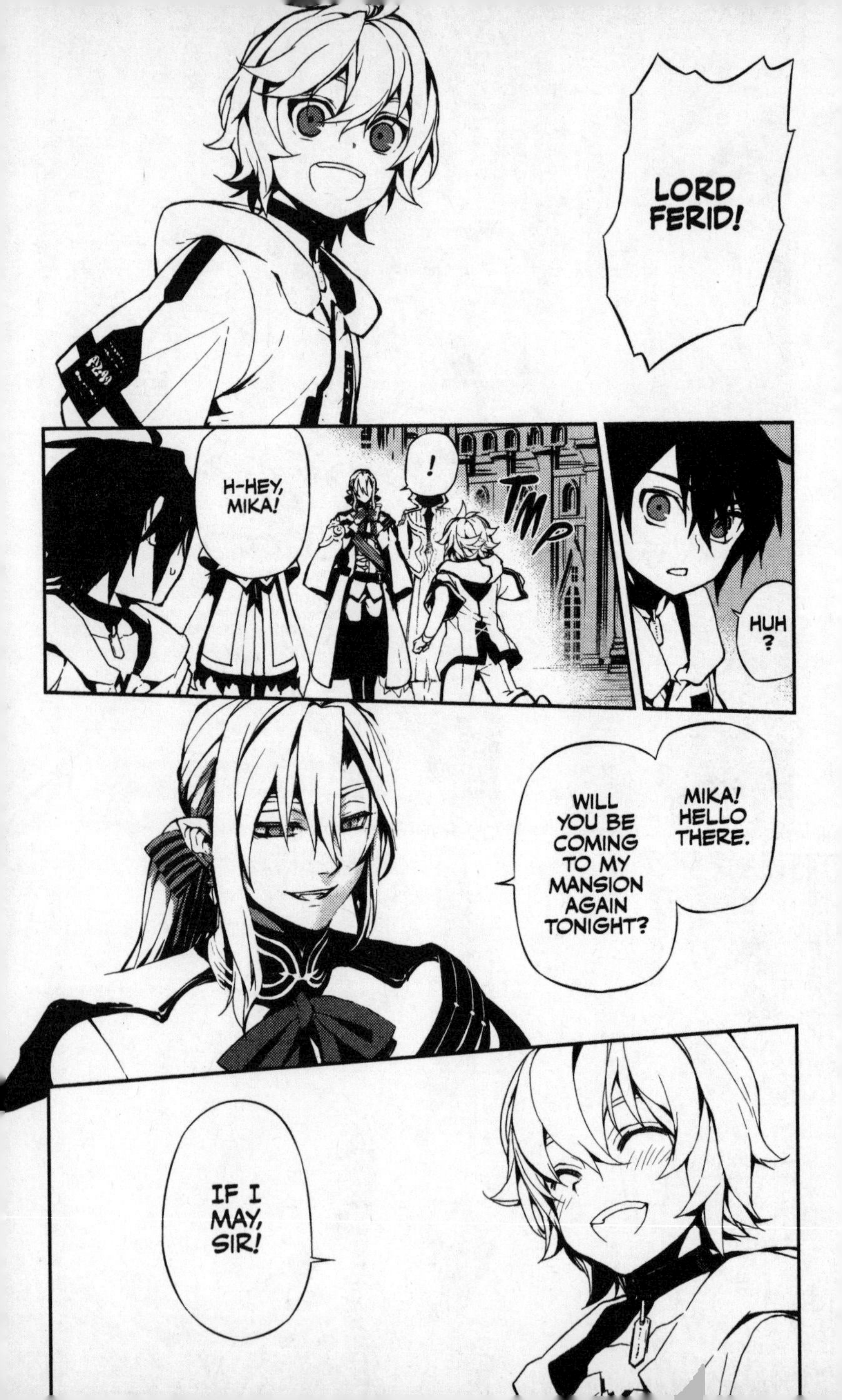
LORD FERID!
HUH?
!
TMP
H-HEY, MIKA!
MIKA! HELLO THERE.
WILL YOU BE COMING TO MY MANSION AGAIN TONIGHT?
IF I MAY, SIR!

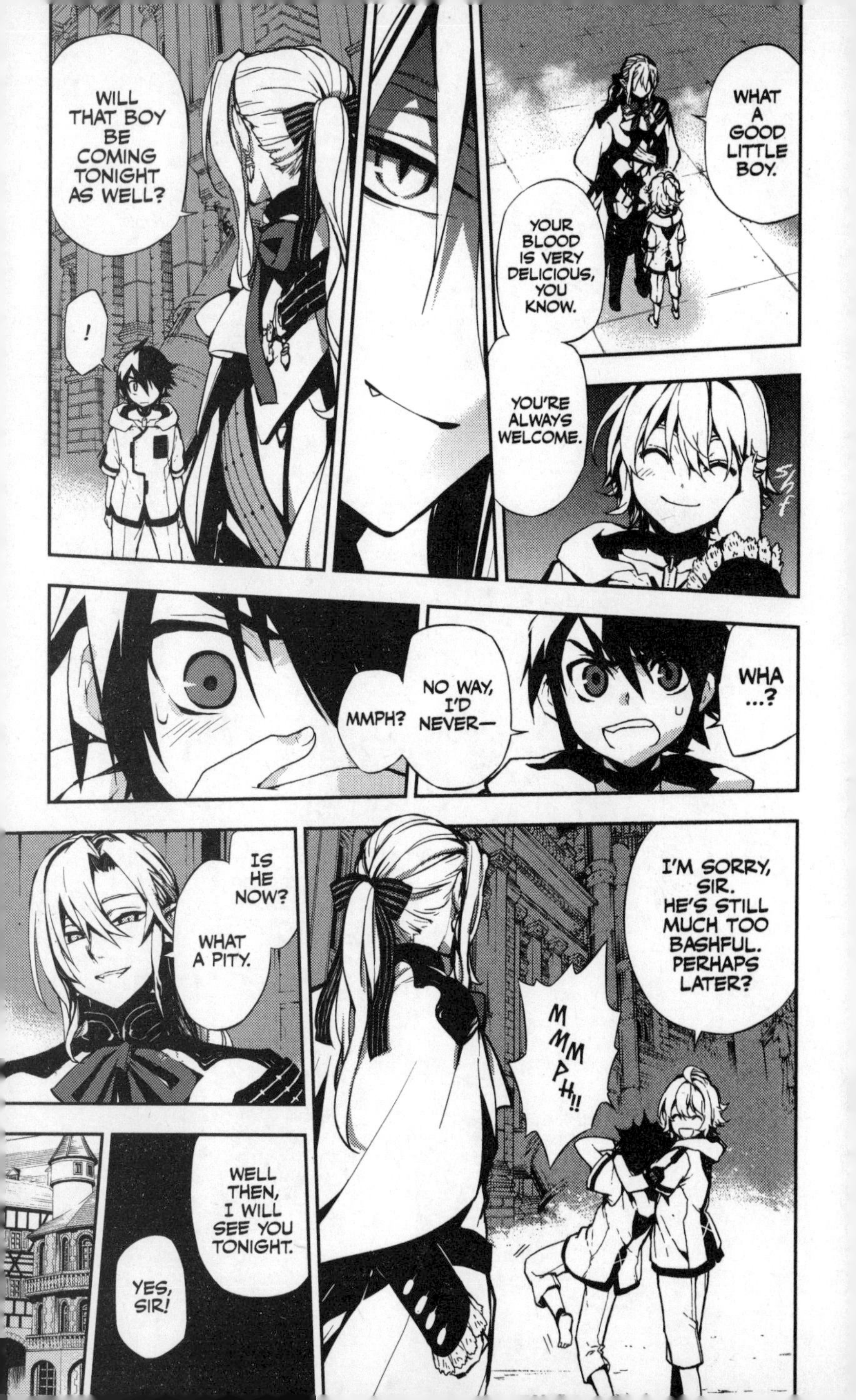
WHAT A GOOD LITTLE BOY.
YOUR BLOOD IS VERY DELICIOUS, YOU KNOW.
YOU'RE ALWAYS WELCOME.
shf
WILL THAT BOY BE COMING TONIGHT AS WELL?
!
WHA ...?
NO WAY, I'D NEVER—
MMPH?
I'M SORRY, SIR. HE'S STILL MUCH TOO BASHFUL. PERHAPS LATER?
MMMPH!!
IS HE NOW?
WHAT A PITY.
WELL THEN, I WILL SEE YOU TONIGHT.
YES, SIR!

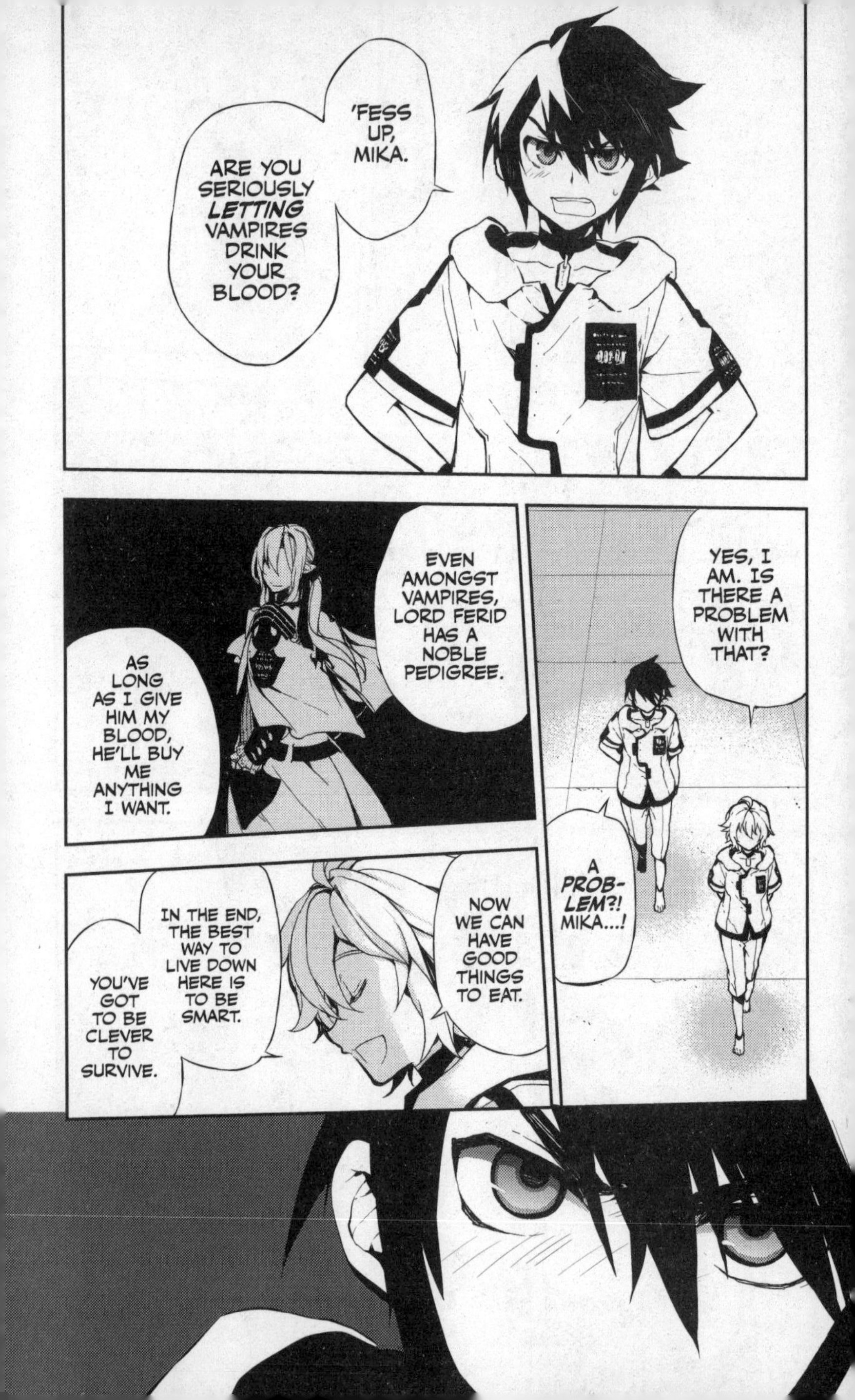
'FESS UP, MIKA.
ARE YOU SERIOUSLY *LETTING* VAMPIRES DRINK YOUR BLOOD?
YES, I AM. IS THERE A PROBLEM WITH THAT?
A *PROBLEM*?! MIKA...!
EVEN AMONGST VAMPIRES, LORD FERID HAS A NOBLE PEDIGREE.
AS LONG AS I GIVE HIM MY BLOOD, HE'LL BUY ME ANYTHING I WANT.
NOW WE CAN HAVE GOOD THINGS TO EAT.
IN THE END, THE BEST WAY TO LIVE DOWN HERE IS TO BE SMART.
YOU'VE GOT TO BE CLEVER TO SURVIVE.

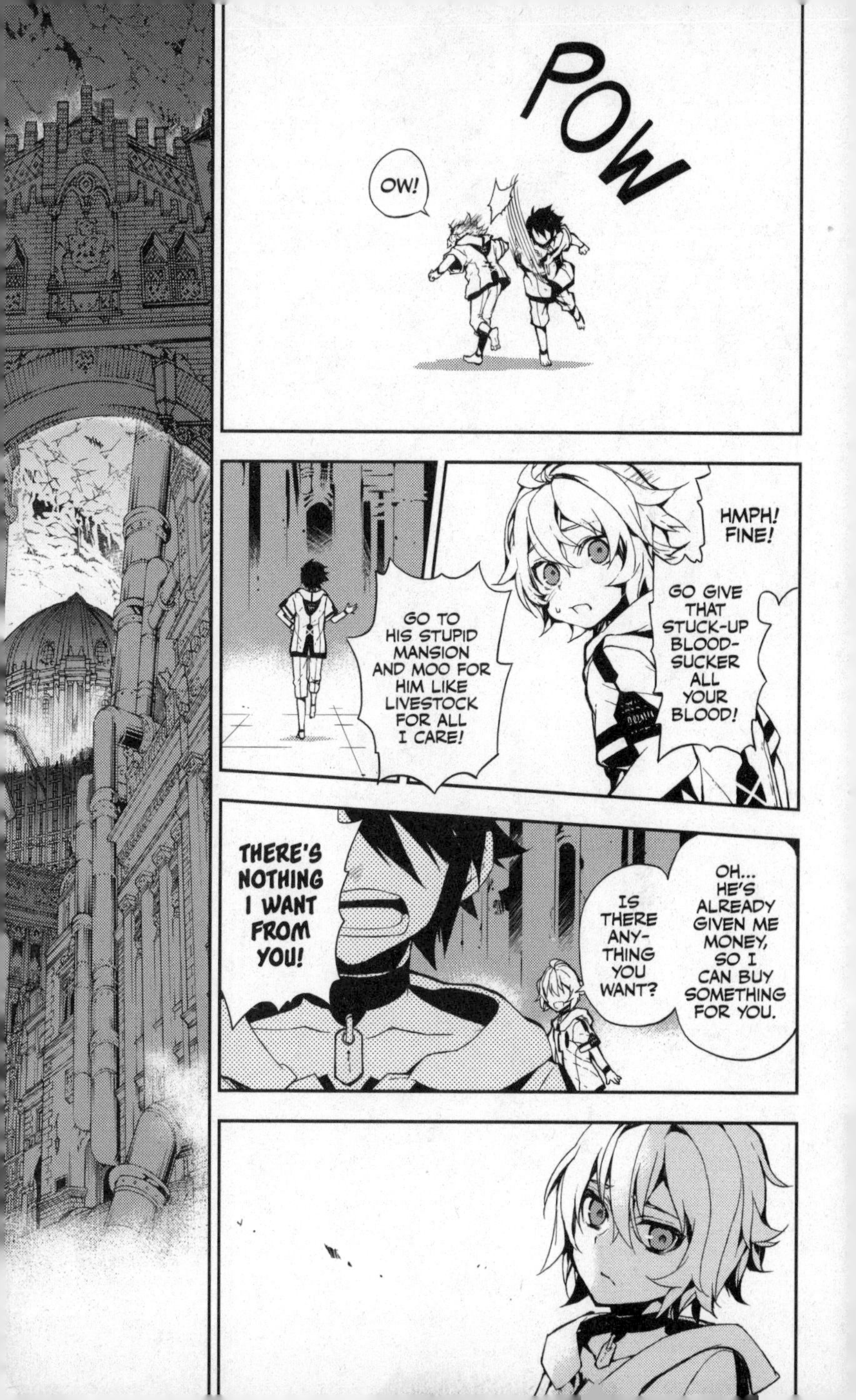
POW
OW!
HMPH! FINE!
GO GIVE THAT STUCK-UP BLOOD-SUCKER ALL YOUR BLOOD!
GO TO HIS STUPID MANSION AND MOO FOR HIM LIKE LIVESTOCK FOR ALL I CARE!
OH... HE'S ALREADY GIVEN ME MONEY, SO I CAN BUY SOMETHING FOR YOU.
IS THERE ANYTHING YOU WANT?
THERE'S NOTHING I WANT FROM YOU!

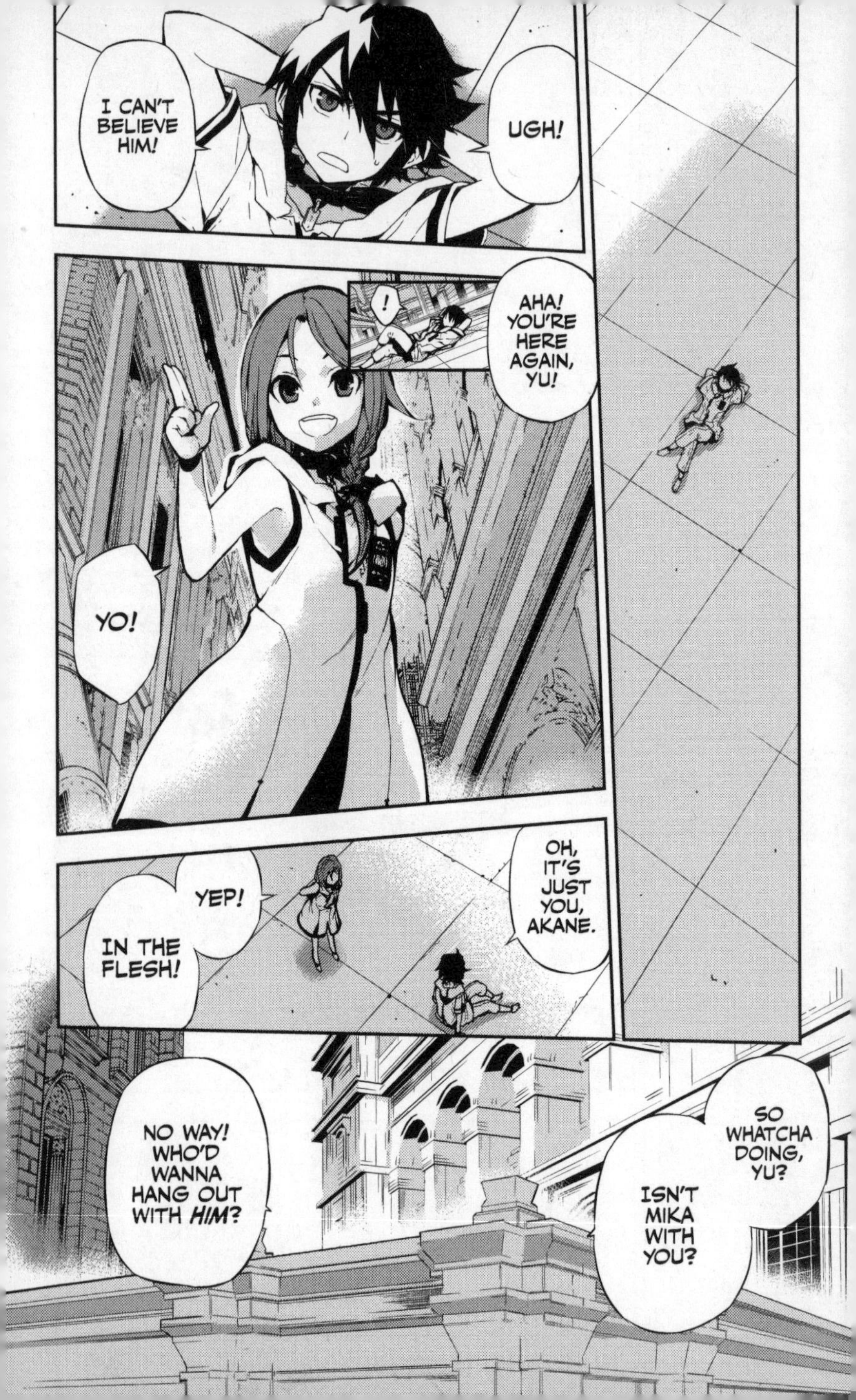
UGH!
I CAN'T BELIEVE HIM!
AHA! YOU'RE HERE AGAIN, YU!
!
YO!
OH, IT'S JUST YOU, AKANE.
YEP! IN THE FLESH!
SO WHATCHA DOING, YU?
ISN'T MIKA WITH YOU?
NO WAY! WHO'D WANNA HANG OUT WITH *HIM*?

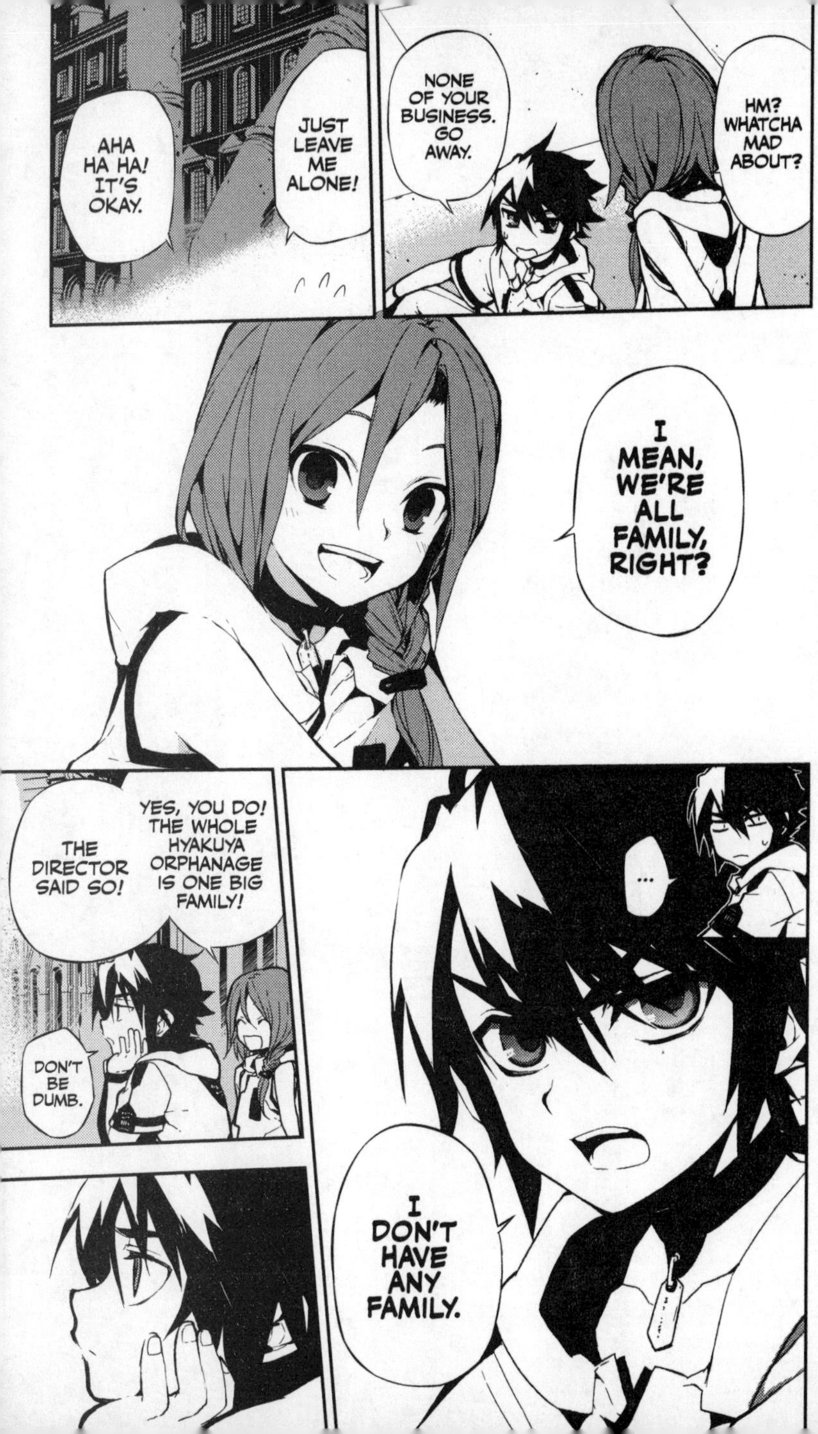
HM? WHATCHA MAD ABOUT?
NONE OF YOUR BUSINESS. GO AWAY.
JUST LEAVE ME ALONE!
AHA HA HA! IT'S OKAY.
I MEAN, WE'RE ALL FAMILY, RIGHT?
...
I DON'T HAVE ANY FAMILY.
YES, YOU DO! THE WHOLE HYAKUYA ORPHANAGE IS ONE BIG FAMILY!
THE DIRECTOR SAID SO!
DON'T BE DUMB.

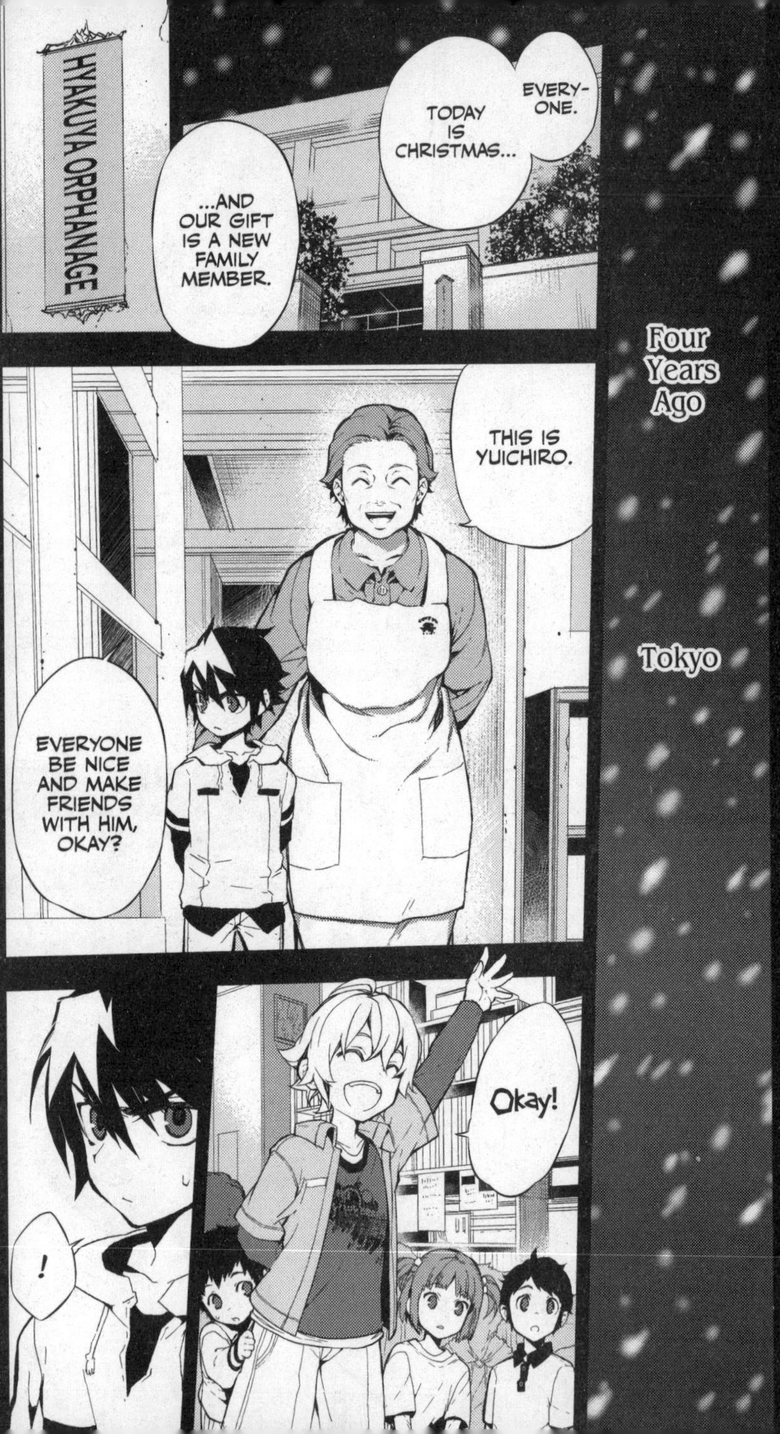
Four Years Ago
Tokyo
EVERY-ONE.
TODAY IS CHRISTMAS...
...AND OUR GIFT IS A NEW FAMILY MEMBER.
HYAKUYA ORPHANAGE
THIS IS YUICHIRO.
EVERYONE BE NICE AND MAKE FRIENDS WITH HIM, OKAY?
Okay!
!

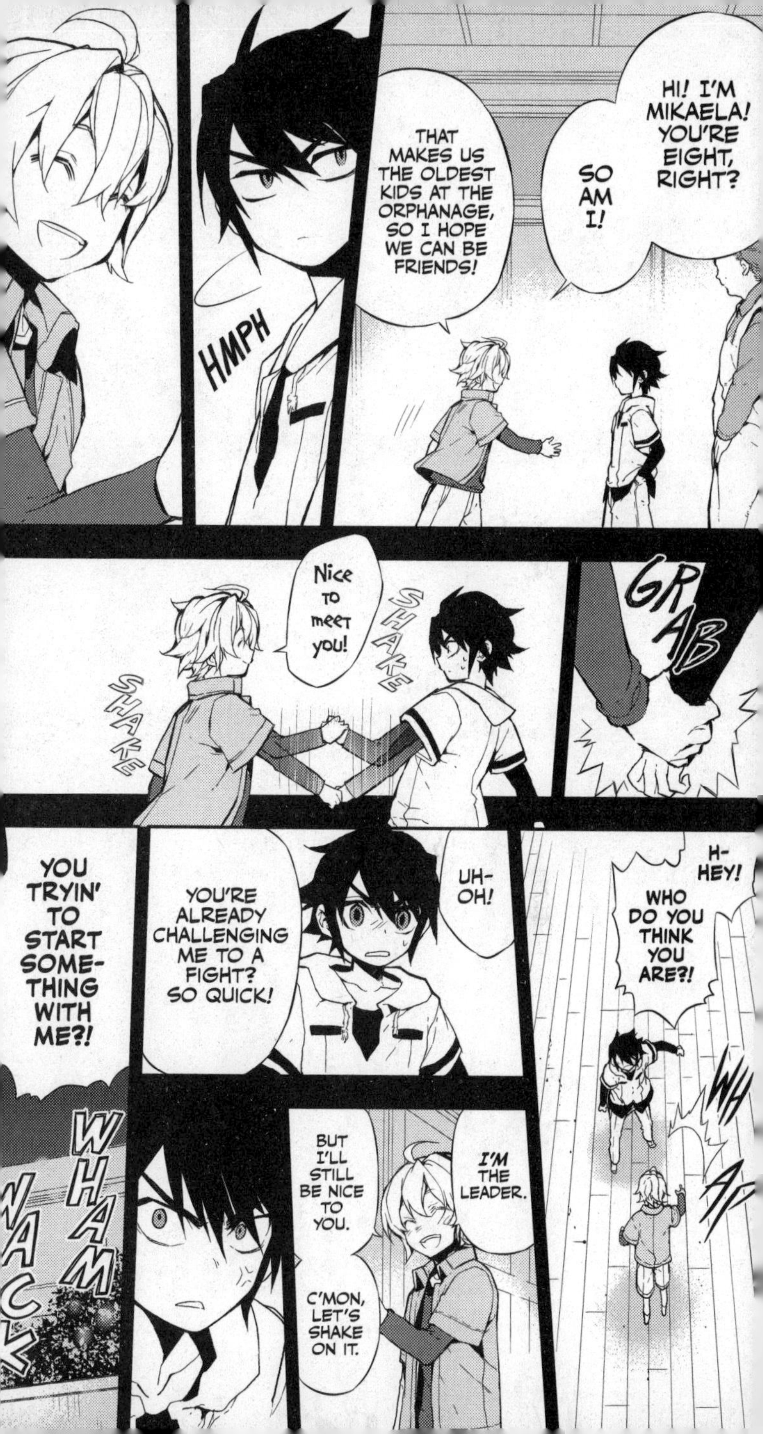
HI! I'M MIKAELA! YOU'RE EIGHT, RIGHT?
SO AM I!
THAT MAKES US THE OLDEST KIDS AT THE ORPHANAGE, SO I HOPE WE CAN BE FRIENDS!
HMPH
GRAB
Nice to meet you!
SHAKE
SHAKE
H-HEY!
WHO DO YOU THINK YOU ARE?!
WHAP
UH-OH!
YOU'RE ALREADY CHALLENGING ME TO A FIGHT? SO QUICK!
YOU TRYIN' TO START SOME-THING WITH ME?!
I'M THE LEADER.
BUT I'LL STILL BE NICE TO YOU.
C'MON, LET'S SHAKE ON IT.
WHAM
WHACK

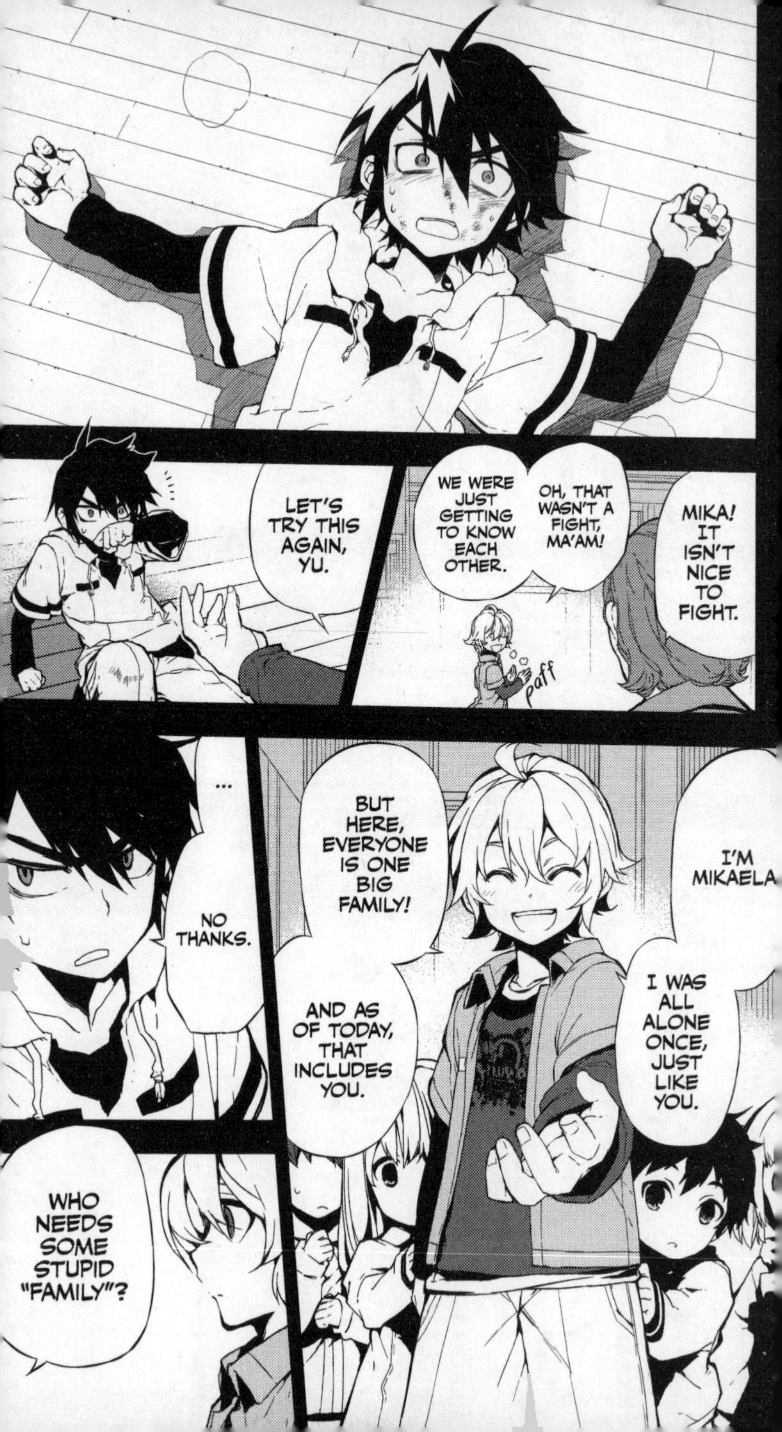
MIKA! IT ISN'T NICE TO FIGHT.
OH, THAT WASN'T A FIGHT, MA'AM!
WE WERE JUST GETTING TO KNOW EACH OTHER.
paff
LET'S TRY THIS AGAIN, YU.
I'M MIKAELA
I WAS ALL ALONE ONCE, JUST LIKE YOU.
BUT HERE, EVERYONE IS ONE BIG FAMILY!
AND AS OF TODAY, THAT INCLUDES YOU.
...
NO THANKS.
WHO NEEDS SOME STUPID "FAMILY"?

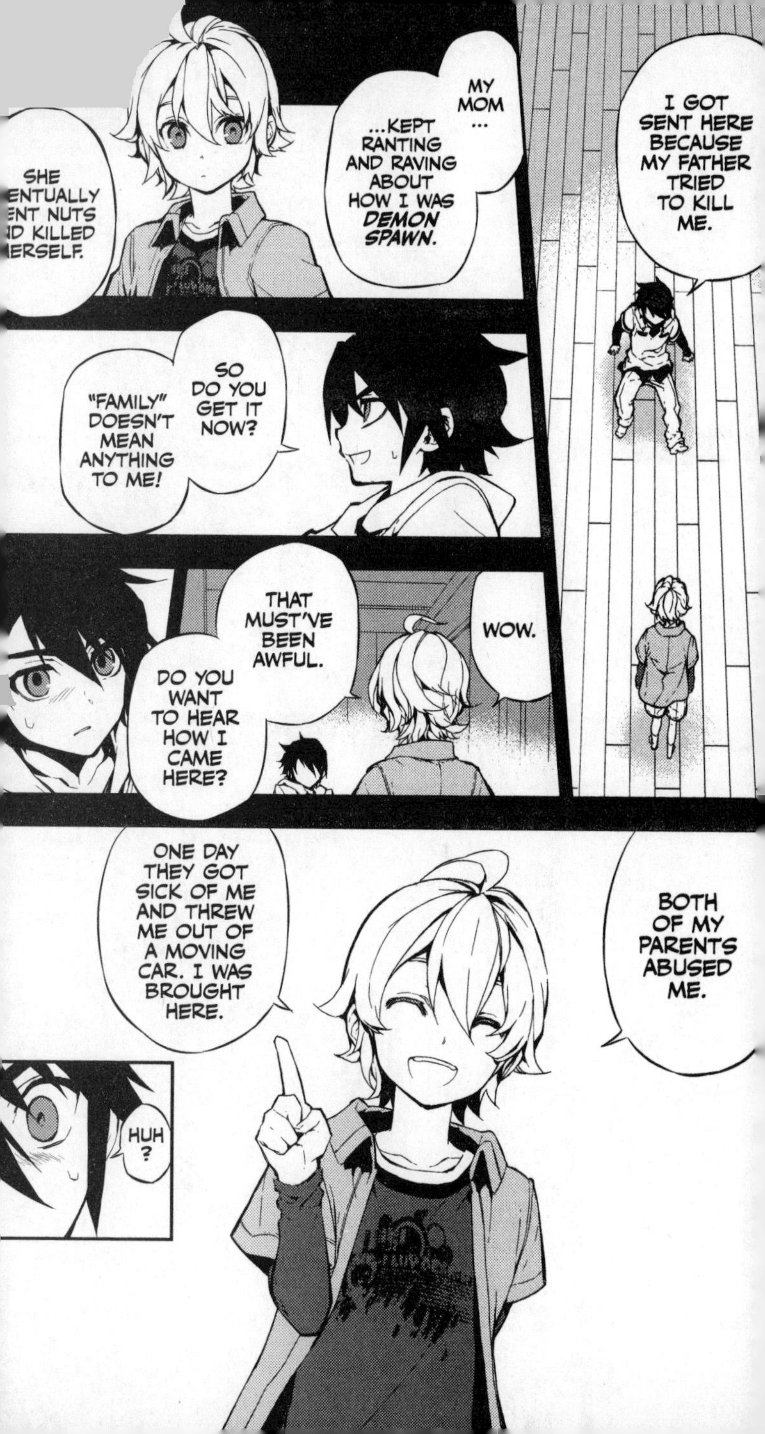
I GOT SENT HERE BECAUSE MY FATHER TRIED TO KILL ME.
MY MOM ...
...KEPT RANTING AND RAVING ABOUT HOW I WAS *DEMON SPAWN.*
SHE ENTUALLY ENT NUTS ID KILLED ERSELF.
SO DO YOU GET IT NOW?
"FAMILY" DOESN'T MEAN ANYTHING TO ME!
WOW.
THAT MUST'VE BEEN AWFUL.
DO YOU WANT TO HEAR HOW I CAME HERE?
BOTH OF MY PARENTS ABUSED ME.
ONE DAY THEY GOT SICK OF ME AND THREW ME OUT OF A MOVING CAR. I WAS BROUGHT HERE.
HUH?

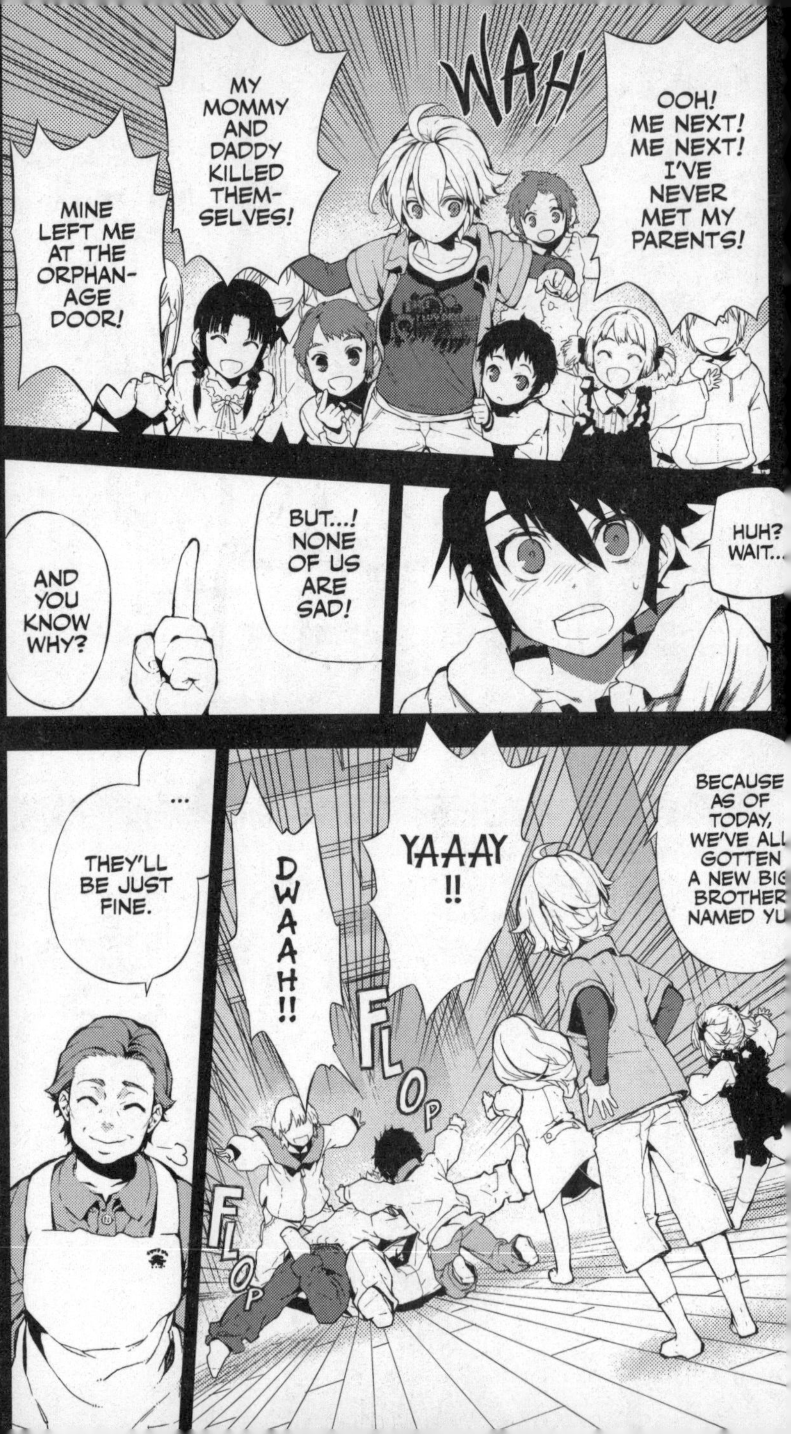
OOH! ME NEXT! ME NEXT! I'VE NEVER MET MY PARENTS!
WAH
MY MOMMY AND DADDY KILLED THEM-SELVES!
MINE LEFT ME AT THE ORPHAN-AGE DOOR!
HUH? WAIT...
BUT...! NONE OF US ARE SAD!
AND YOU KNOW WHY?
BECAUSE AS OF TODAY, WE'VE ALL GOTTEN A NEW BIG BROTHER NAMED YU
YAAAY!!
DWAAAH!!
FLOP
FLOP
...
THEY'LL BE JUST FINE.

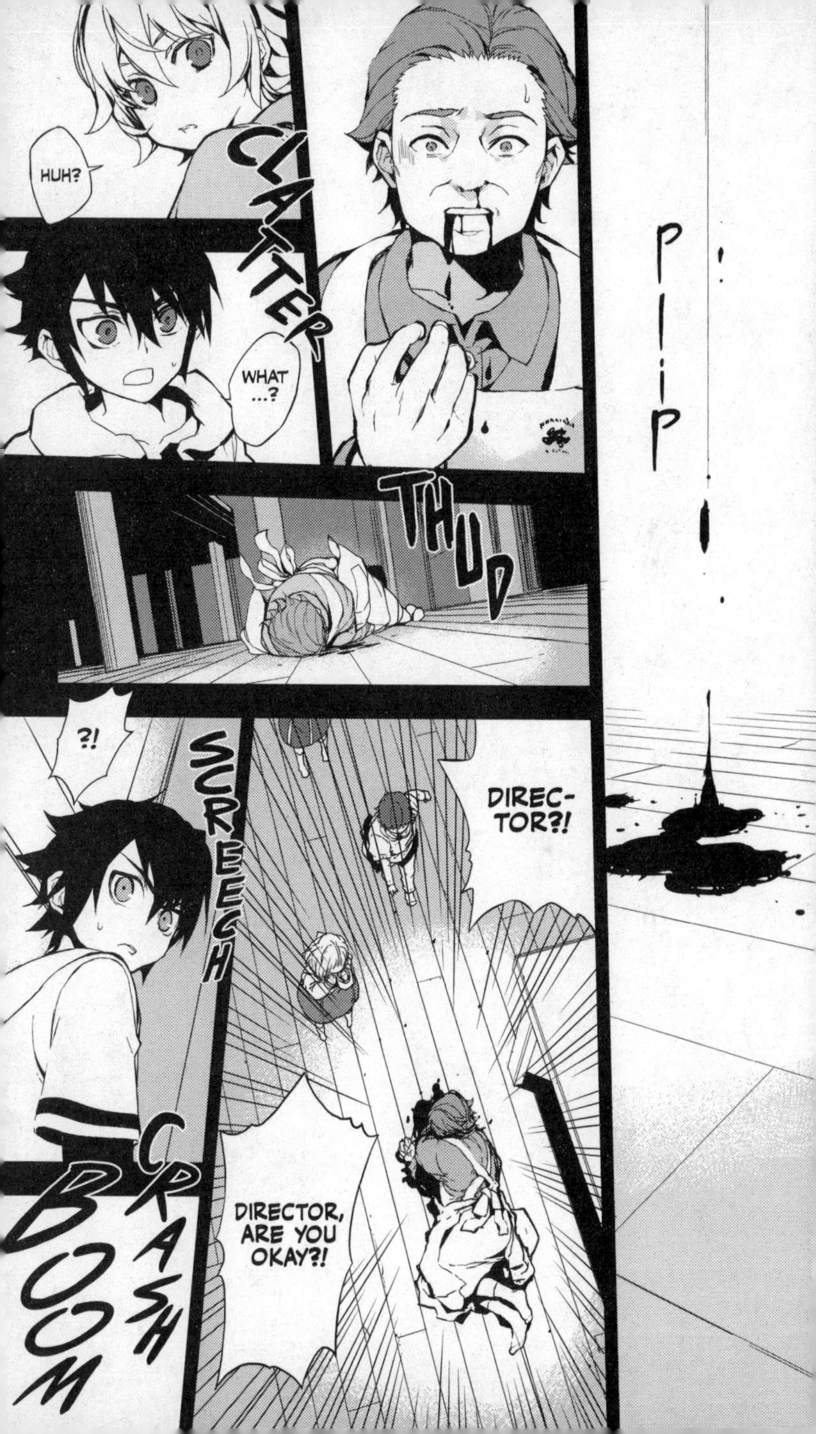
PIP
CLATTER
HUH?
WHAT ...?
THUD
DIRECTOR?!
DIRECTOR, ARE YOU OKAY?!
?!
SCREEECH
CRASH
BOOM

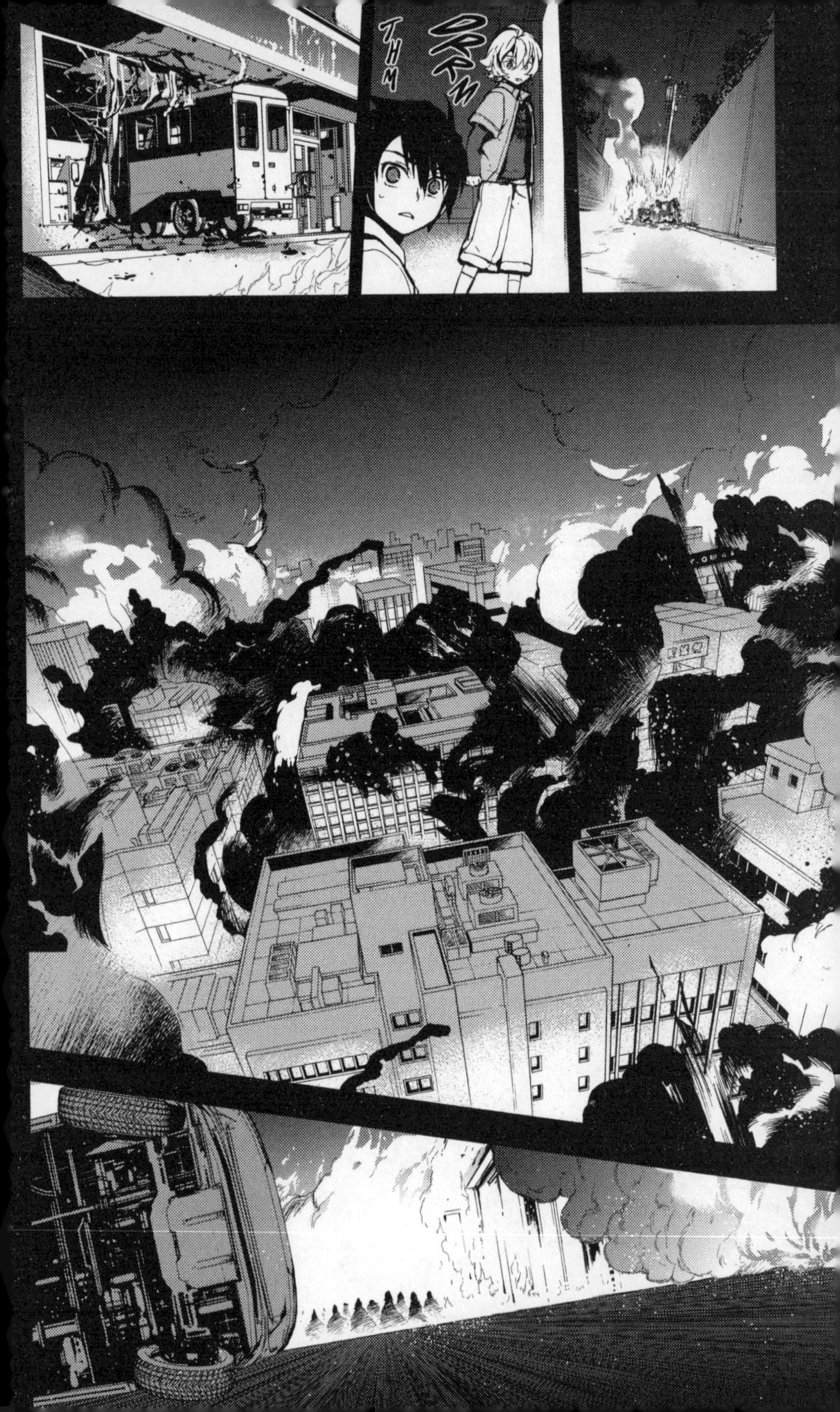
DRRM
THM

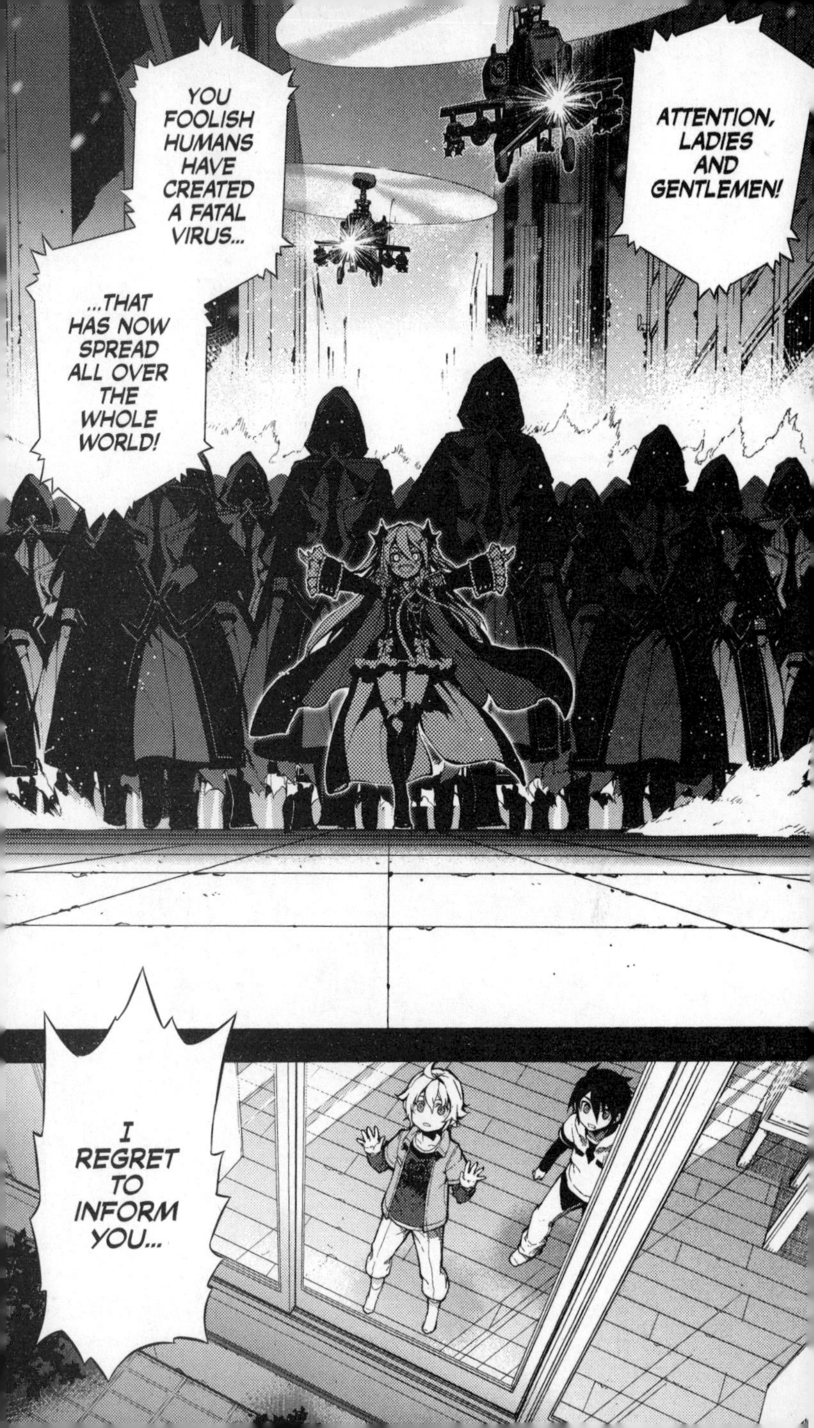
ATTENTION, LADIES AND GENTLEMEN!
YOU FOOLISH HUMANS HAVE CREATED A FATAL VIRUS...
...THAT HAS NOW SPREAD ALL OVER THE WHOLE WORLD!
I REGRET TO INFORM YOU...

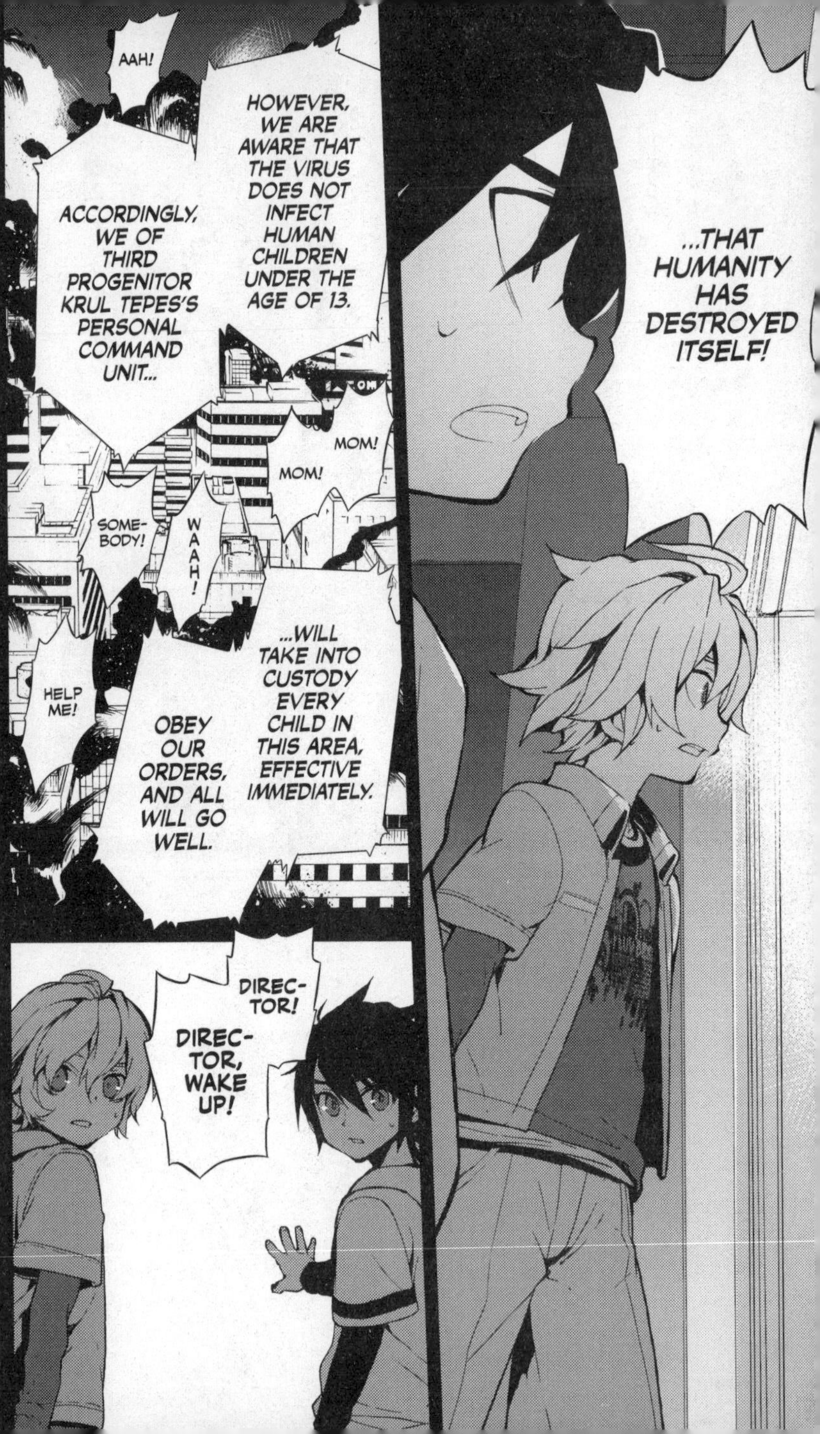
...THAT HUMANITY HAS DESTROYED ITSELF!
HOWEVER, WE ARE AWARE THAT THE VIRUS DOES NOT INFECT HUMAN CHILDREN UNDER THE AGE OF 13.
AAH!
ACCORDINGLY, WE OF THIRD PROGENITOR KRUL TEPES'S PERSONAL COMMAND UNIT...
MOM!
MOM!
WAAH!
SOME-BODY!
...WILL TAKE INTO CUSTODY EVERY CHILD IN THIS AREA, EFFECTIVE IMMEDIATELY.
OBEY OUR ORDERS, AND ALL WILL GO WELL.
HELP ME!
DIREC-TOR!
DIREC-TOR, WAKE UP!

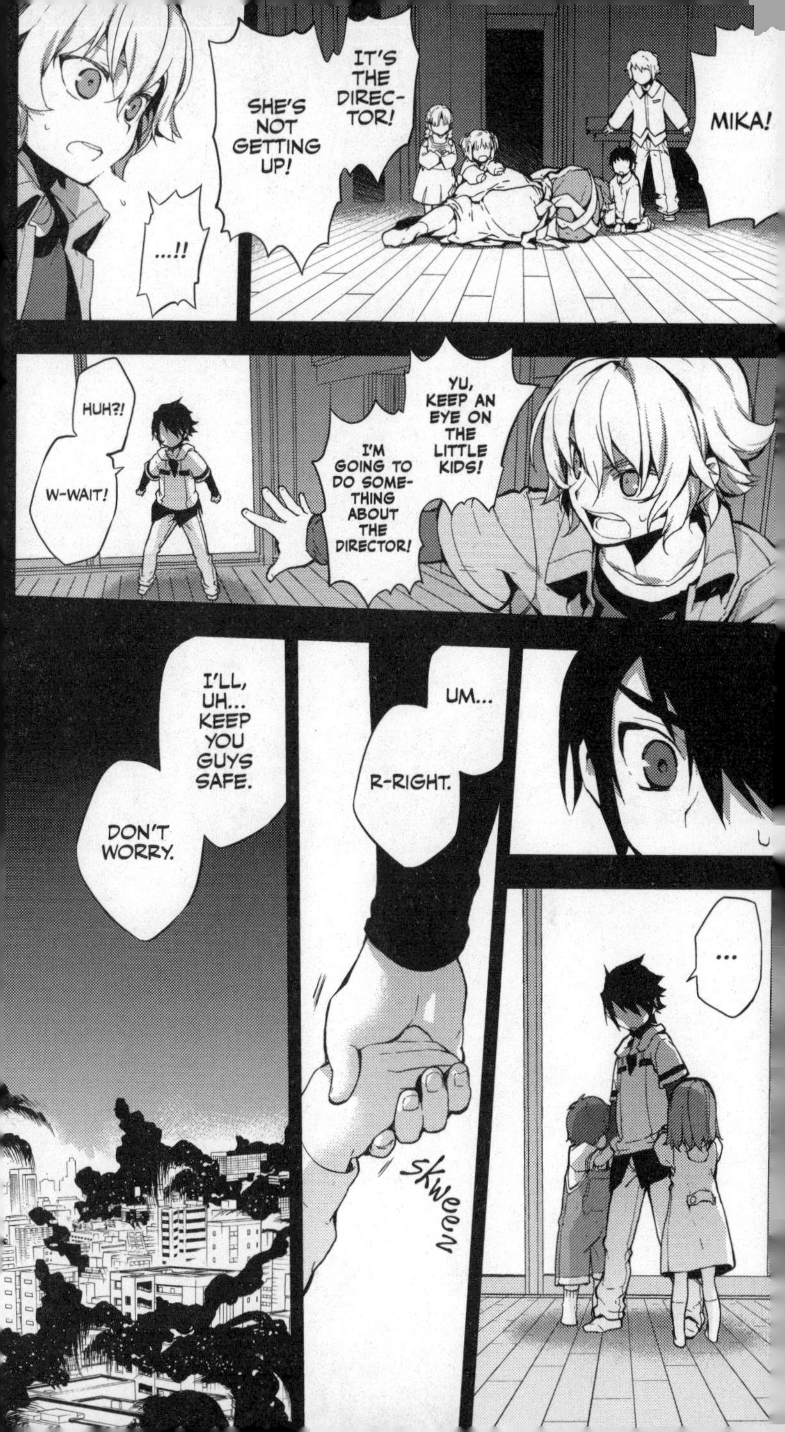
MIKA!
IT'S THE DIREC-TOR!
SHE'S NOT GETTING UP!
...!!
YU, KEEP AN EYE ON THE LITTLE KIDS!
I'M GOING TO DO SOME-THING ABOUT THE DIRECTOR!
HUH?!
W-WAIT!
...
UM...
R-RIGHT.
skween
I'LL, UH... KEEP YOU GUYS SAFE.
DON'T WORRY.

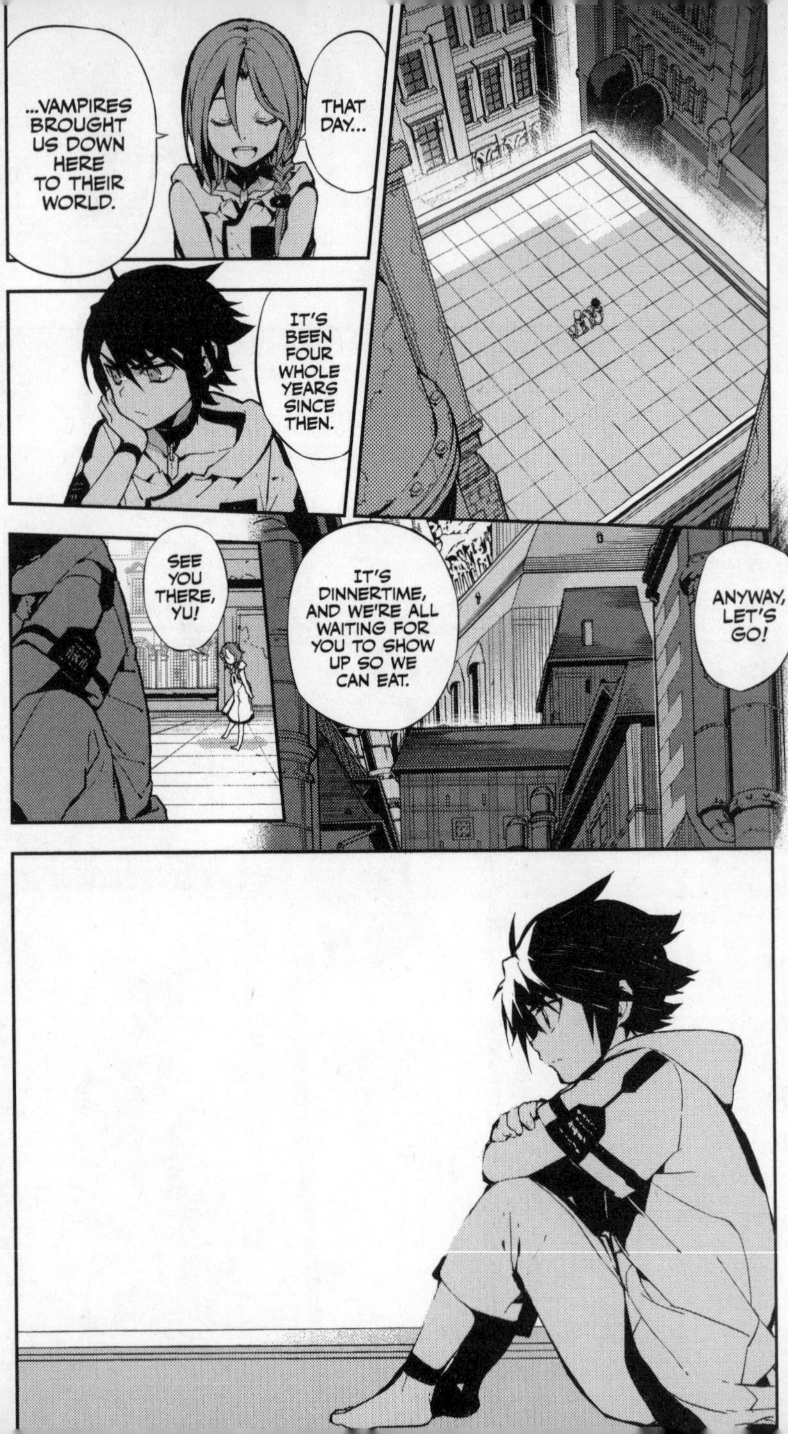
THAT DAY...
...VAMPIRES BROUGHT US DOWN HERE TO THEIR WORLD.
IT'S BEEN FOUR WHOLE YEARS SINCE THEN.
ANYWAY, LET'S GO!
IT'S DINNERTIME, AND WE'RE ALL WAITING FOR YOU TO SHOW UP SO WE CAN EAT.
SEE YOU THERE, YU!

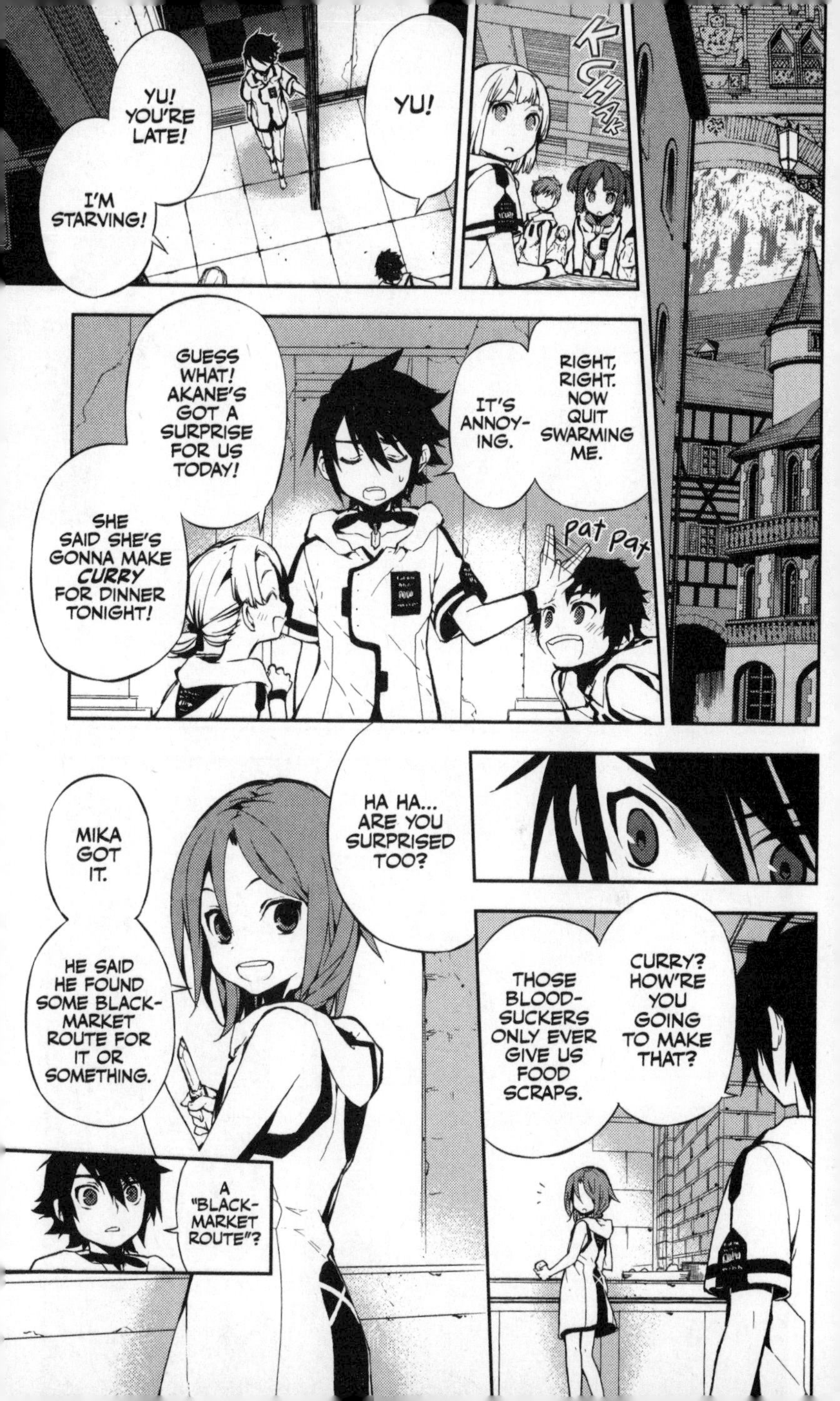
KCHAK
YU!
YU! YOU'RE LATE!
I'M STARVING!
RIGHT, RIGHT. NOW QUIT SWARMING ME.
IT'S ANNOY-ING.
pat pat
GUESS WHAT! AKANE'S GOT A SURPRISE FOR US TODAY!
SHE SAID SHE'S GONNA MAKE *CURRY* FOR DINNER TONIGHT!
CURRY? HOW'RE YOU GOING TO MAKE THAT?
THOSE BLOOD-SUCKERS ONLY EVER GIVE US FOOD SCRAPS.
HA HA... ARE YOU SURPRISED TOO?
MIKA GOT IT.
HE SAID HE FOUND SOME BLACK-MARKET ROUTE FOR IT OR SOMETHING.
A "BLACK-MARKET ROUTE"?

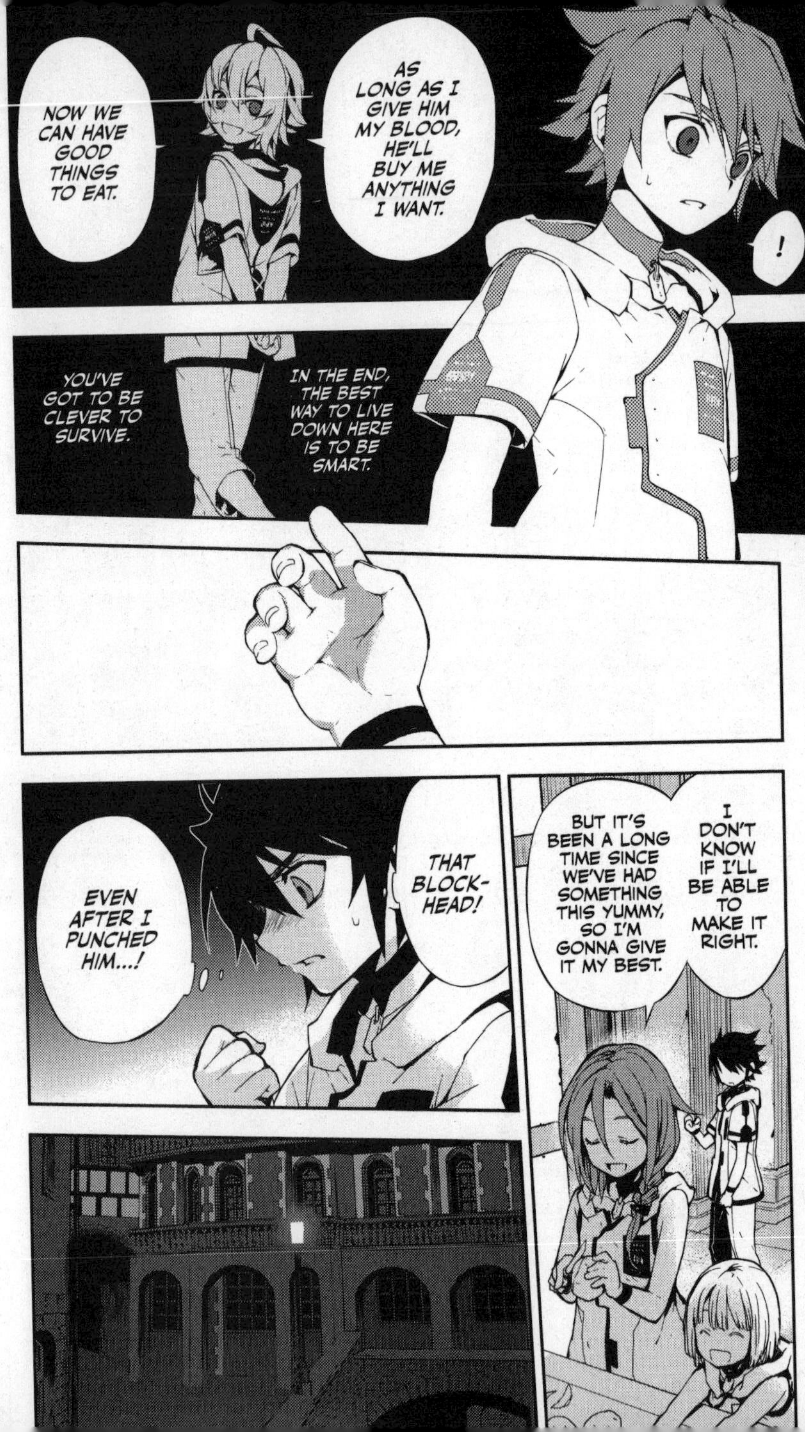
!
AS LONG AS I GIVE HIM MY BLOOD, HE'LL BUY ME ANYTHING I WANT.
NOW WE CAN HAVE GOOD THINGS TO EAT.
IN THE END, THE BEST WAY TO LIVE DOWN HERE IS TO BE SMART.
YOU'VE GOT TO BE CLEVER TO SURVIVE.
I DON'T KNOW IF I'LL BE ABLE TO MAKE IT RIGHT.
BUT IT'S BEEN A LONG TIME SINCE WE'VE HAD SOMETHING THIS YUMMY, SO I'M GONNA GIVE IT MY BEST.
THAT BLOCK-HEAD!
EVEN AFTER I PUNCHED HIM...!

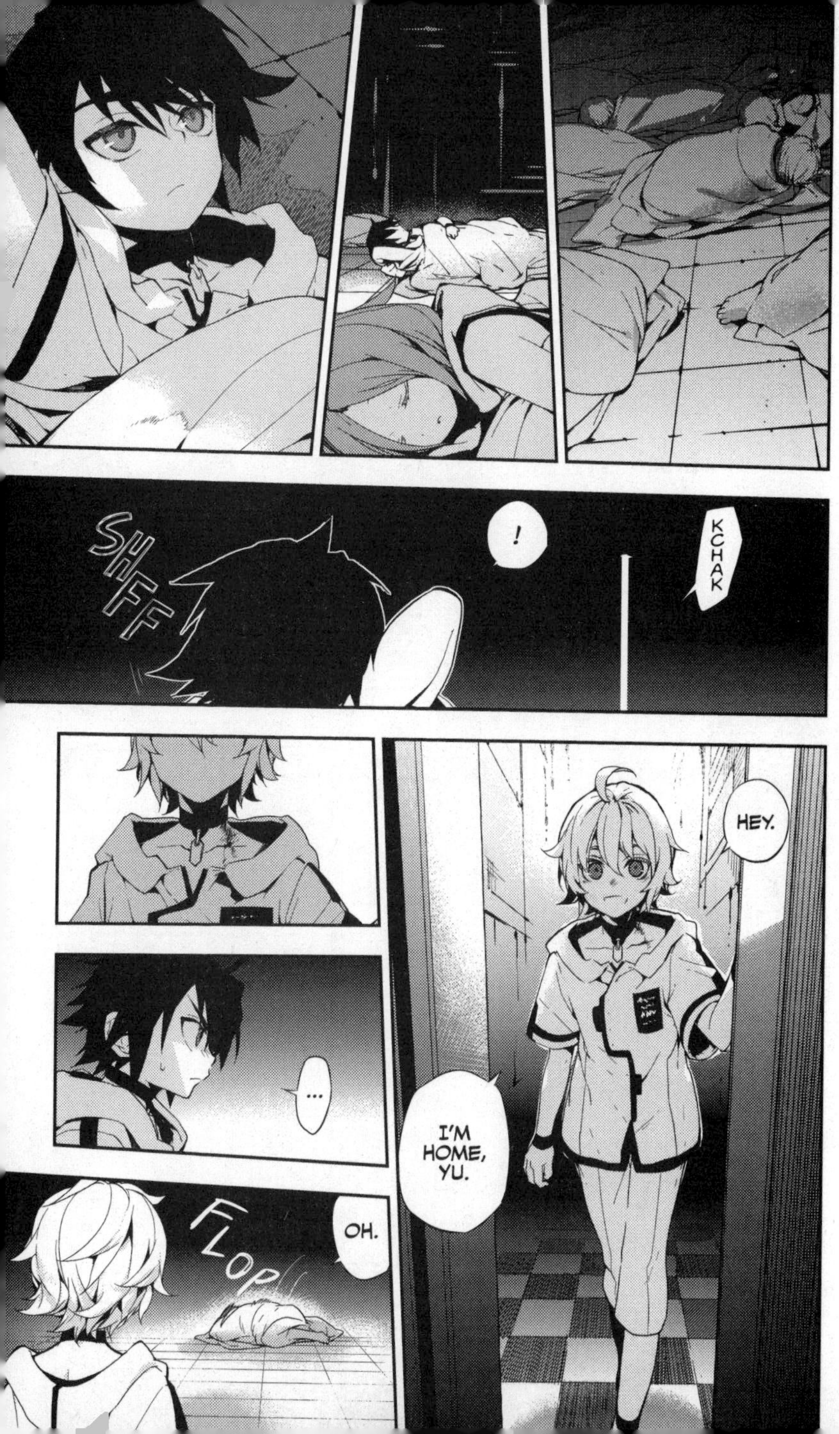
KCHAK
!
SHFF
HEY.
I'M HOME, YU.
...
OH.
FLOP

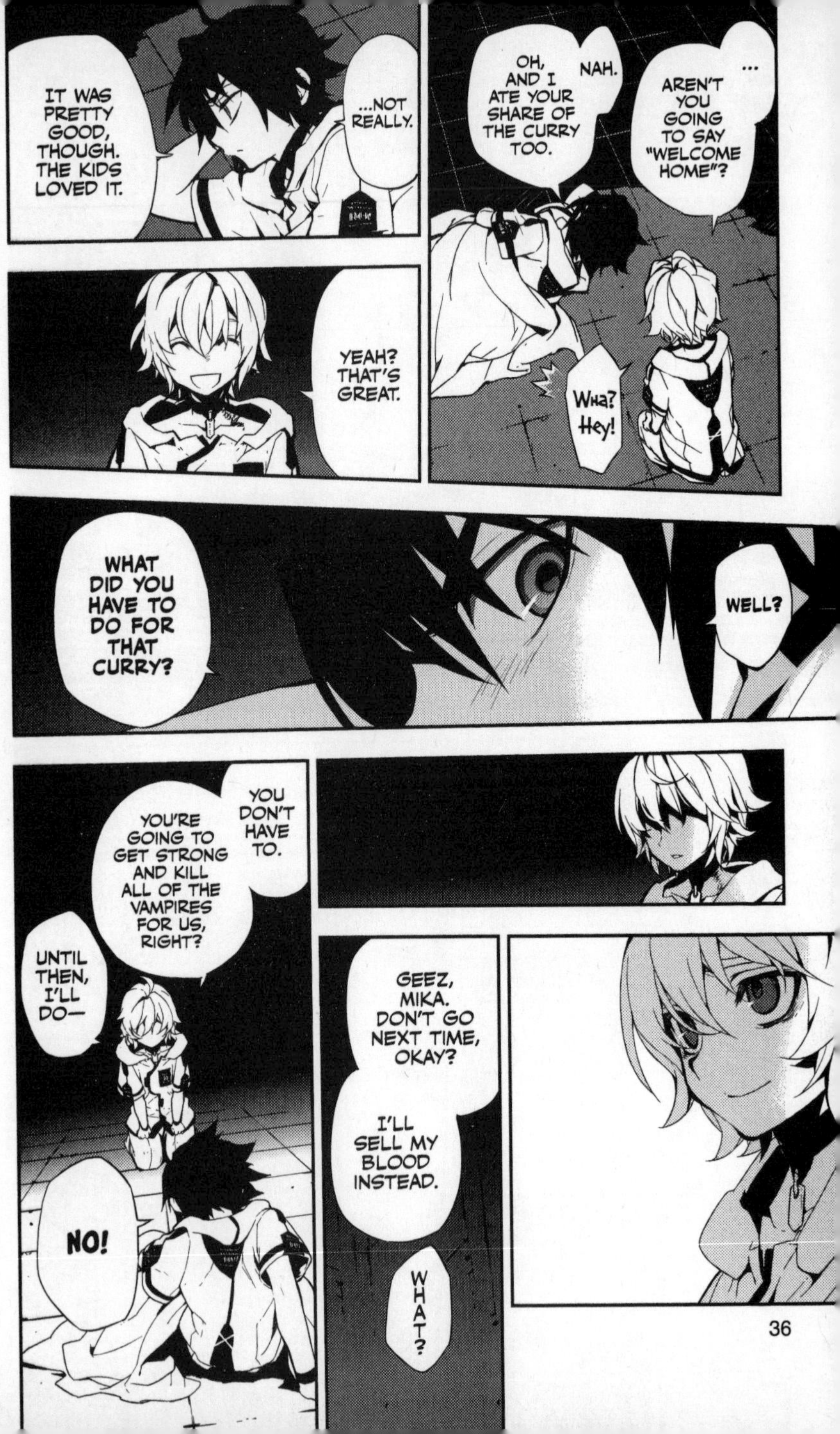
...
AREN'T YOU GOING TO SAY "WELCOME HOME"?
NAH.
OH, AND I ATE YOUR SHARE OF THE CURRY TOO.
Wha? Hey!
...NOT REALLY.
IT WAS PRETTY GOOD, THOUGH. THE KIDS LOVED IT.
YEAH? THAT'S GREAT.
WELL?
WHAT DID YOU HAVE TO DO FOR THAT CURRY?
GEEZ, MIKA. DON'T GO NEXT TIME, OKAY?
I'LL SELL MY BLOOD INSTEAD.
WHAT?
YOU DON'T HAVE TO.
YOU'RE GOING TO GET STRONG AND KILL ALL OF THE VAMPIRES FOR US, RIGHT?
UNTIL THEN, I'LL DO—
NO!

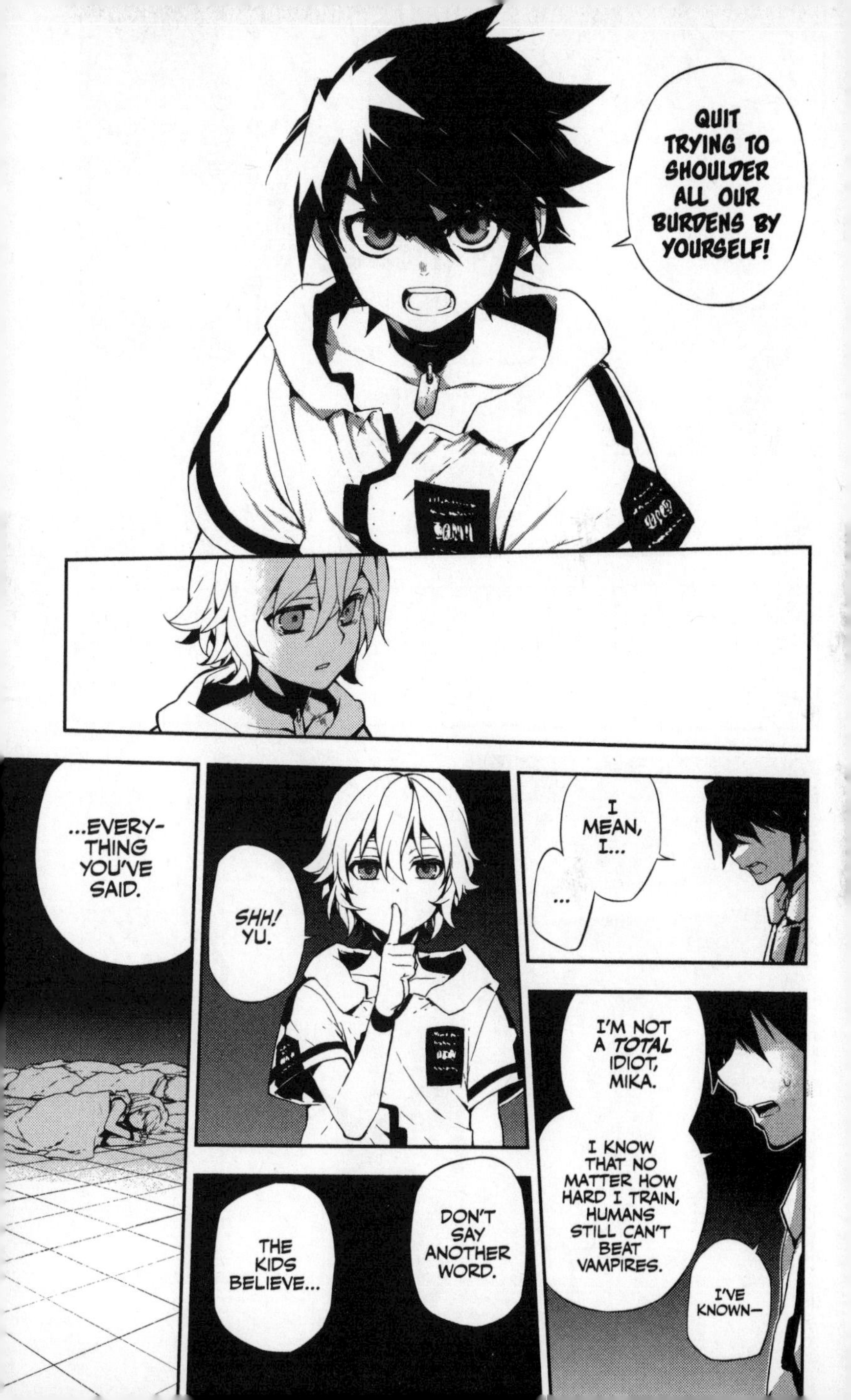
QUIT TRYING TO SHOULDER ALL OUR BURDENS BY YOURSELF!
I MEAN, I...
...
SHH! YU.
I'M NOT A *TOTAL* IDIOT, MIKA.
I KNOW THAT NO MATTER HOW HARD I TRAIN, HUMANS STILL CAN'T BEAT VAMPIRES.
I'VE KNOWN—
DON'T SAY ANOTHER WORD.
THE KIDS BELIEVE...
...EVERY-THING YOU'VE SAID.

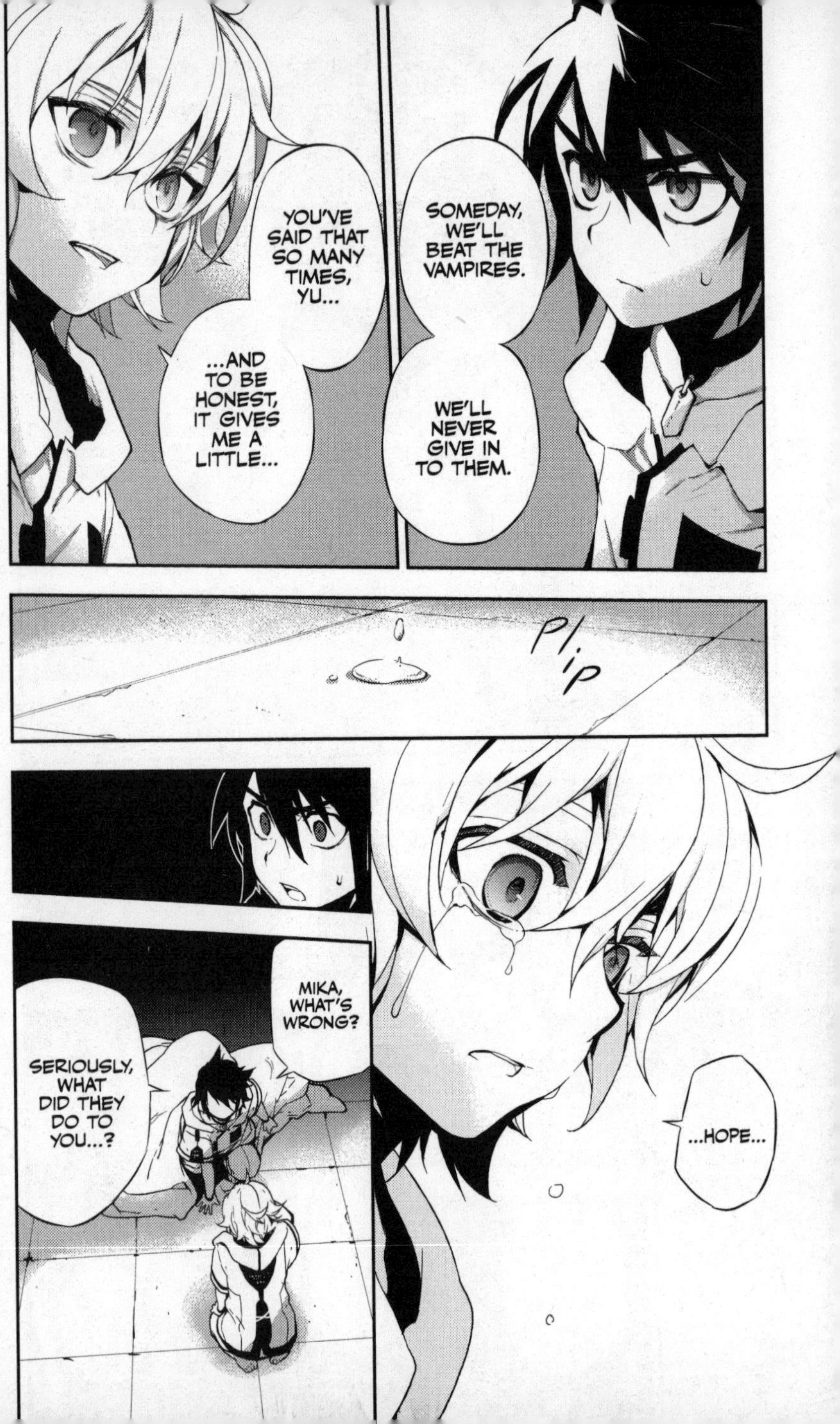
SOMEDAY, WE'LL BEAT THE VAMPIRES.
WE'LL NEVER GIVE IN TO THEM.
YOU'VE SAID THAT SO MANY TIMES, YU...
...AND TO BE HONEST, IT GIVES ME A LITTLE...
Plip
...HOPE...
MIKA, WHAT'S WRONG?
SERIOUSLY, WHAT DID THEY DO TO YOU...?

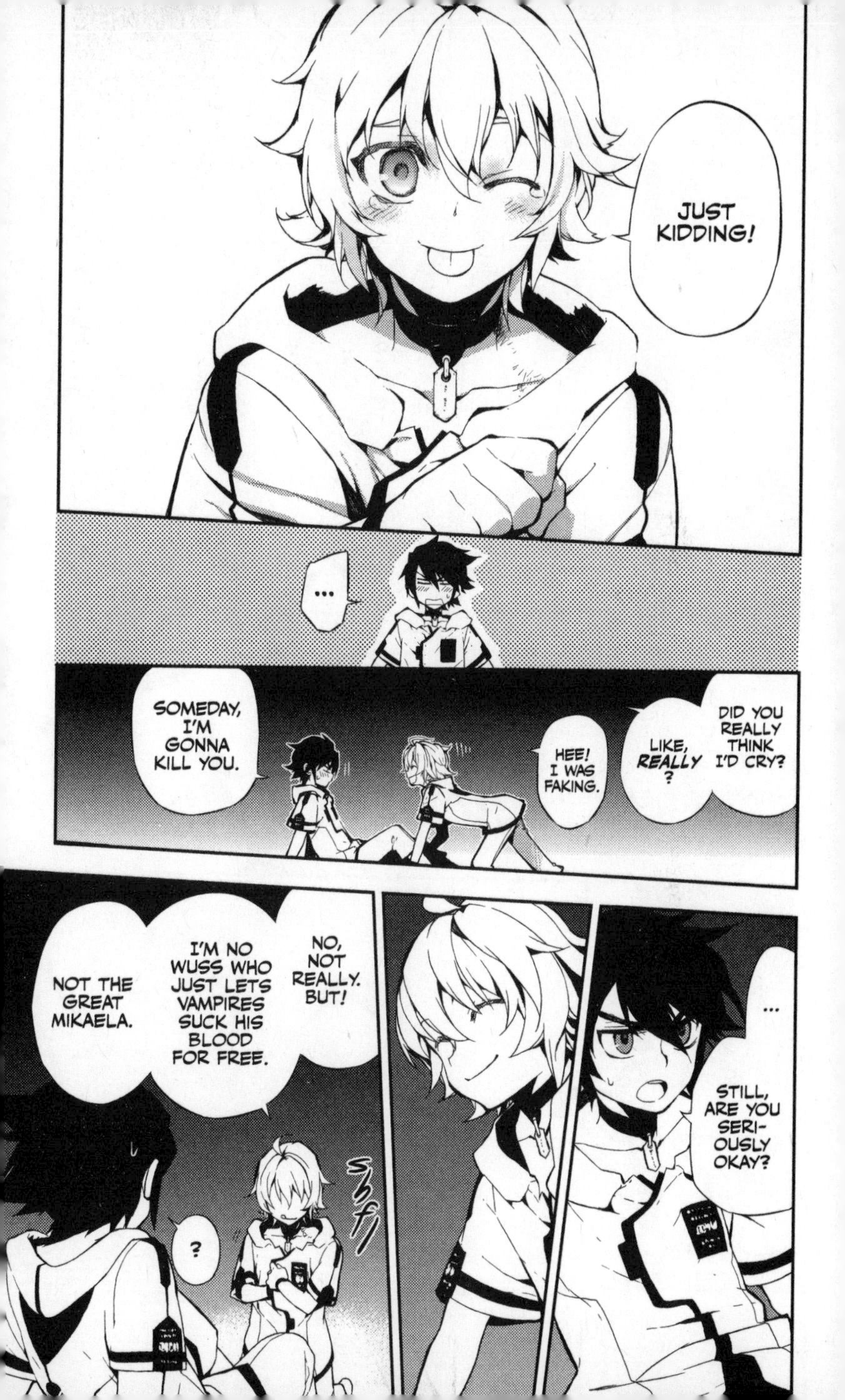
JUST KIDDING!
...
DID YOU REALLY THINK I'D CRY?
LIKE, REALLY?
HEE! I WAS FAKING.
SOMEDAY, I'M GONNA KILL YOU.
...
STILL, ARE YOU SERI-OUSLY OKAY?
NO, NOT REALLY. BUT!
I'M NO WUSS WHO JUST LETS VAMPIRES SUCK HIS BLOOD FOR FREE.
NOT THE GREAT MIKAELA.
?

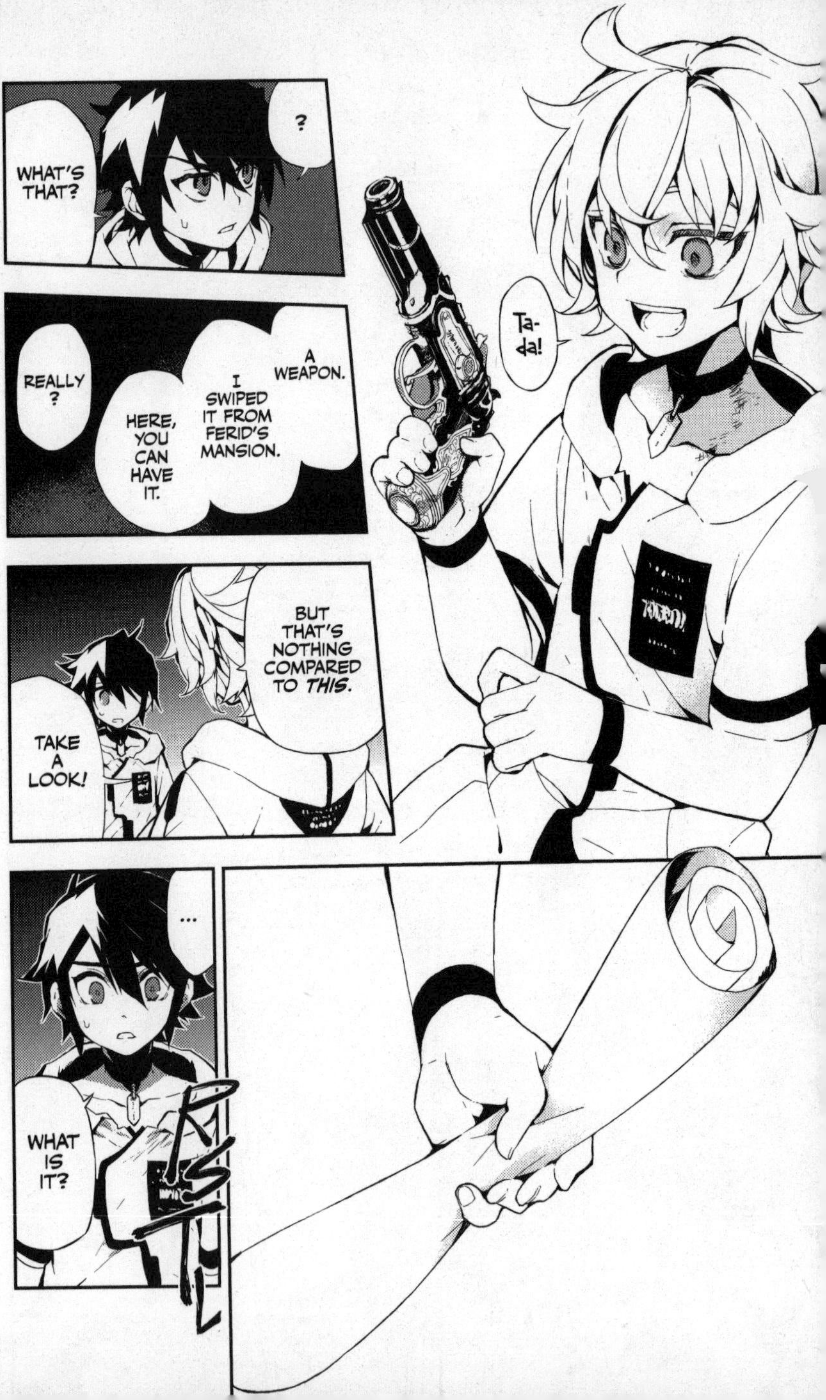

Ta-da!
?
WHAT'S THAT?
A WEAPON.
I SWIPED IT FROM FERID'S MANSION.
HERE, YOU CAN HAVE IT.
REALLY?
BUT THAT'S NOTHING COMPARED TO *THIS*.
TAKE A LOOK!
...
WHAT IS IT?

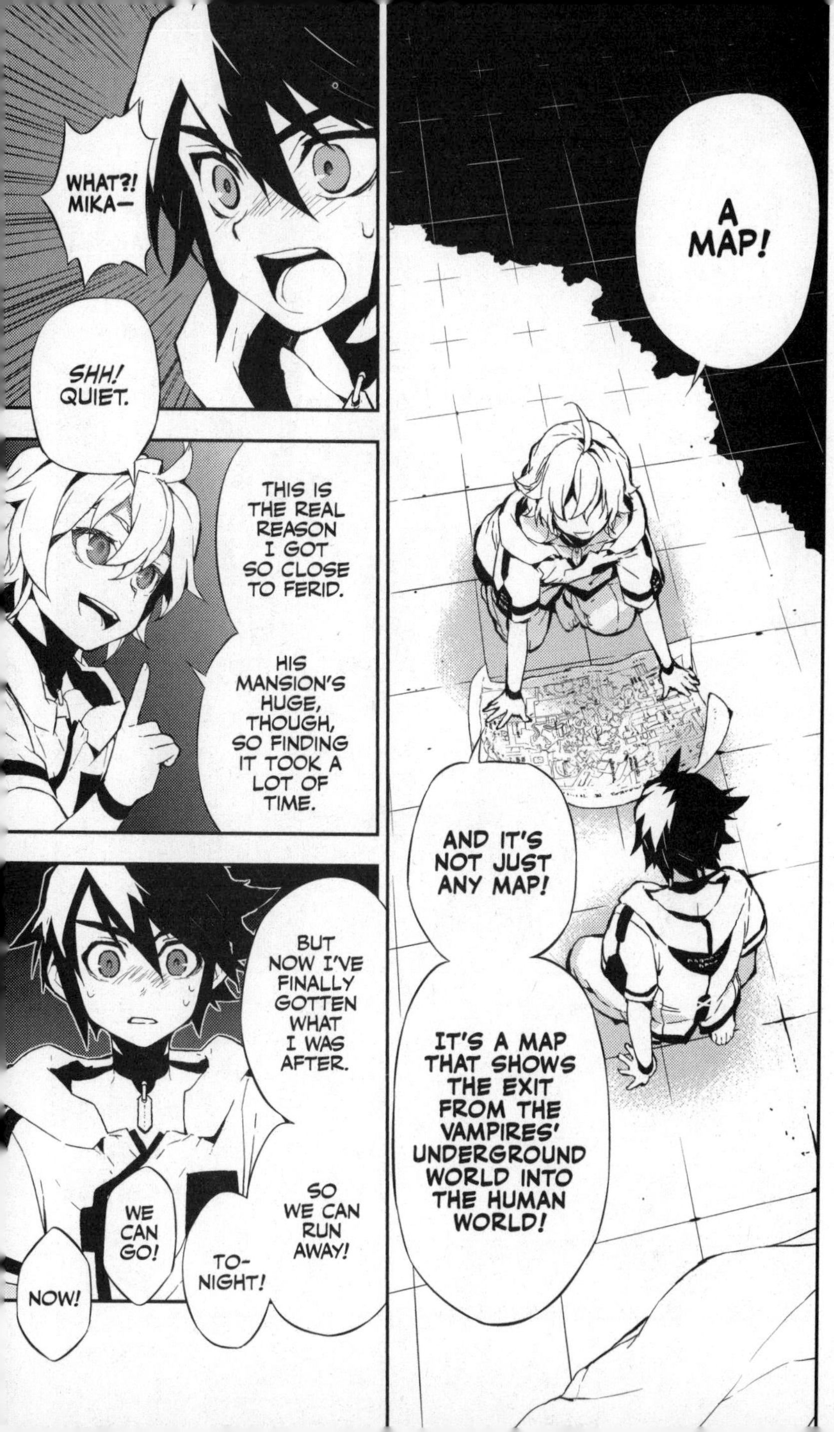
A MAP!
AND IT'S NOT JUST ANY MAP!
IT'S A MAP THAT SHOWS THE EXIT FROM THE VAMPIRES' UNDERGROUND WORLD INTO THE HUMAN WORLD!
WHAT?! MIKA—
SHH! QUIET.
THIS IS THE REAL REASON I GOT SO CLOSE TO FERID.
HIS MANSION'S HUGE, THOUGH, SO FINDING IT TOOK A LOT OF TIME.
BUT NOW I'VE FINALLY GOTTEN WHAT I WAS AFTER.
SO WE CAN RUN AWAY!
TO-NIGHT!
WE CAN GO!
NOW!

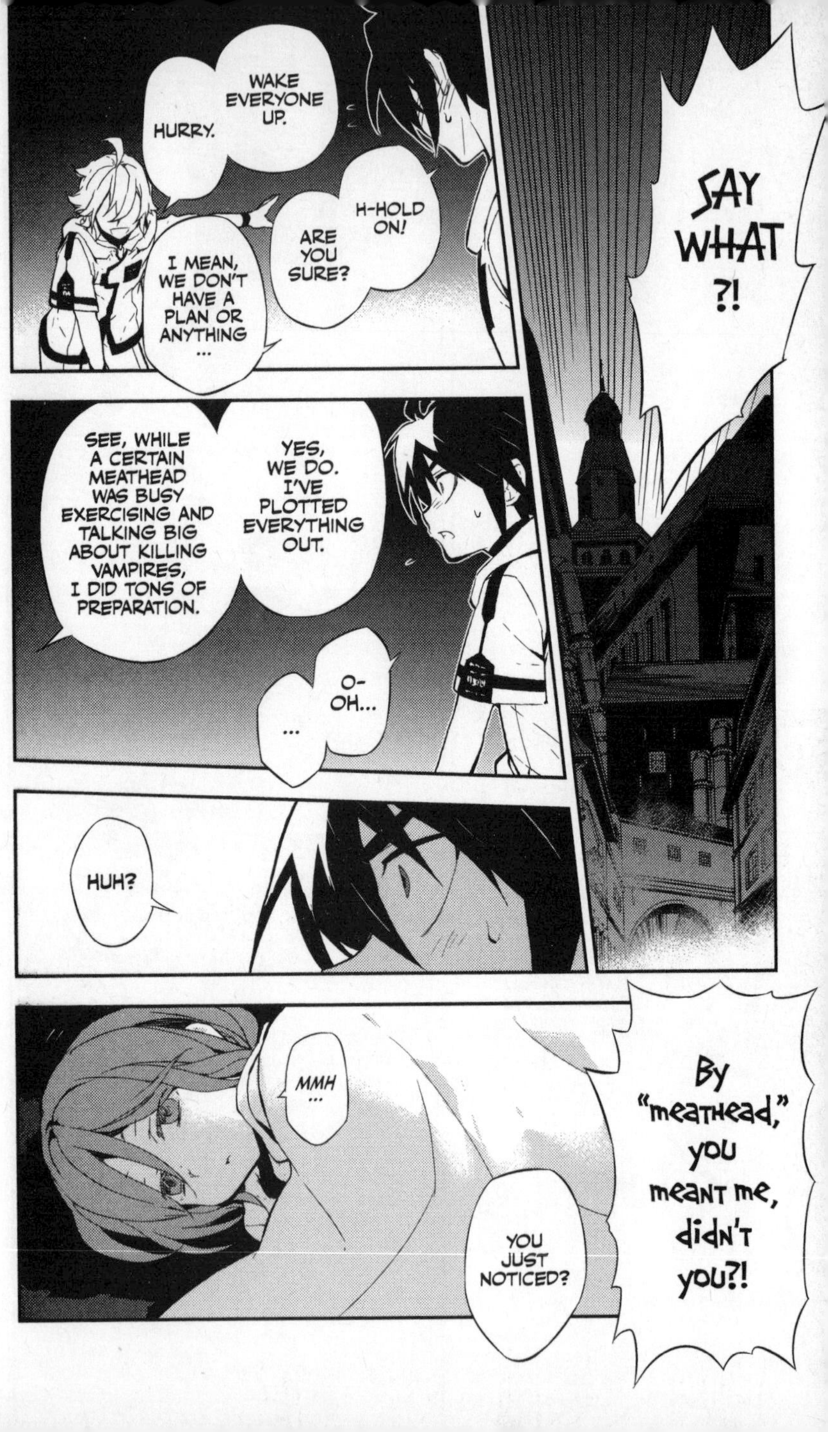
SAY WHAT ?!
WAKE EVERYONE UP.
HURRY.
H-HOLD ON! ARE YOU SURE?
I MEAN, WE DON'T HAVE A PLAN OR ANYTHING ...
YES, WE DO. I'VE PLOTTED EVERYTHING OUT.
SEE, WHILE A CERTAIN MEATHEAD WAS BUSY EXERCISING AND TALKING BIG ABOUT KILLING VAMPIRES, I DID TONS OF PREPARATION.
O-OH... ...
HUH?
By "meathead," you meant me, didn't you?!
MMH ...
YOU JUST NOTICED?

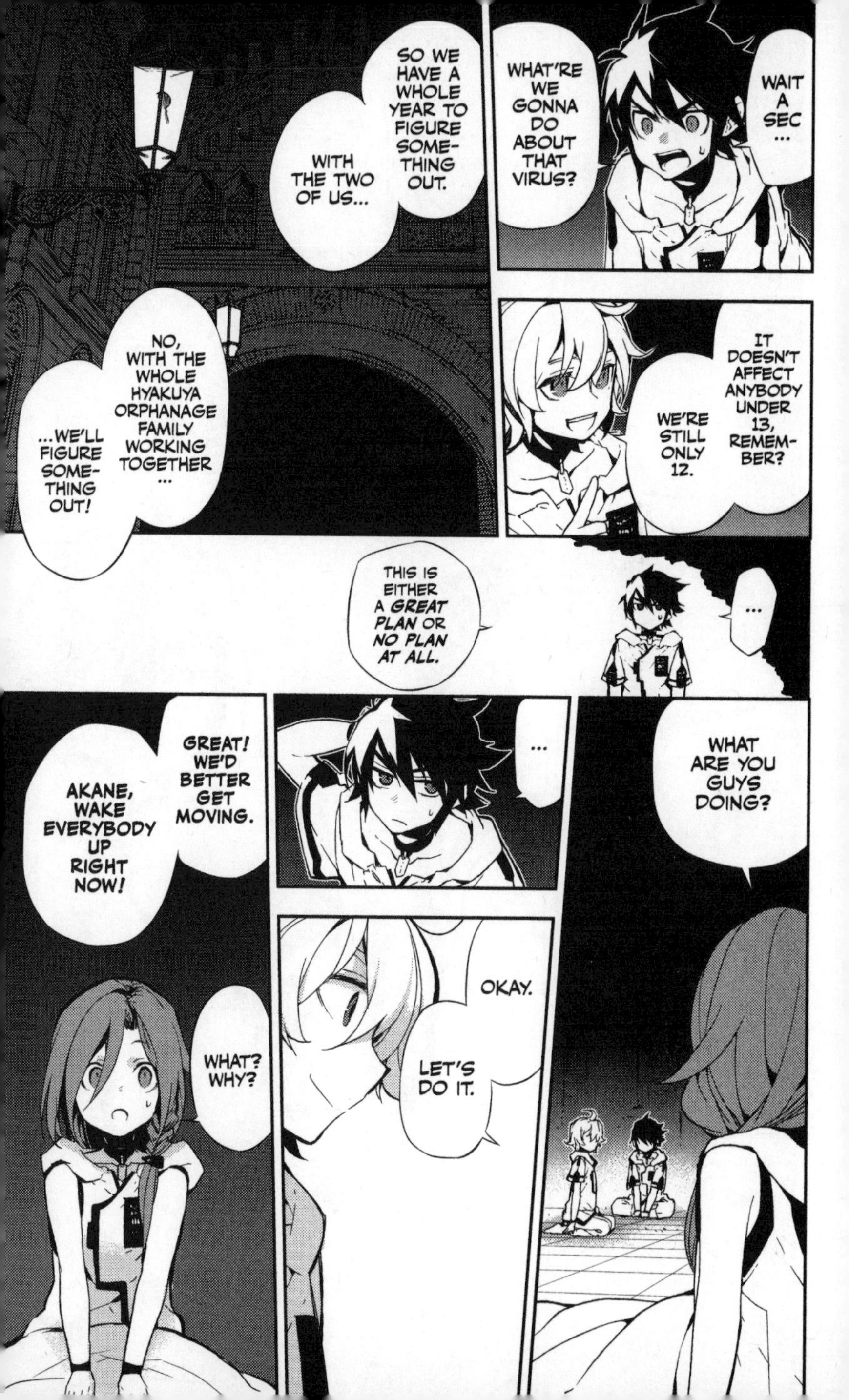
WAIT A SEC ...
WHAT'RE WE GONNA DO ABOUT THAT VIRUS?
IT DOESN'T AFFECT ANYBODY UNDER 13, REMEMBER?
WE'RE STILL ONLY 12.
SO WE HAVE A WHOLE YEAR TO FIGURE SOMETHING OUT.
WITH THE TWO OF US...
NO, WITH THE WHOLE HYAKUYA ORPHANAGE FAMILY WORKING TOGETHER ...
...WE'LL FIGURE SOMETHING OUT!
...
THIS IS EITHER A *GREAT PLAN* OR *NO PLAN AT ALL.*
WHAT ARE YOU GUYS DOING?
...
OKAY.
LET'S DO IT.
GREAT! WE'D BETTER GET MOVING.
AKANE, WAKE EVERYBODY UP RIGHT NOW!
WHAT? WHY?

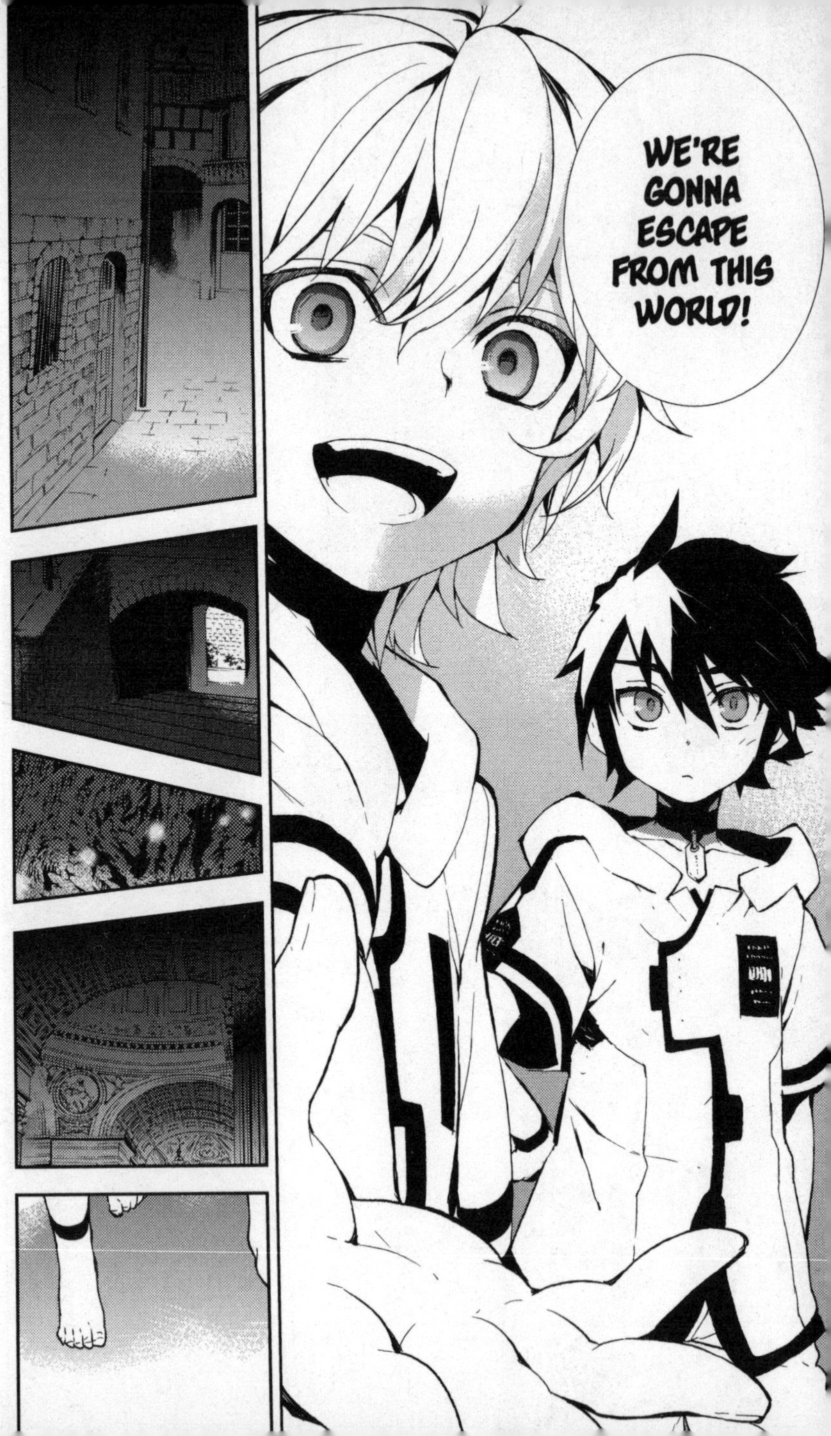
WE'RE GONNA ESCAPE FROM THIS WORLD!

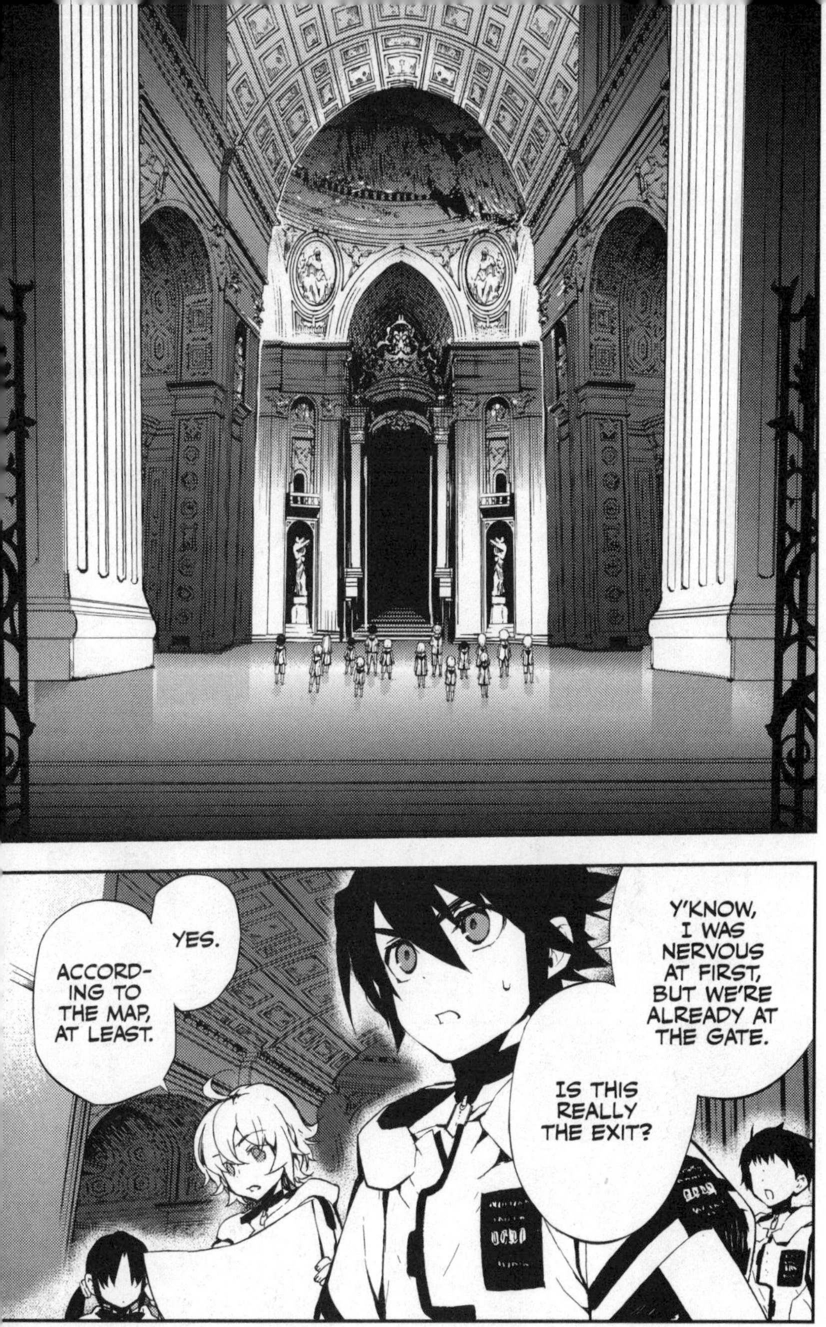
Y'KNOW, I WAS NERVOUS AT FIRST, BUT WE'RE ALREADY AT THE GATE.
IS THIS REALLY THE EXIT?
YES.
ACCORD-ING TO THE MAP, AT LEAST.

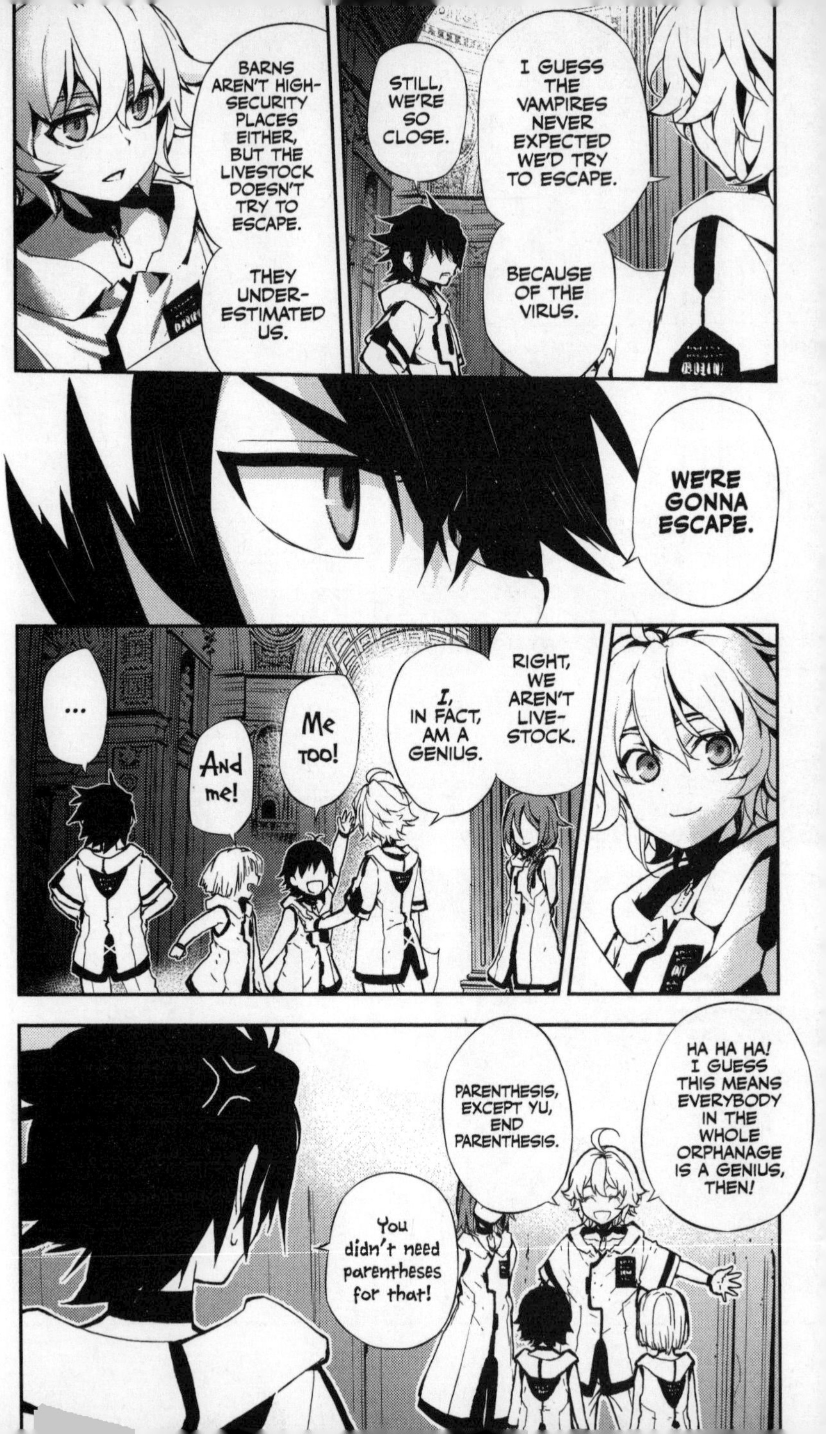
I GUESS THE VAMPIRES NEVER EXPECTED WE'D TRY TO ESCAPE.
BECAUSE OF THE VIRUS.
STILL, WE'RE SO CLOSE.
BARNS AREN'T HIGH-SECURITY PLACES EITHER, BUT THE LIVESTOCK DOESN'T TRY TO ESCAPE.
THEY UNDER-ESTIMATED US.
WE'RE GONNA ESCAPE.
RIGHT, WE AREN'T LIVE-STOCK.
I, IN FACT, AM A GENIUS.
Me too!
And me!
...
HA HA HA! I GUESS THIS MEANS EVERYBODY IN THE WHOLE ORPHANAGE IS A GENIUS, THEN!
PARENTHESIS, EXCEPT YU, END PARENTHESIS.
You didn't need parentheses for that!

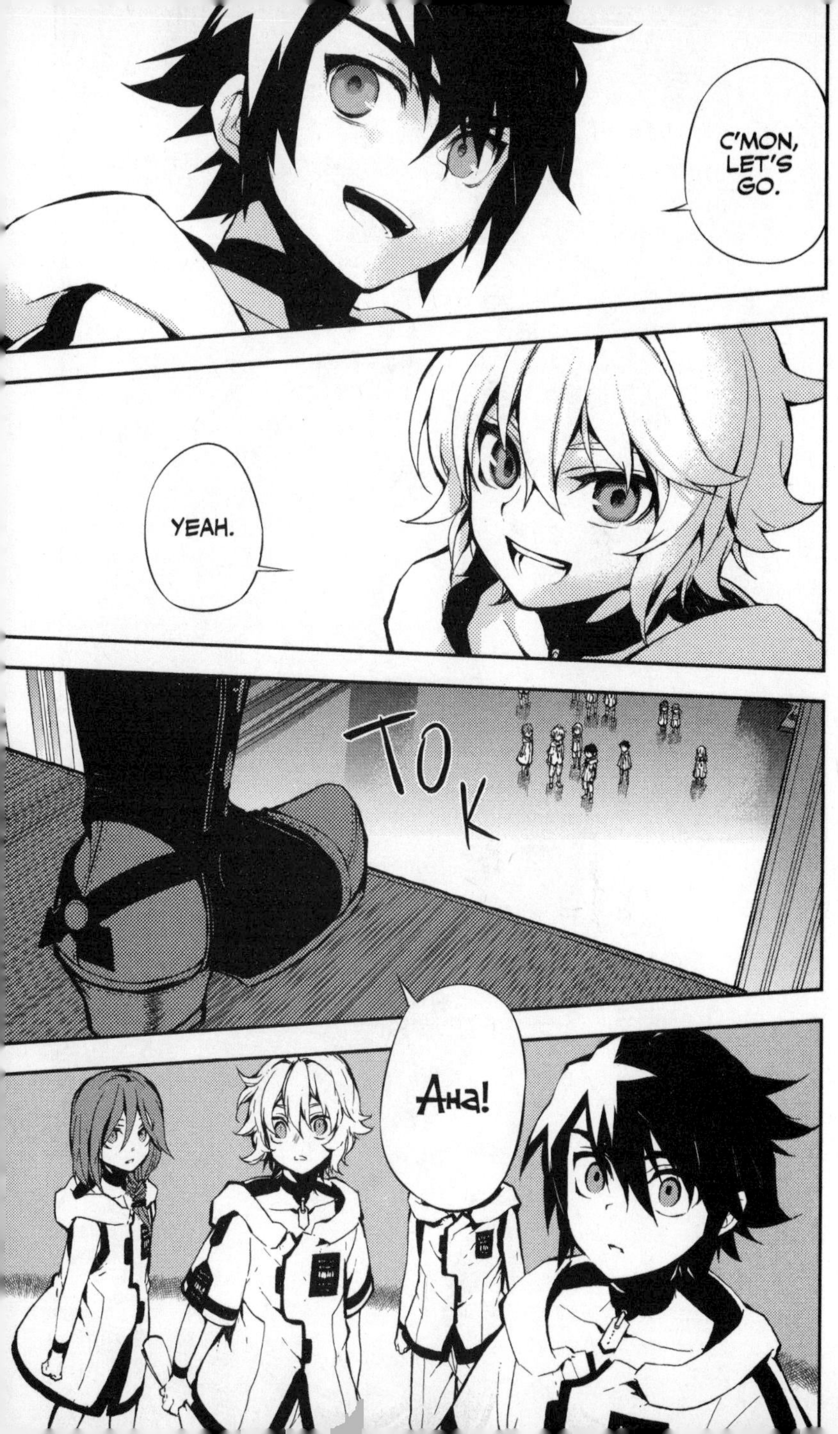
C'MON, LET'S GO.
YEAH.
TOK
AHA!

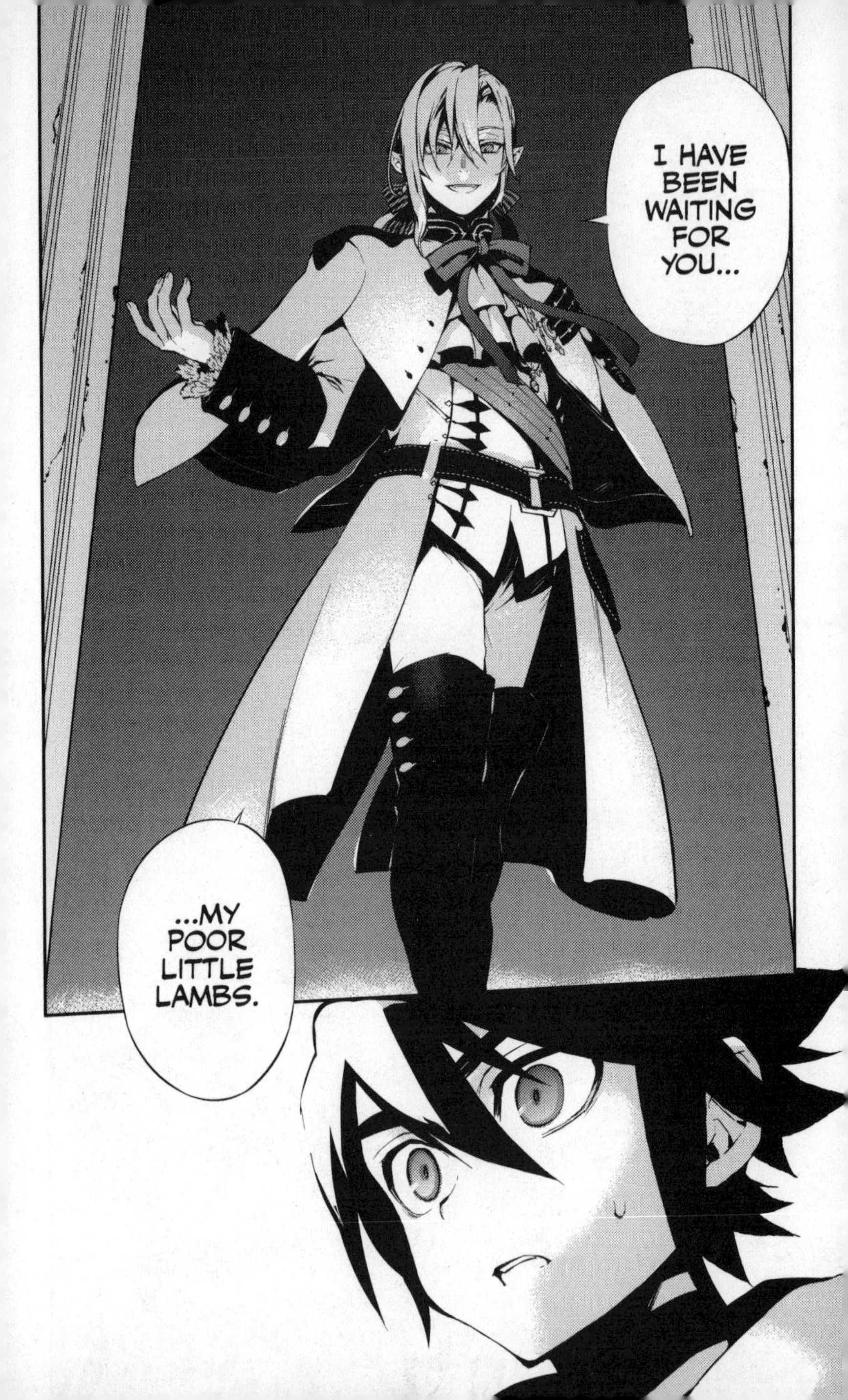
I HAVE BEEN WAITING FOR YOU...
...MY POOR LITTLE LAMBS.

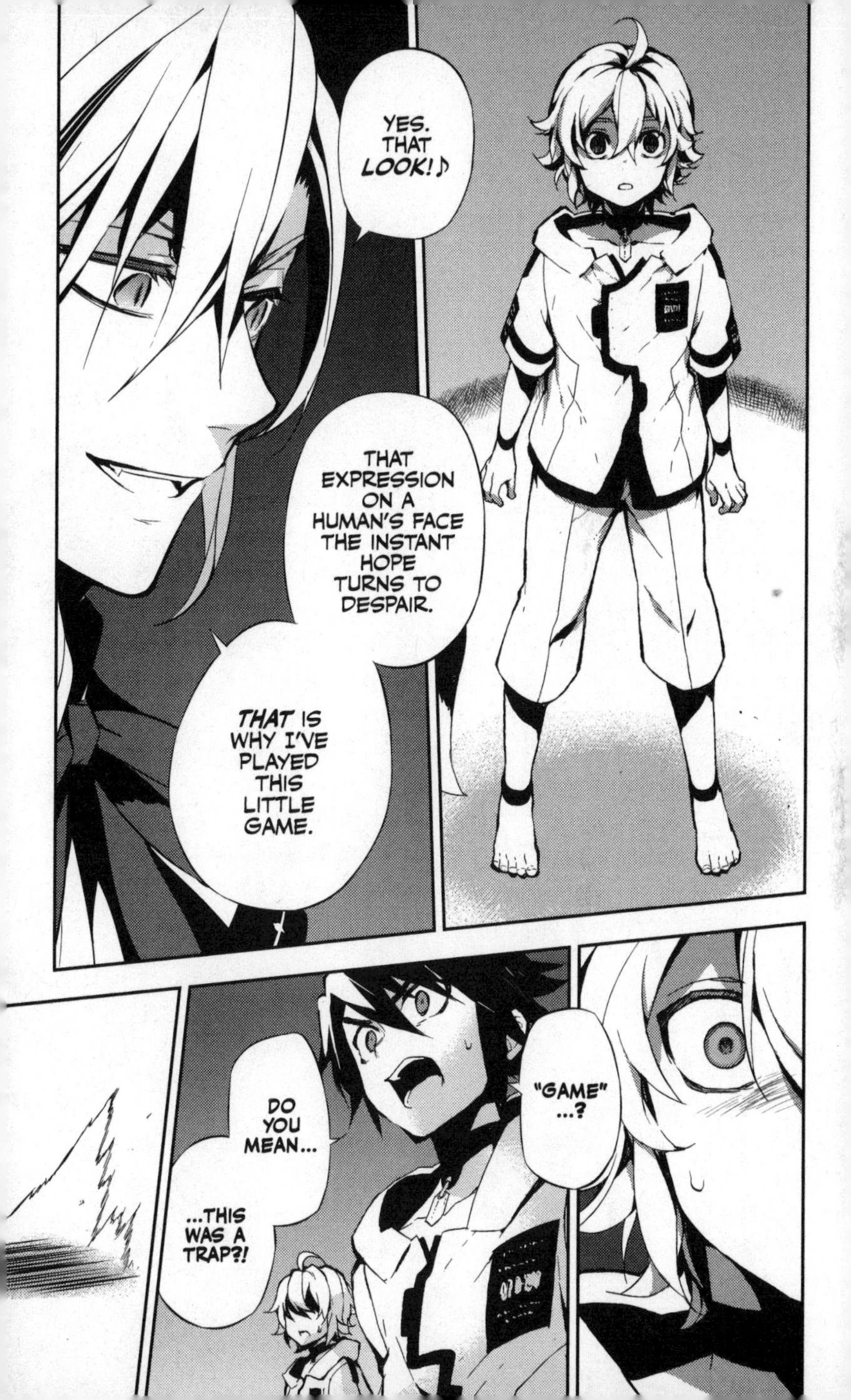
YES. THAT LOOK!♪
THAT EXPRESSION ON A HUMAN'S FACE THE INSTANT HOPE TURNS TO DESPAIR.
THAT IS WHY I'VE PLAYED THIS LITTLE GAME.
"GAME" ...?
DO YOU MEAN...
...THIS WAS A TRAP?!

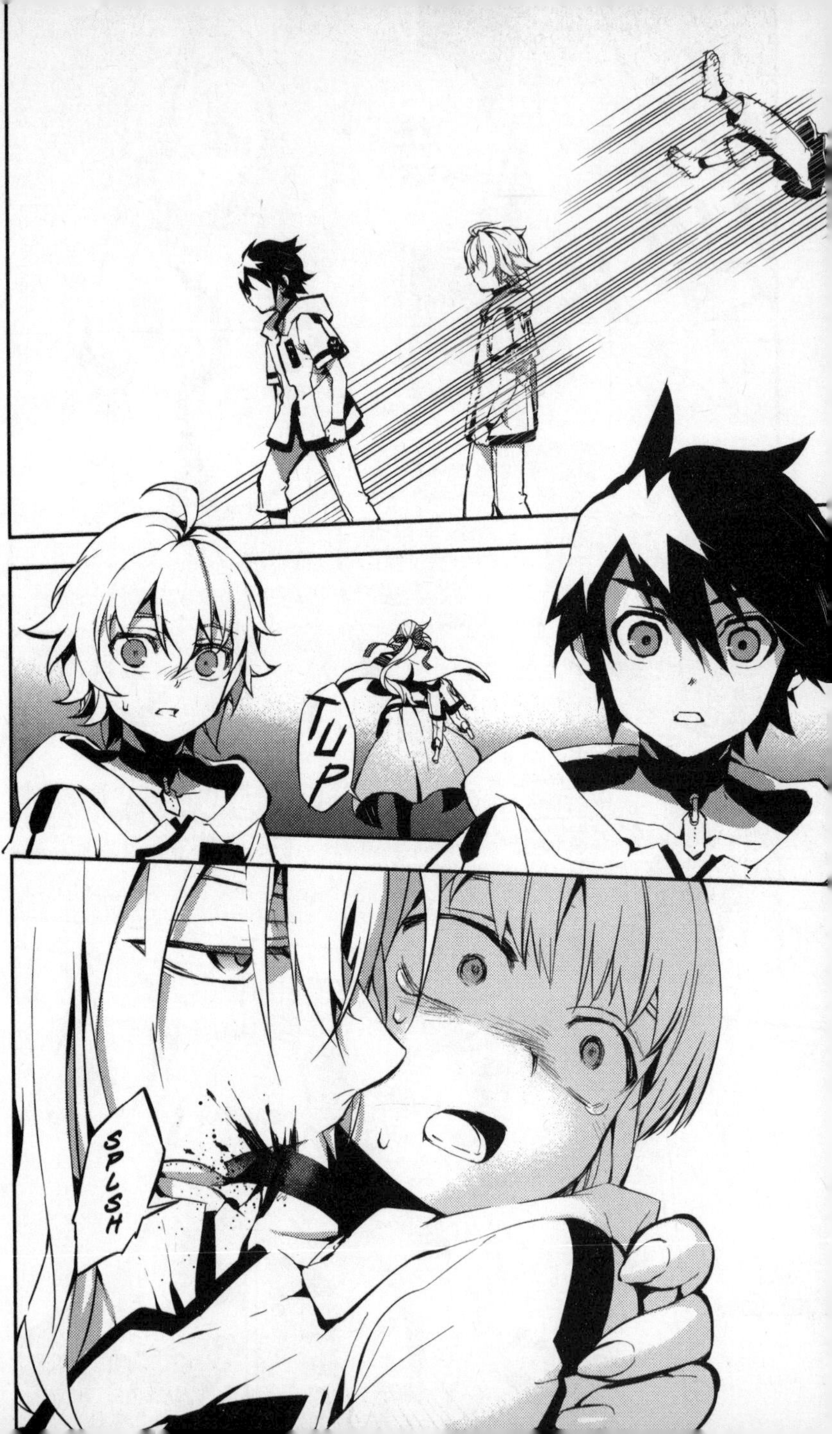
TUP
SPLSH

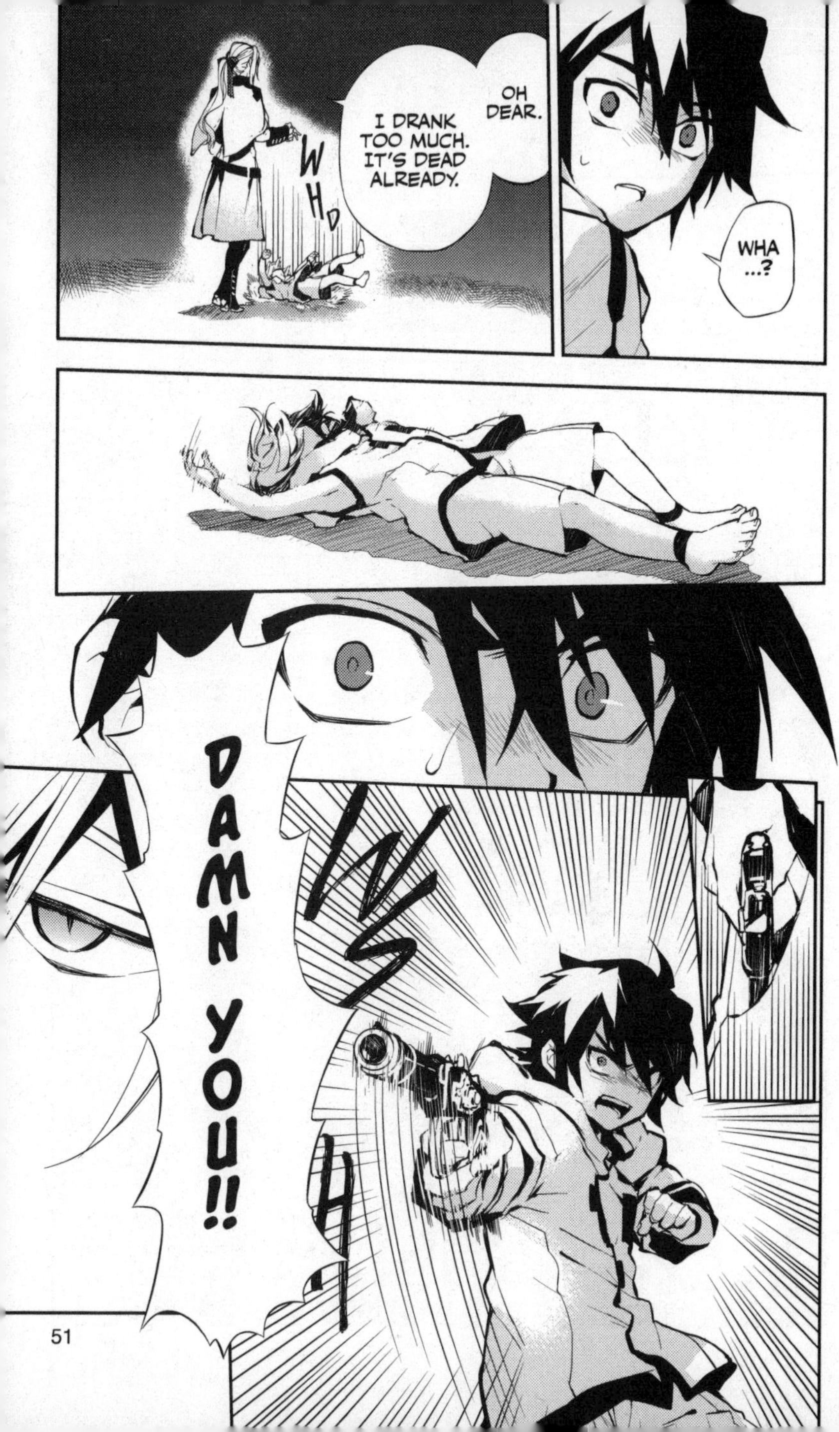
WHA ...?
OH DEAR.
I DRANK TOO MUCH. IT'S DEAD ALREADY.
WHD
DAMN YOU!!

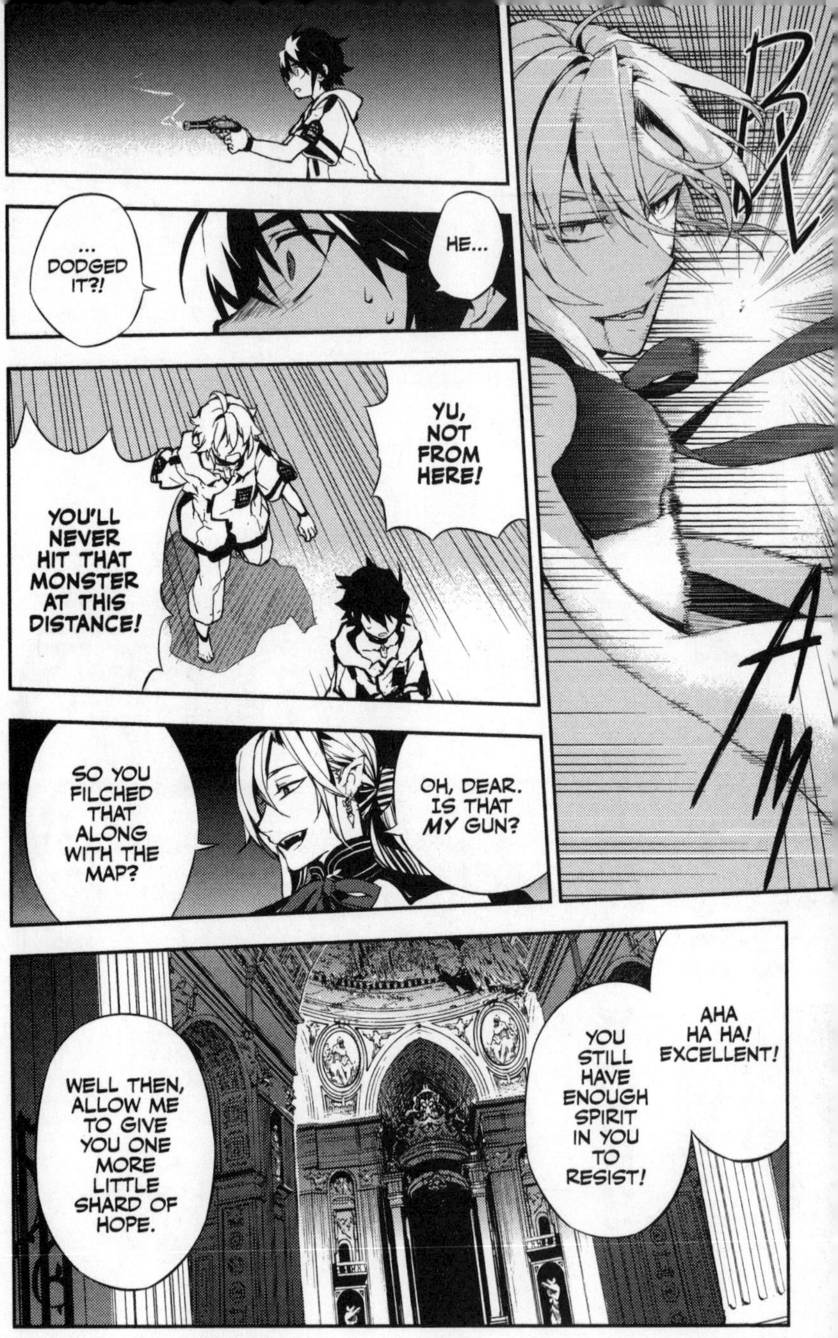
BLAM
HE...
...DODGED IT?!
YU, NOT FROM HERE!
YOU'LL NEVER HIT THAT MONSTER AT THIS DISTANCE!
OH, DEAR. IS THAT *MY* GUN?
SO YOU FILCHED THAT ALONG WITH THE MAP?
AHA HA HA! EXCELLENT!
YOU STILL HAVE ENOUGH SPIRIT IN YOU TO RESIST!
WELL THEN, ALLOW ME TO GIVE YOU ONE MORE LITTLE SHARD OF HOPE.

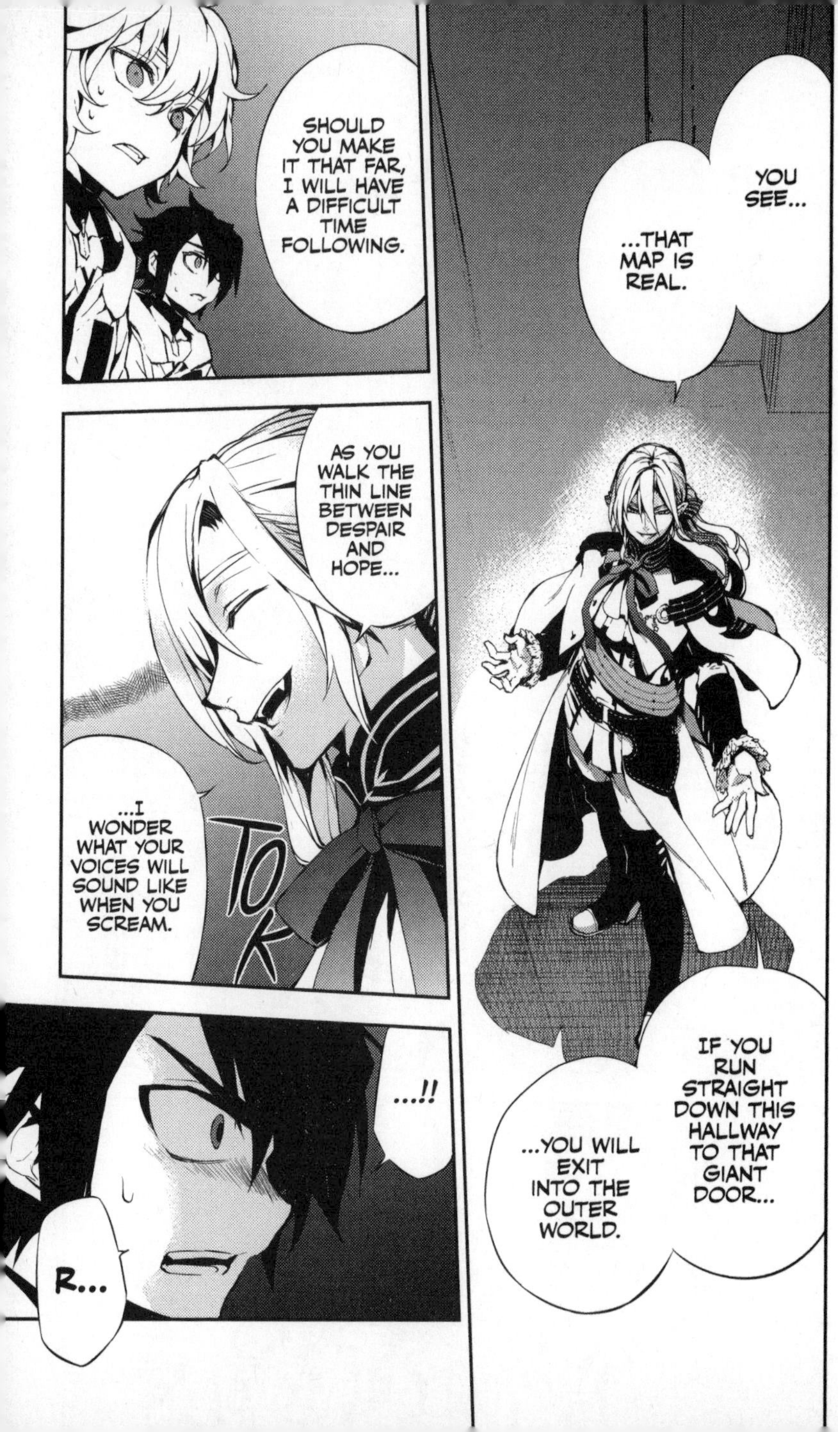
YOU SEE...
...THAT MAP IS REAL.
IF YOU RUN STRAIGHT DOWN THIS HALLWAY TO THAT GIANT DOOR...
...YOU WILL EXIT INTO THE OUTER WORLD.
SHOULD YOU MAKE IT THAT FAR, I WILL HAVE A DIFFICULT TIME FOLLOWING.
AS YOU WALK THE THIN LINE BETWEEN DESPAIR AND HOPE...
...I WONDER WHAT YOUR VOICES WILL SOUND LIKE WHEN YOU SCREAM.
TOK
...!!
R...

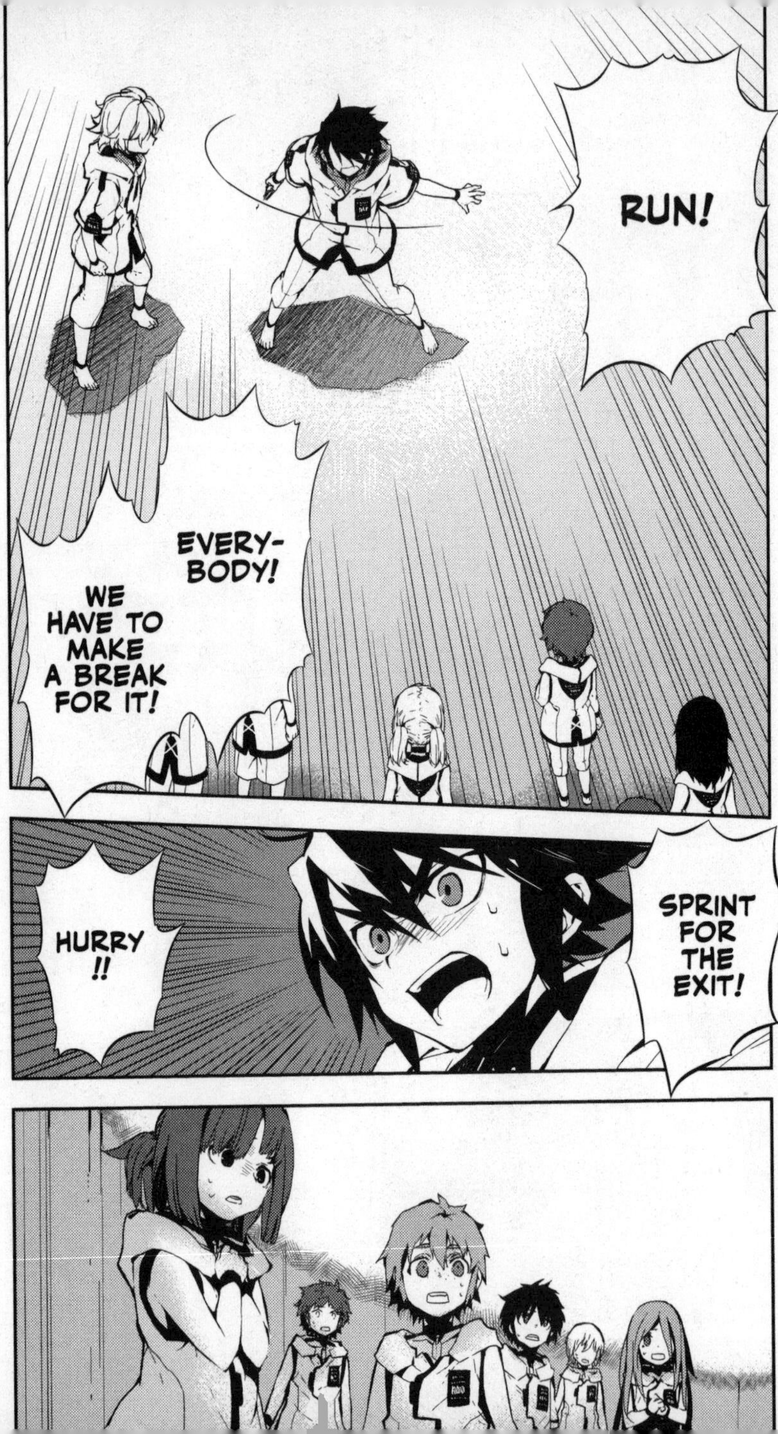
RUN!
EVERY-BODY!
WE HAVE TO MAKE A BREAK FOR IT!
SPRINT FOR THE EXIT!
HURRY!!

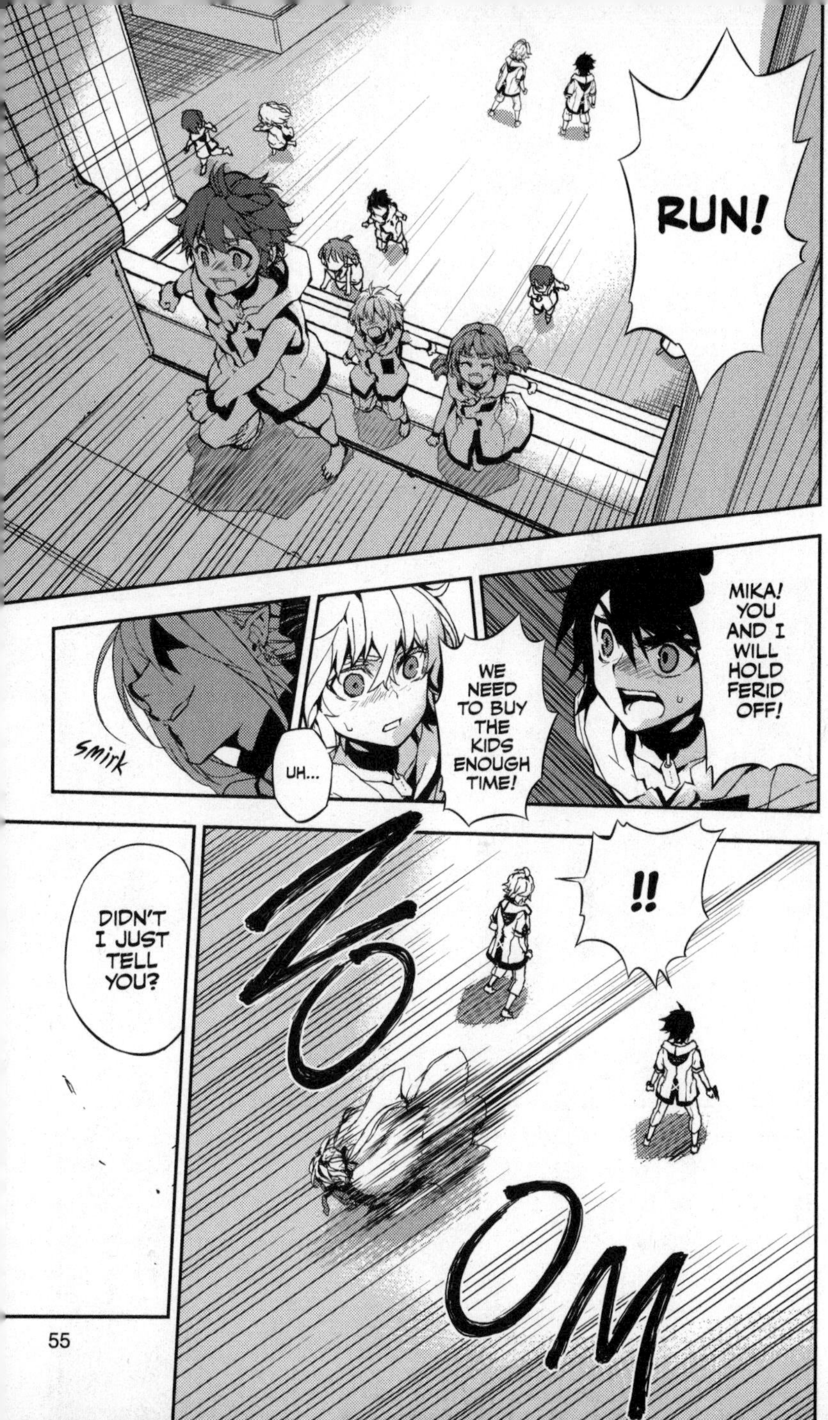
RUN!
MIKA! YOU AND I WILL HOLD FERID OFF!
WE NEED TO BUY THE KIDS ENOUGH TIME!
UH...
smirk
!!
DIDN'T I JUST TELL YOU?

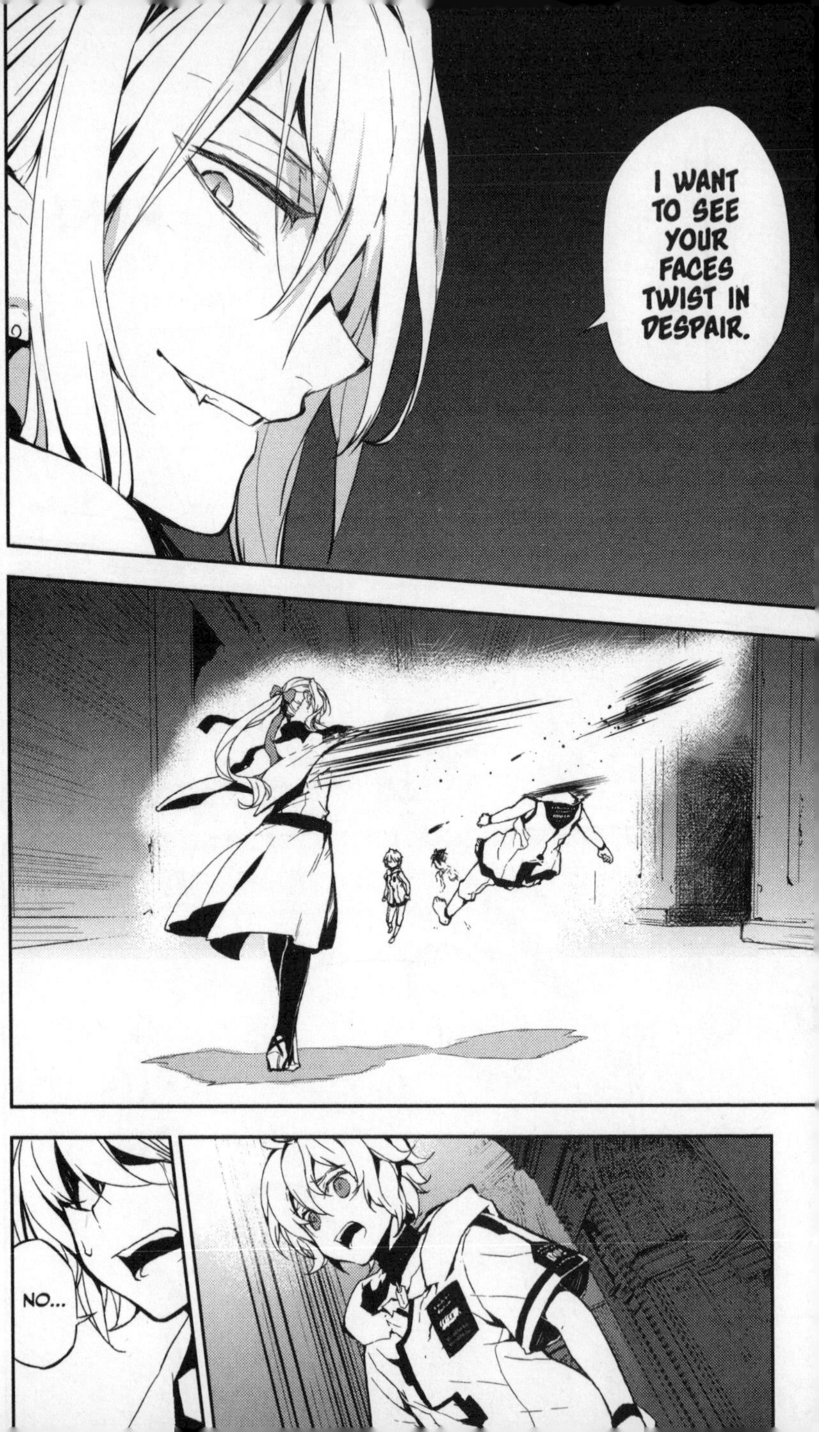
I WANT TO SEE YOUR FACES TWIST IN DESPAIR.
NO...

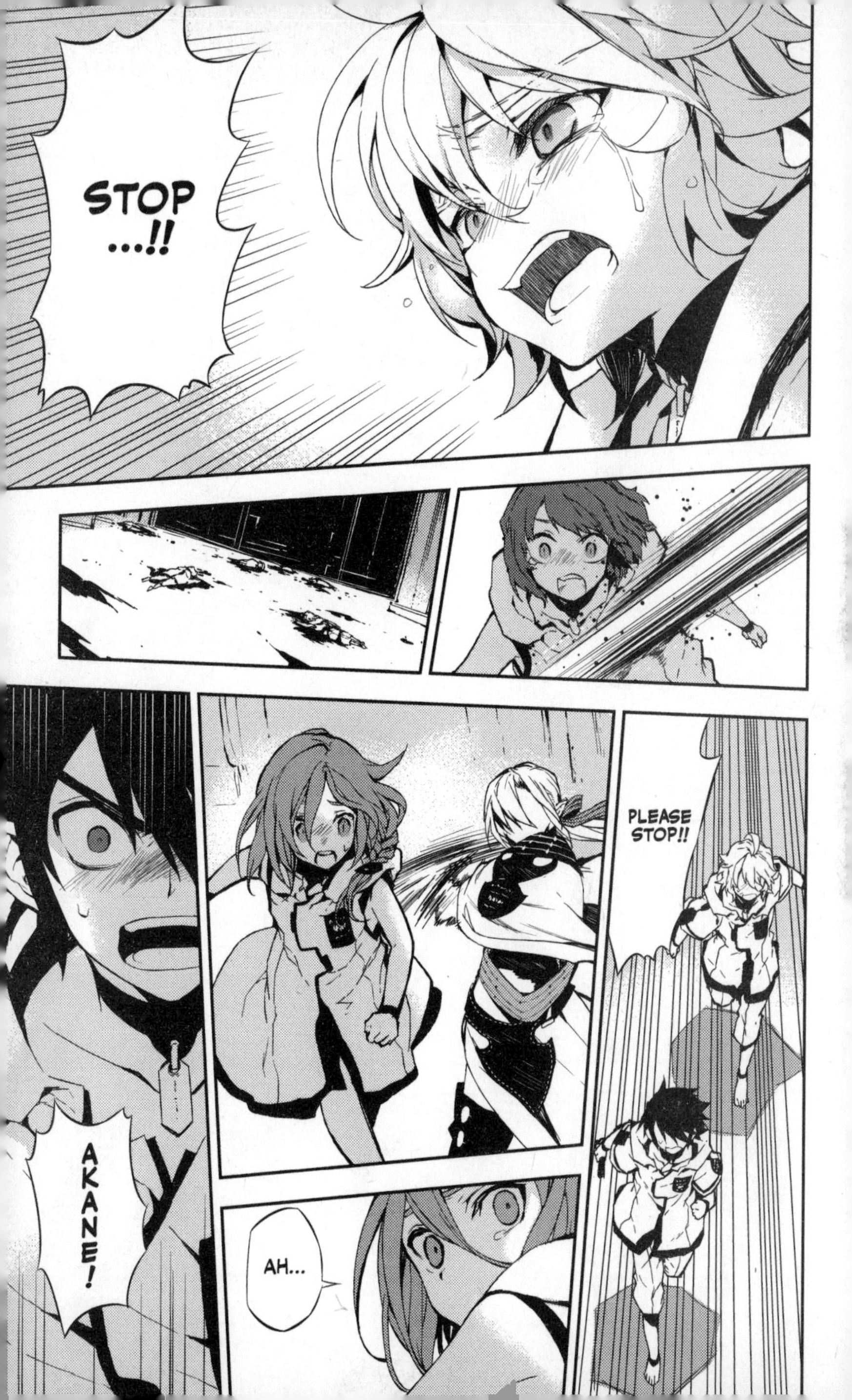
STOP ...!!
PLEASE STOP!!
AH...
AKANE!

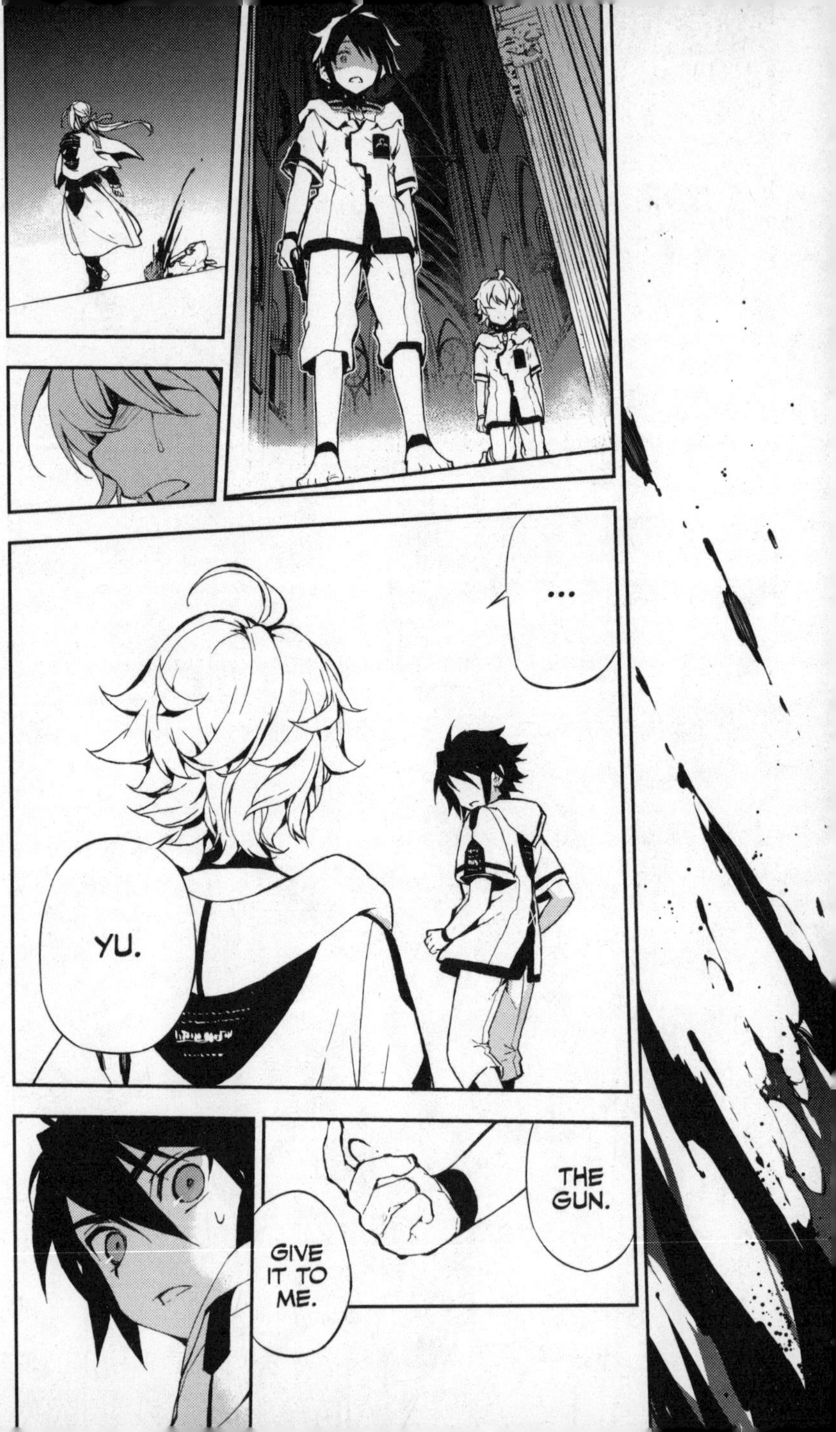
...
YU.
THE GUN.
GIVE IT TO ME.

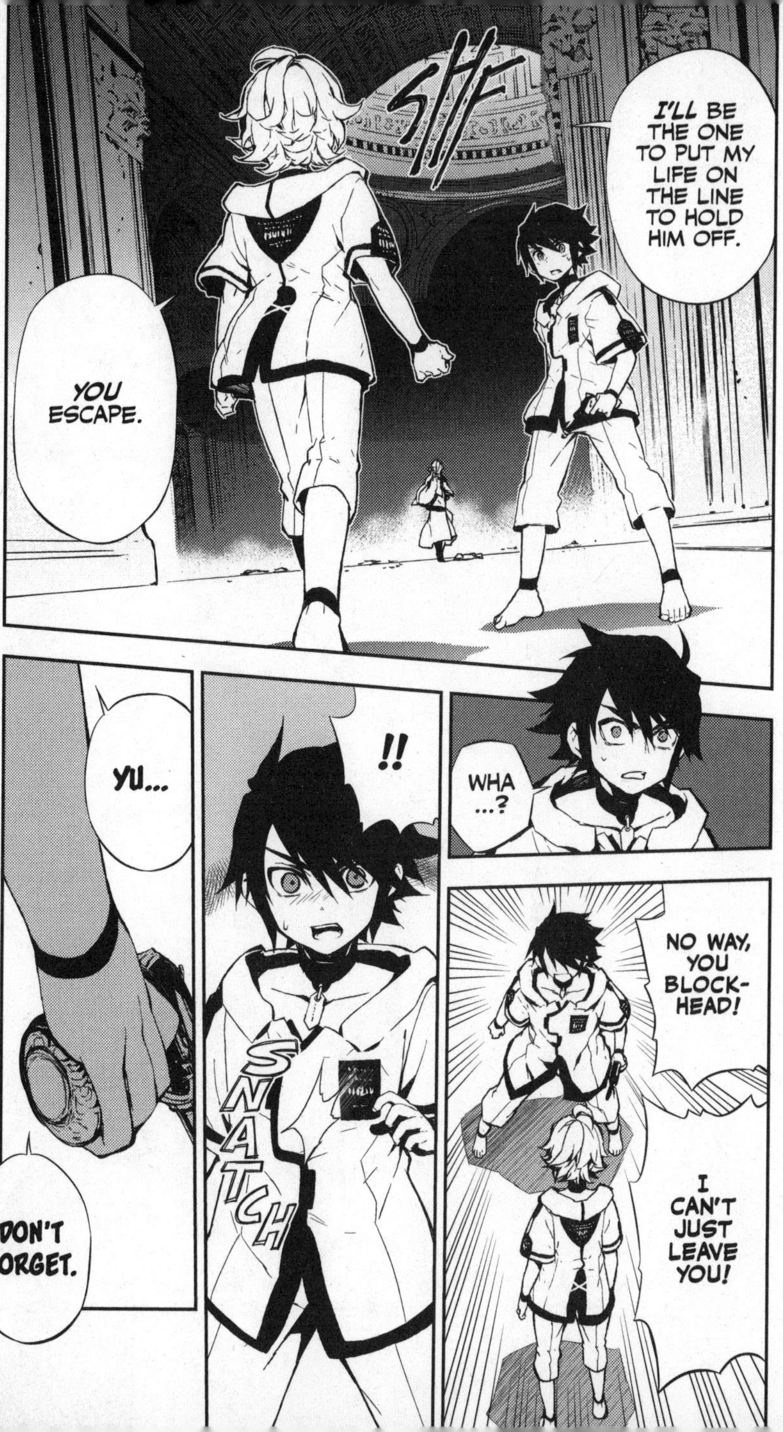
I'LL BE THE ONE TO PUT MY LIFE ON THE LINE TO HOLD HIM OFF.
SHF
YOU ESCAPE.
WHA ...?
NO WAY, YOU BLOCK-HEAD!
I CAN'T JUST LEAVE YOU!
!!
SNATCH
YU...
DON'T FORGET.

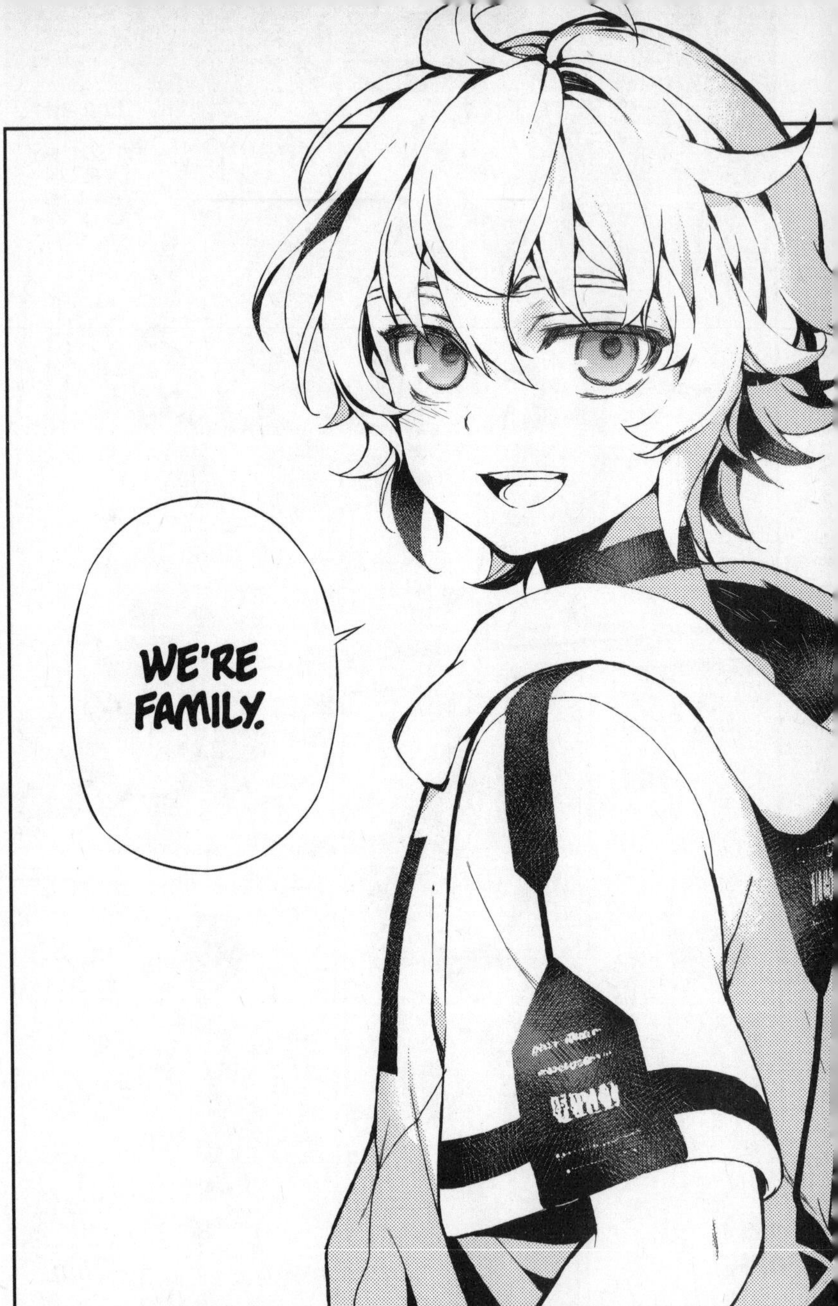
WE'RE FAMILY.

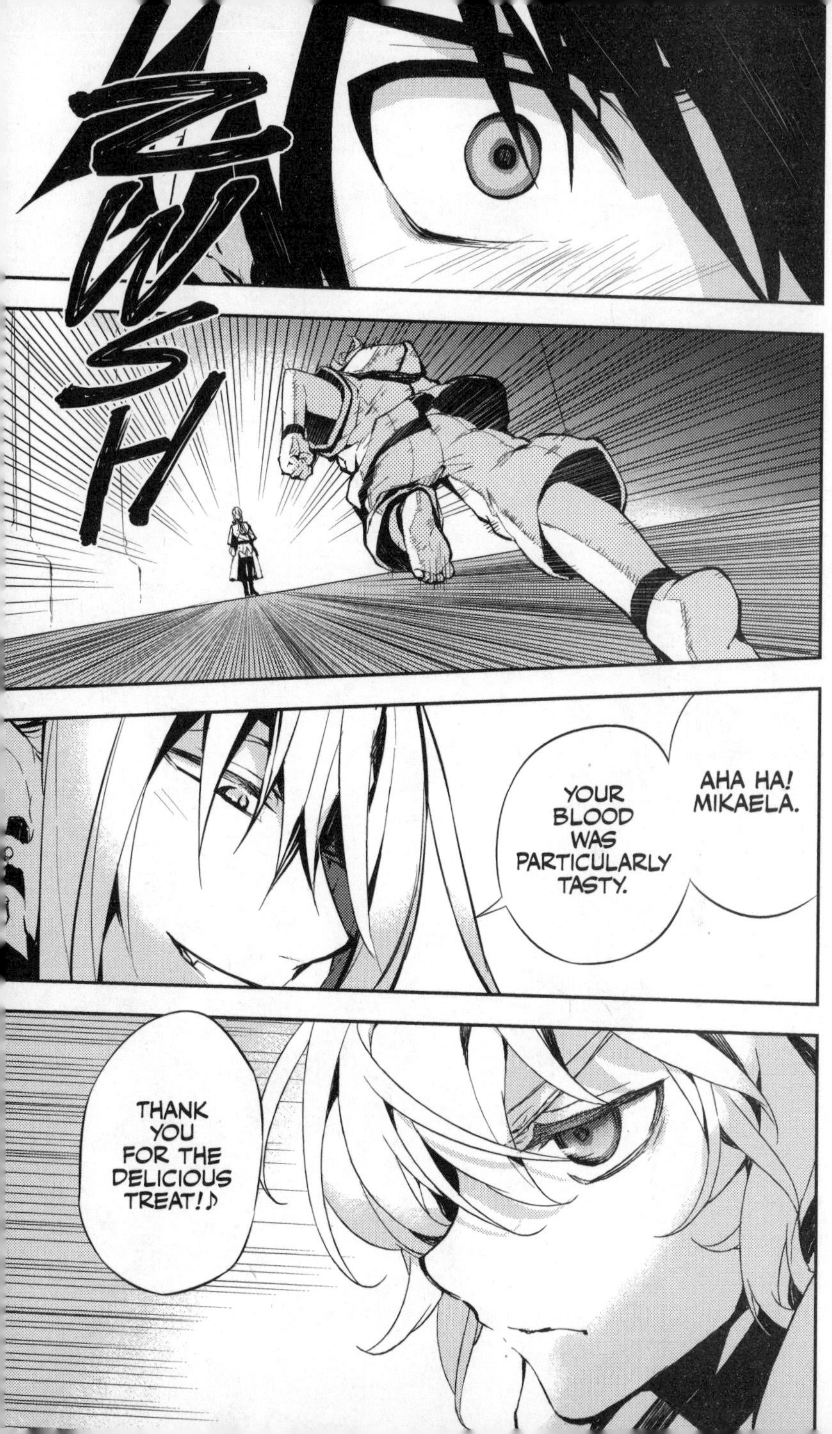

WHSH
AHA HA! MIKAELA.
YOUR BLOOD WAS PARTICULARLY TASTY.
THANK YOU FOR THE DELICIOUS TREAT!♪

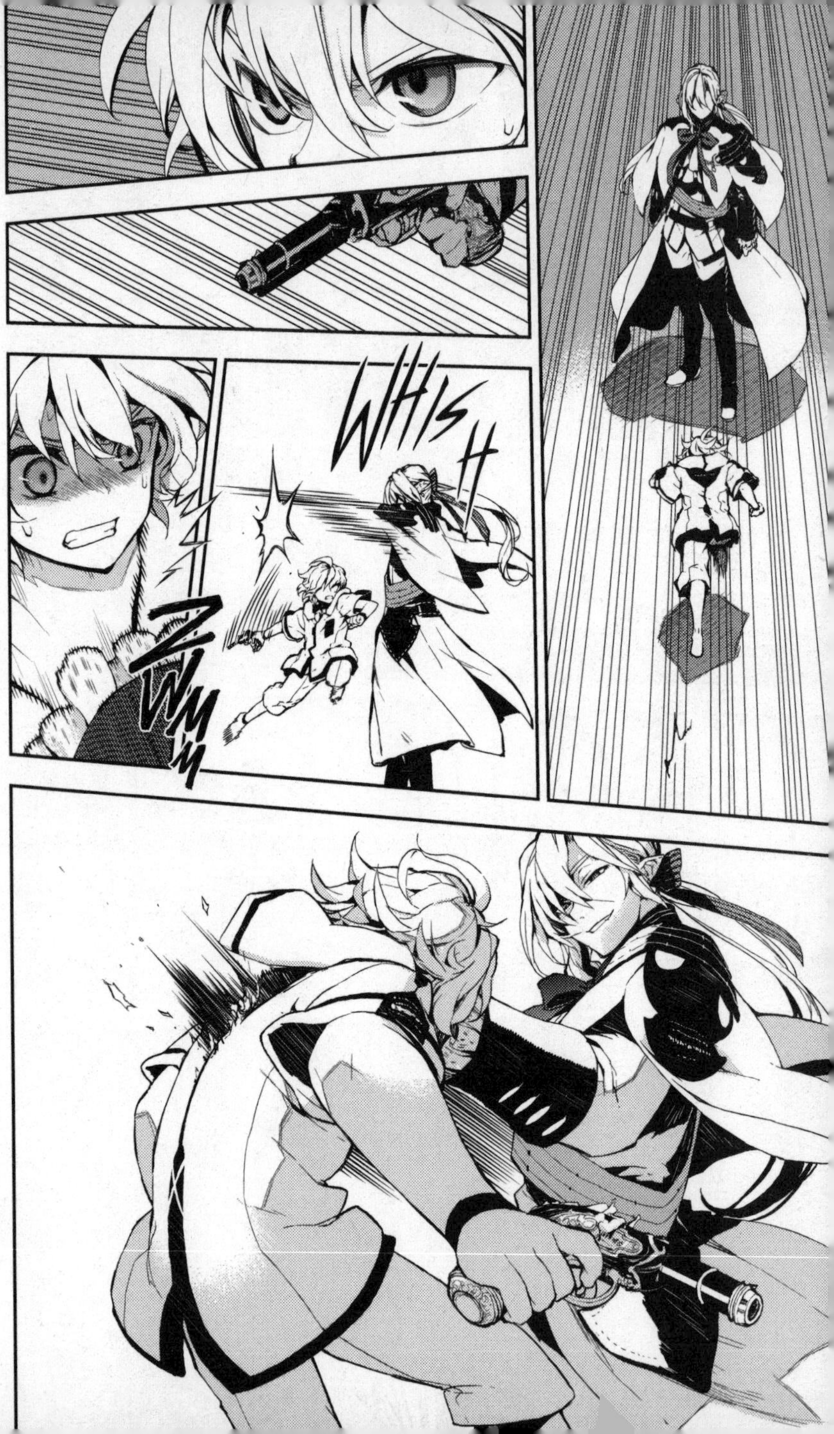
WHISH
ZWMM

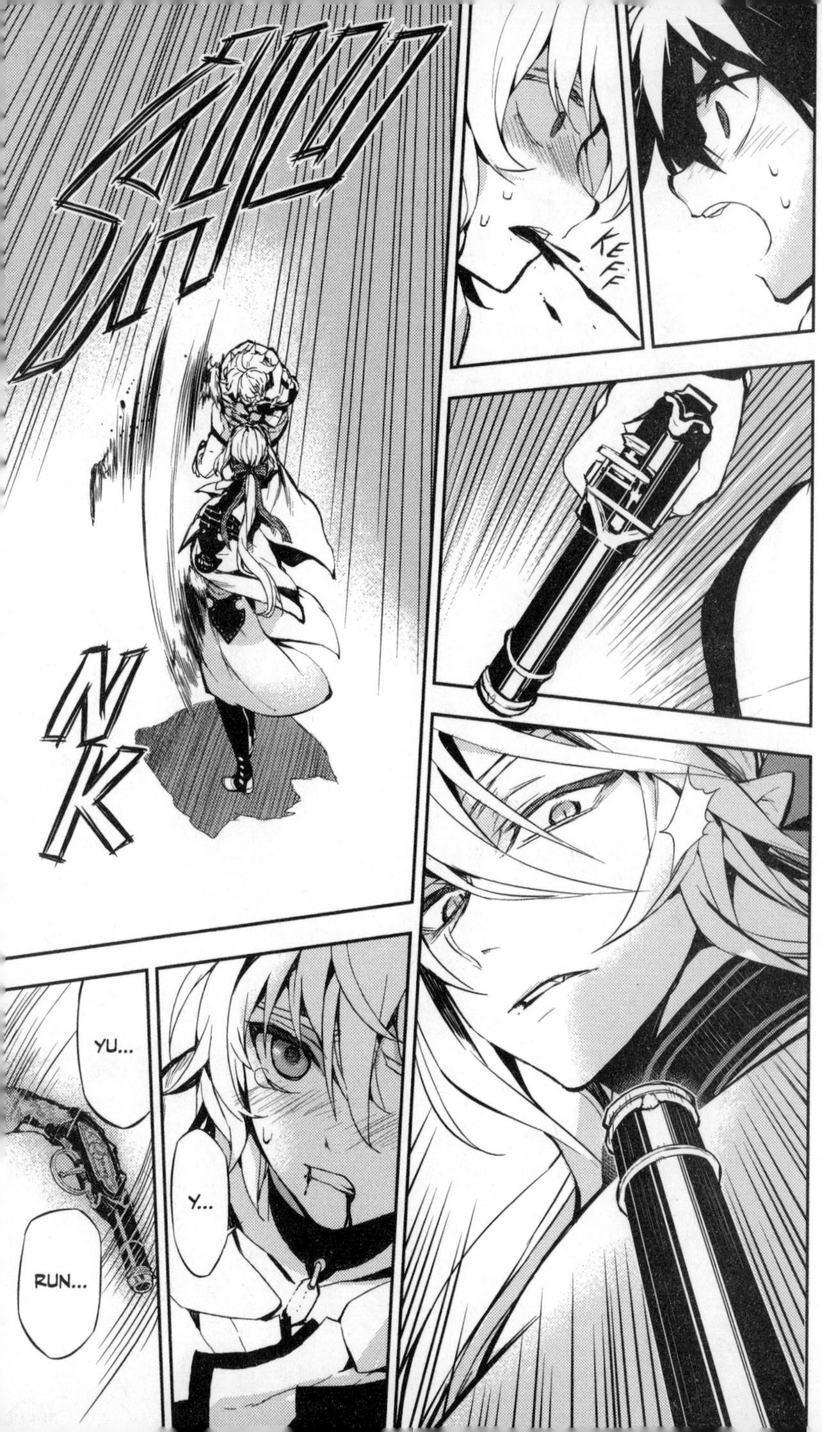
KEFF
SHUNK
YU...
Y...
RUN...

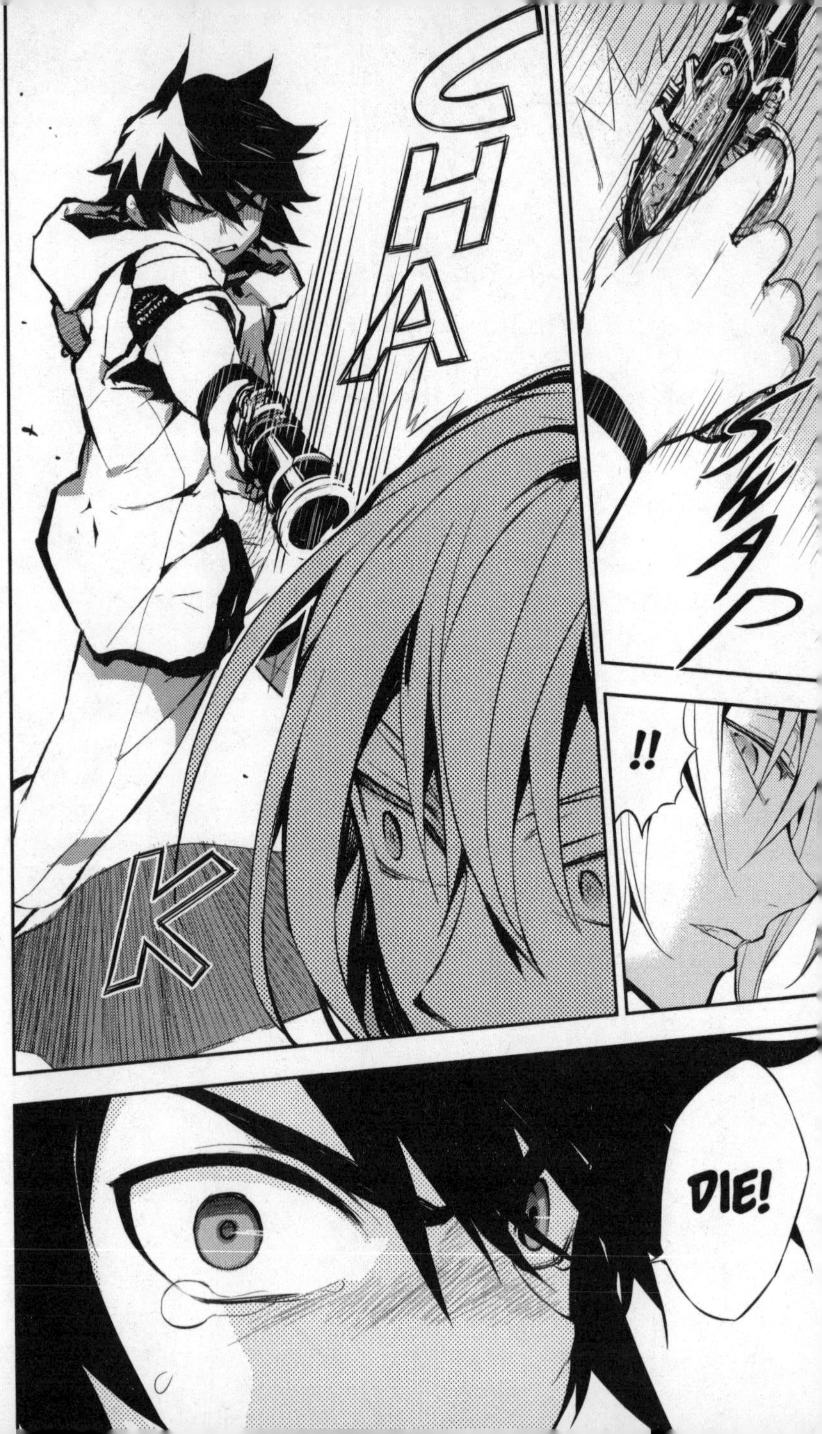
SWAP
!!
CHAK
DIE!

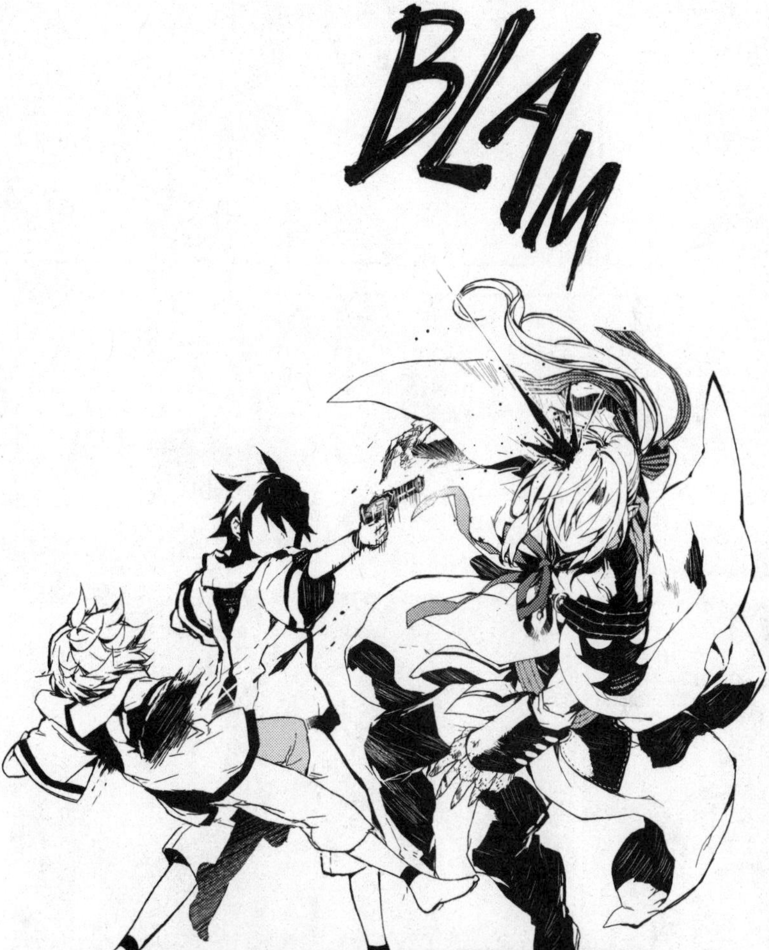
BLAM

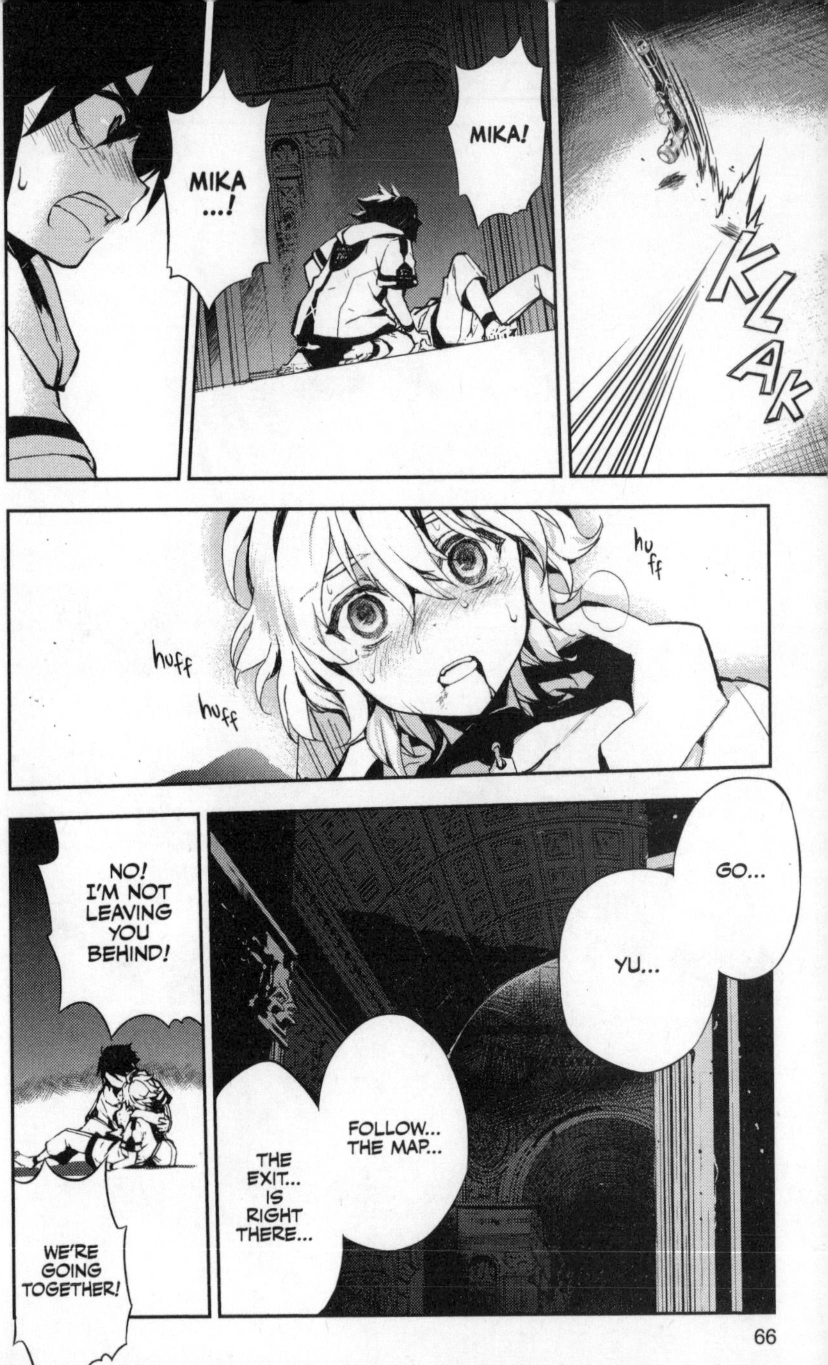
KLAK
MIKA!
MIKA ...!
huff
huff
huff
GO...
YU...
FOLLOW... THE MAP...
THE EXIT... IS RIGHT THERE...
NO! I'M NOT LEAVING YOU BEHIND!
WE'RE GOING TOGETHER!

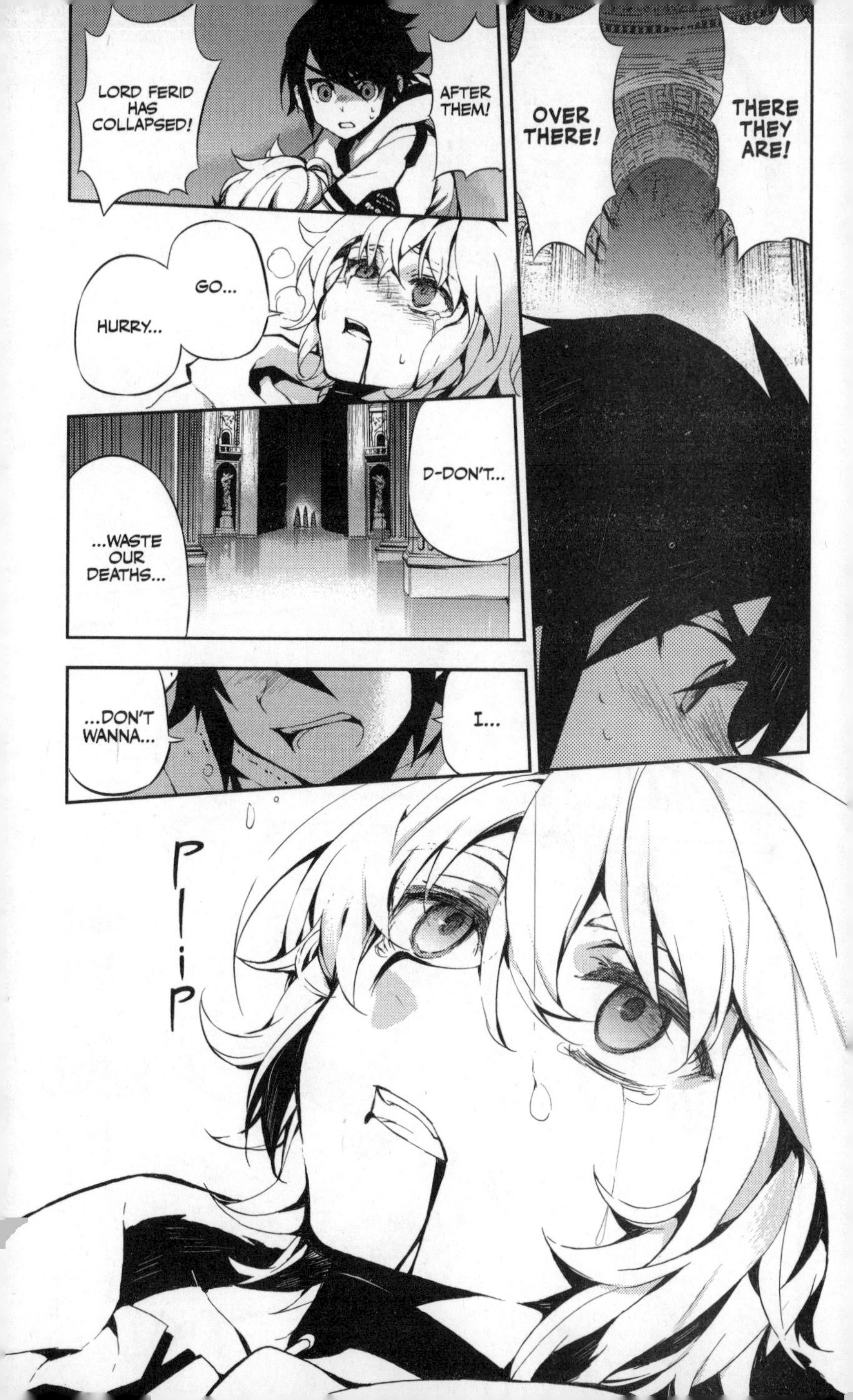
THERE THEY ARE!
OVER THERE!
AFTER THEM!
LORD FERID HAS COLLAPSED!
GO...
HURRY...
D-DON'T...
...WASTE OUR DEATHS...
I...
...DON'T WANNA...
PLIP

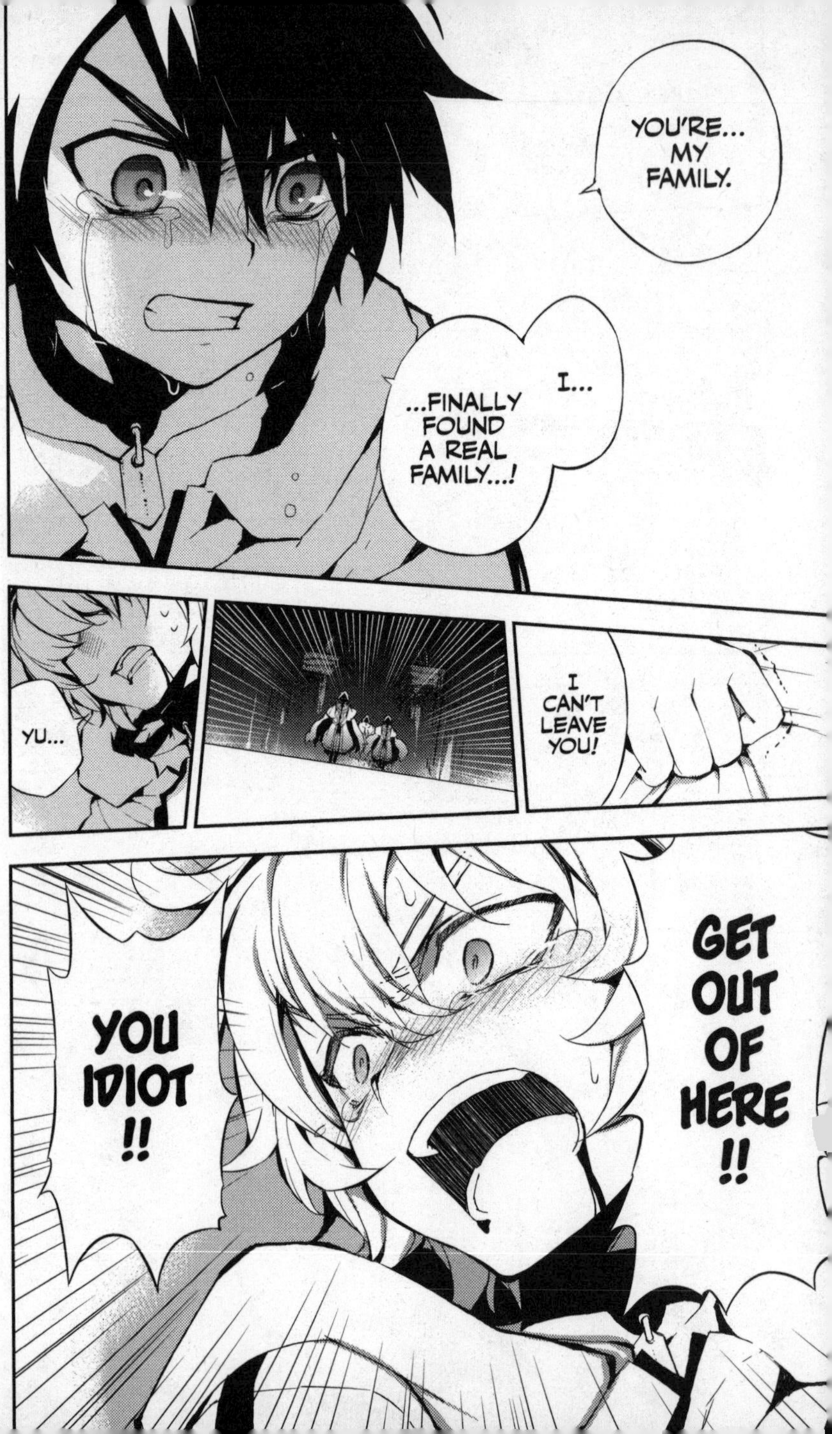
YOU'RE... MY FAMILY.
I...
...FINALLY FOUND A REAL FAMILY...!
I CAN'T LEAVE YOU!
YU...
GET OUT OF HERE!!
YOU IDIOT!!

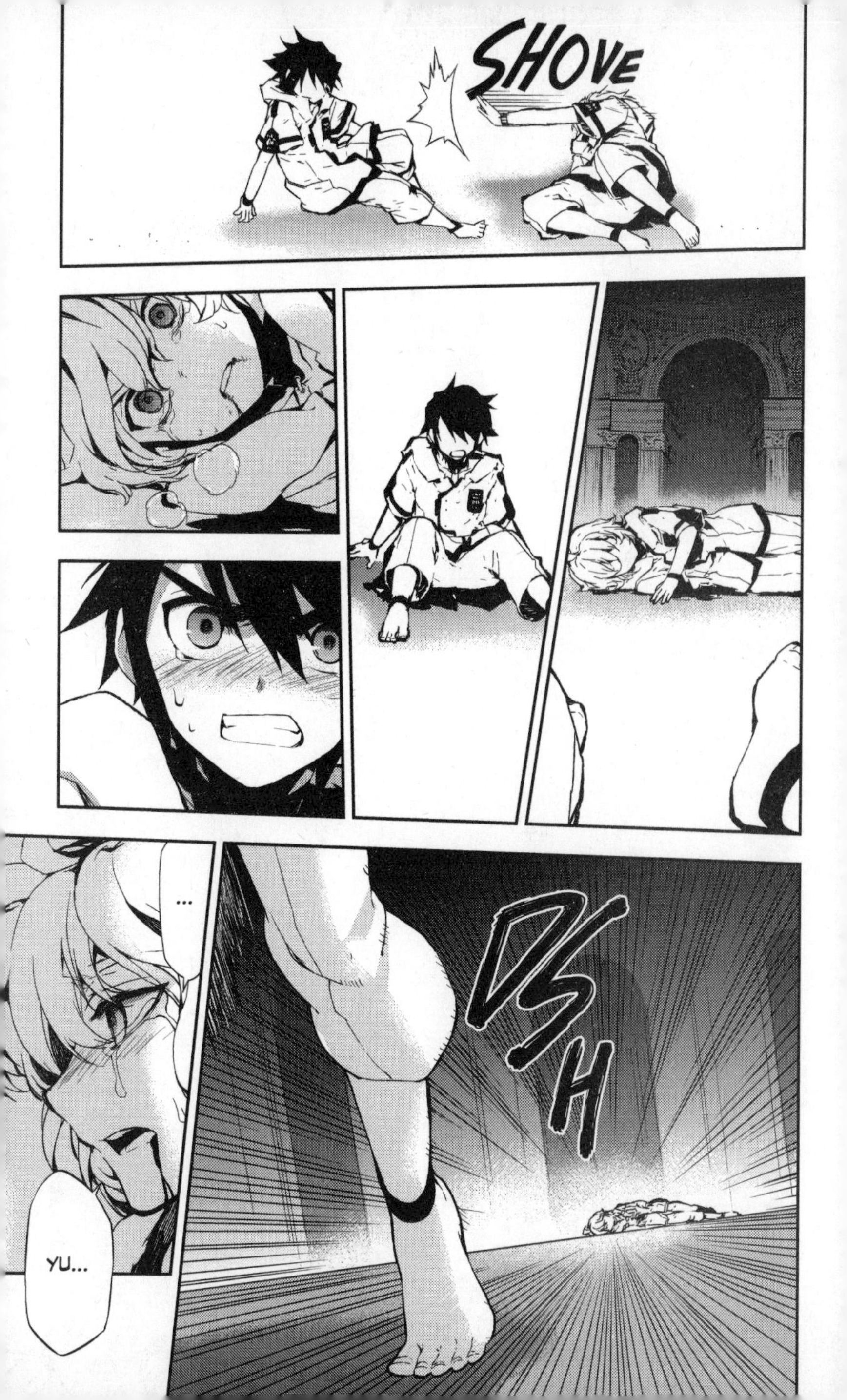
SHOVE
...
DSH
YU...

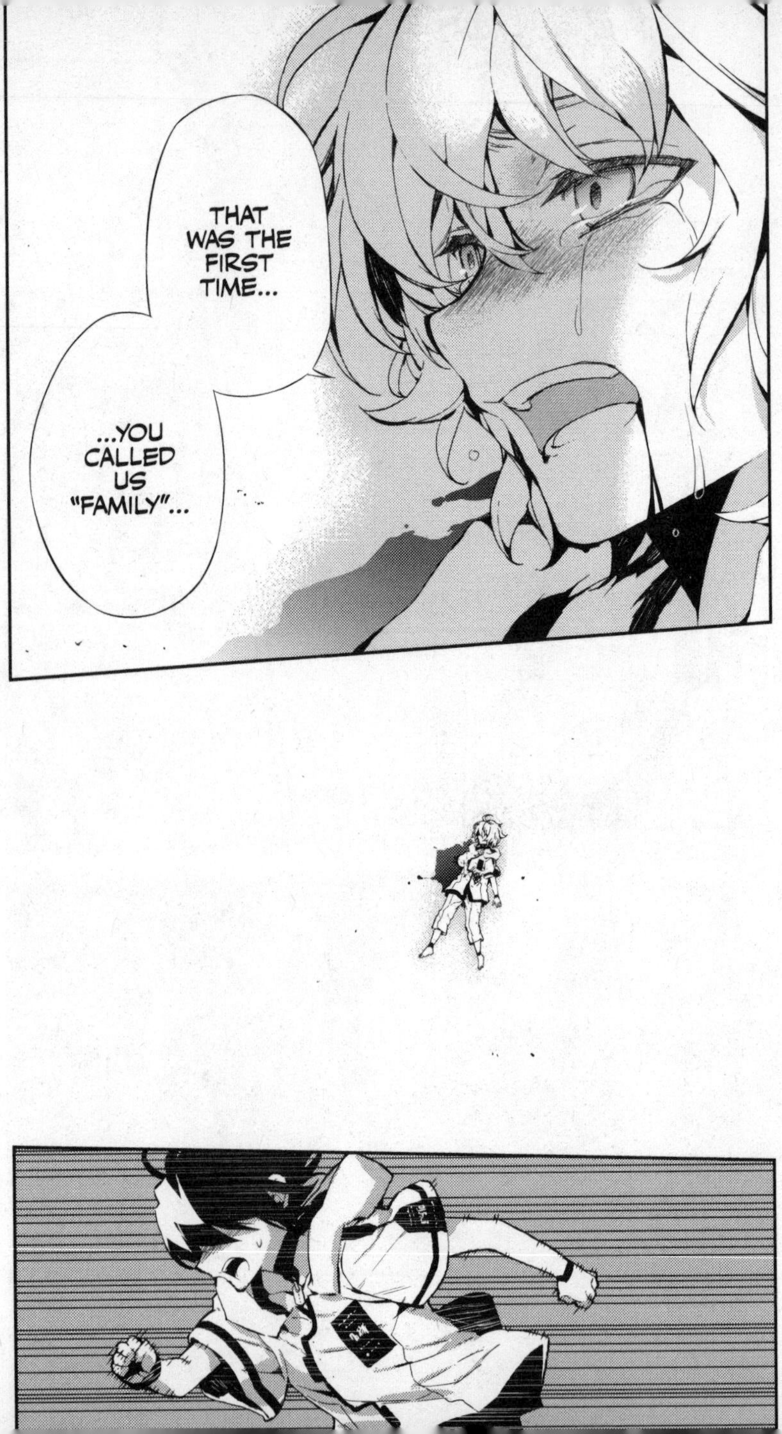
THAT WAS THE FIRST TIME...
...YOU CALLED US "FAMILY"...

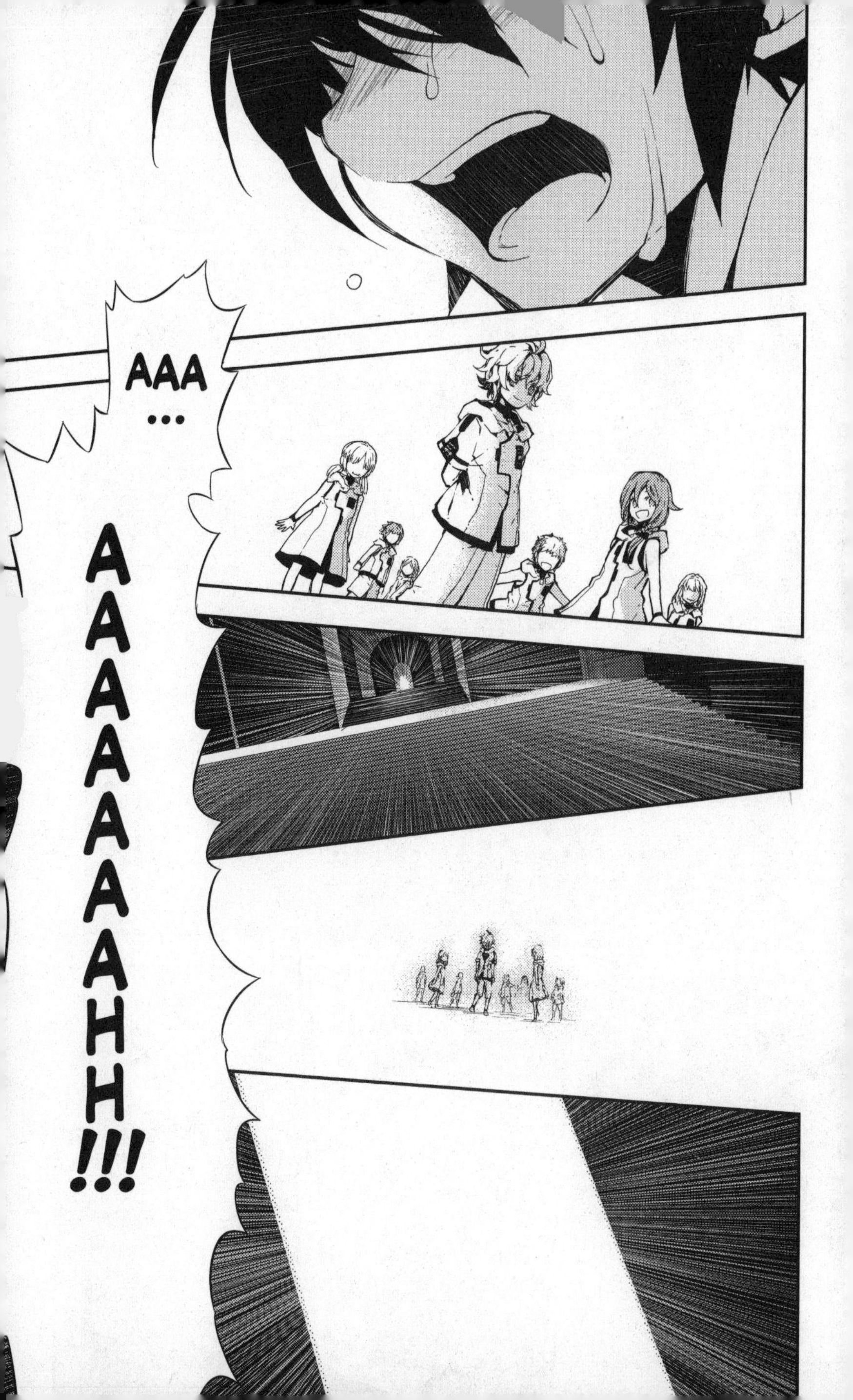
AAA...
AAAAAAAAH!!!

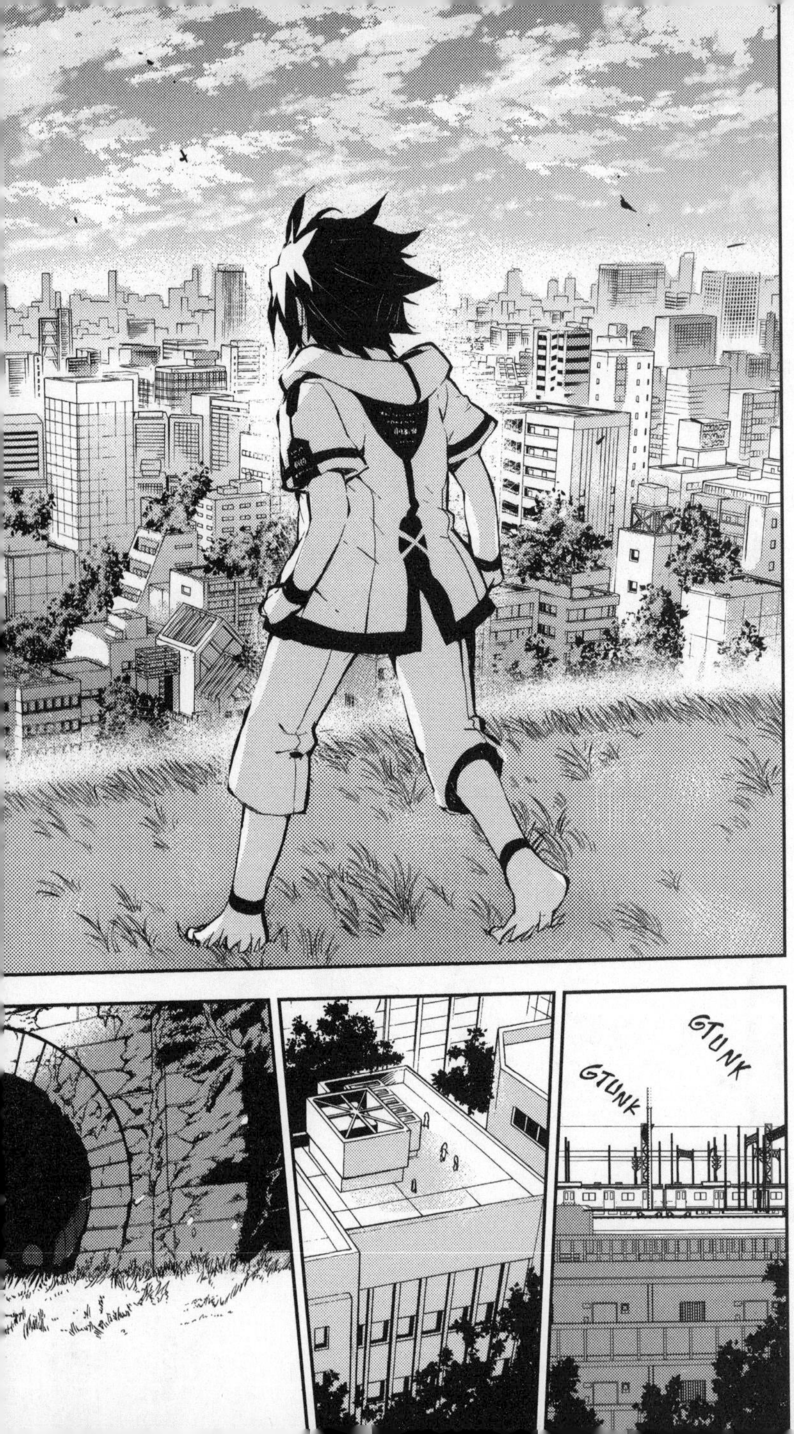
GTUNK
GTUNK

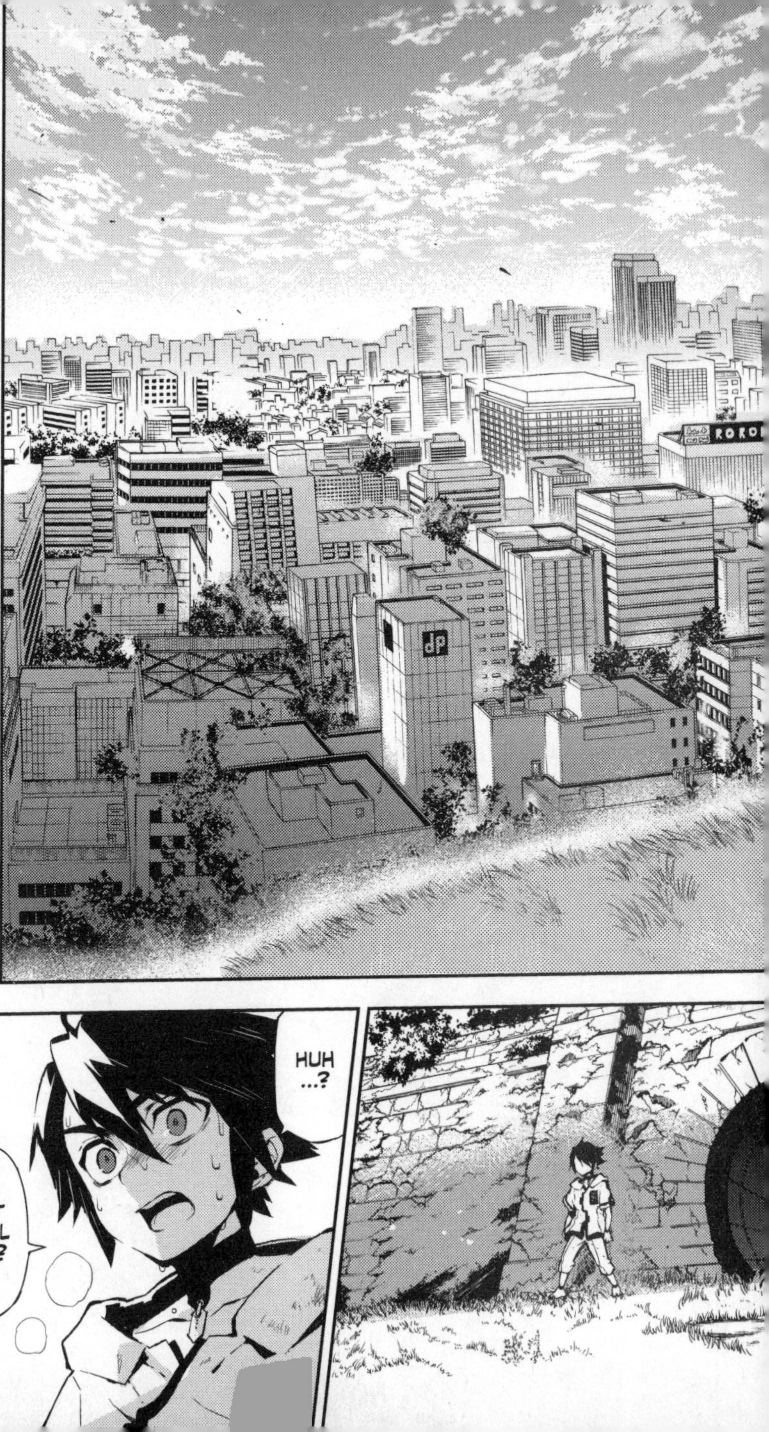
HUH ...?
WHAT IS ALL THIS?

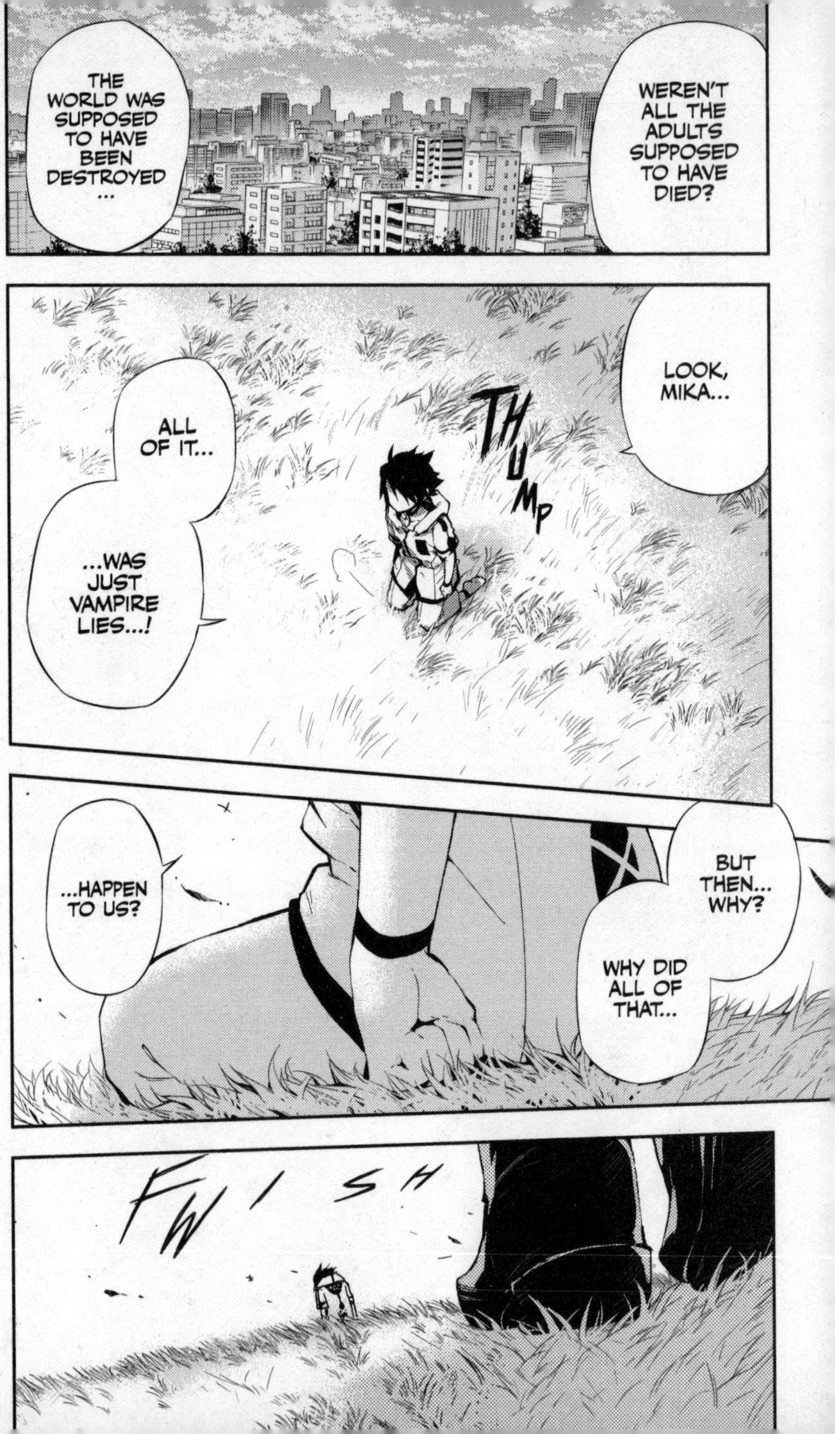
WEREN'T ALL THE ADULTS SUPPOSED TO HAVE DIED?
THE WORLD WAS SUPPOSED TO HAVE BEEN DESTROYED ...
LOOK, MIKA...
THUMP
ALL OF IT...
...WAS JUST VAMPIRE LIES...!
BUT THEN... WHY?
WHY DID ALL OF THAT...
...HAPPEN TO US?
FWISH

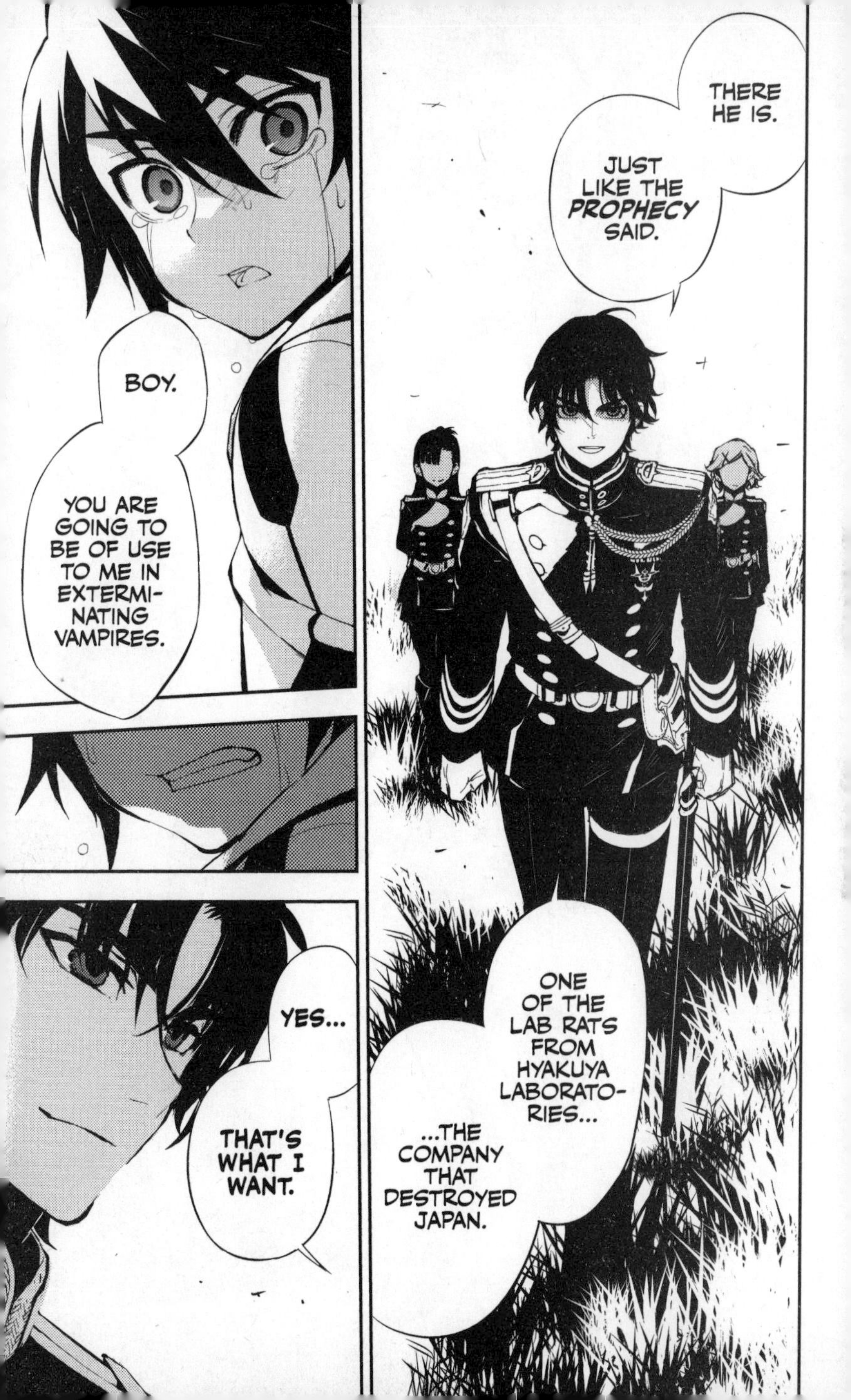
THERE HE IS.
JUST LIKE THE PROPHECY SAID.
ONE OF THE LAB RATS FROM HYAKUYA LABORATORIES...
...THE COMPANY THAT DESTROYED JAPAN.
BOY.
YOU ARE GOING TO BE OF USE TO ME IN EXTERMINATING VAMPIRES.
YES...
THAT'S WHAT I WANT.

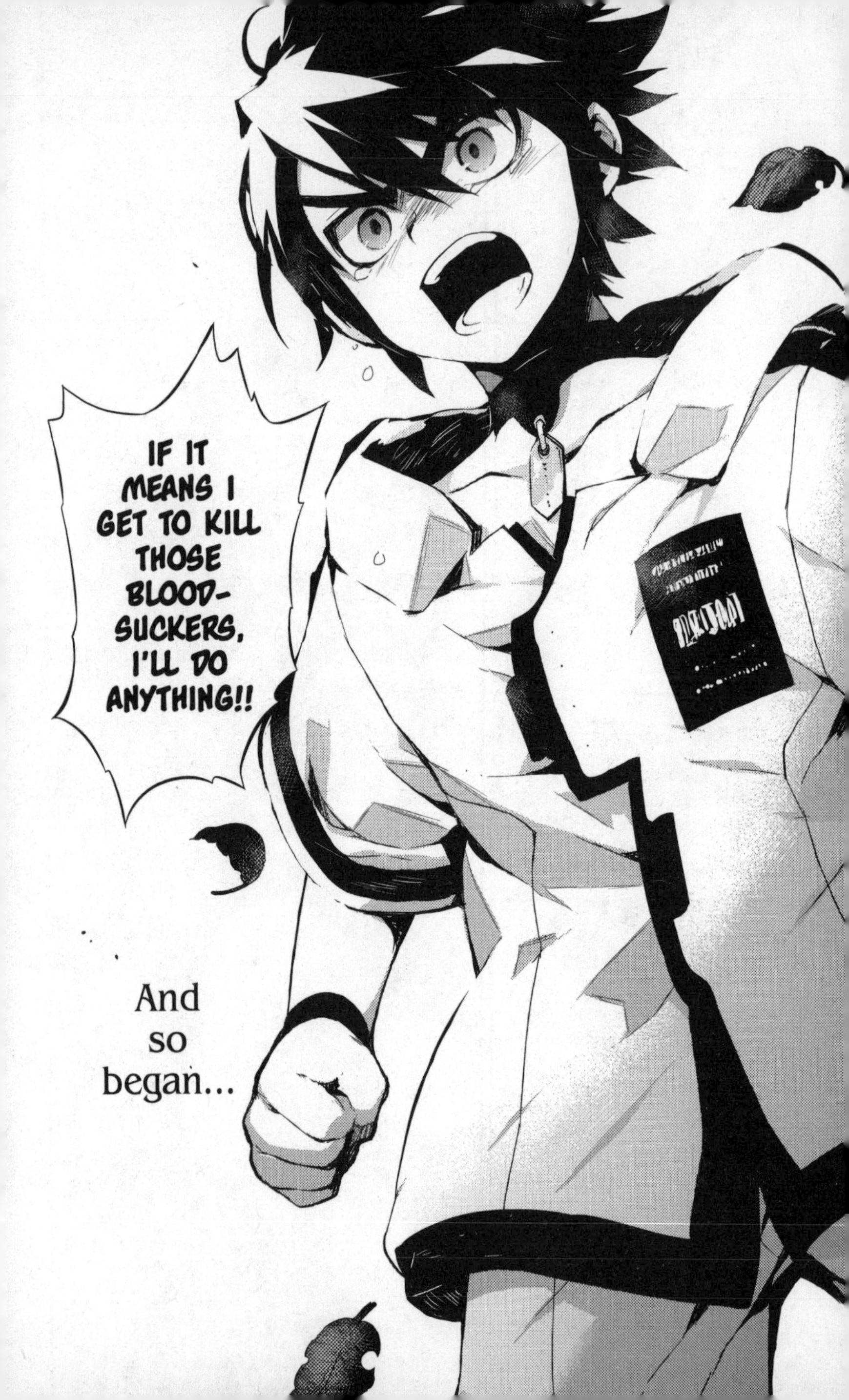
IF IT MEANS I GET TO KILL THOSE BLOOD-SUCKERS, I'LL DO ANYTHING!!
And so began...

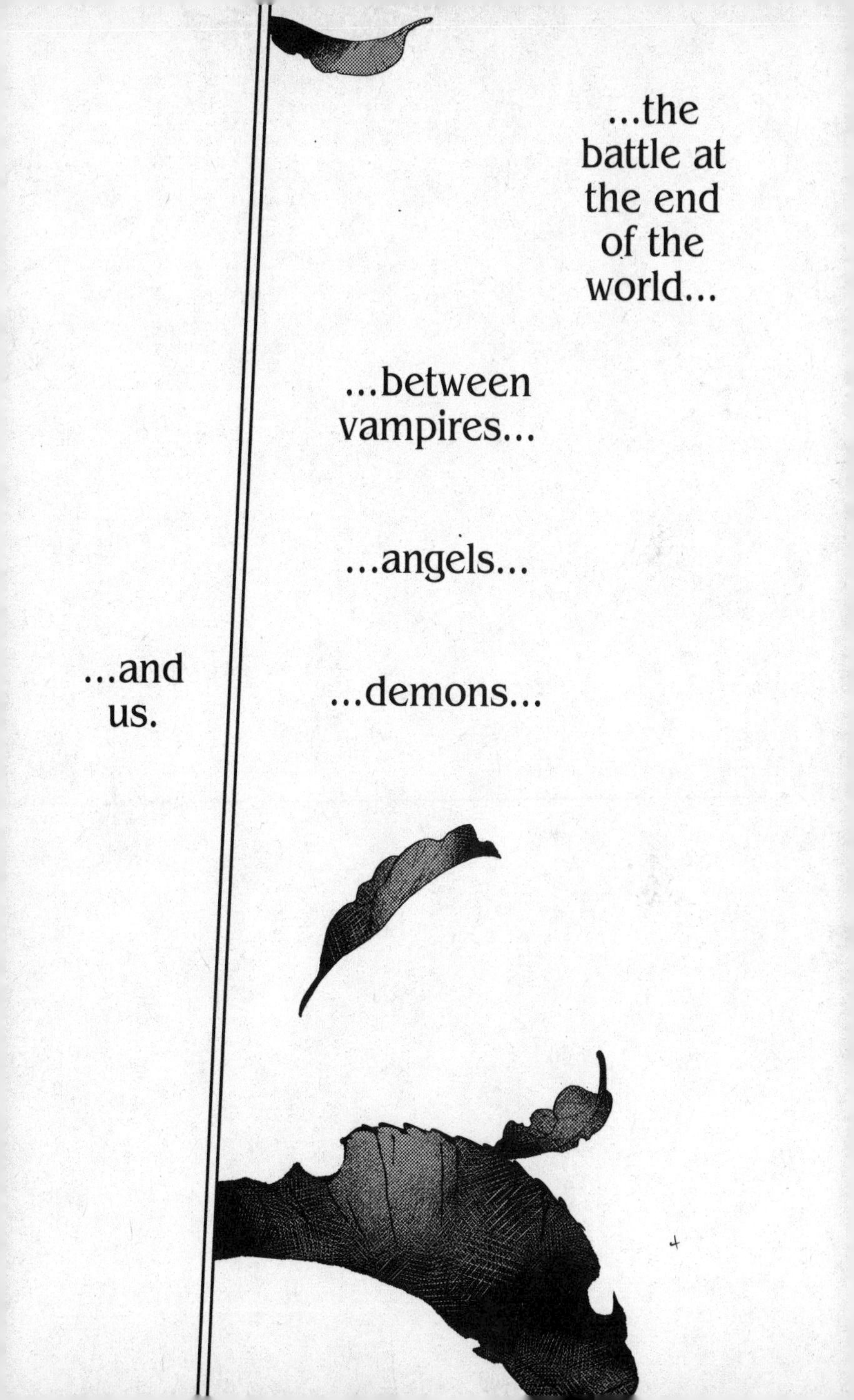
...the battle at the end of the world...
...between vampires...
...angels...
...demons...
...and us.

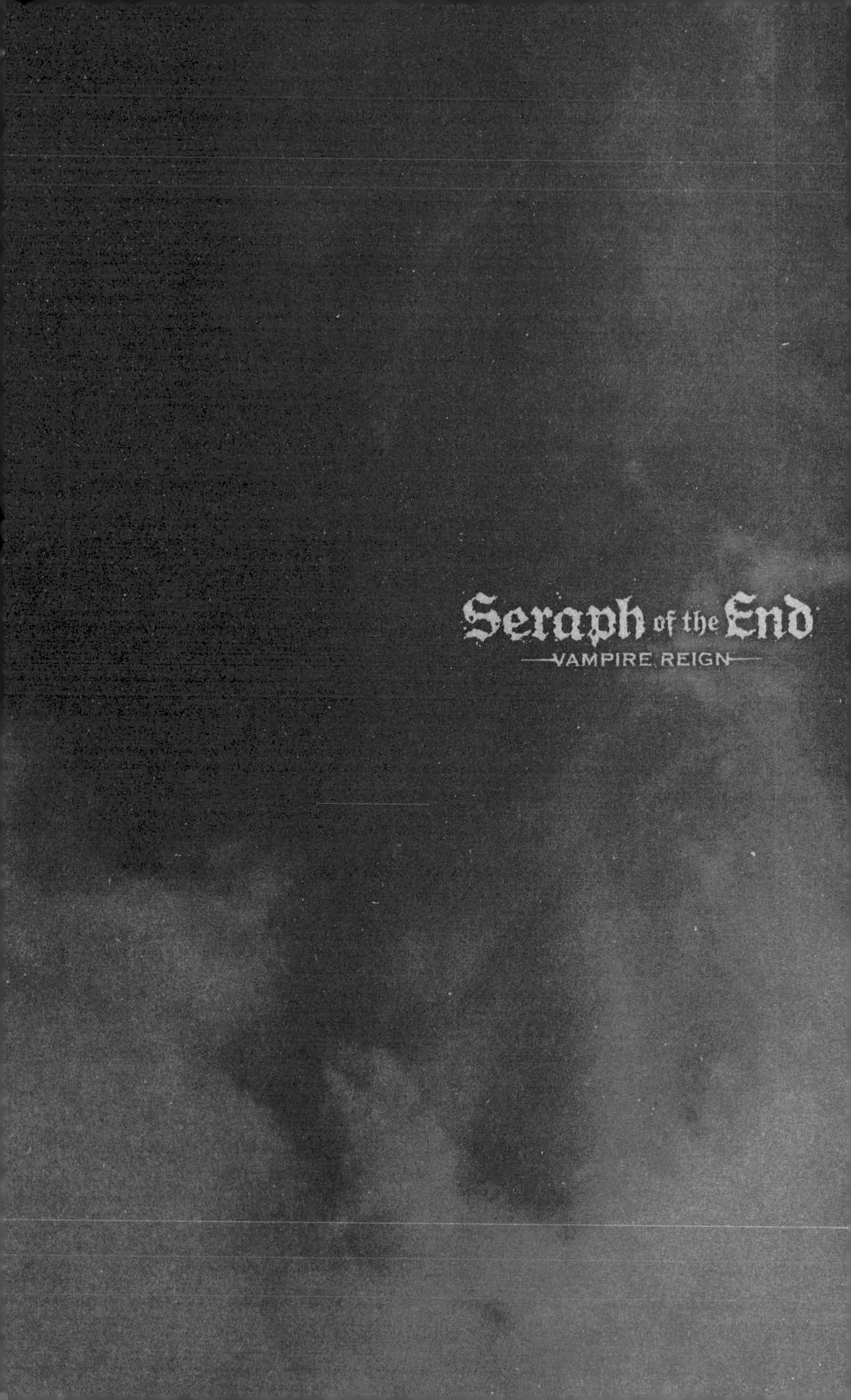
Seraph of the End
VAMPIRE REIGN

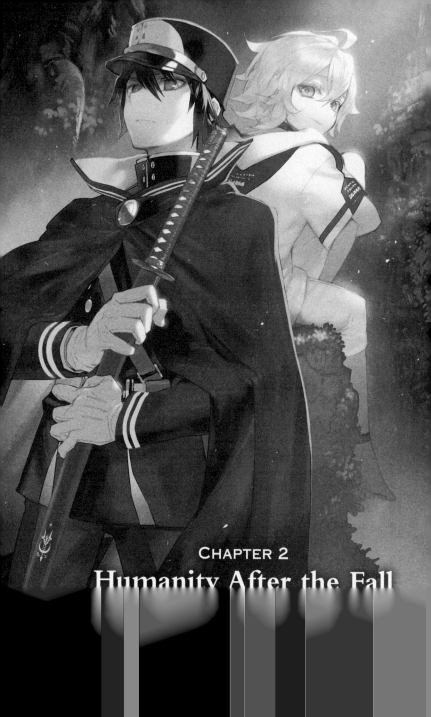

CHAPTER 2
Humanity After the Fall

Seraph of the End
VAMPIRE REIGN

I SEE THE SAME SCENE EVERY TIME I CLOSE MY EYES.

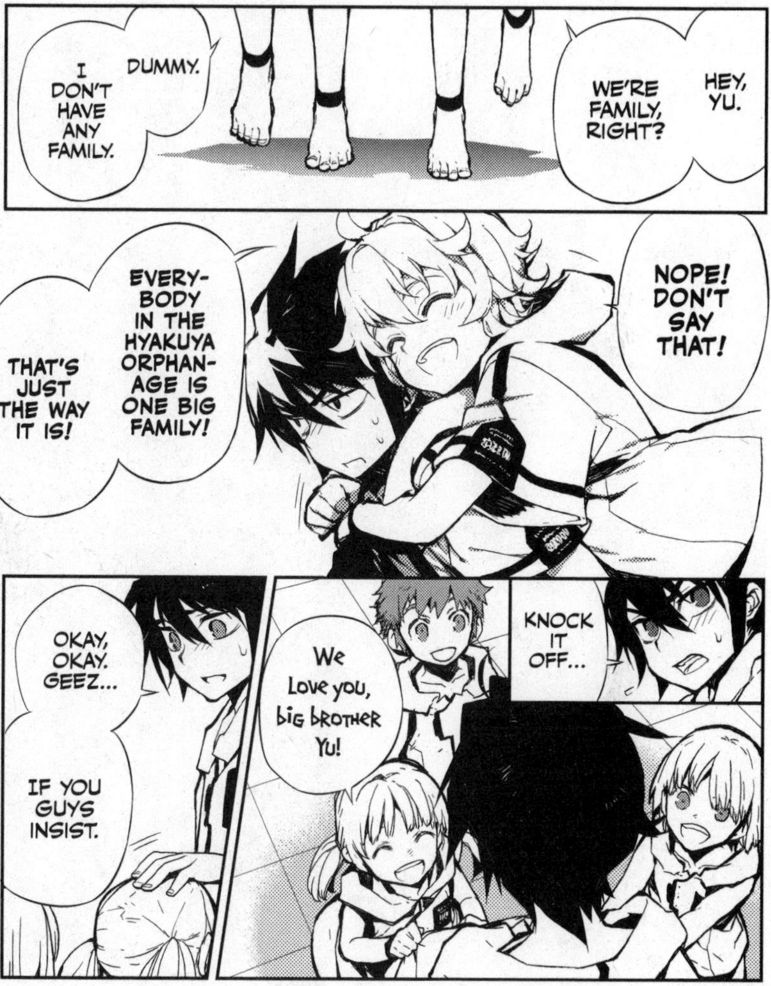
HEY, YU.
WE'RE FAMILY, RIGHT?
DUMMY.
I DON'T HAVE ANY FAMILY.
NOPE! DON'T SAY THAT!
EVERYBODY IN THE HYAKUYA ORPHANAGE IS ONE BIG FAMILY!
THAT'S JUST THE WAY IT IS!
KNOCK IT OFF...
We Love you, big brother Yu!
OKAY, OKAY. GEEZ...
IF YOU GUYS INSIST.

I SEE THE SMILING FACES OF MY FRIENDS...
MY PRECIOUS FAMILY...

AND THEN—

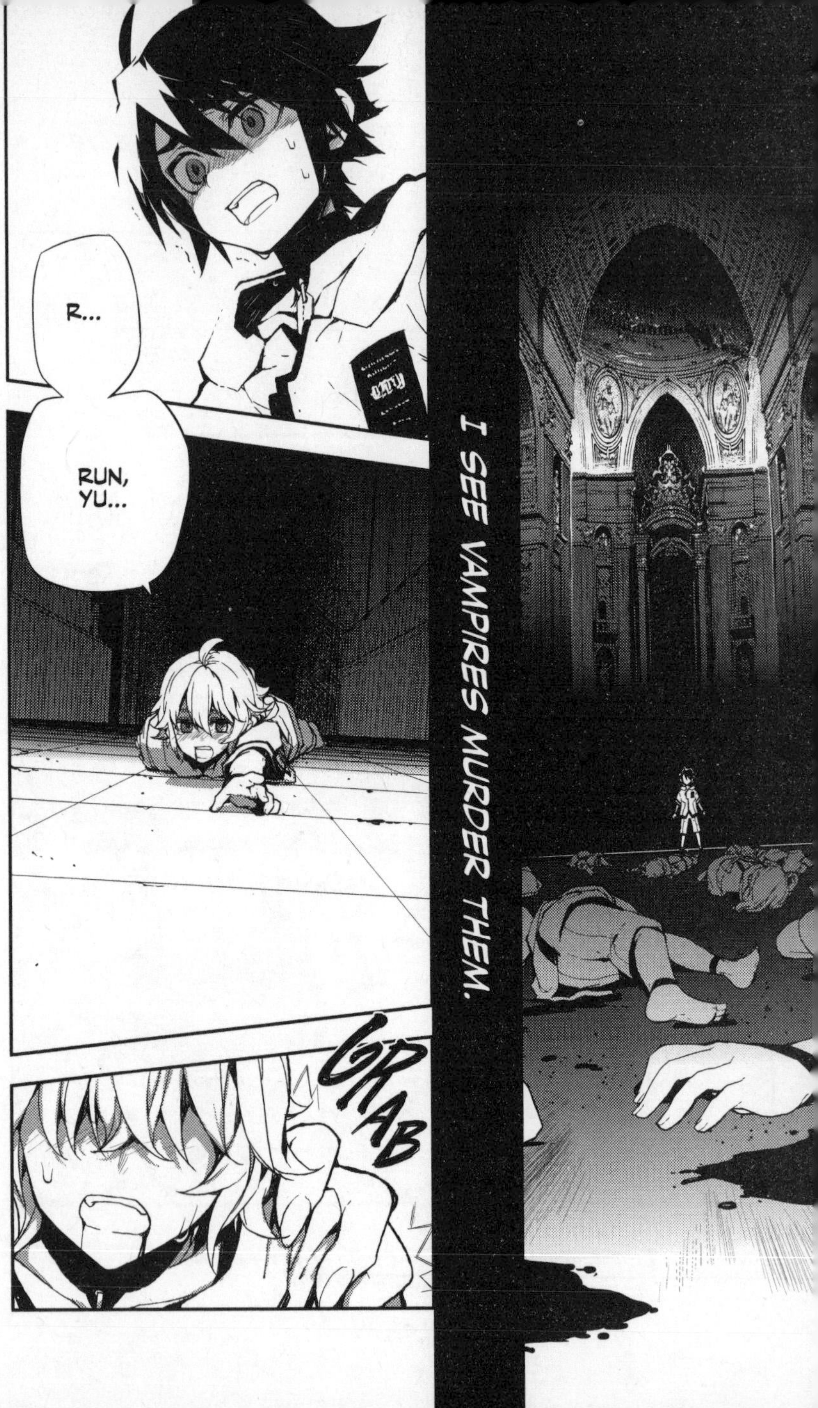
I SEE VAMPIRES MURDER THEM.
R...
RUN, YU...
GRAB

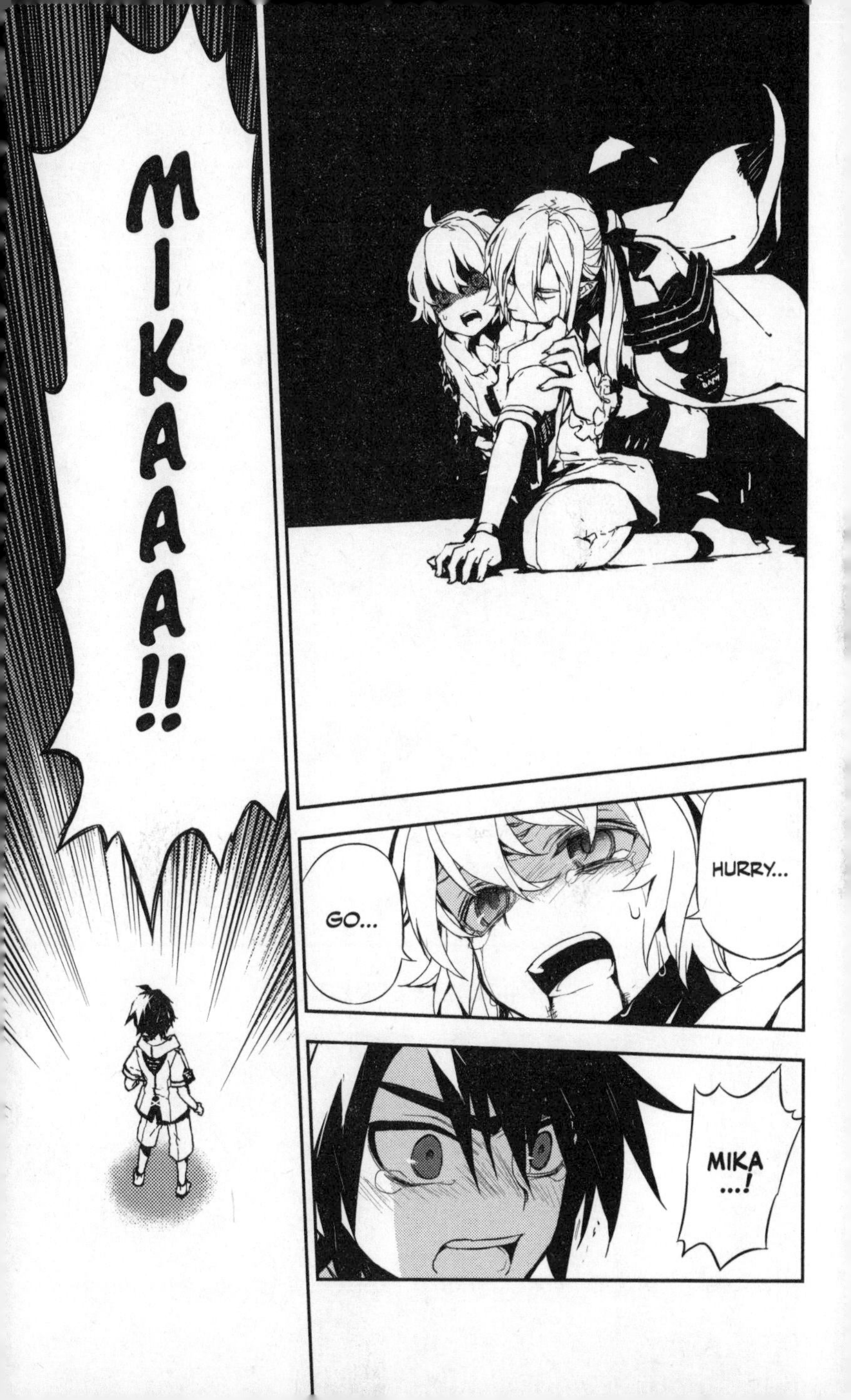
HURRY...
GO...
MIKA ...!
MIKAAA!!

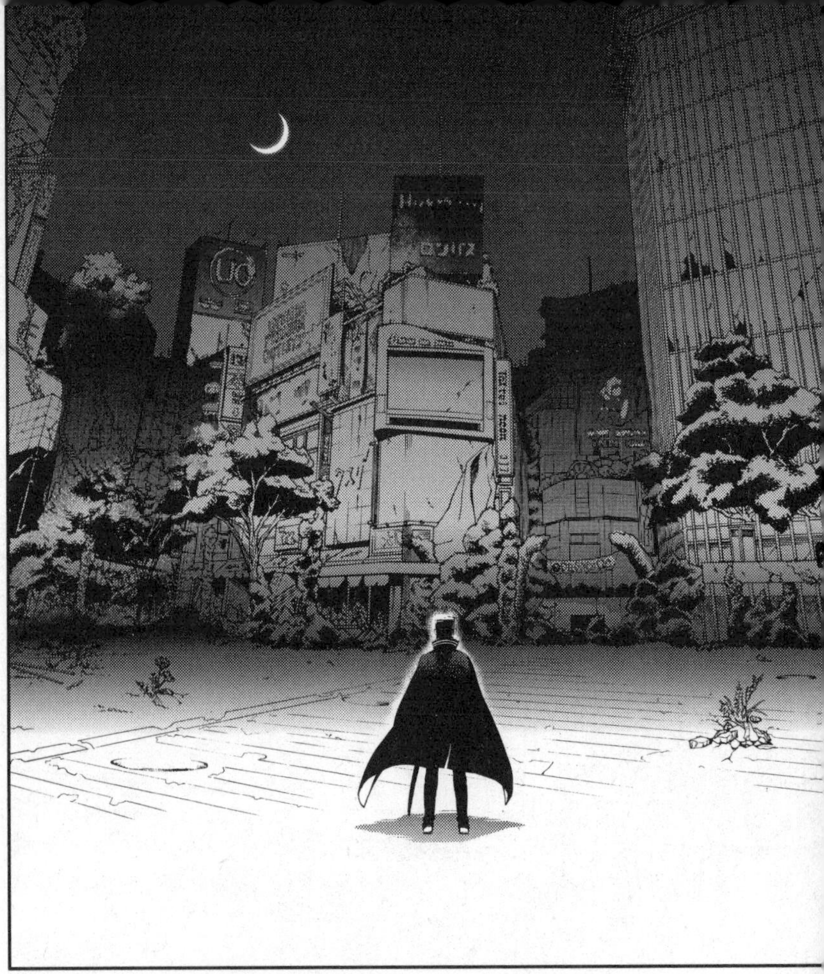

Four Years Later

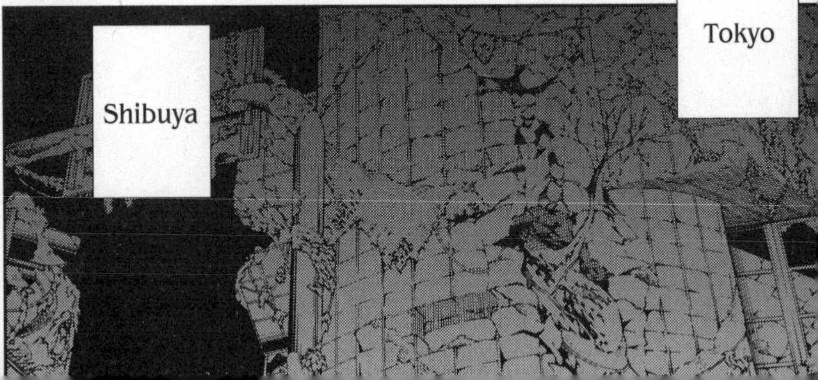
Tokyo
Shibuya

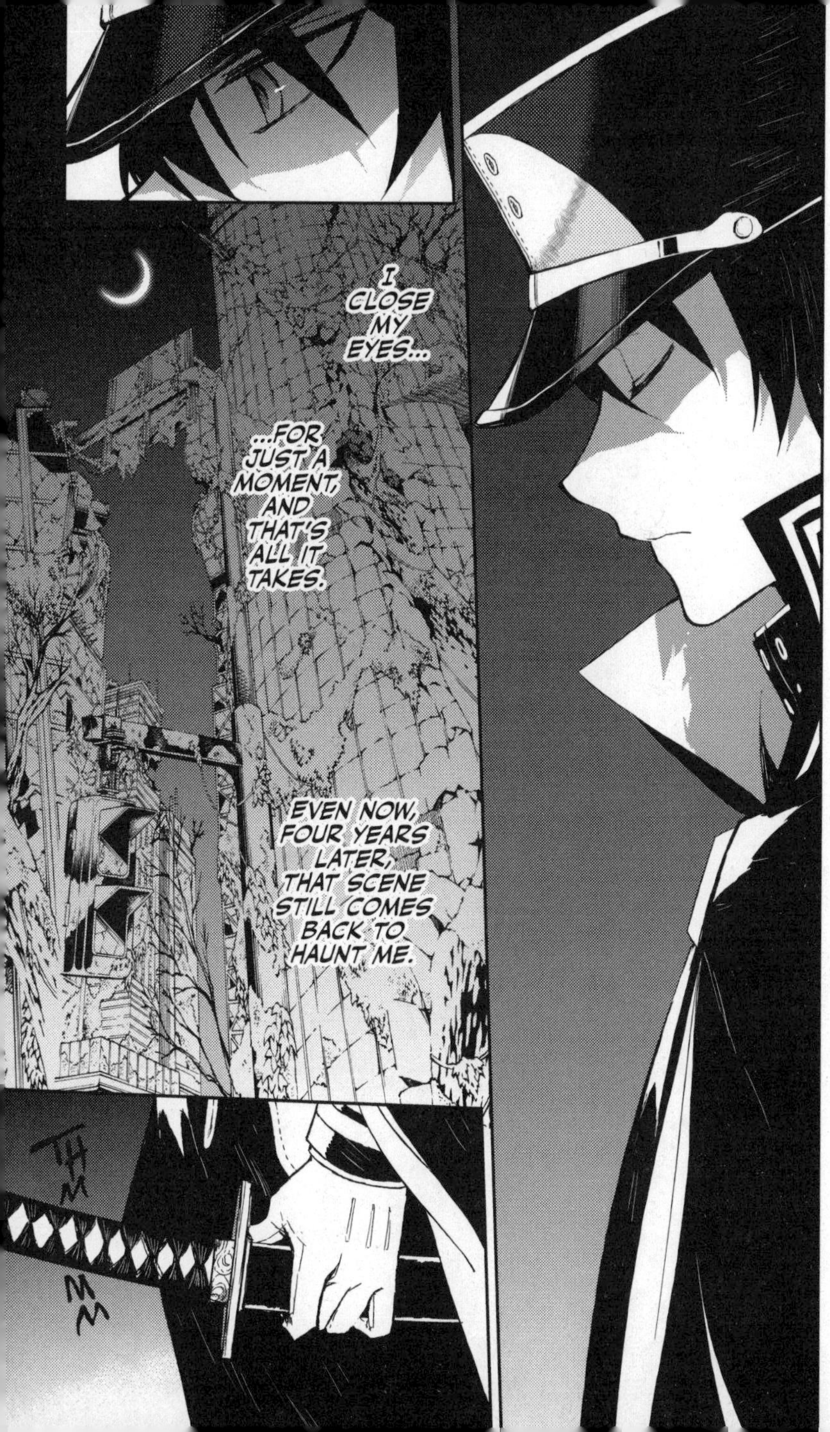
I CLOSE MY EYES...
...FOR JUST A MOMENT, AND THAT'S ALL IT TAKES.
EVEN NOW, FOUR YEARS LATER, THAT SCENE STILL COMES BACK TO HAUNT ME.
THMMM

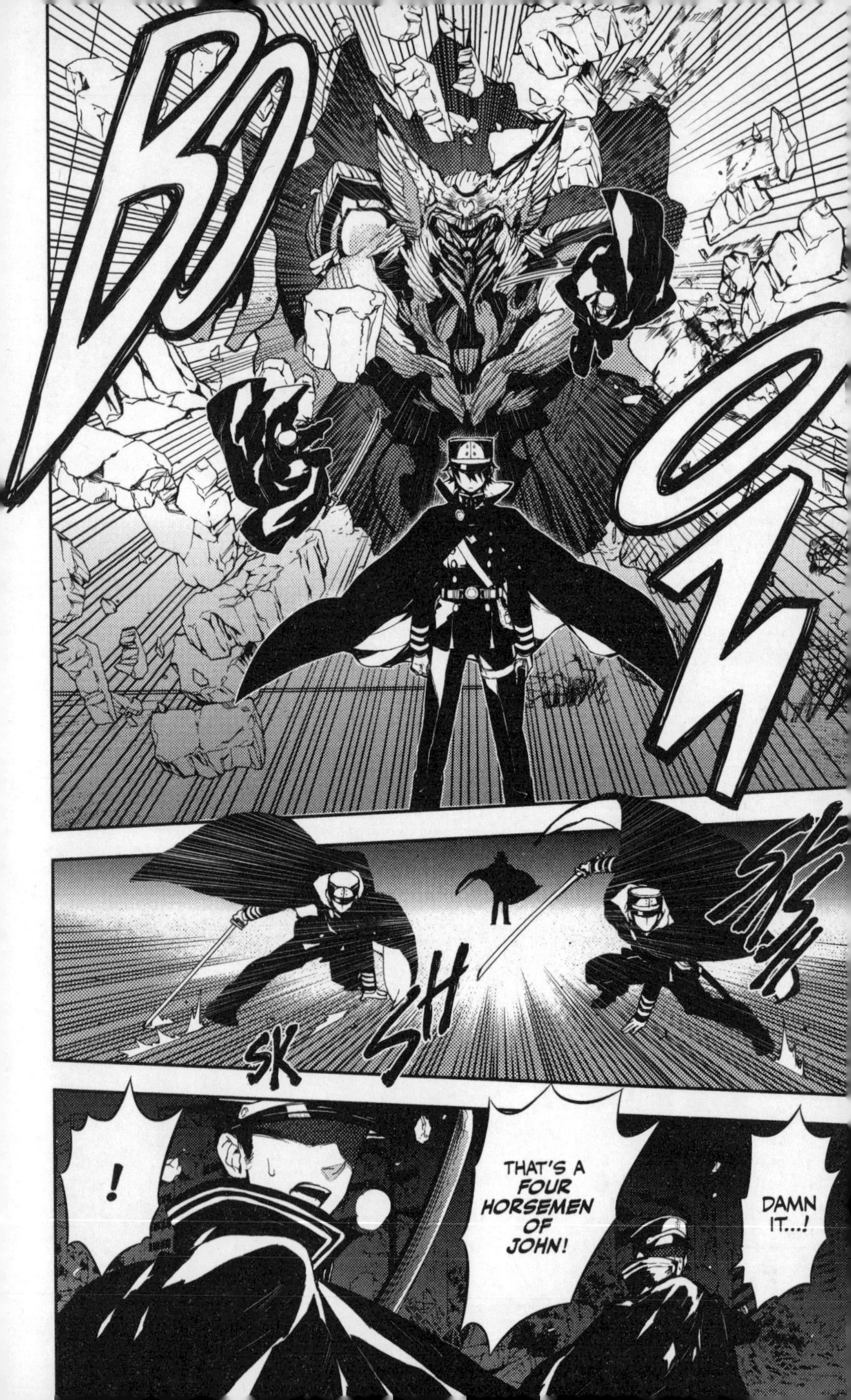
BOOOM
SKSH
SKSH
DAMN IT...!
THAT'S A FOUR HORSEMEN OF JOHN!
!

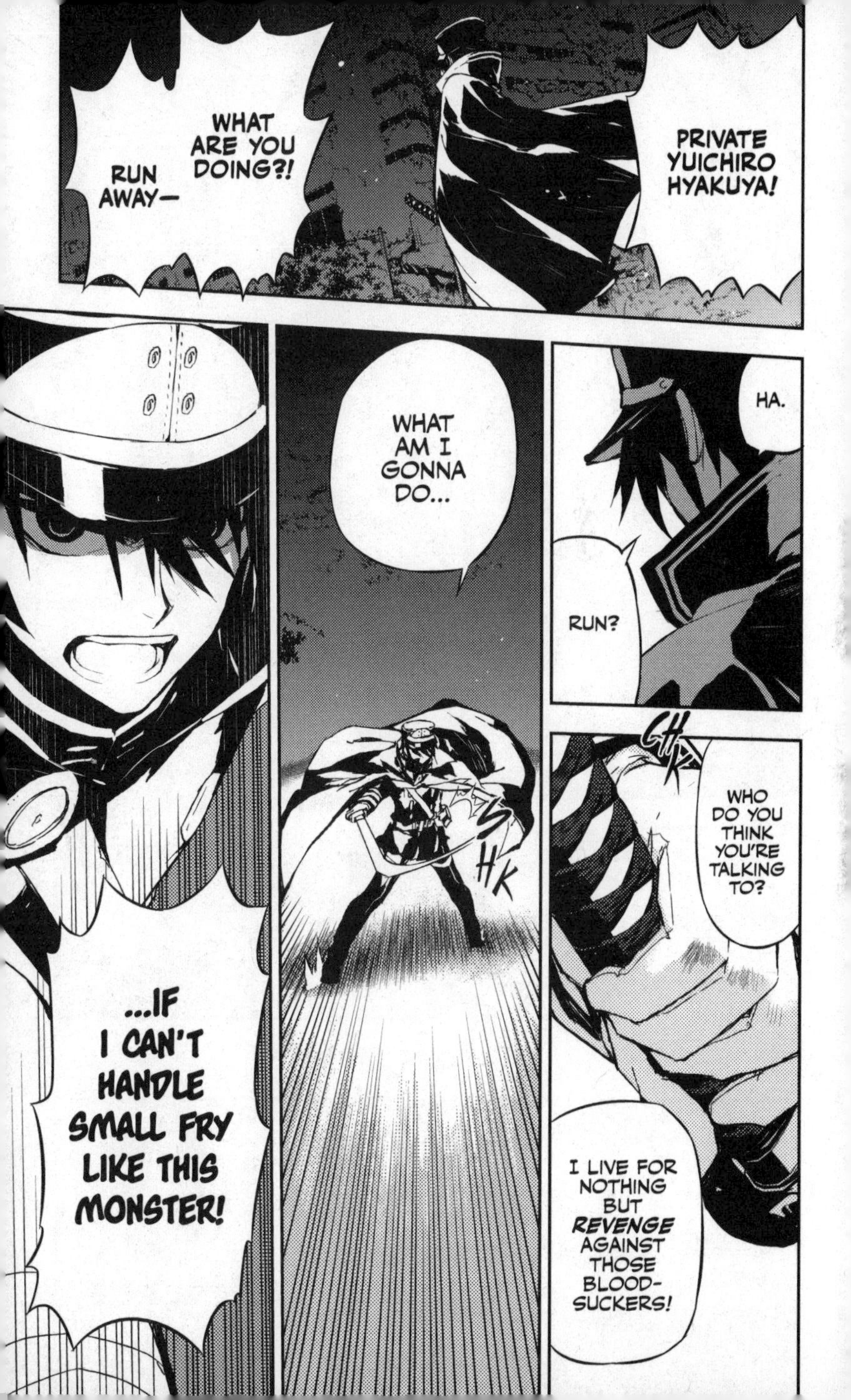
PRIVATE YUICHIRO HYAKUYA!
WHAT ARE YOU DOING?!
RUN AWAY—
HA.
RUN?
CHK
WHO DO YOU THINK YOU'RE TALKING TO?
I LIVE FOR NOTHING BUT *REVENGE* AGAINST THOSE BLOOD-SUCKERS!
WHAT AM I GONNA DO...
...IF I CAN'T HANDLE SMALL FRY LIKE THIS MONSTER!

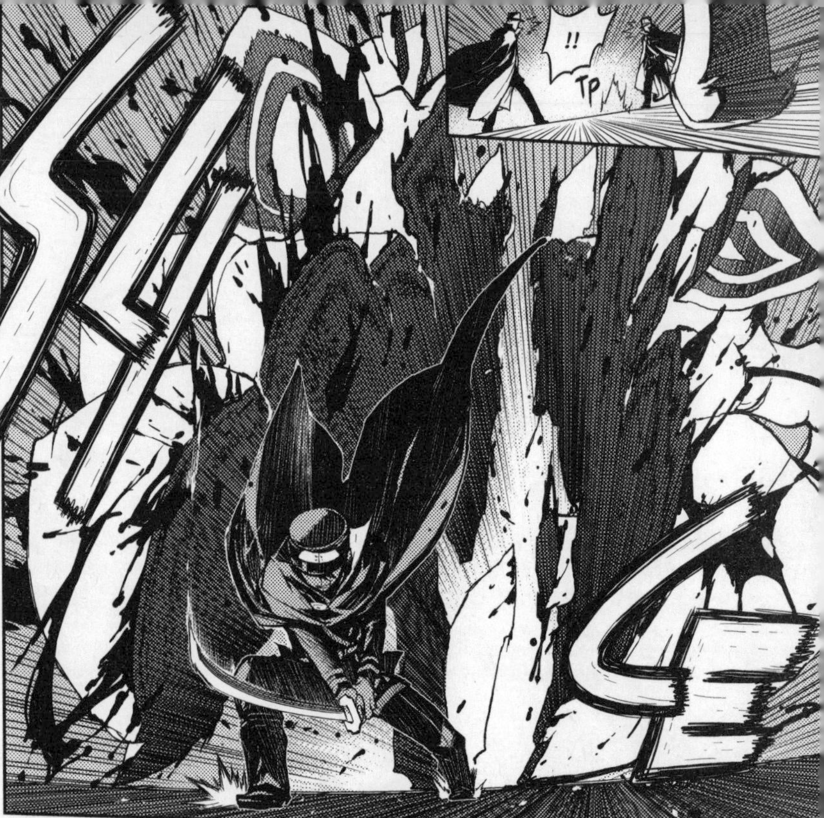
!!
TP

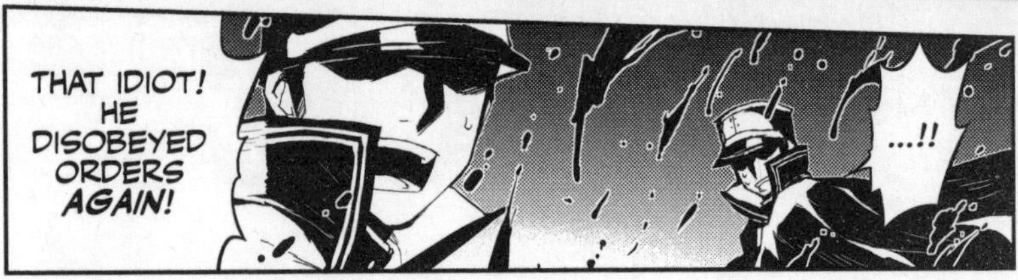
...!!
THAT IDIOT! HE DISOBEYED ORDERS AGAIN!

The Next Day

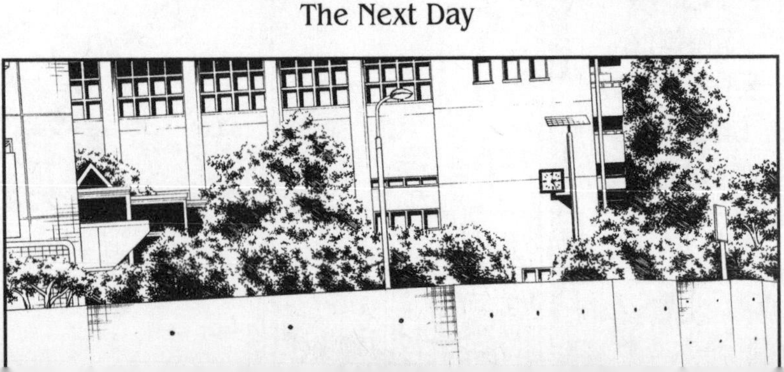

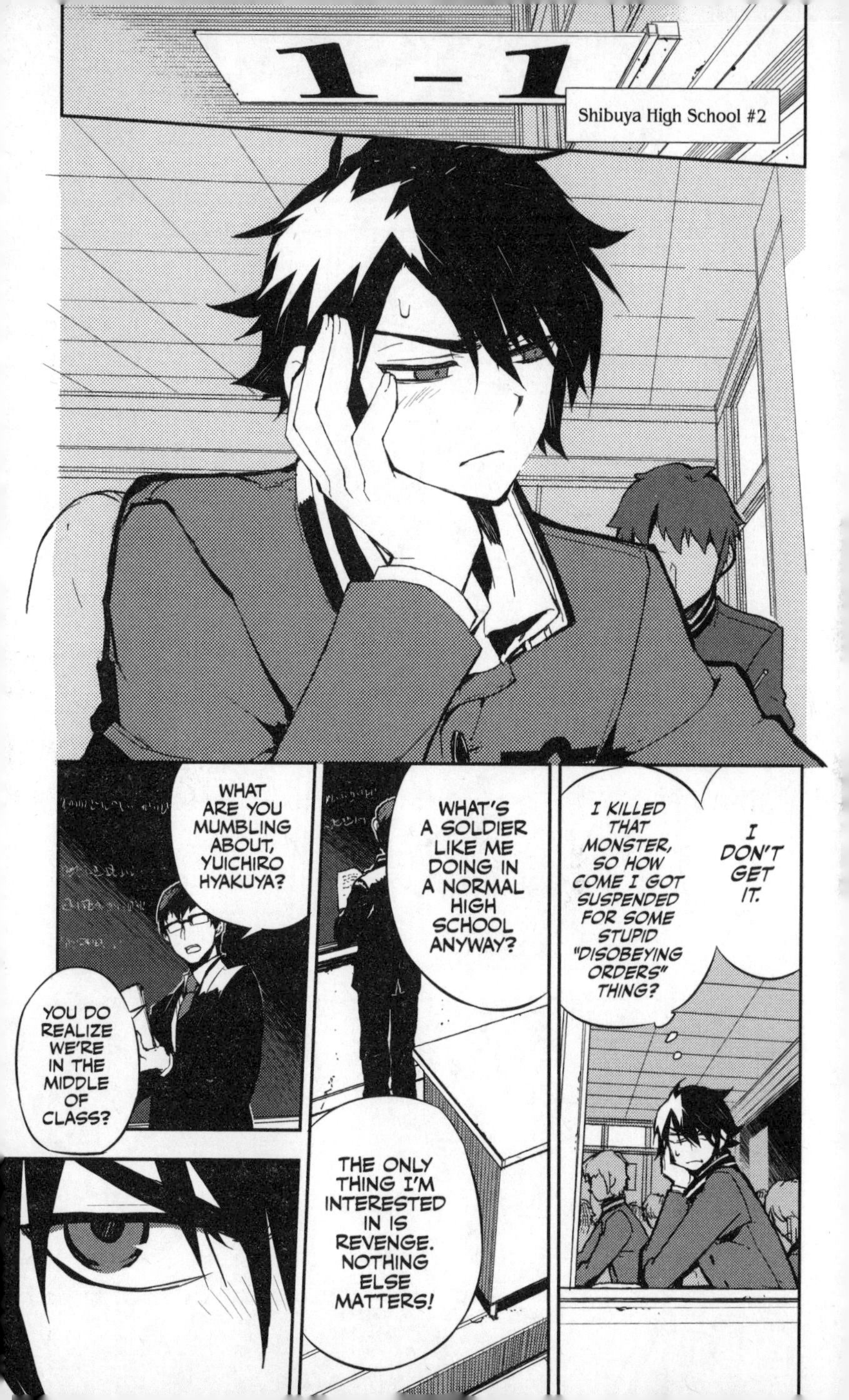
1-1
Shibuya High School #2
I DON'T GET IT.
I KILLED THAT MONSTER, SO HOW COME I GOT SUSPENDED FOR SOME STUPID "DISOBEYING ORDERS" THING?
WHAT'S A SOLDIER LIKE ME DOING IN A NORMAL HIGH SCHOOL ANYWAY?
WHAT ARE YOU MUMBLING ABOUT, YUICHIRO HYAKUYA?
YOU DO REALIZE WE'RE IN THE MIDDLE OF CLASS?
THE ONLY THING I'M INTERESTED IN IS REVENGE. NOTHING ELSE MATTERS!

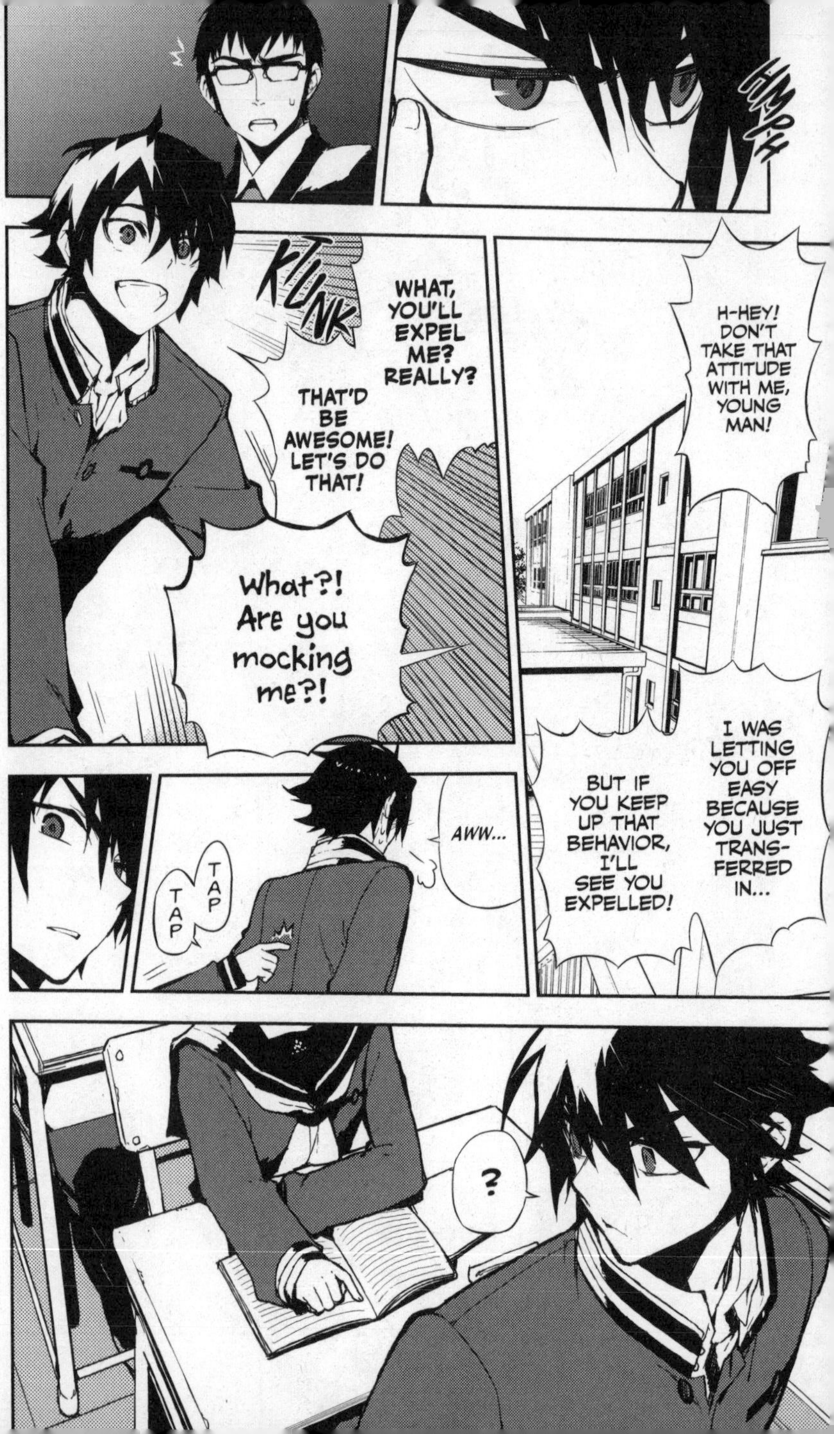
HMPH
H-HEY! DON'T TAKE THAT ATTITUDE WITH ME, YOUNG MAN!
I WAS LETTING YOU OFF EASY BECAUSE YOU JUST TRANS-FERRED IN...
BUT IF YOU KEEP UP THAT BEHAVIOR, I'LL SEE YOU EXPELLED!
KLUNK
WHAT, YOU'LL EXPEL ME? REALLY?
THAT'D BE AWESOME! LET'S DO THAT!
What?! Are you mocking me?!
AWW...
TAP TAP
?

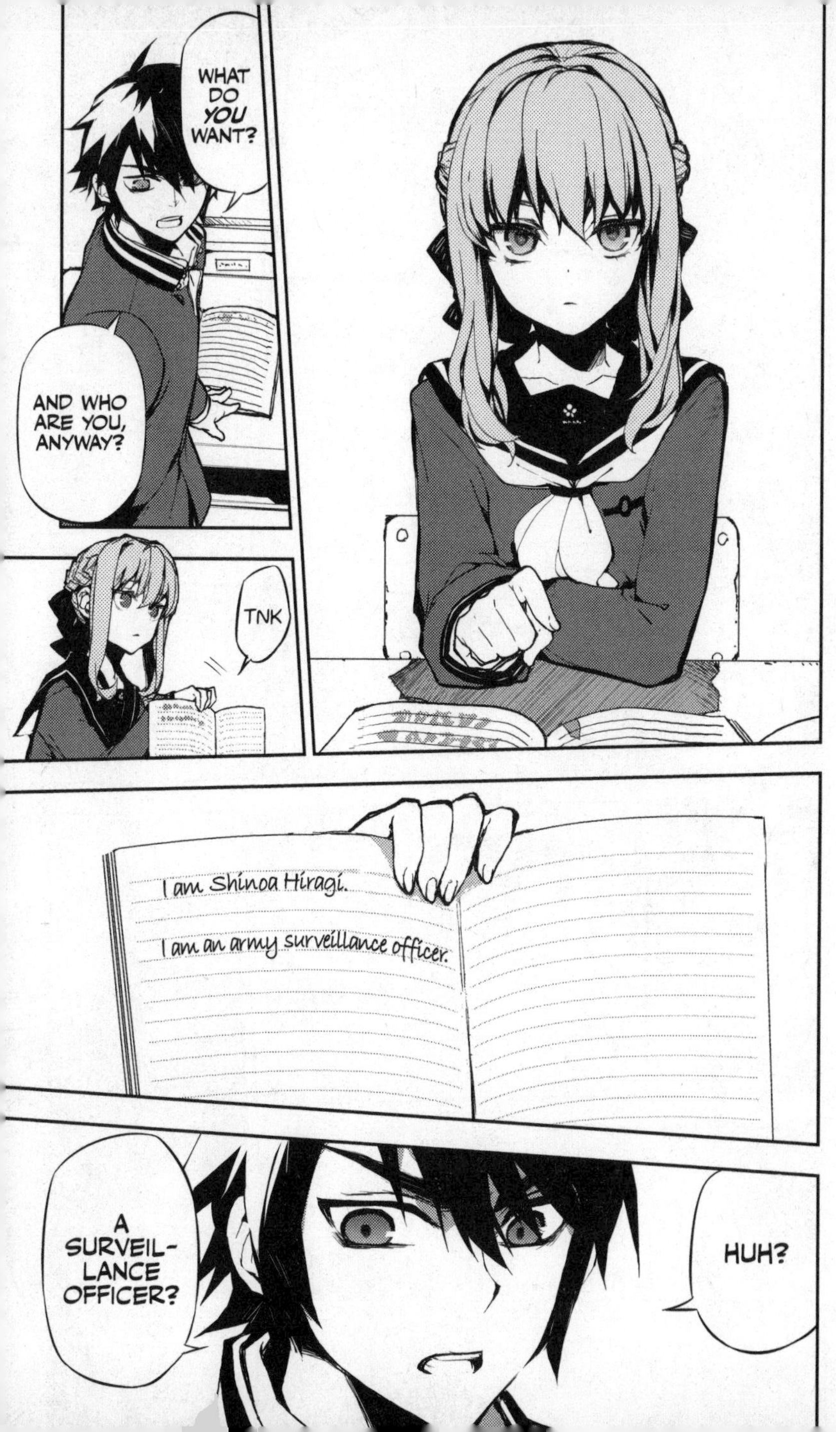
WHAT DO *YOU* WANT?
AND WHO ARE YOU, ANYWAY?
TNK
I am Shinoa Hiragi.
I am an army surveillance officer.
HUH?
A SURVEIL-LANCE OFFICER?

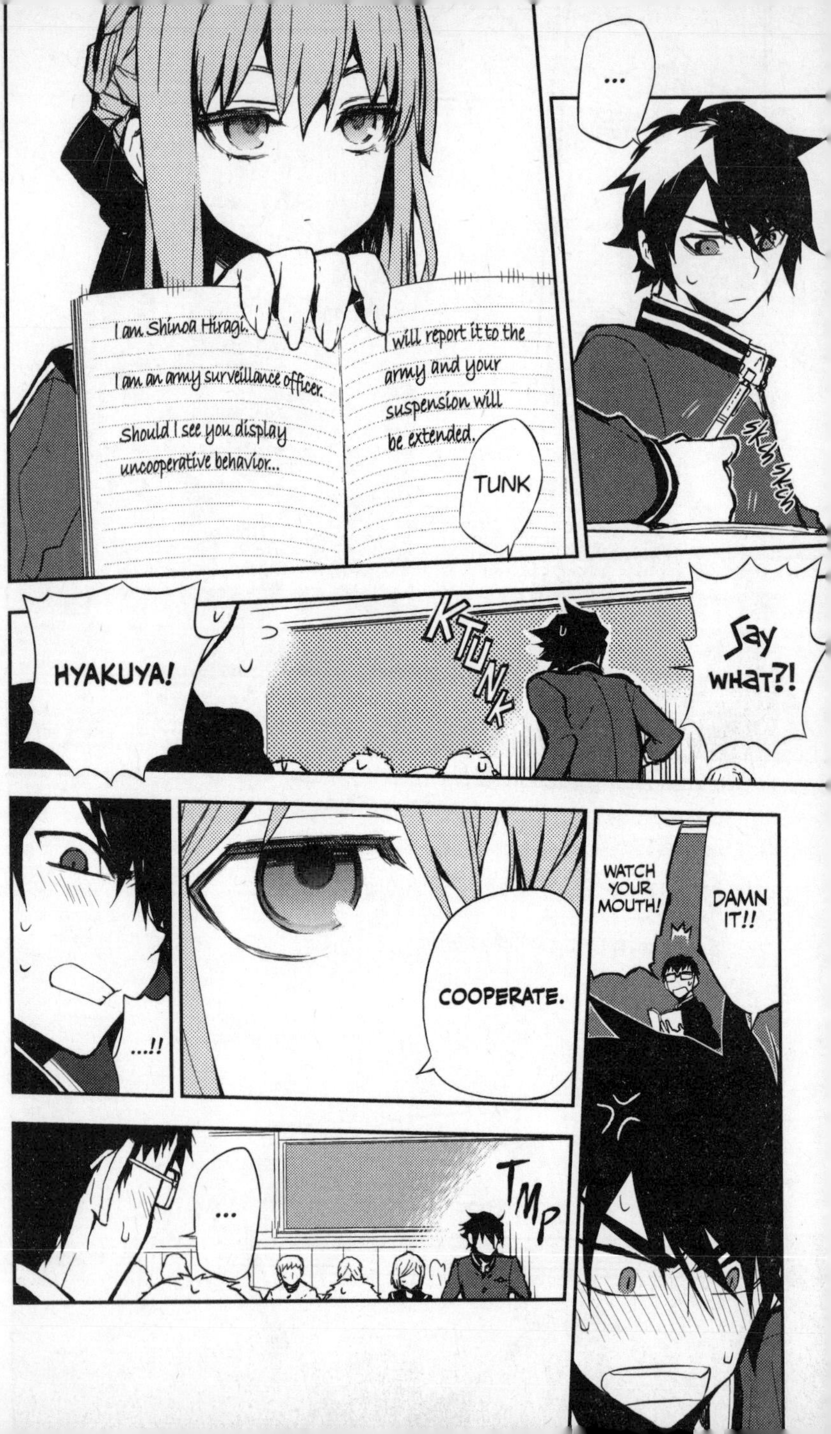

...
skish skish
I am Shinoa Hiragi.
I am an army surveillance officer.
Should I see you display uncooperative behavior...
I will report it to the army and your suspension will be extended.
TUNK
Say WHAT?!
KTUNK
HYAKUYA!
DAMN IT!!
WATCH YOUR MOUTH!
COOPERATE.
...!!
TMP
...

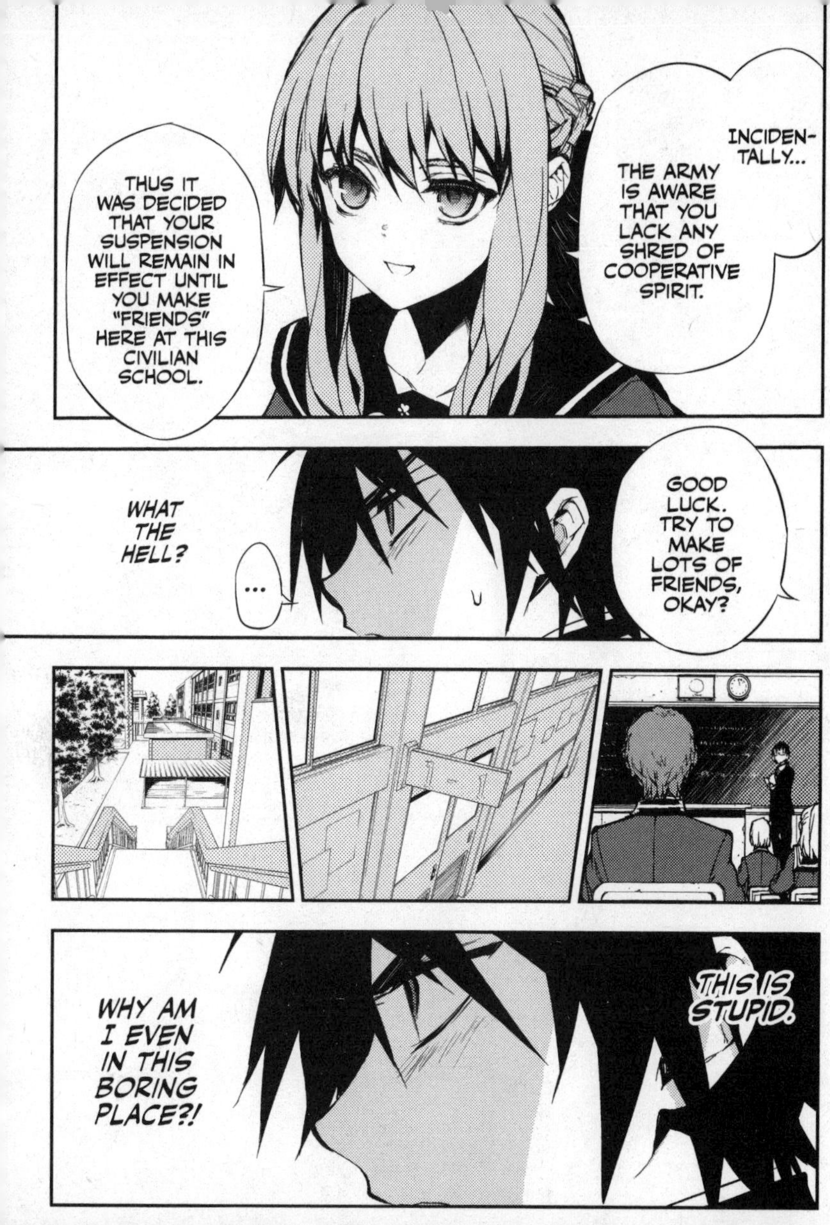
INCIDENTALLY...
THE ARMY IS AWARE THAT YOU LACK ANY SHRED OF COOPERATIVE SPIRIT.
THUS IT WAS DECIDED THAT YOUR SUSPENSION WILL REMAIN IN EFFECT UNTIL YOU MAKE "FRIENDS" HERE AT THIS CIVILIAN SCHOOL.
GOOD LUCK. TRY TO MAKE LOTS OF FRIENDS, OKAY?
...
WHAT THE HELL?
THIS IS STUPID.
WHY AM I EVEN IN THIS BORING PLACE?!

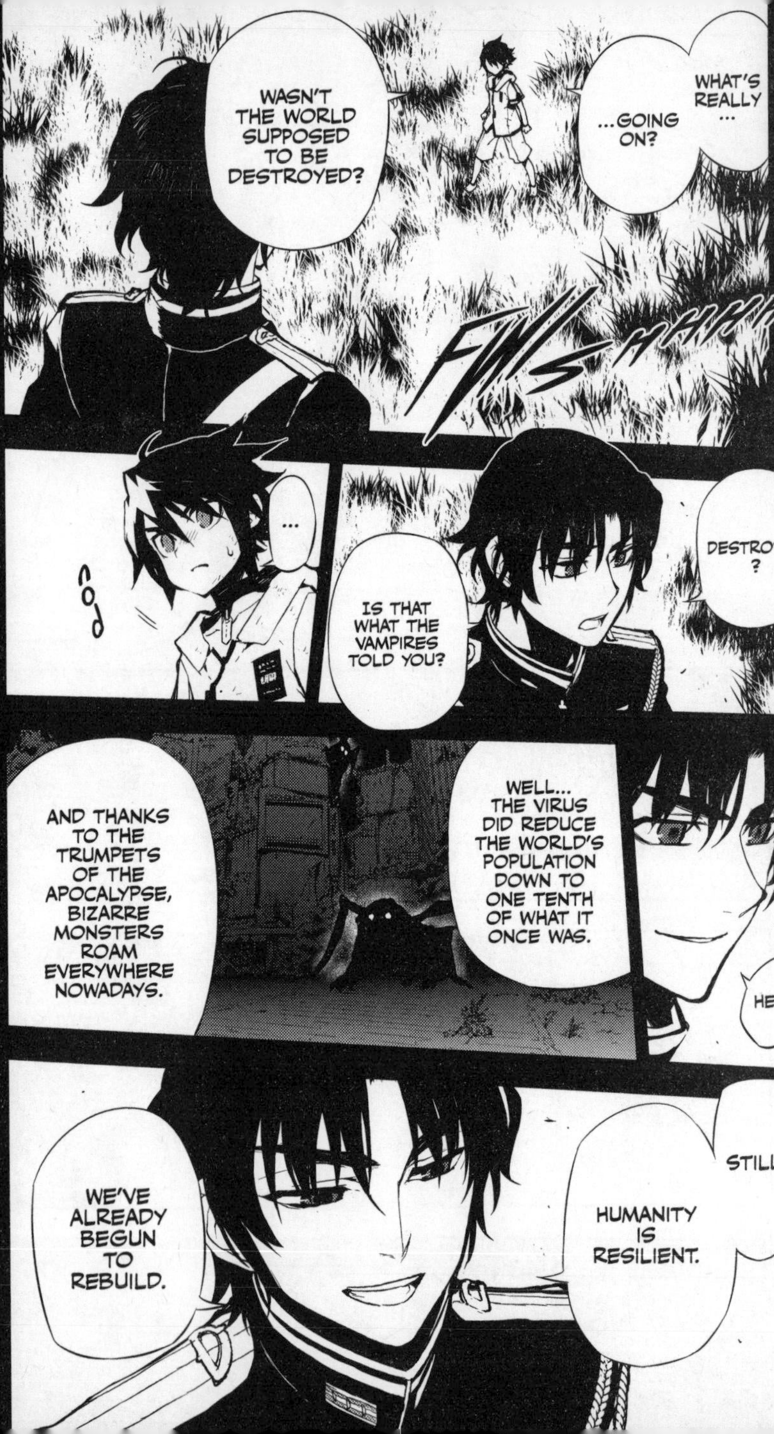
WHAT'S REALLY ...
...GOING ON?
WASN'T THE WORLD SUPPOSED TO BE DESTROYED?
DESTROYED?
IS THAT WHAT THE VAMPIRES TOLD YOU?
...
HEH.
WELL... THE VIRUS DID REDUCE THE WORLD'S POPULATION DOWN TO ONE TENTH OF WHAT IT ONCE WAS.
AND THANKS TO THE TRUMPETS OF THE APOCALYPSE, BIZARRE MONSTERS ROAM EVERYWHERE NOWADAYS.
STILL...
HUMANITY IS RESILIENT.
WE'VE ALREADY BEGUN TO REBUILD.

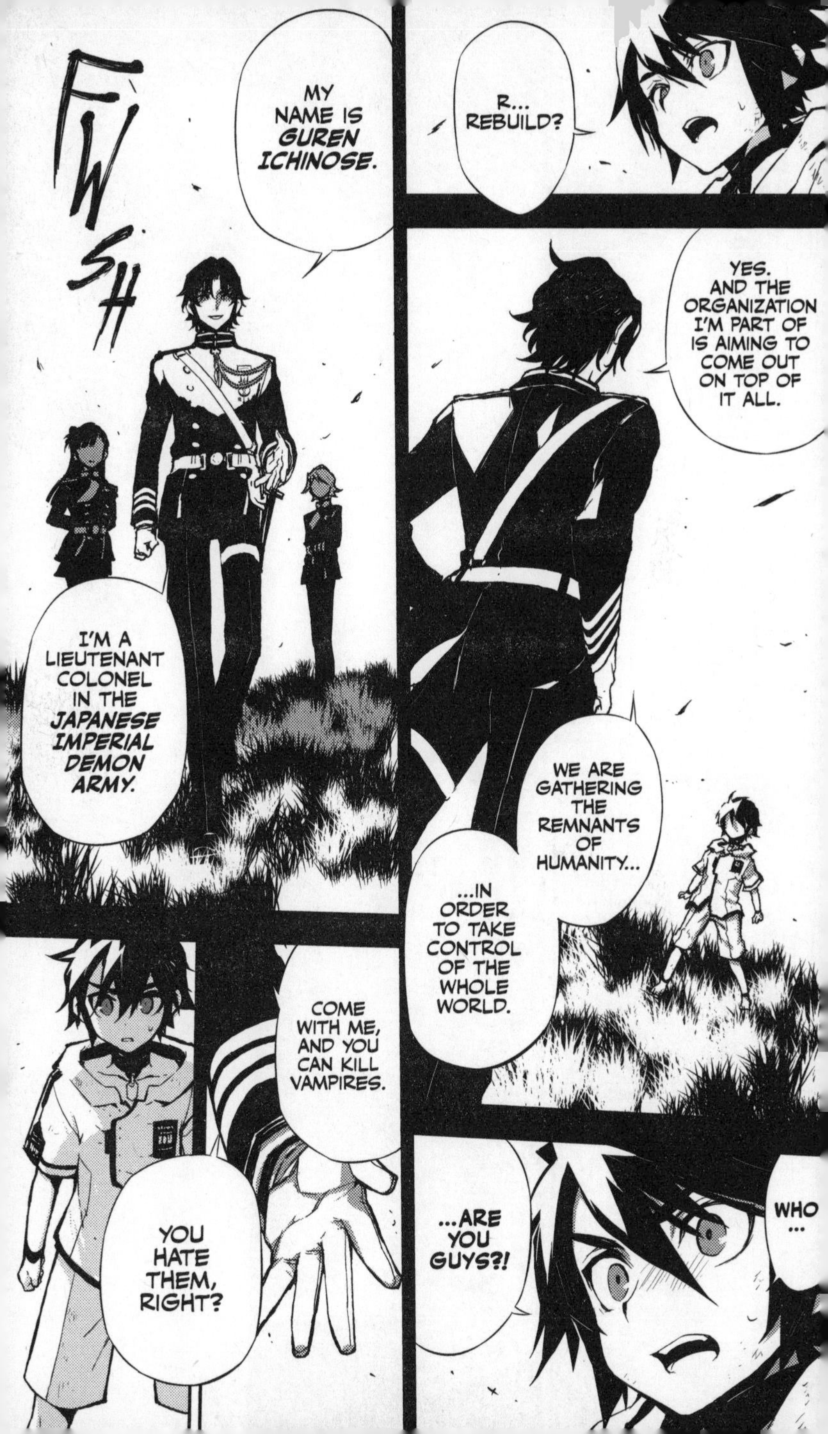
R... REBUILD?
YES. AND THE ORGANIZATION I'M PART OF IS AIMING TO COME OUT ON TOP OF IT ALL.
WE ARE GATHERING THE REMNANTS OF HUMANITY...
...IN ORDER TO TAKE CONTROL OF THE WHOLE WORLD.
WHO...
...ARE YOU GUYS?!
FWSH
MY NAME IS GUREN ICHINOSE.
I'M A LIEUTENANT COLONEL IN THE JAPANESE IMPERIAL DEMON ARMY.
COME WITH ME, AND YOU CAN KILL VAMPIRES.
YOU HATE THEM, RIGHT?

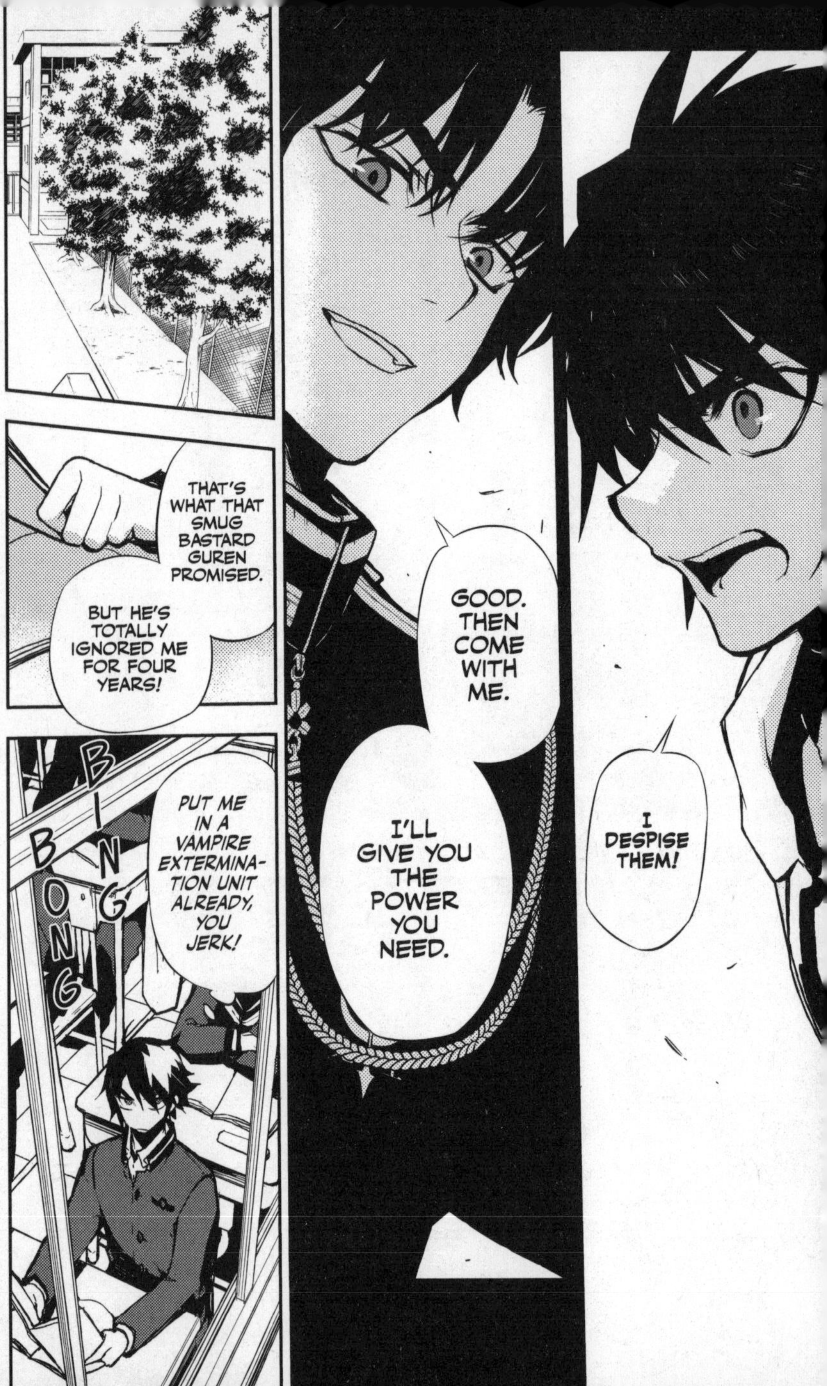
I DESPISE THEM!
GOOD. THEN COME WITH ME.
I'LL GIVE YOU THE POWER YOU NEED.
THAT'S WHAT THAT SMUG BASTARD GUREN PROMISED.
BUT HE'S TOTALLY IGNORED ME FOR FOUR YEARS!
PUT ME IN A VAMPIRE EXTERMINATION UNIT ALREADY, YOU JERK!
BING
BONG

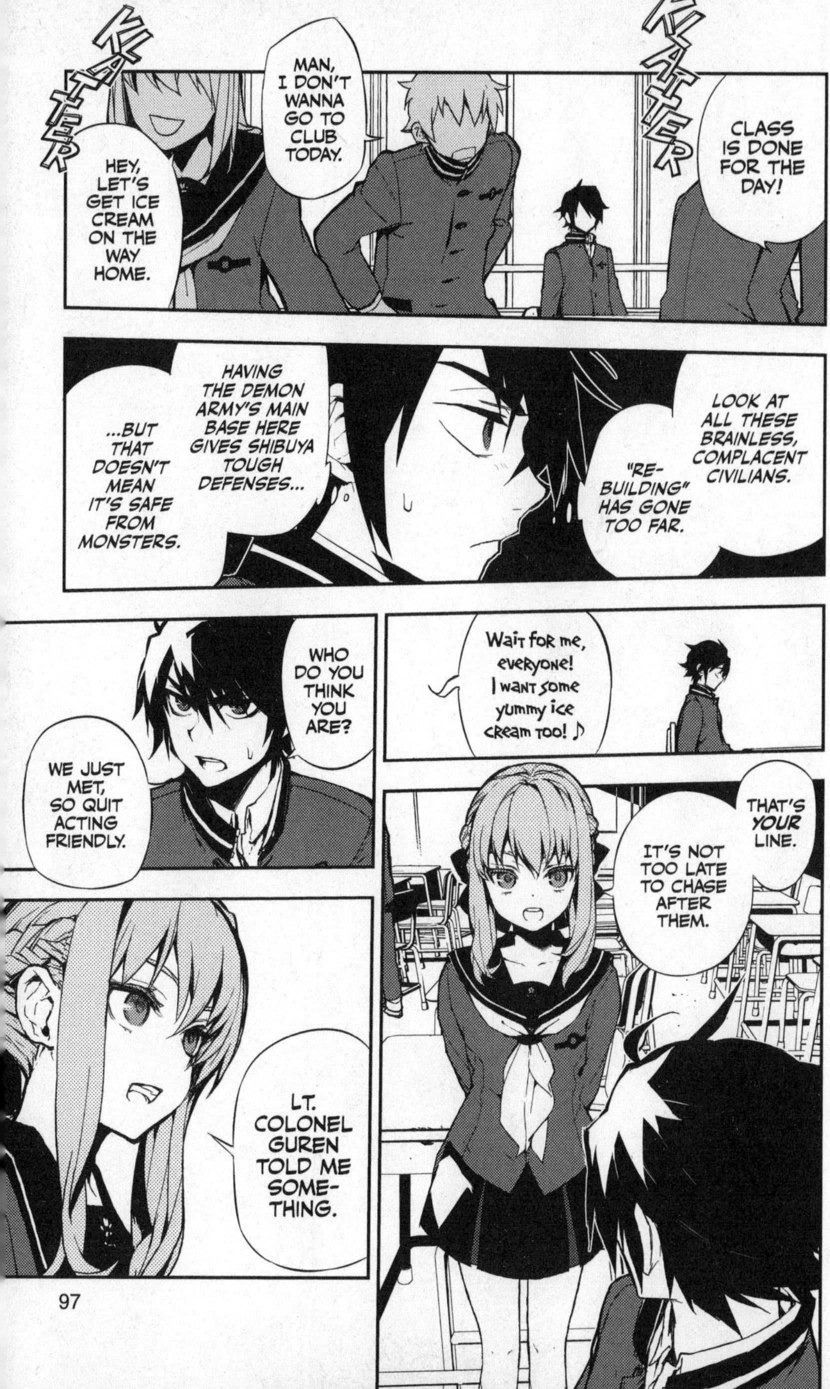
KLATTER
CLASS IS DONE FOR THE DAY!
MAN, I DON'T WANNA GO TO CLUB TODAY.
KLATTER
HEY, LET'S GET ICE CREAM ON THE WAY HOME.
LOOK AT ALL THESE BRAINLESS, COMPLACENT CIVILIANS.
"RE-BUILDING" HAS GONE TOO FAR.
HAVING THE DEMON ARMY'S MAIN BASE HERE GIVES SHIBUYA TOUGH DEFENSES...
...BUT THAT DOESN'T MEAN IT'S SAFE FROM MONSTERS.
Wait for me, everyone! I want some yummy ice cream too! ♪
WHO DO YOU THINK YOU ARE?
WE JUST MET, SO QUIT ACTING FRIENDLY.
THAT'S *YOUR* LINE.
IT'S NOT TOO LATE TO CHASE AFTER THEM.
LT. COLONEL GUREN TOLD ME SOME-THING.

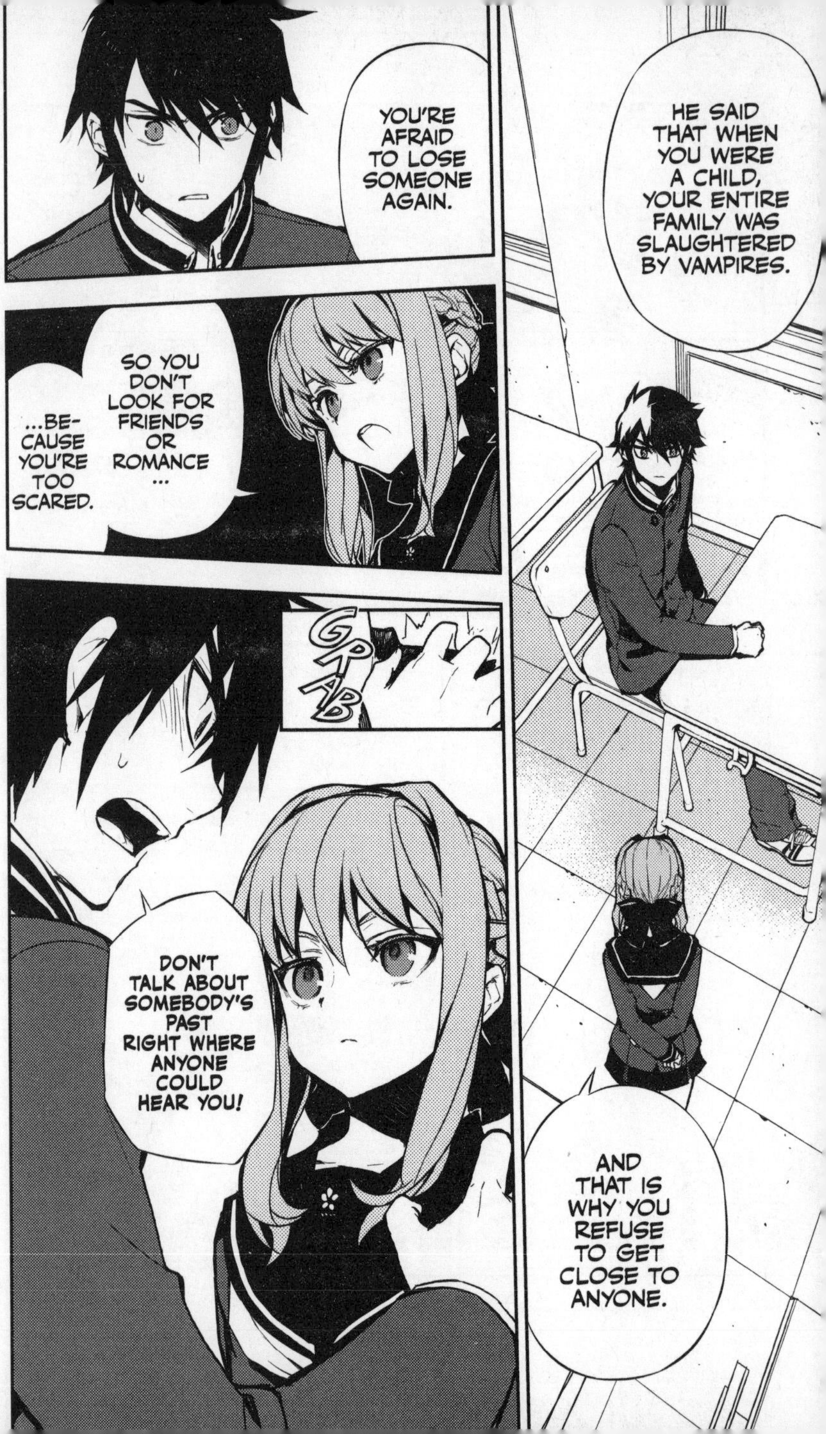
HE SAID THAT WHEN YOU WERE A CHILD, YOUR ENTIRE FAMILY WAS SLAUGHTERED BY VAMPIRES.
AND THAT IS WHY YOU REFUSE TO GET CLOSE TO ANYONE.
YOU'RE AFRAID TO LOSE SOMEONE AGAIN.
SO YOU DON'T LOOK FOR FRIENDS OR ROMANCE...
...BE-CAUSE YOU'RE TOO SCARED.
GRAB
DON'T TALK ABOUT SOMEBODY'S PAST RIGHT WHERE ANYONE COULD HEAR YOU!

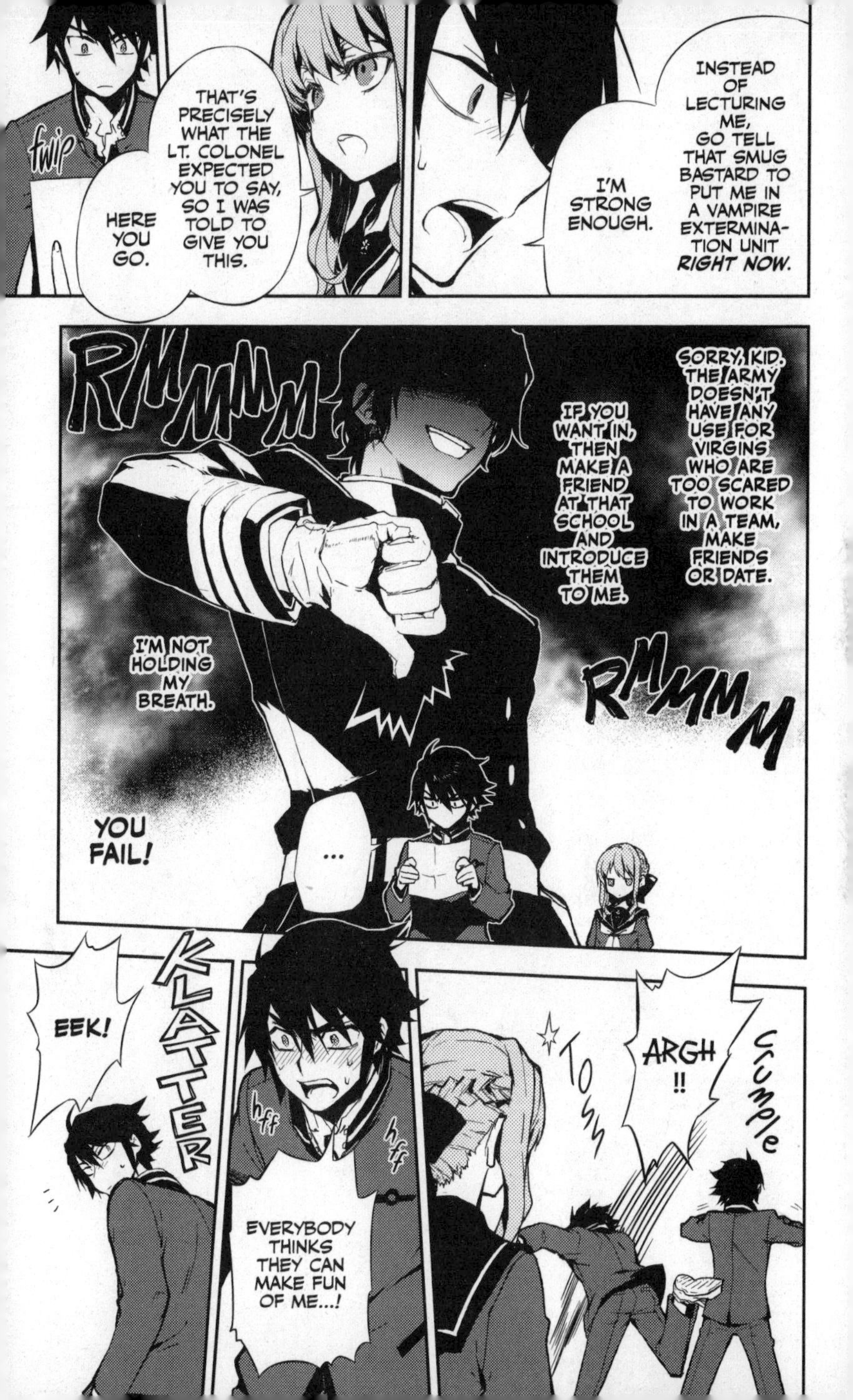
INSTEAD OF LECTURING ME, GO TELL THAT SMUG BASTARD TO PUT ME IN A VAMPIRE EXTERMINATION UNIT *RIGHT NOW.*
I'M STRONG ENOUGH.
THAT'S PRECISELY WHAT THE LT. COLONEL EXPECTED YOU TO SAY, SO I WAS TOLD TO GIVE YOU THIS.
HERE YOU GO.
fwip
RMMMM
SORRY, KID. THE ARMY DOESN'T HAVE ANY USE FOR VIRGINS WHO ARE TOO SCARED TO WORK IN A TEAM, MAKE FRIENDS OR DATE.
IF YOU WANT IN, THEN MAKE A FRIEND AT THAT SCHOOL AND INTRODUCE THEM TO ME.
RMMMMM
I'M NOT HOLDING MY BREATH.
YOU FAIL!
...
ARGH!!
crumple
TOSS
KLATTER
hff
hff
EVERYBODY THINKS THEY CAN MAKE FUN OF ME...!
EEK!

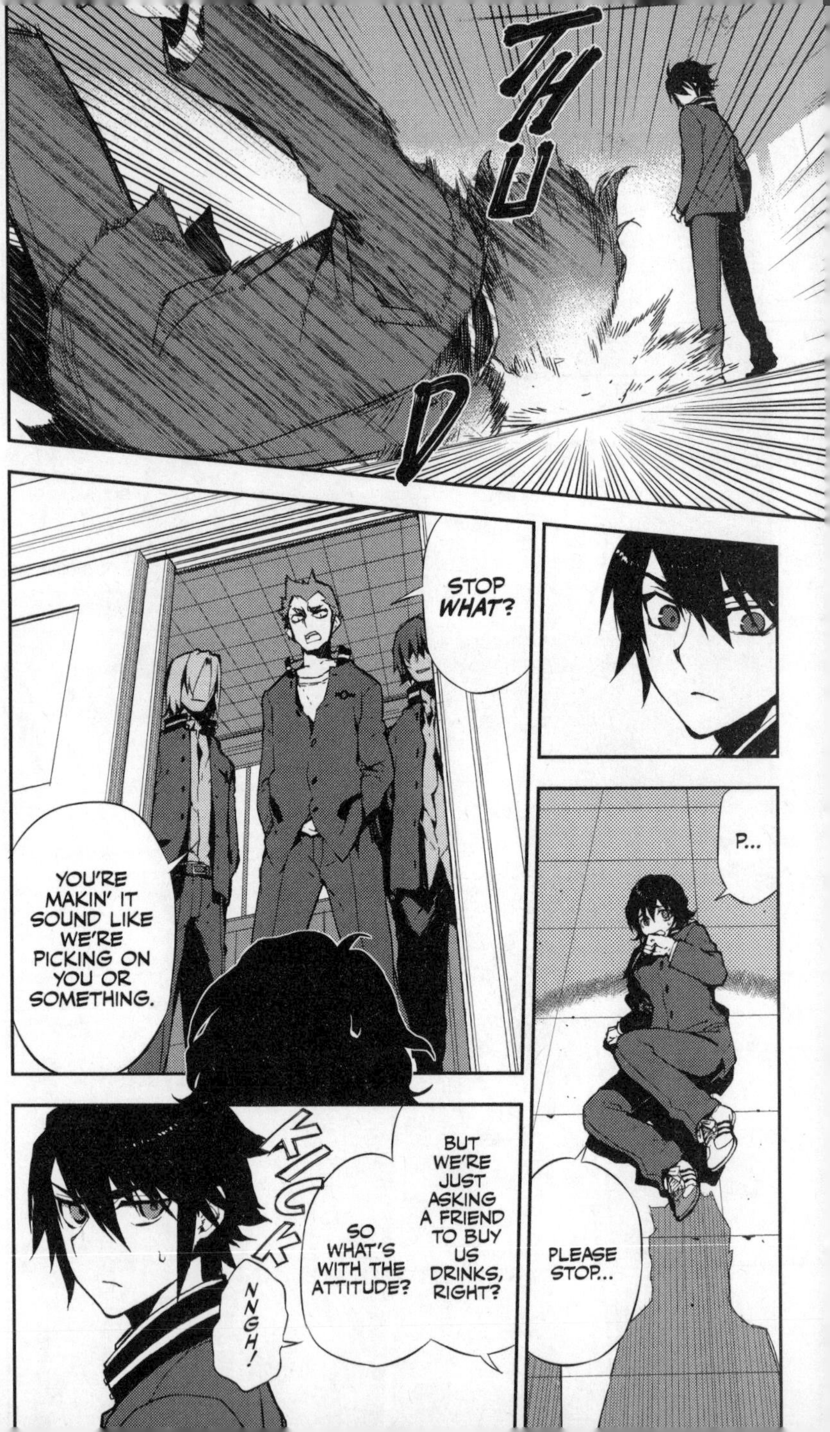
THUD
P...
PLEASE STOP...
STOP WHAT?
YOU'RE MAKIN' IT SOUND LIKE WE'RE PICKING ON YOU OR SOMETHING.
BUT WE'RE JUST ASKING A FRIEND TO BUY US DRINKS, RIGHT?
SO WHAT'S WITH THE ATTITUDE?
KICK
NNGH!

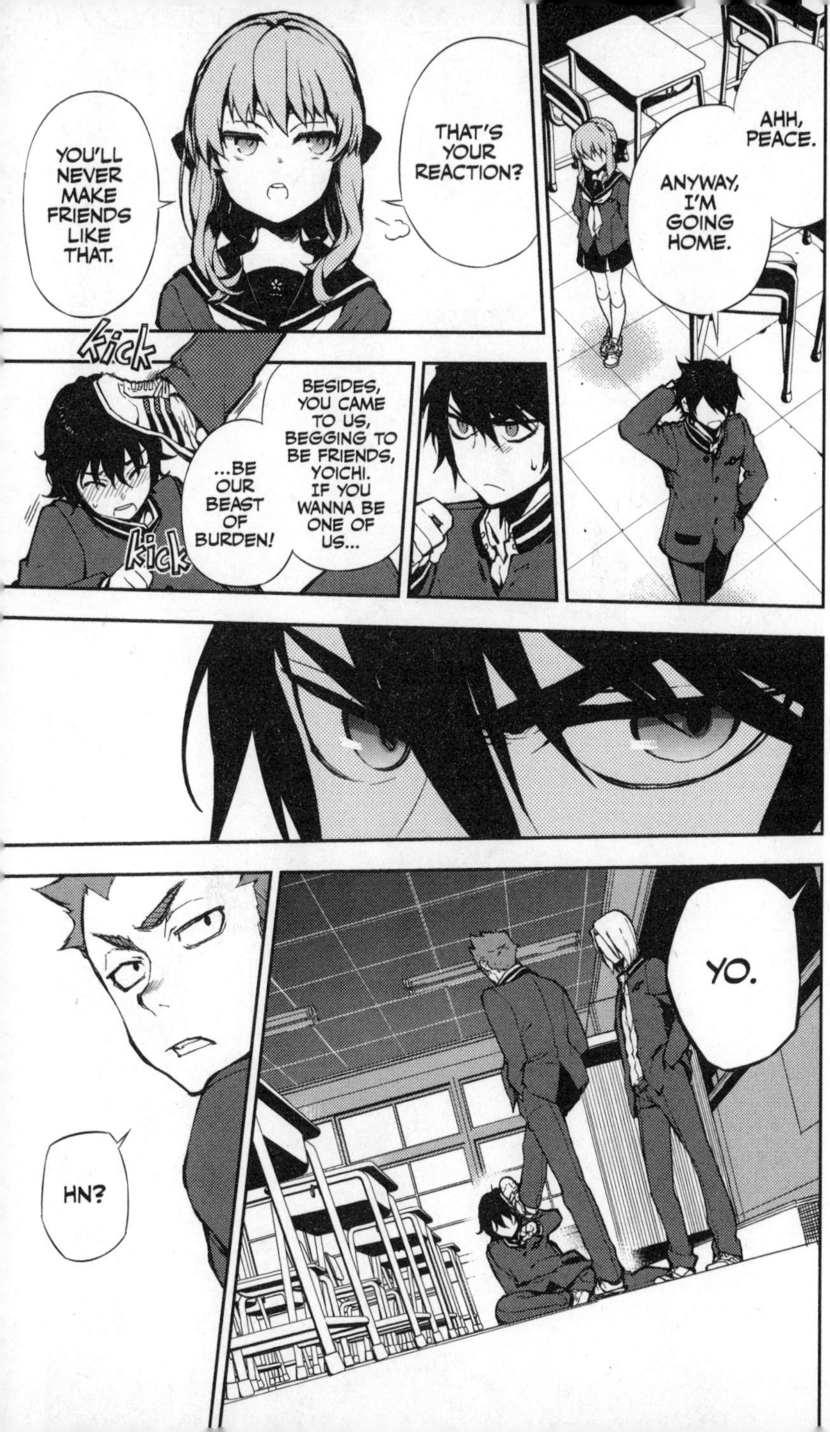
AHH, PEACE.
ANYWAY, I'M GOING HOME.
THAT'S YOUR REACTION?
YOU'LL NEVER MAKE FRIENDS LIKE THAT.
KICK
BESIDES, YOU CAME TO US, BEGGING TO BE FRIENDS, YOICHI. IF YOU WANNA BE ONE OF US...
...BE OUR BEAST OF BURDEN!
KICK
YO.
HN?

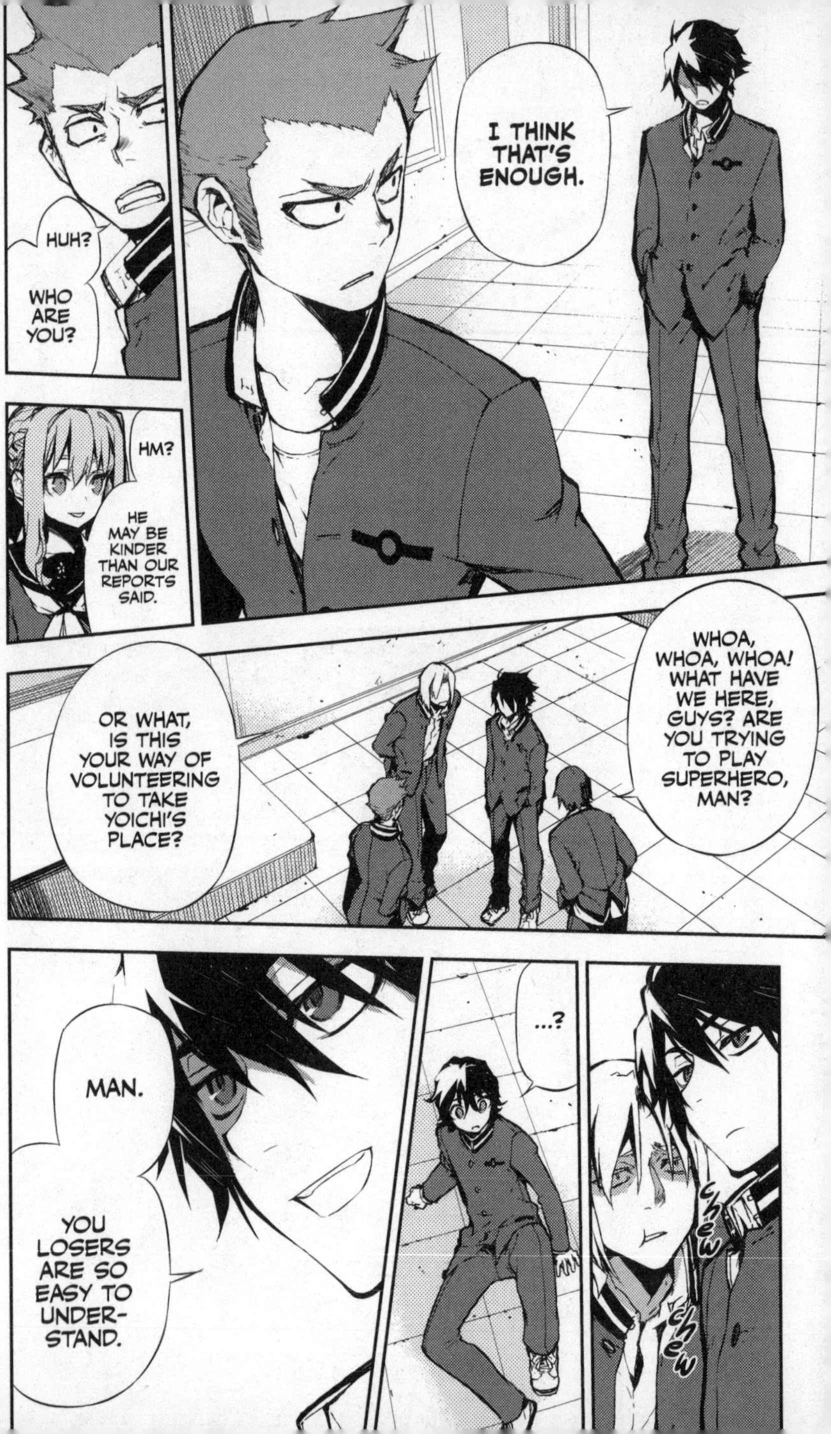
I THINK THAT'S ENOUGH.
HUH?
WHO ARE YOU?
HM?
HE MAY BE KINDER THAN OUR REPORTS SAID.
WHOA, WHOA, WHOA! WHAT HAVE WE HERE, GUYS? ARE YOU TRYING TO PLAY SUPERHERO, MAN?
OR WHAT, IS THIS YOUR WAY OF VOLUNTEERING TO TAKE YOICHI'S PLACE?
chew
chew
...?
MAN.
YOU LOSERS ARE SO EASY TO UNDER-STAND.

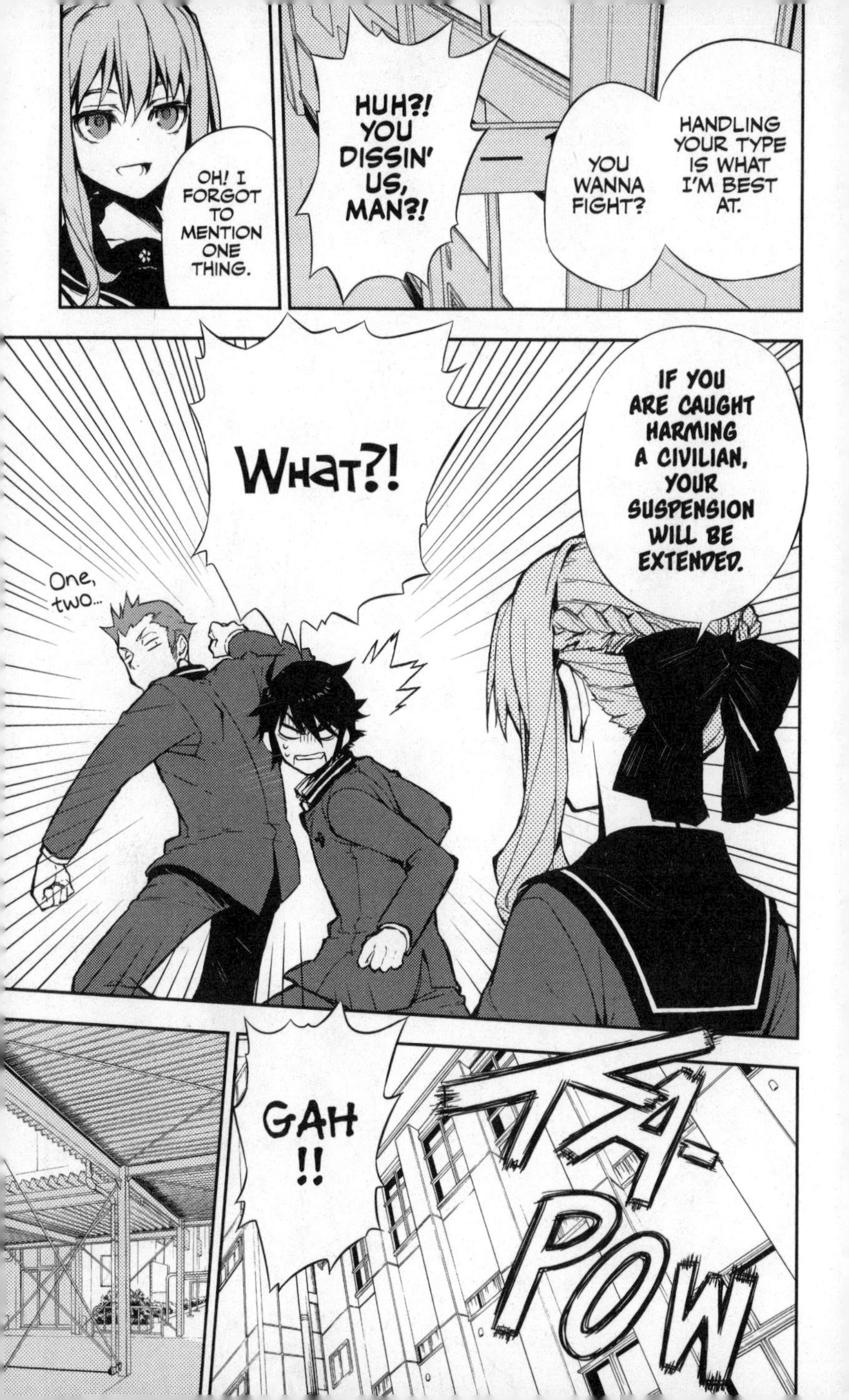
HANDLING YOUR TYPE IS WHAT I'M BEST AT.
YOU WANNA FIGHT?
HUH?! YOU DISSIN' US, MAN?!
OH! I FORGOT TO MENTION ONE THING.
IF YOU ARE CAUGHT HARMING A CIVILIAN, YOUR SUSPENSION WILL BE EXTENDED.
WHAT?!
One, two...
KA-POW
GAH !!

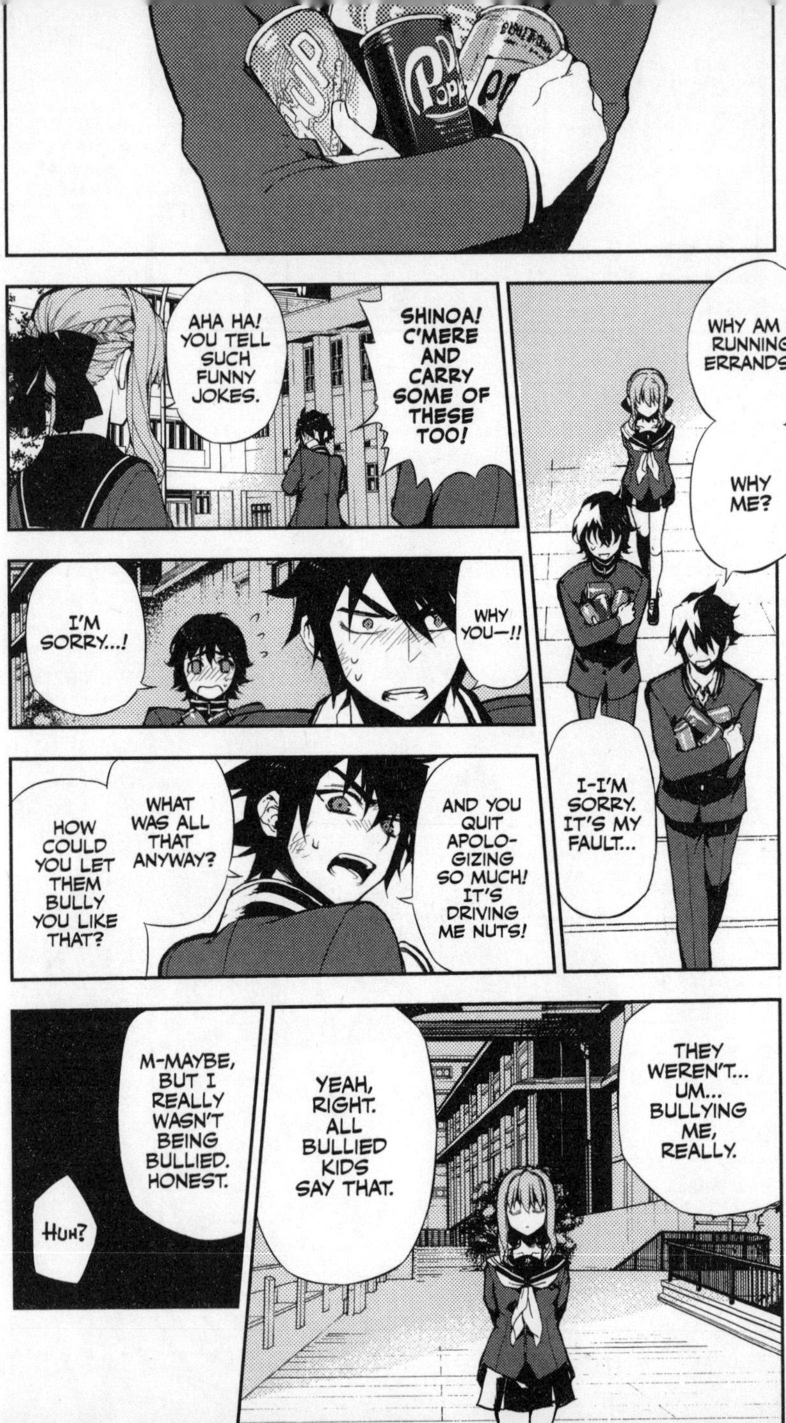
Pop
WHY AM I RUNNING ERRANDS?
WHY ME?
I-I'M SORRY. IT'S MY FAULT...
SHINOA! C'MERE AND CARRY SOME OF THESE TOO!
AHA HA! YOU TELL SUCH FUNNY JOKES.
WHY YOU—!!
I'M SORRY...!
AND YOU QUIT APOLO-GIZING SO MUCH! IT'S DRIVING ME NUTS!
WHAT WAS ALL THAT ANYWAY?
HOW COULD YOU LET THEM BULLY YOU LIKE THAT?
THEY WEREN'T... UM... BULLYING ME, REALLY.
YEAH, RIGHT. ALL BULLIED KIDS SAY THAT.
M-MAYBE, BUT I REALLY WASN'T BEING BULLIED. HONEST.
HUH?

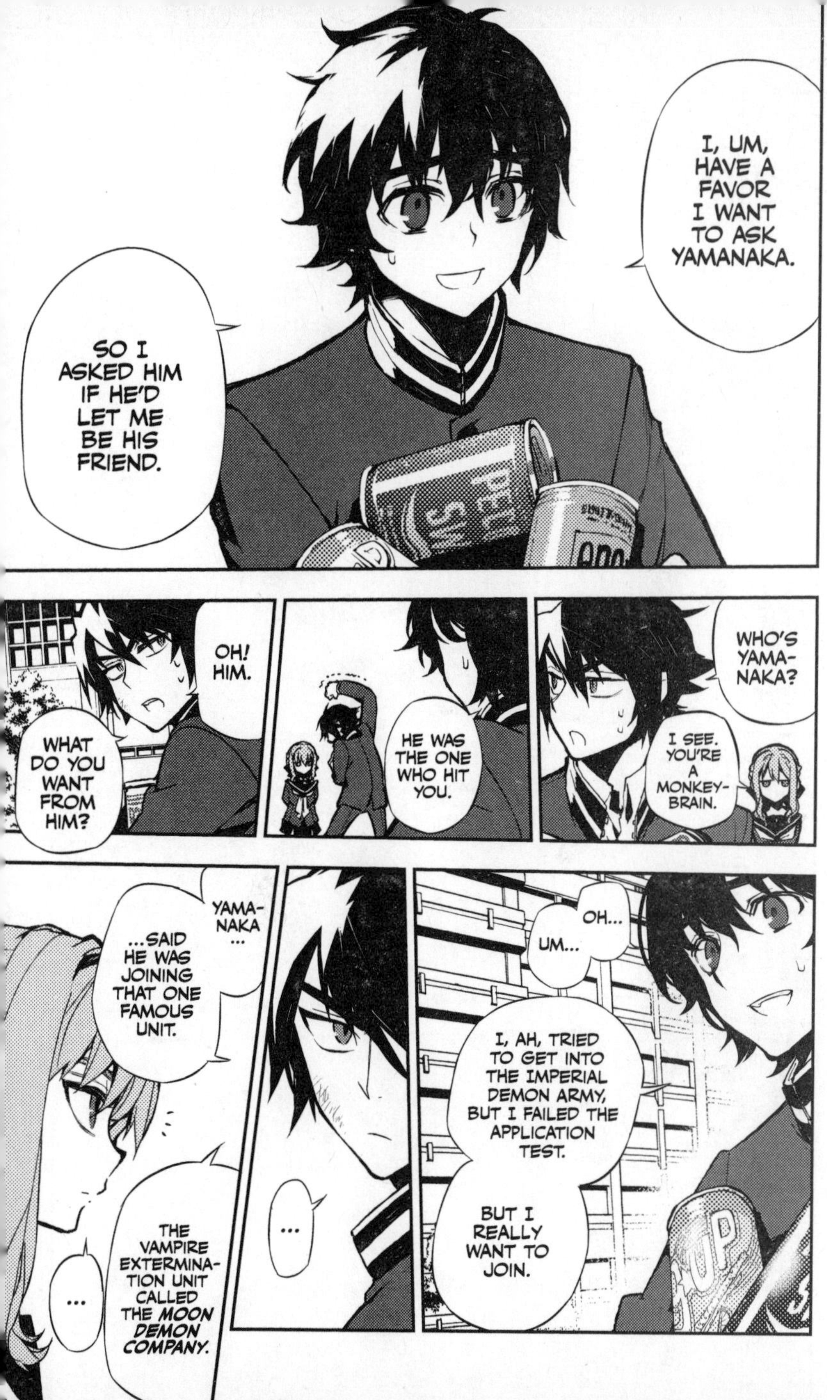
I, UM, HAVE A FAVOR I WANT TO ASK YAMANAKA.
SO I ASKED HIM IF HE'D LET ME BE HIS FRIEND.
WHO'S YAMANAKA?
I SEE. YOU'RE A MONKEY-BRAIN.
HE WAS THE ONE WHO HIT YOU.
OH! HIM.
WHAT DO YOU WANT FROM HIM?
OH...
UM...
I, AH, TRIED TO GET INTO THE IMPERIAL DEMON ARMY, BUT I FAILED THE APPLICATION TEST.
BUT I REALLY WANT TO JOIN.
...
YAMANAKA...
...SAID HE WAS JOINING THAT ONE FAMOUS UNIT.
THE VAMPIRE EXTERMINATION UNIT CALLED THE *MOON DEMON COMPANY*.
...

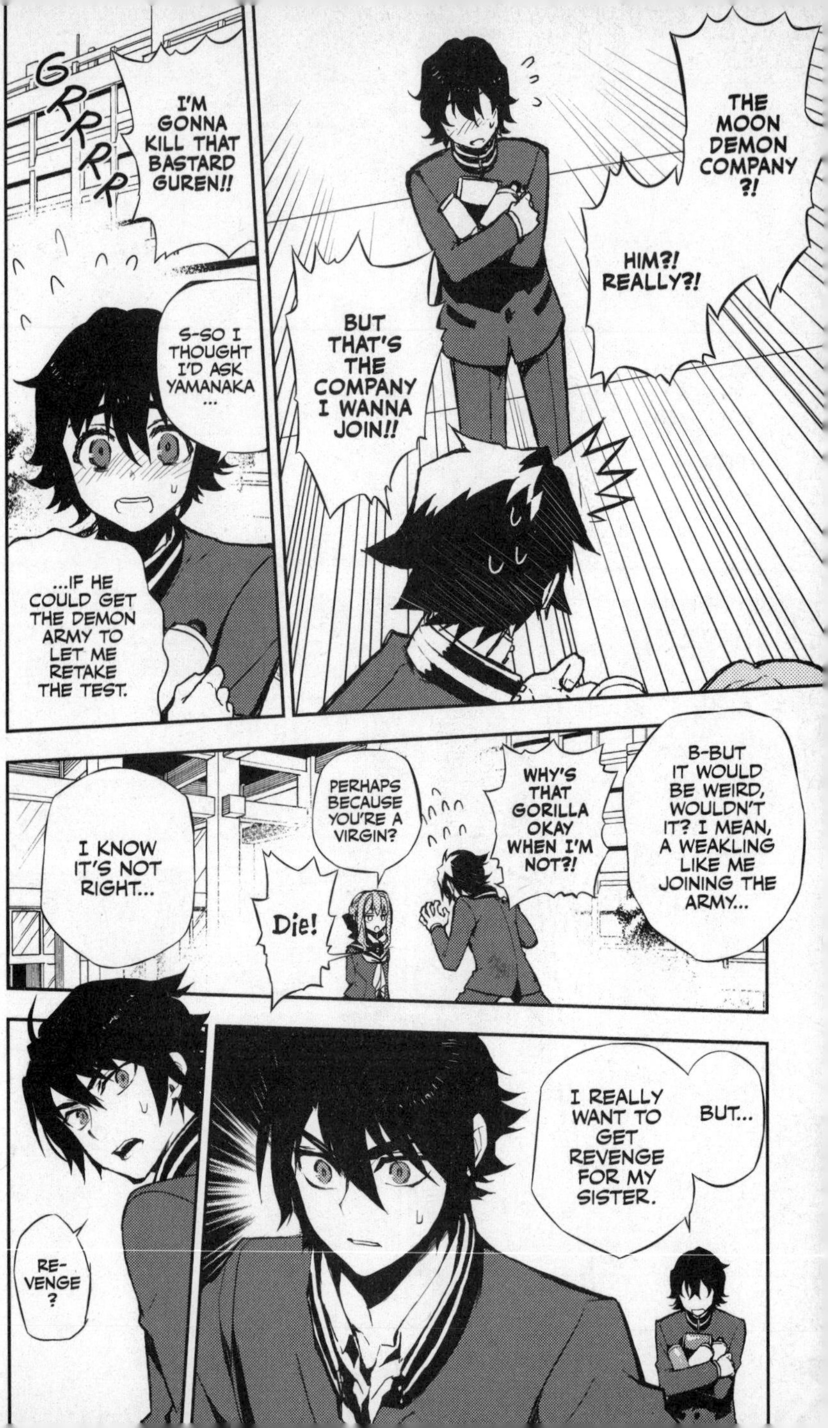
THE MOON DEMON COMPANY?!
HIM?! REALLY?!
BUT THAT'S THE COMPANY I WANNA JOIN!!
I'M GONNA KILL THAT BASTARD GUREN!!
GRRRR
S-SO I THOUGHT I'D ASK YAMANAKA...
...IF HE COULD GET THE DEMON ARMY TO LET ME RETAKE THE TEST.
B-BUT IT WOULD BE WEIRD, WOULDN'T IT? I MEAN, A WEAKLING LIKE ME JOINING THE ARMY...
WHY'S THAT GORILLA OKAY WHEN I'M NOT?!
PERHAPS BECAUSE YOU'RE A VIRGIN?
Die!
I KNOW IT'S NOT RIGHT...
BUT...
I REALLY WANT TO GET REVENGE FOR MY SISTER.
RE-VENGE?

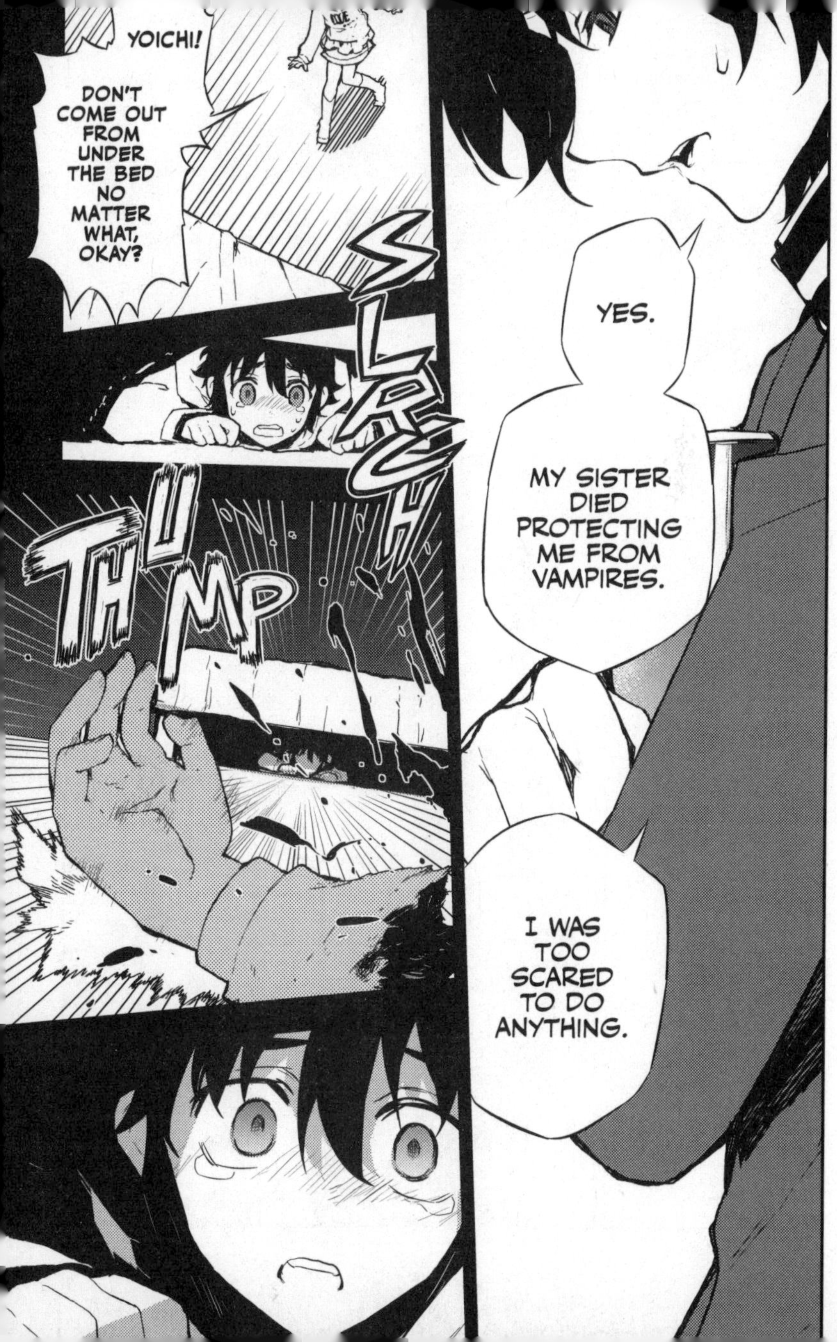
YES.
MY SISTER DIED PROTECTING ME FROM VAMPIRES.
I WAS TOO SCARED TO DO ANYTHING.
YOICHI!
DON'T COME OUT FROM UNDER THE BED NO MATTER WHAT, OKAY?
SLRCH
THUMP

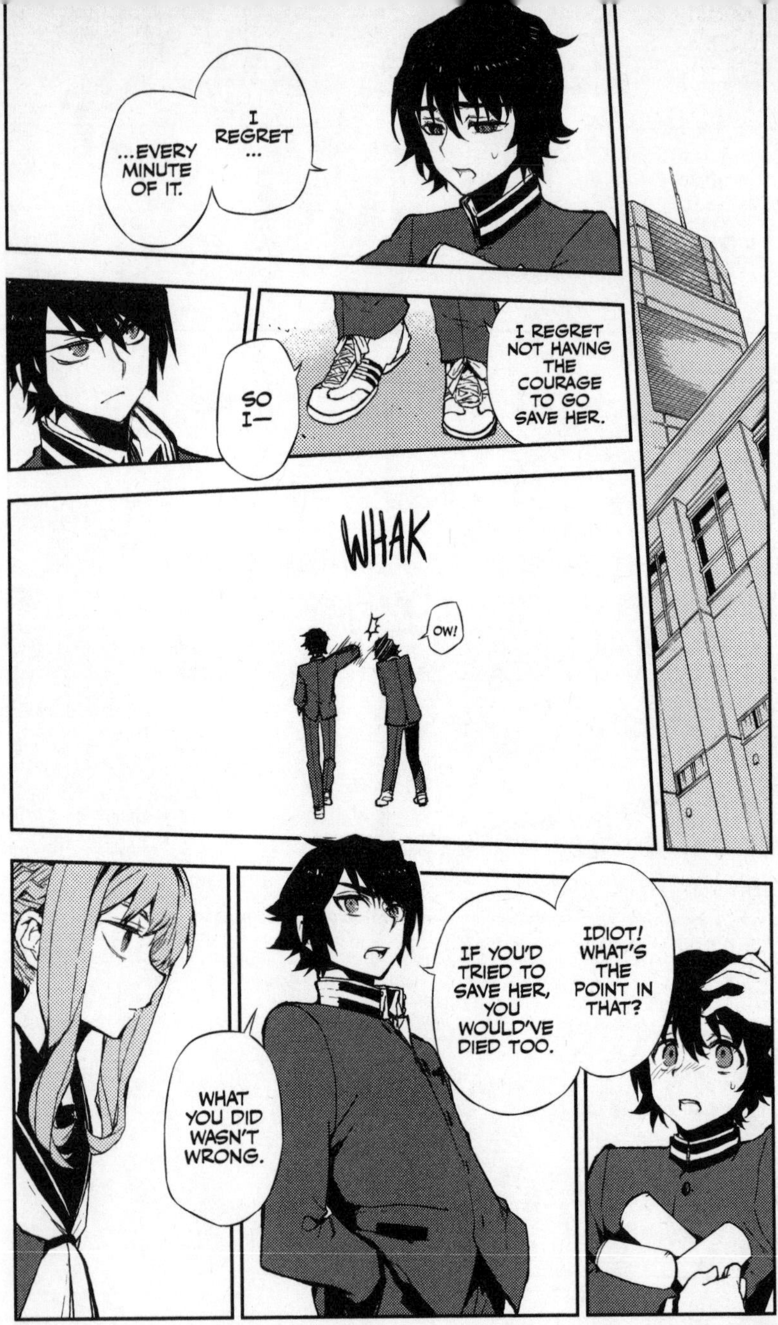
I REGRET...
...EVERY MINUTE OF IT.
I REGRET NOT HAVING THE COURAGE TO GO SAVE HER.
SO I—
WHAK
OW!
IDIOT! WHAT'S THE POINT IN THAT?
IF YOU'D TRIED TO SAVE HER, YOU WOULD'VE DIED TOO.
WHAT YOU DID WASN'T WRONG.

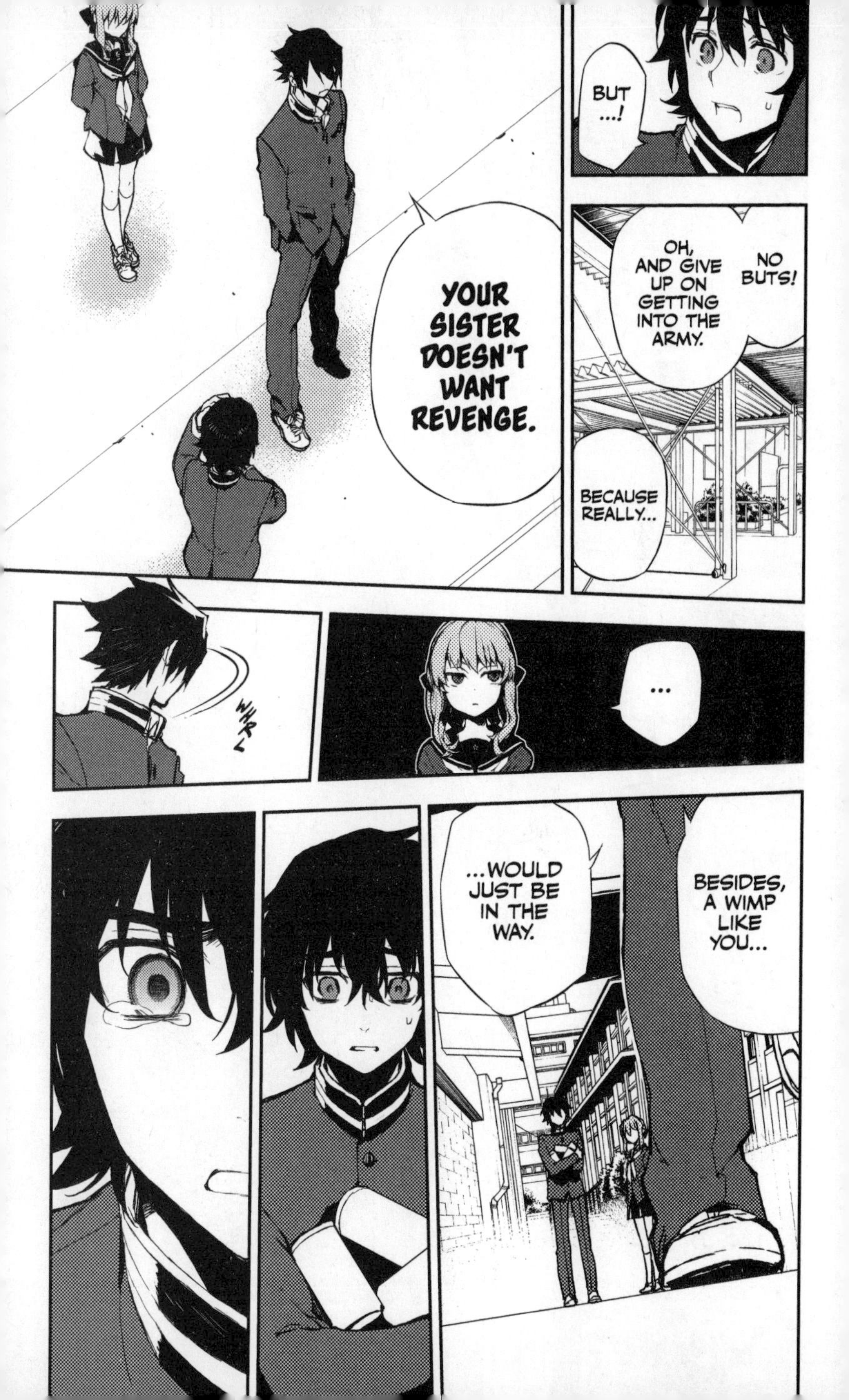
BUT ...!
NO BUTS!
OH, AND GIVE UP ON GETTING INTO THE ARMY.
BECAUSE REALLY...
YOUR SISTER DOESN'T WANT REVENGE.
...
WHIRL
BESIDES, A WIMP LIKE YOU...
...WOULD JUST BE IN THE WAY.

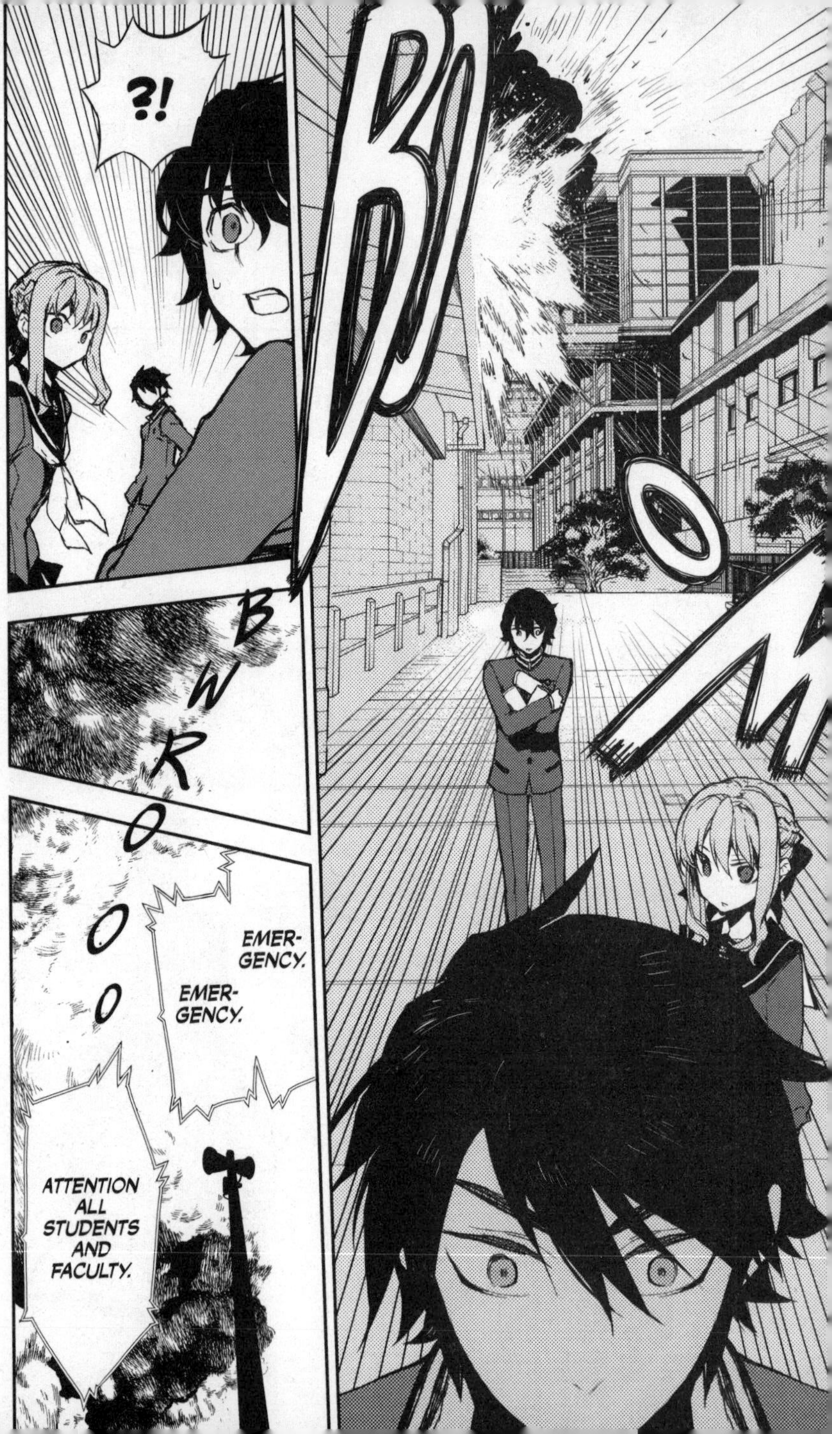
BOOM
?!
BWROOO
EMER-GENCY.
EMER-GENCY.
ATTENTION ALL STUDENTS AND FACULTY.

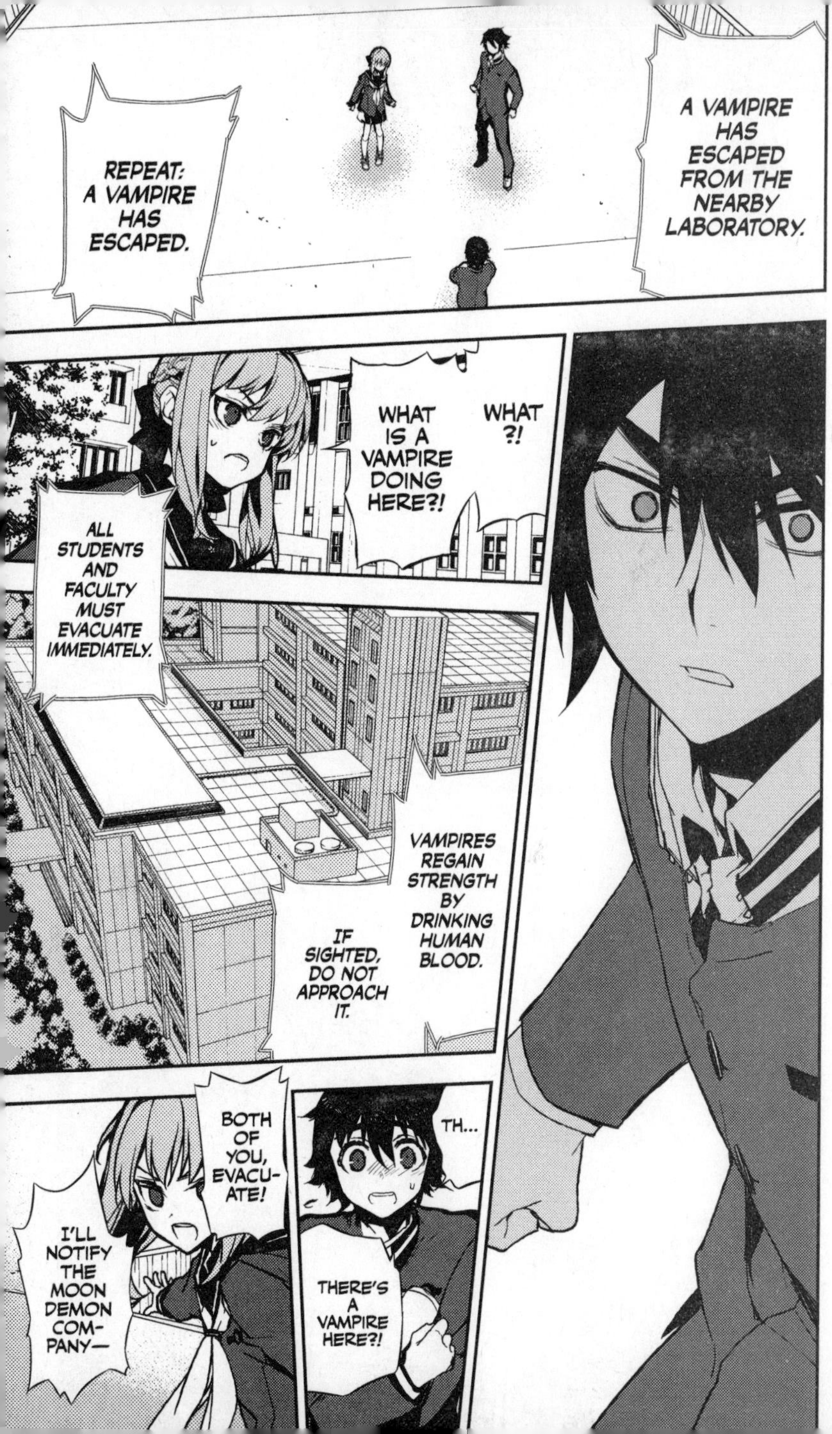
A VAMPIRE HAS ESCAPED FROM THE NEARBY LABORATORY.
REPEAT: A VAMPIRE HAS ESCAPED.
WHAT ?!
WHAT IS A VAMPIRE DOING HERE?!
ALL STUDENTS AND FACULTY MUST EVACUATE IMMEDIATELY.
VAMPIRES REGAIN STRENGTH BY DRINKING HUMAN BLOOD.
IF SIGHTED, DO NOT APPROACH IT.
TH...
THERE'S A VAMPIRE HERE?!
BOTH OF YOU, EVACU-ATE!
I'LL NOTIFY THE MOON DEMON COM-PANY—

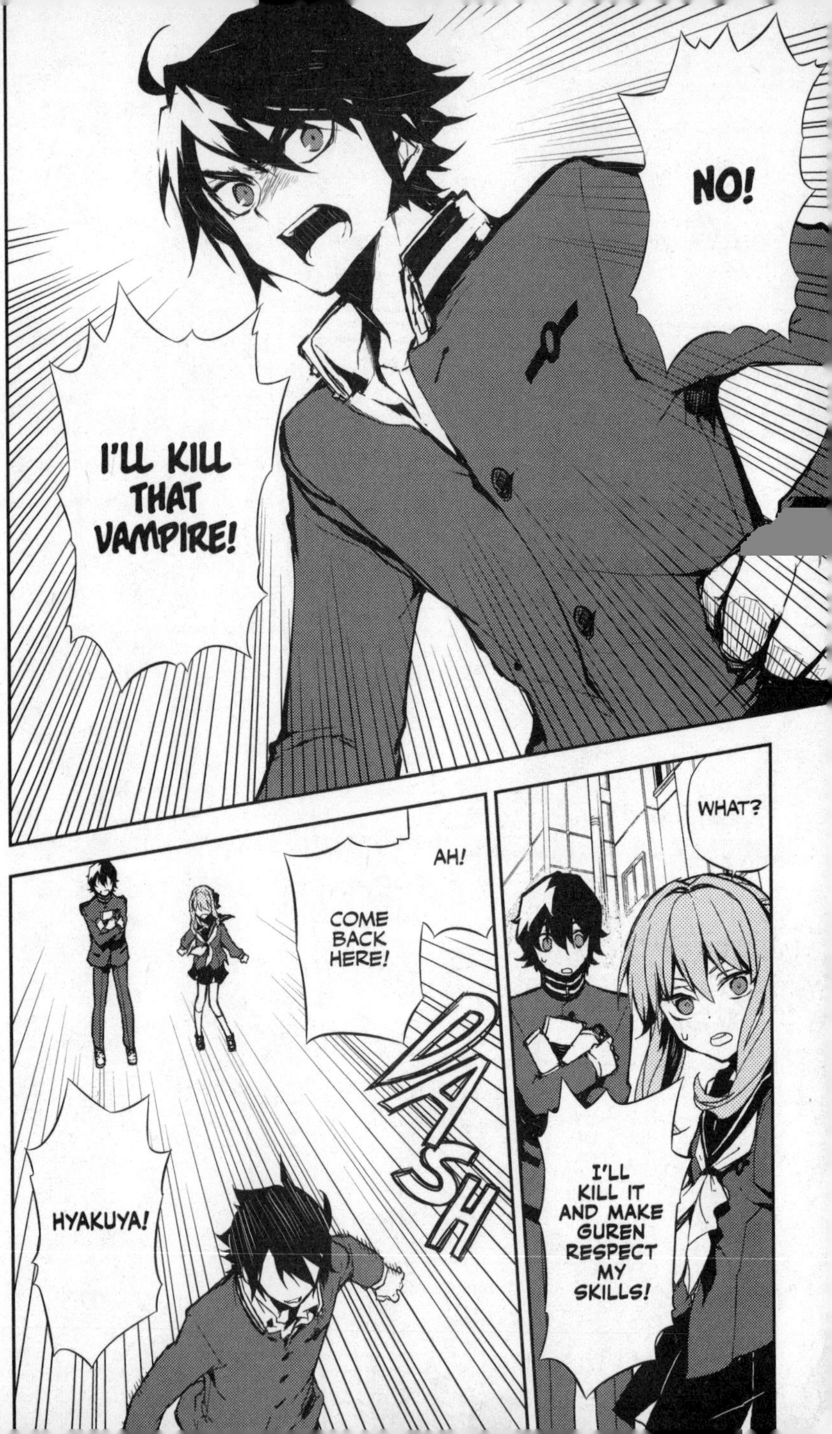
NO!
I'LL KILL THAT VAMPIRE!
WHAT?
I'LL KILL IT AND MAKE GUREN RESPECT MY SKILLS!
AH!
COME BACK HERE!
DASH
HYAKUYA!

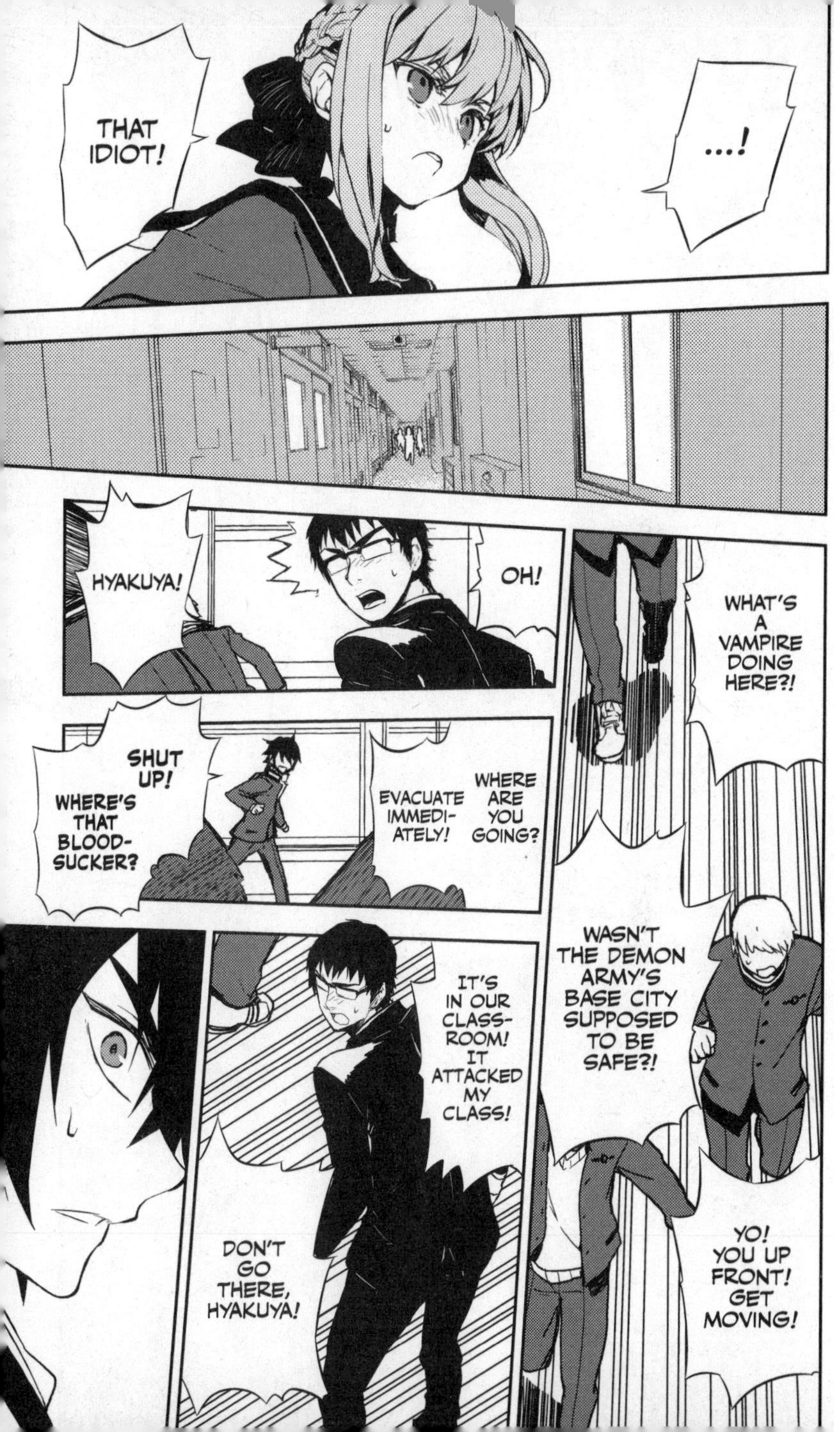
...!
THAT IDIOT!
WHAT'S A VAMPIRE DOING HERE?!
WASN'T THE DEMON ARMY'S BASE CITY SUPPOSED TO BE SAFE?!
YO! YOU UP FRONT! GET MOVING!
OH!
HYAKUYA!
WHERE ARE YOU GOING?
EVACUATE IMMEDIATELY!
SHUT UP! WHERE'S THAT BLOOD-SUCKER?
IT'S IN OUR CLASS-ROOM! IT ATTACKED MY CLASS!
DON'T GO THERE, HYAKUYA!

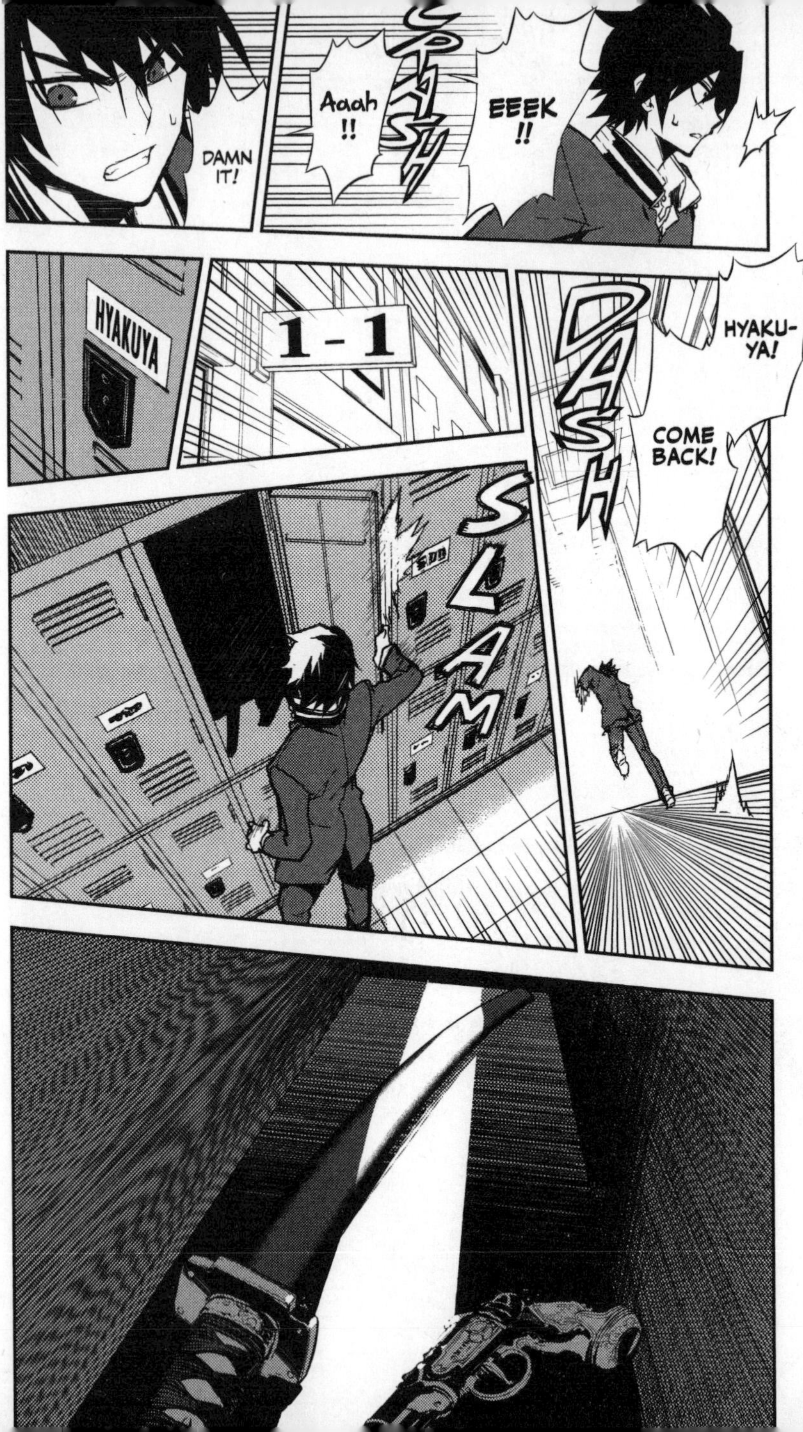
EEEK !!
CRASH
Aaah !!
DAMN IT!
HYAKU-YA!
COME BACK!
DASH
1-1
HYAKUYA
SLAM

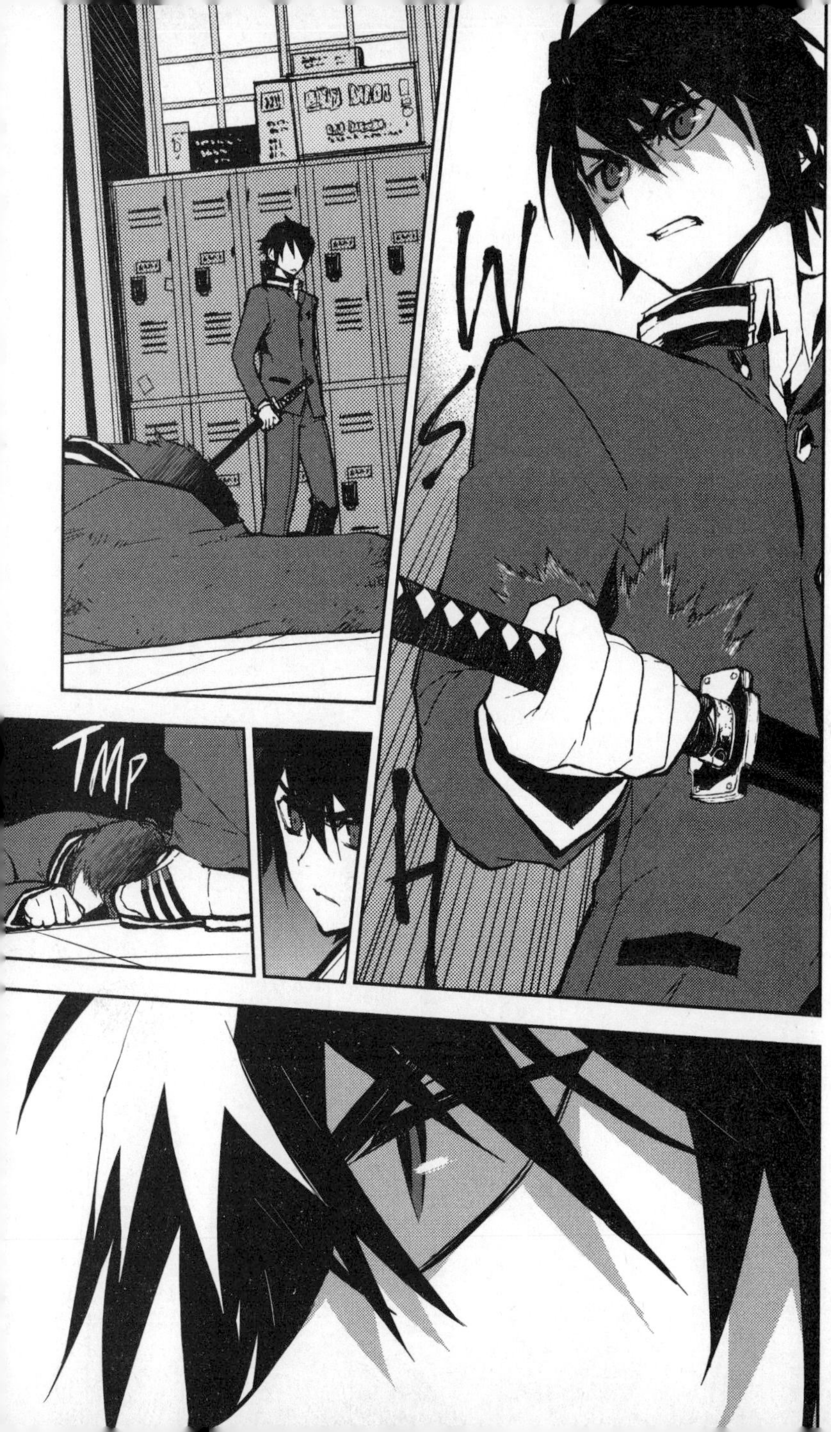
SWSH
TMP

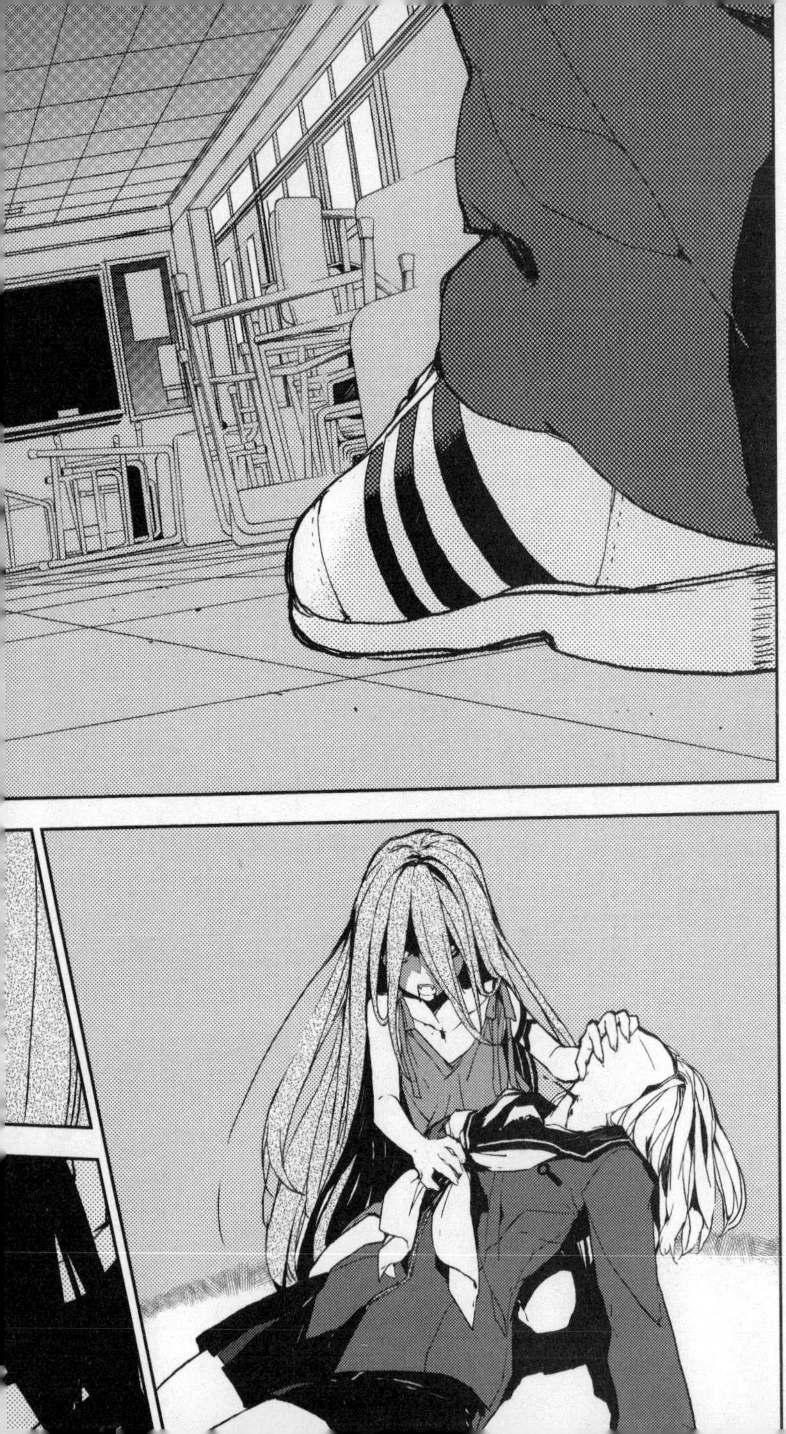

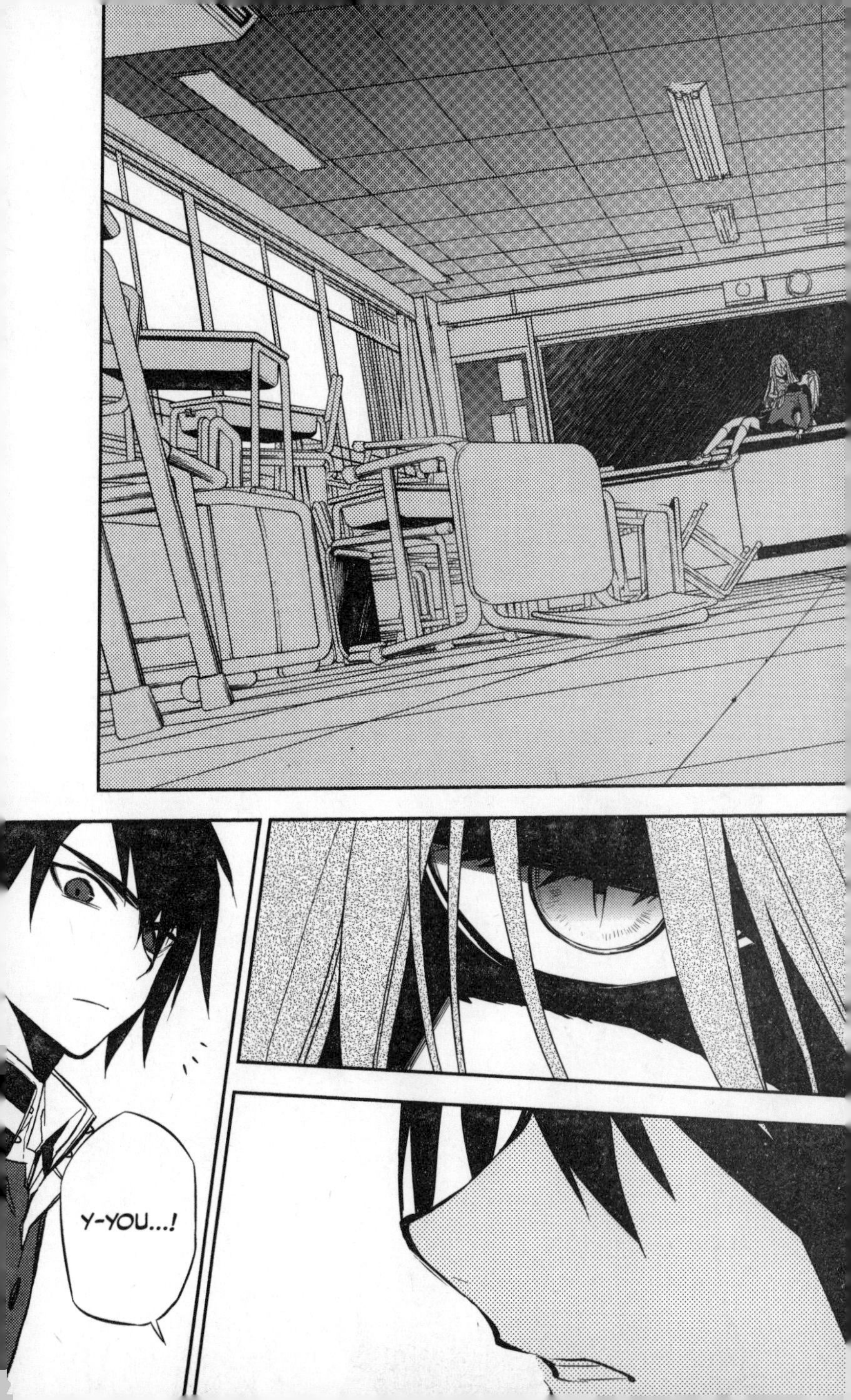
Y-YOU...!

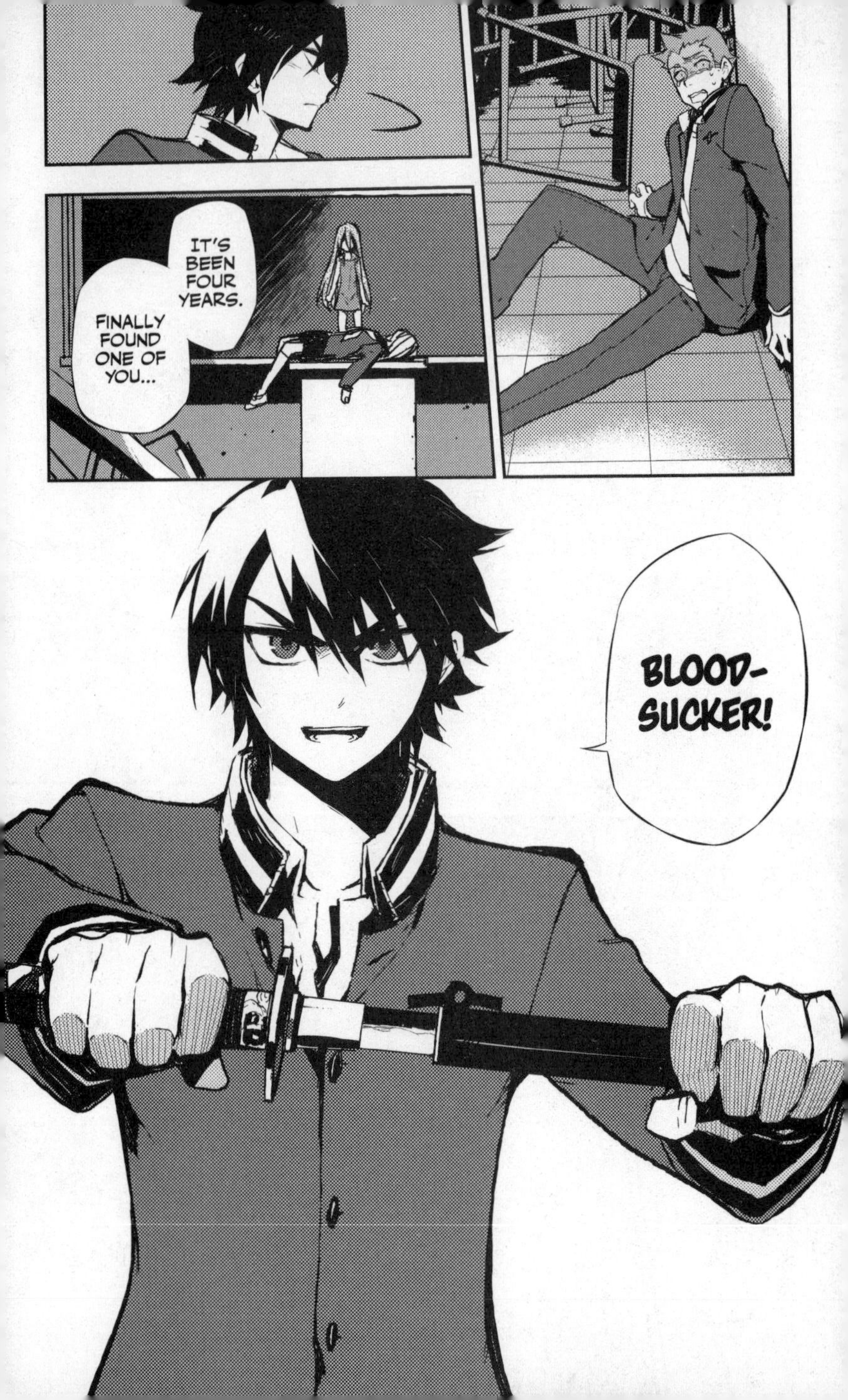
IT'S BEEN FOUR YEARS.
FINALLY FOUND ONE OF YOU...
BLOOD-SUCKER!

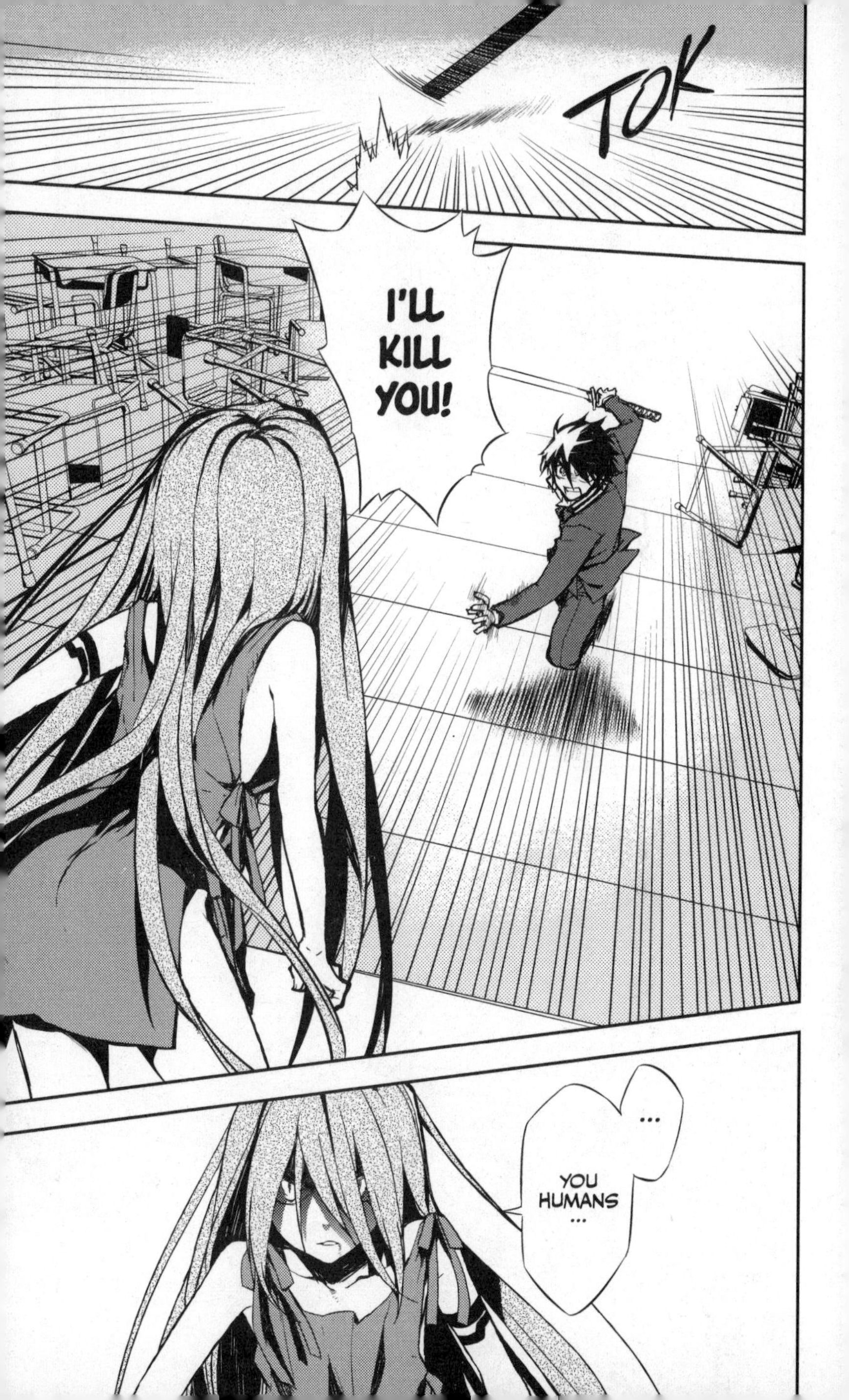
TOK
I'LL KILL YOU!
...
YOU HUMANS ...

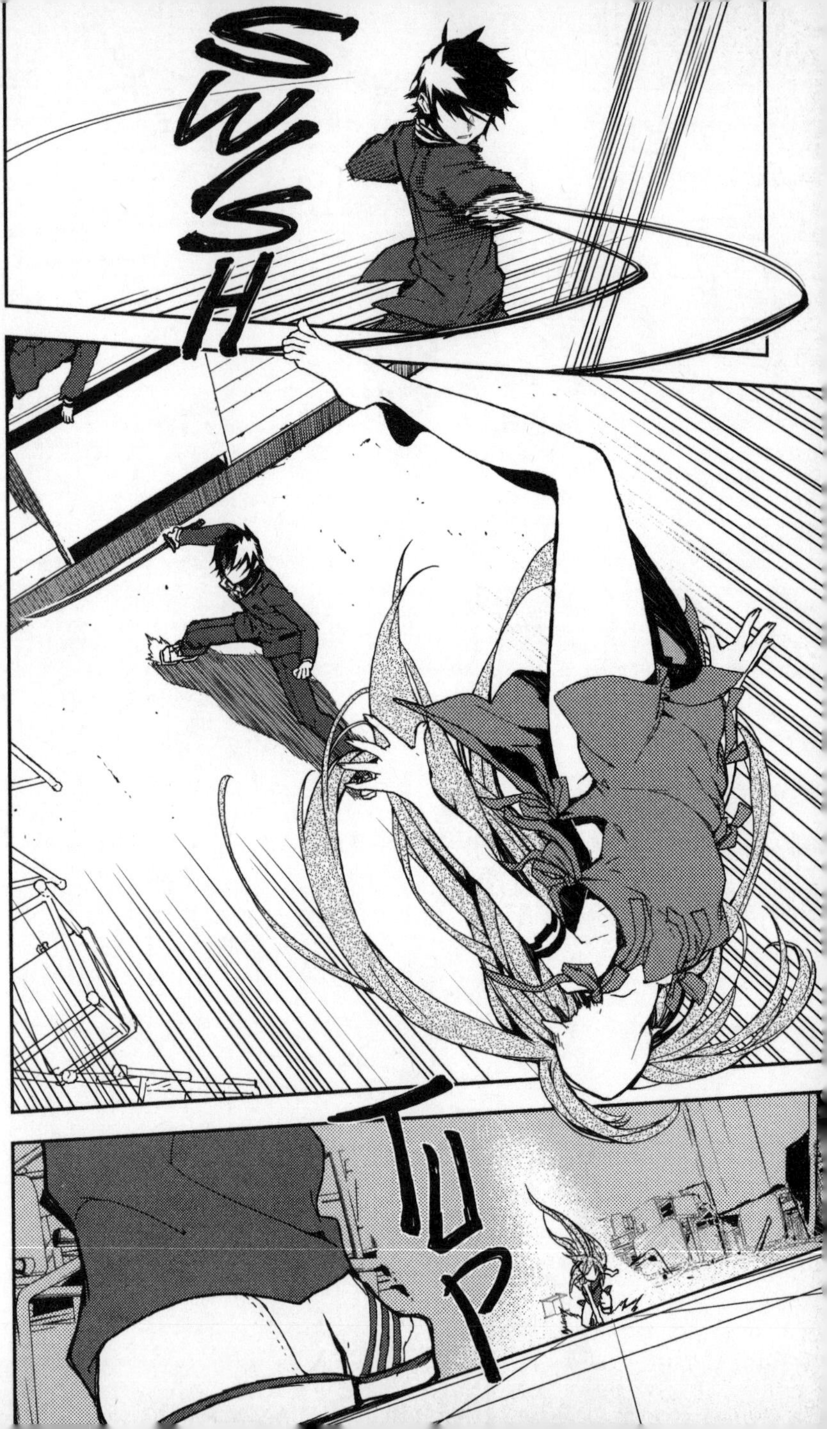
SWISH
TUP

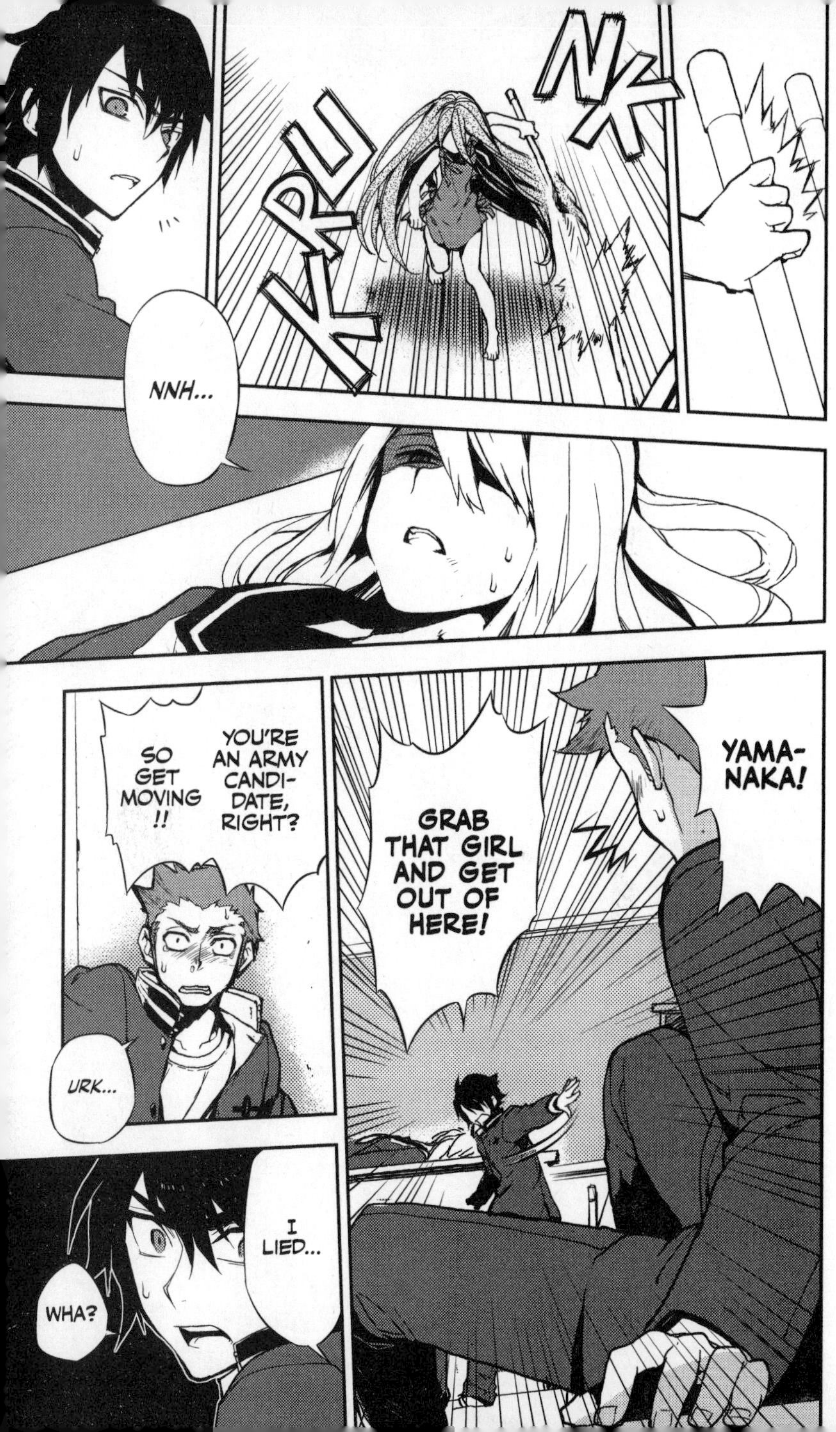
KRUNK
NNH...
YAMA-NAKA!
GRAB THAT GIRL AND GET OUT OF HERE!
YOU'RE AN ARMY CANDIDATE, RIGHT?
SO GET MOVING!!
URK...
I LIED...
WHA?

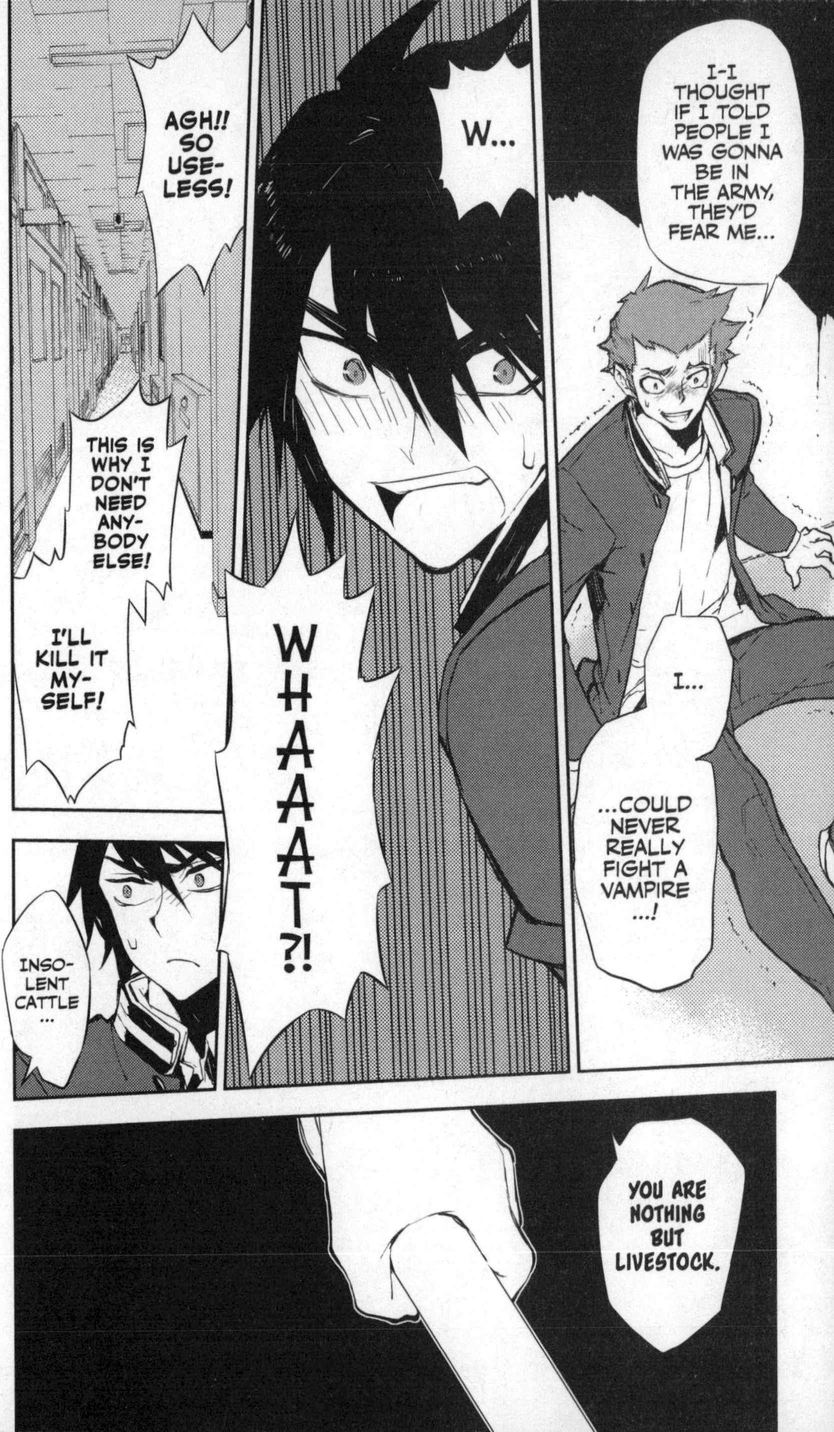
I-I THOUGHT IF I TOLD PEOPLE I WAS GONNA BE IN THE ARMY, THEY'D FEAR ME...
I...
...COULD NEVER REALLY FIGHT A VAMPIRE ...!
W...
WHAAAT?!
AGH!! SO USE-LESS!
THIS IS WHY I DON'T NEED ANY-BODY ELSE!
I'LL KILL IT MY-SELF!
INSO-LENT CATTLE ...
YOU ARE NOTHING BUT LIVESTOCK.

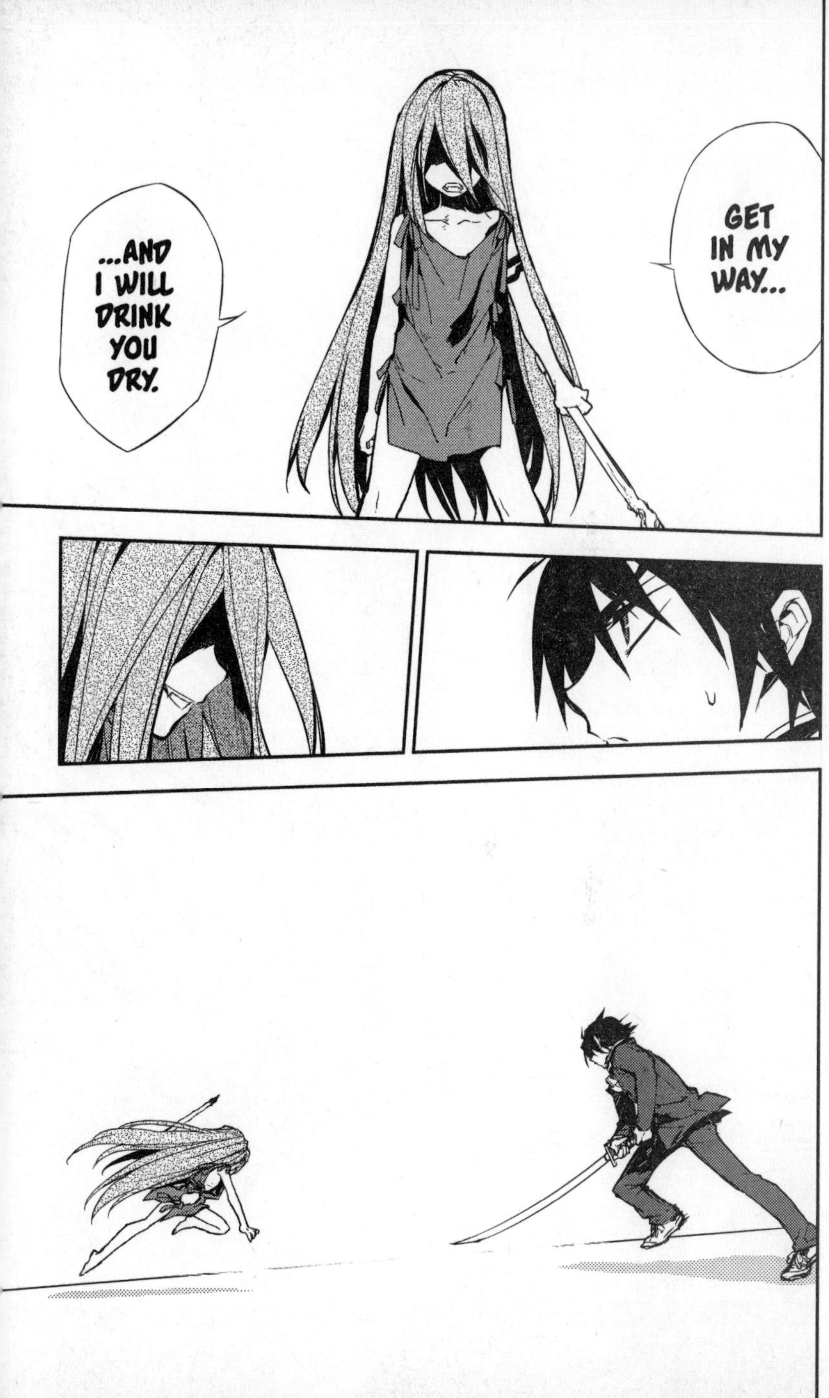
GET IN MY WAY...
...AND I WILL DRINK YOU DRY.

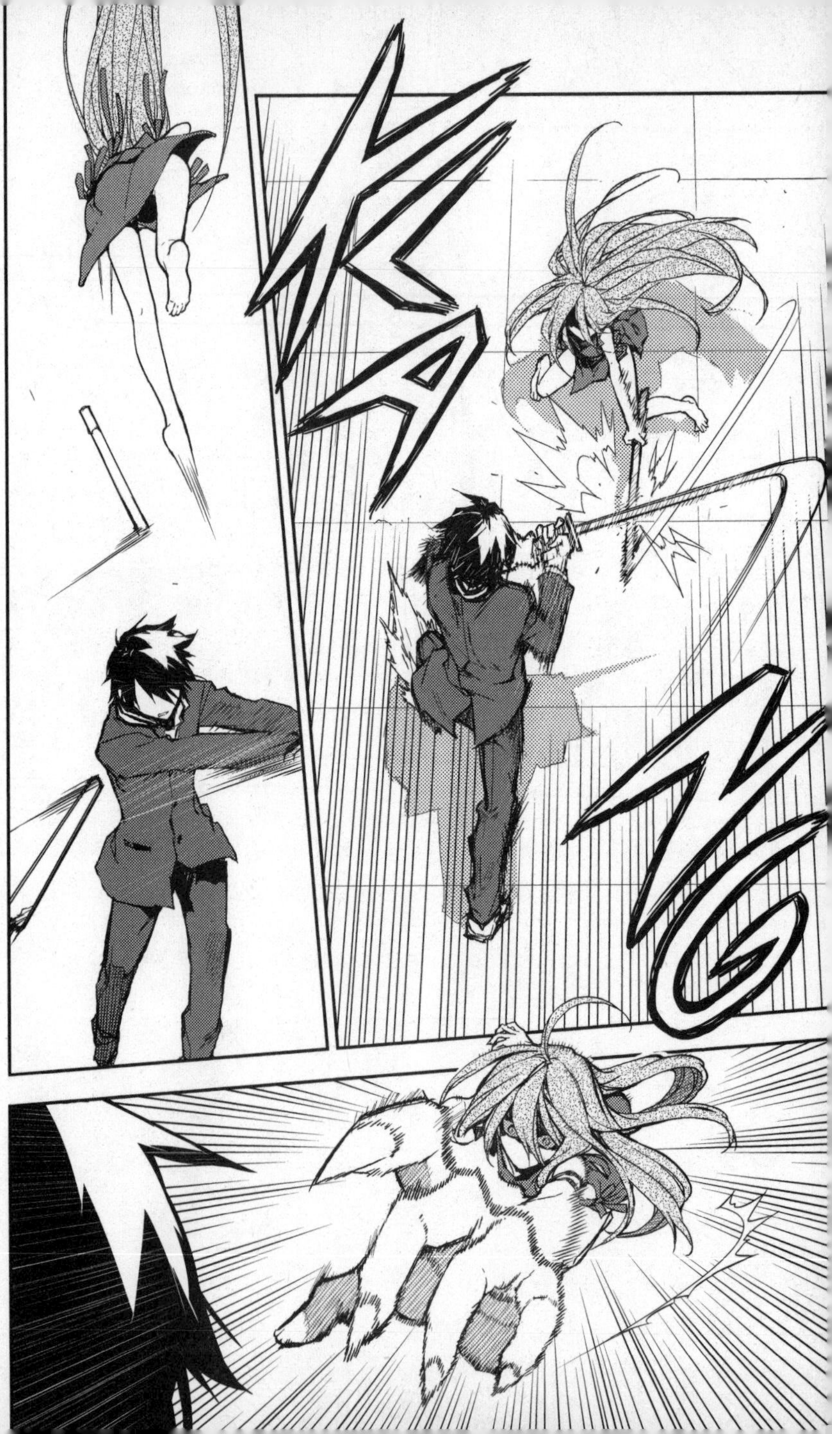
KA
NG

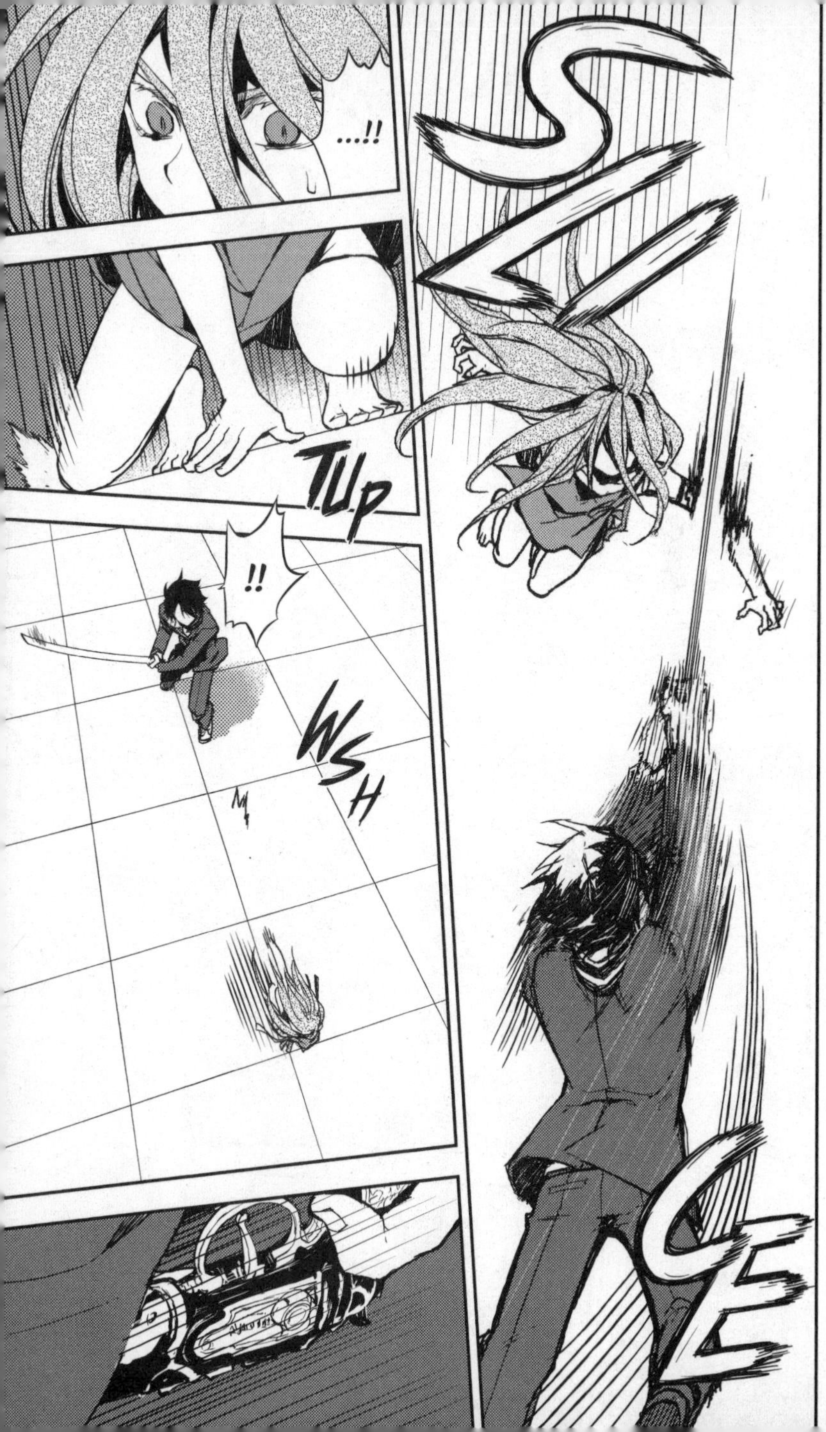
...!!
TUP
!!
WSH

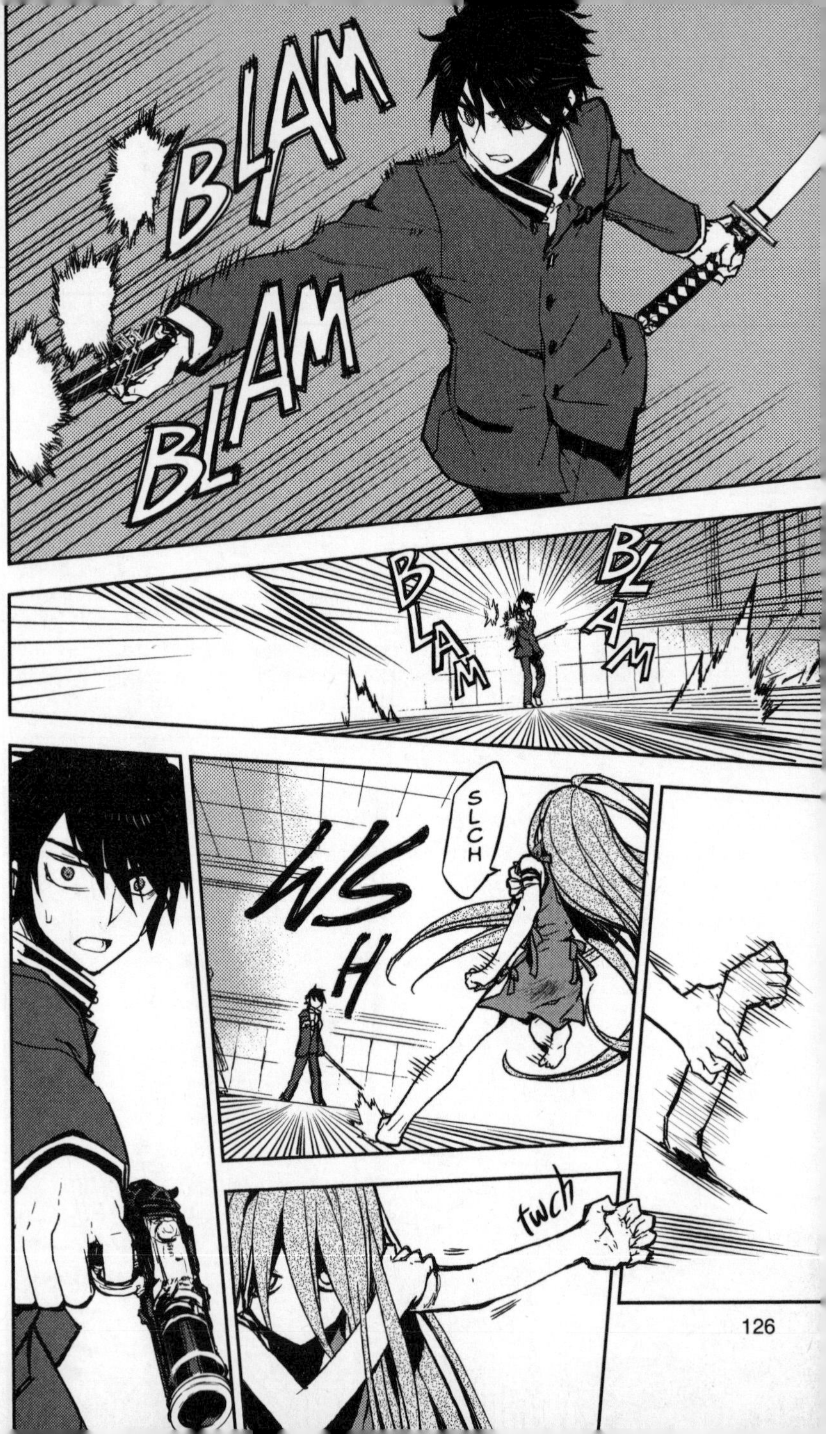
BLAM
BLAM
BLAM
BLAM
SLCH
WSH
twch

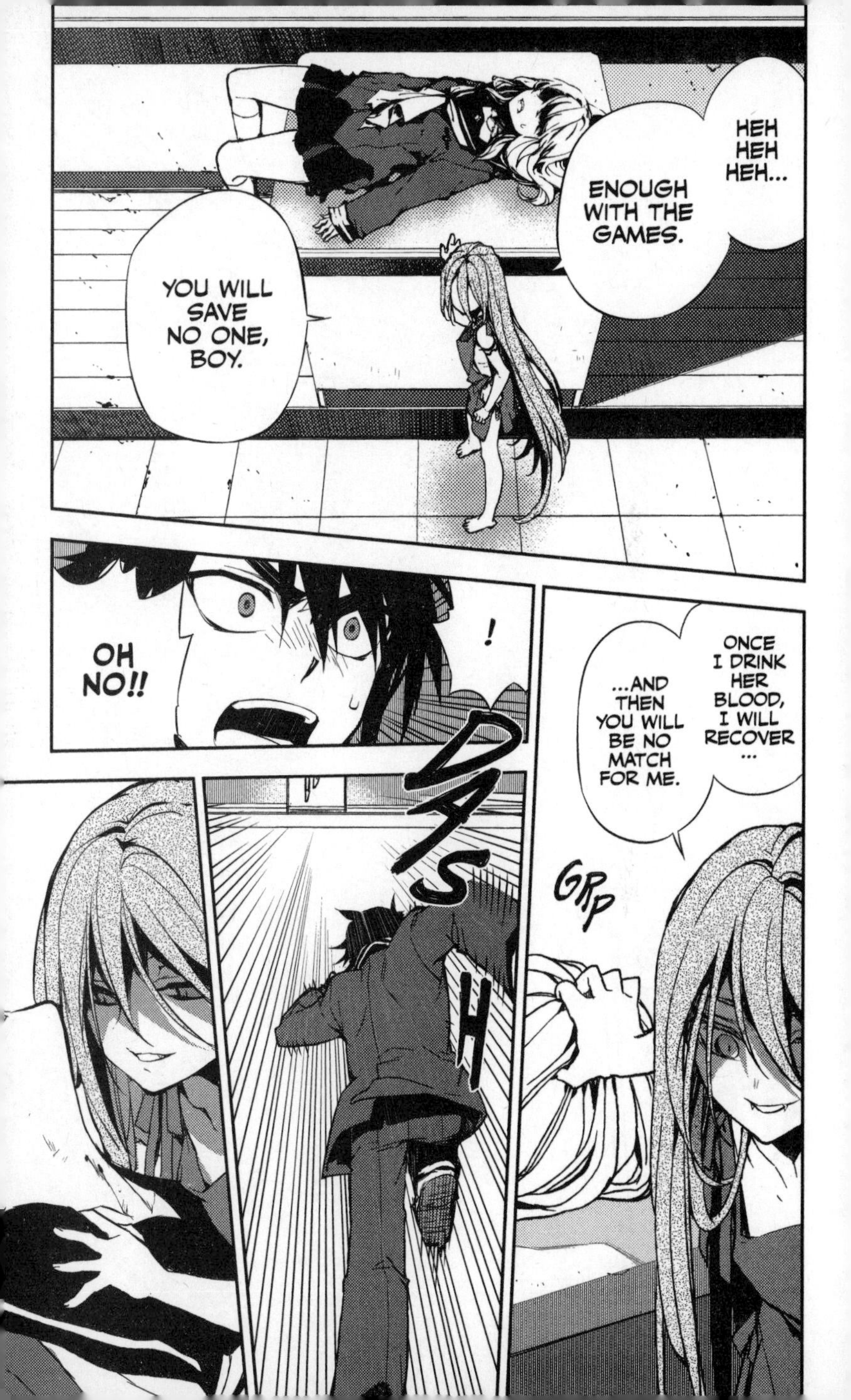
HEH HEH HEH...
ENOUGH WITH THE GAMES.
YOU WILL SAVE NO ONE, BOY.
ONCE I DRINK HER BLOOD, I WILL RECOVER ...
...AND THEN YOU WILL BE NO MATCH FOR ME.
GRP
!
OH NO!!
DASH

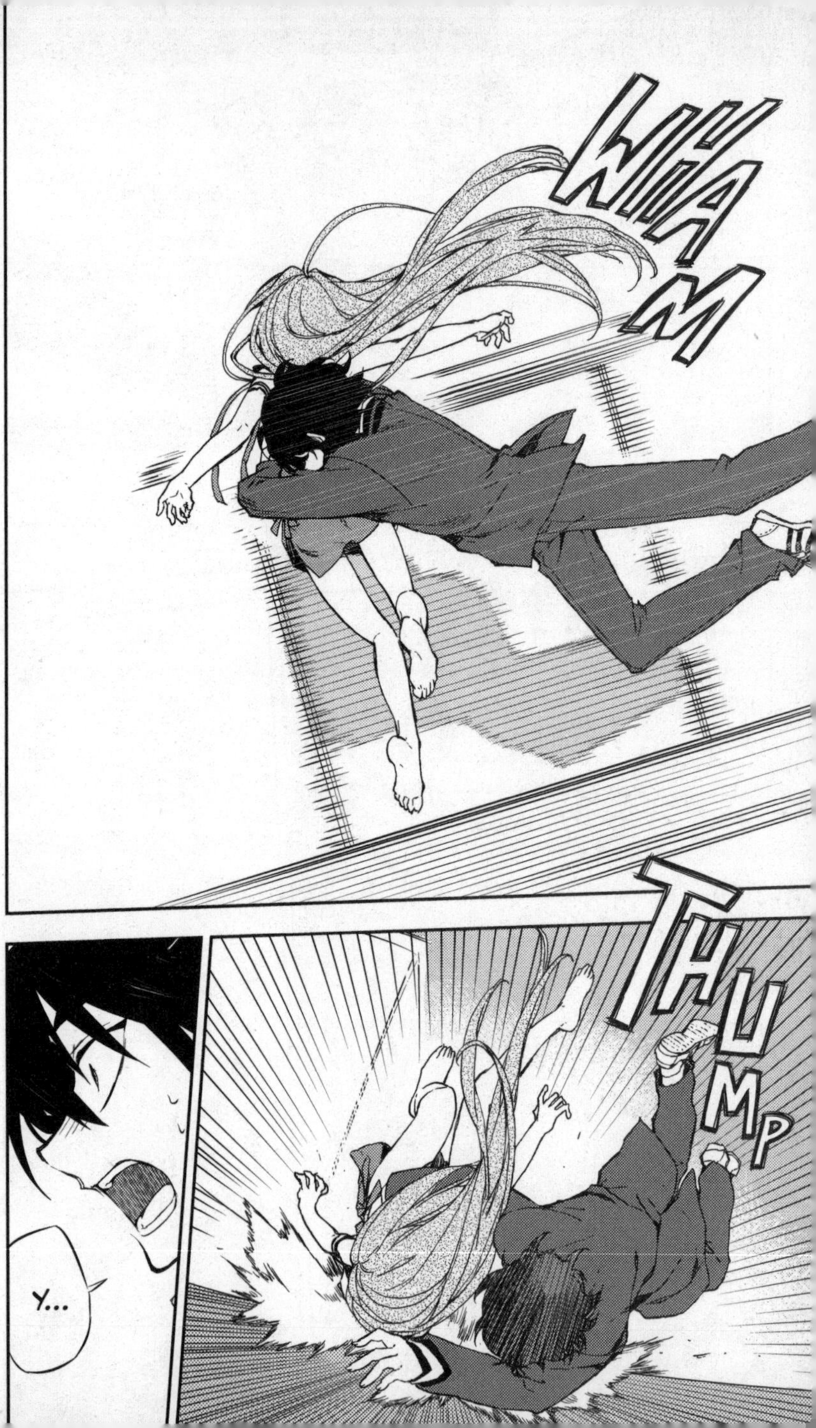
WHAM
THUMP
Y...

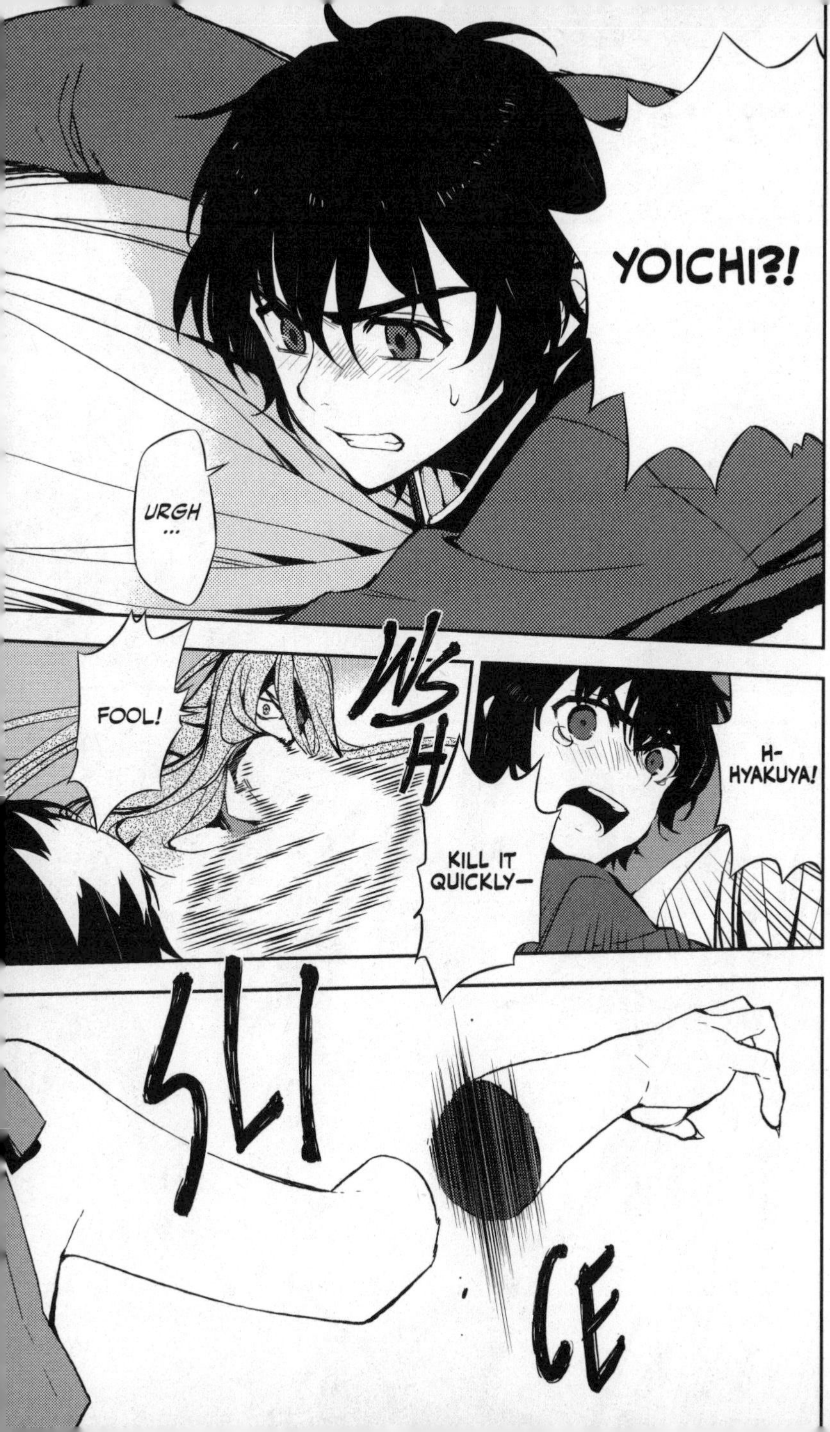
YOICHI?!
URGH...
H-HYAKUYA!
WSH
FOOL!
KILL IT QUICKLY—
SLICE

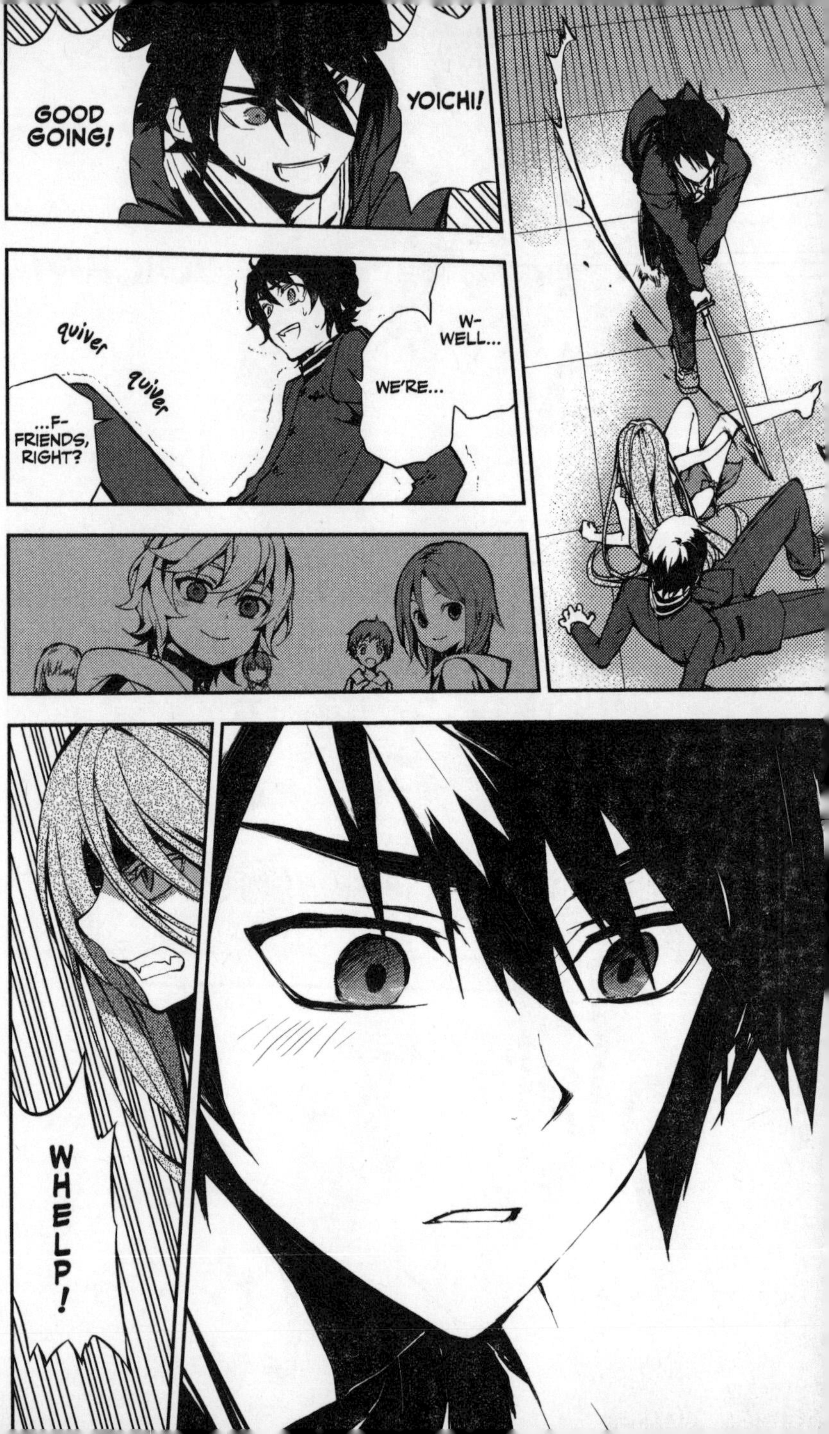
YOICHI!
GOOD GOING!
W-WELL...
WE'RE...
quiver
quiver
...F-FRIENDS, RIGHT?
WHELP!

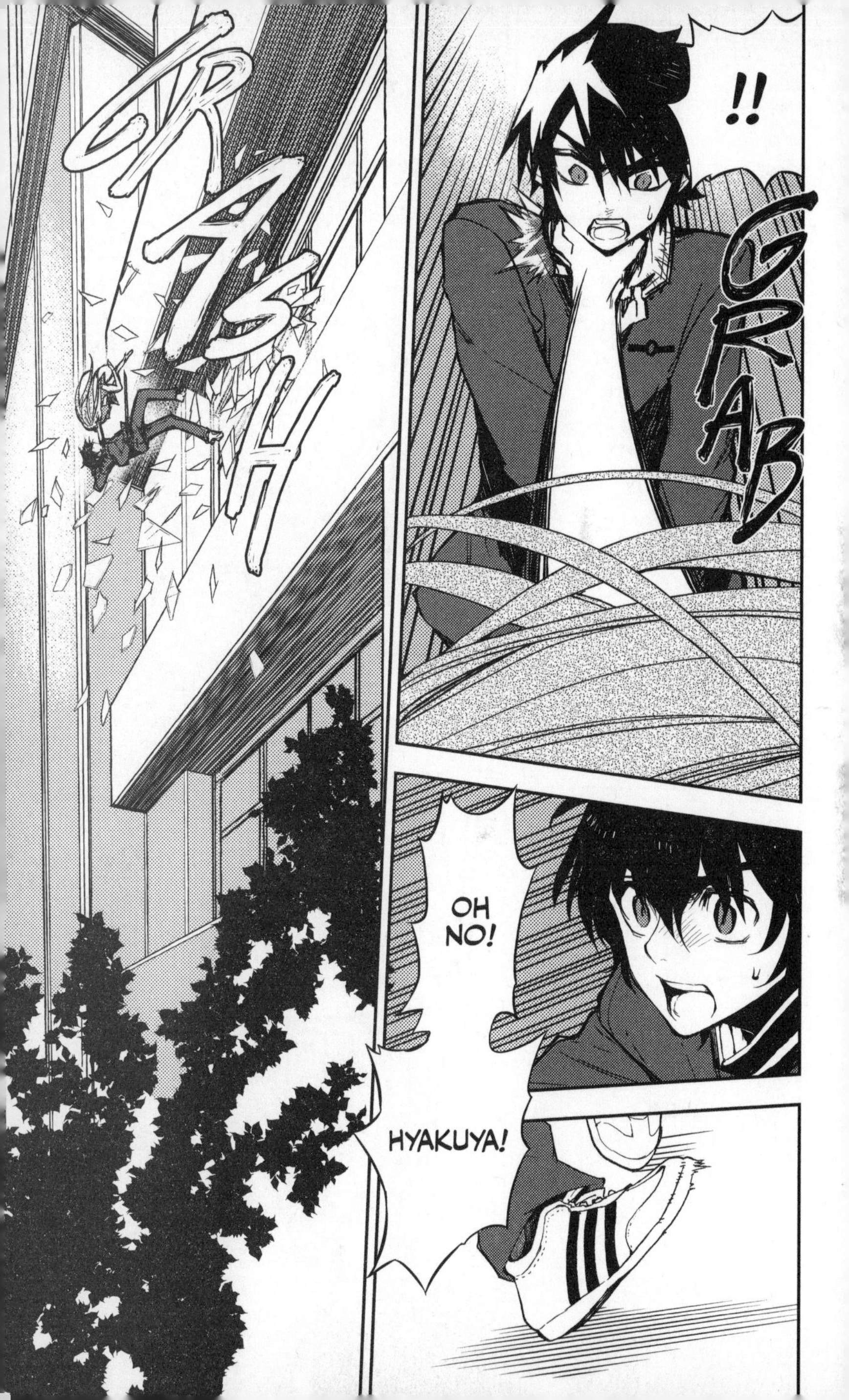
!!
GRAB
OH NO!
HYAKUYA!
CRASH

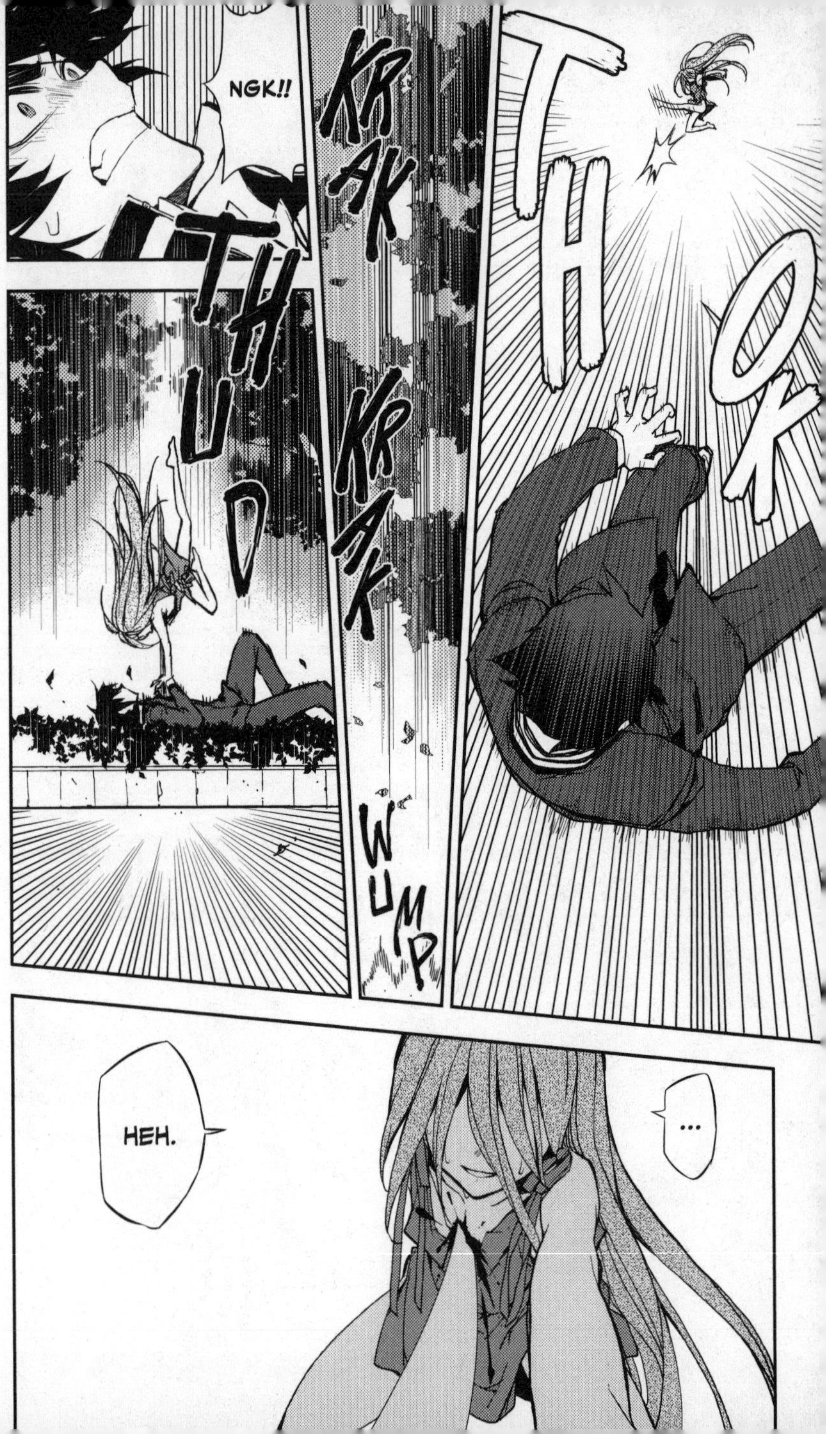
THOK
KRAK
KRAK
WUMP
NGK!!
THUD
...
HEH.

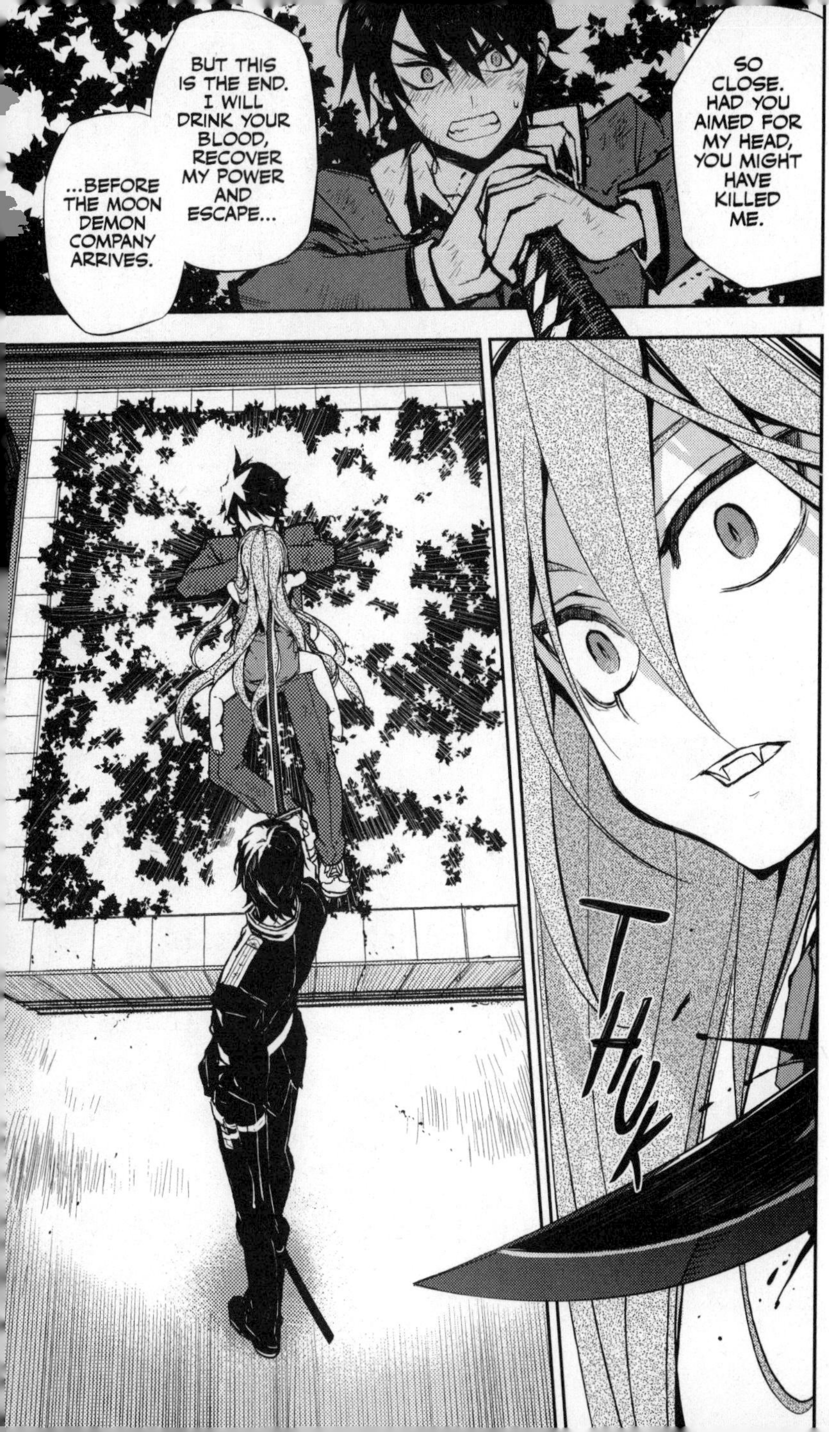
SO CLOSE. HAD YOU AIMED FOR MY HEAD, YOU MIGHT HAVE KILLED ME.
BUT THIS IS THE END. I WILL DRINK YOUR BLOOD, RECOVER MY POWER AND ESCAPE...
...BEFORE THE MOON DEMON COMPANY ARRIVES.
THUK

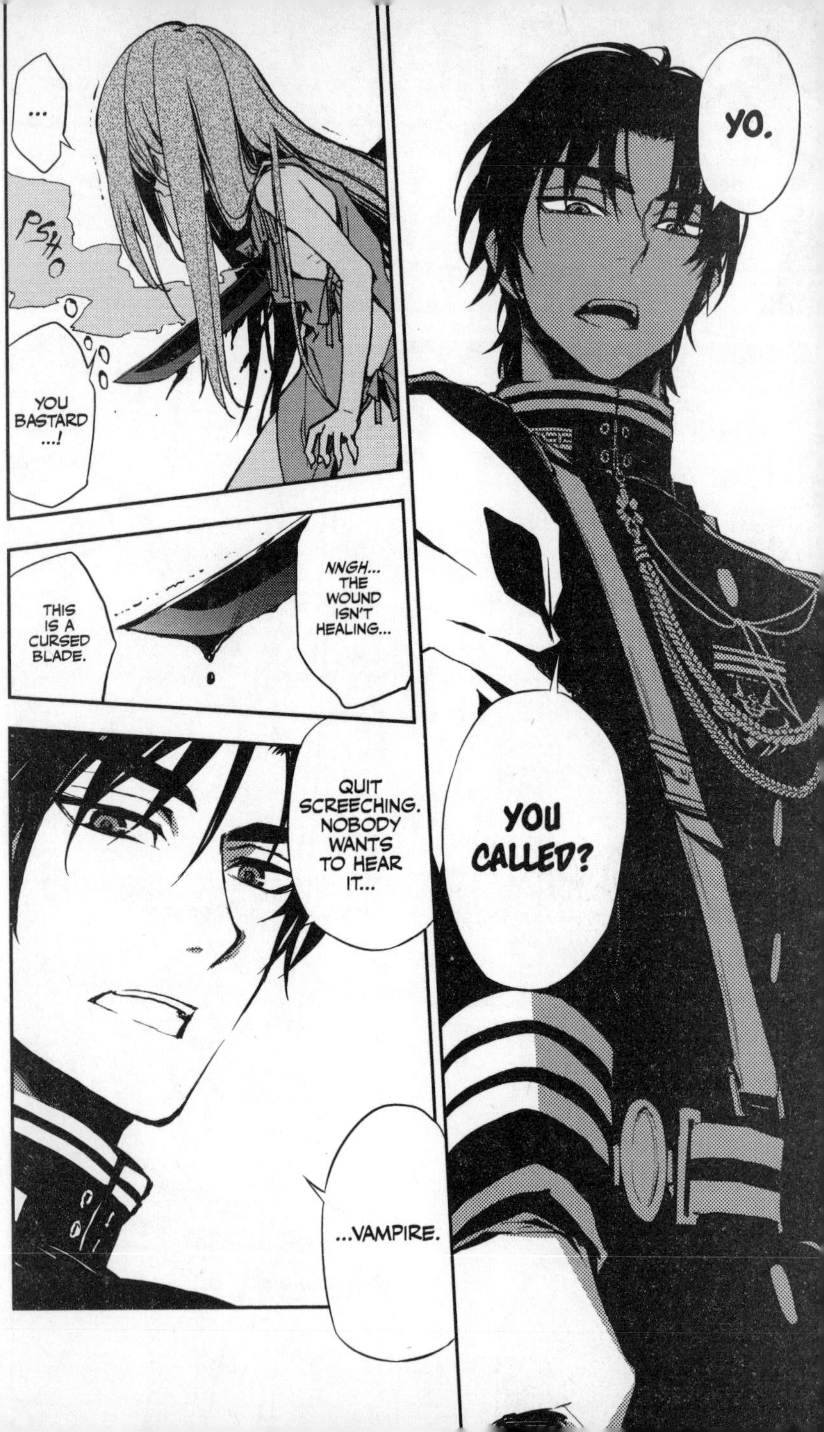
YO.
YOU CALLED?
...
PSHOO
YOU BASTARD ...!
NNGH... THE WOUND ISN'T HEALING...
THIS IS A CURSED BLADE.
QUIT SCREECHING. NOBODY WANTS TO HEAR IT...
...VAMPIRE.

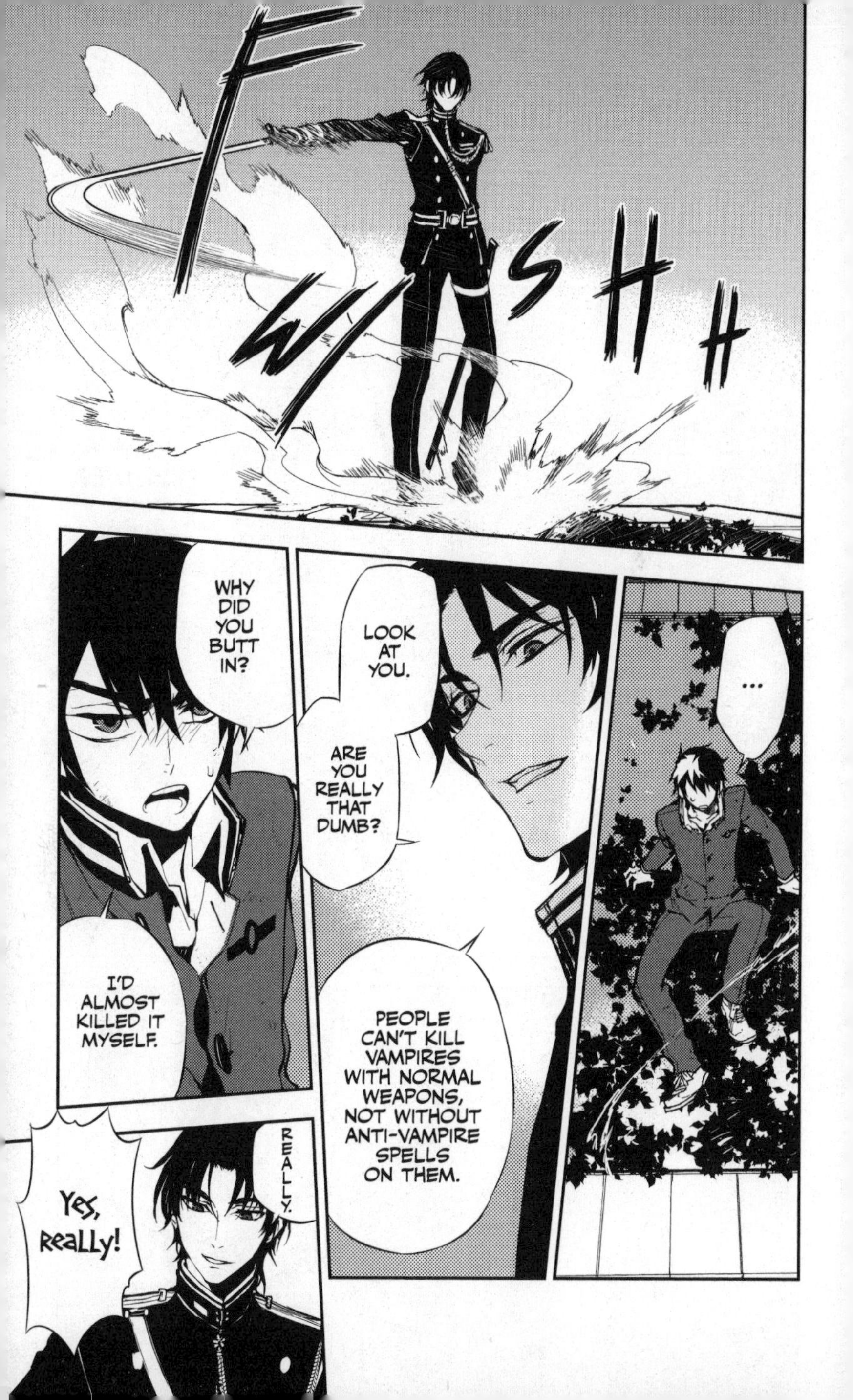
FWISHH
...
LOOK AT YOU.
ARE YOU REALLY THAT DUMB?
PEOPLE CAN'T KILL VAMPIRES WITH NORMAL WEAPONS, NOT WITHOUT ANTI-VAMPIRE SPELLS ON THEM.
WHY DID YOU BUTT IN?
I'D ALMOST KILLED IT MYSELF.
REALLY.
Yes, really!

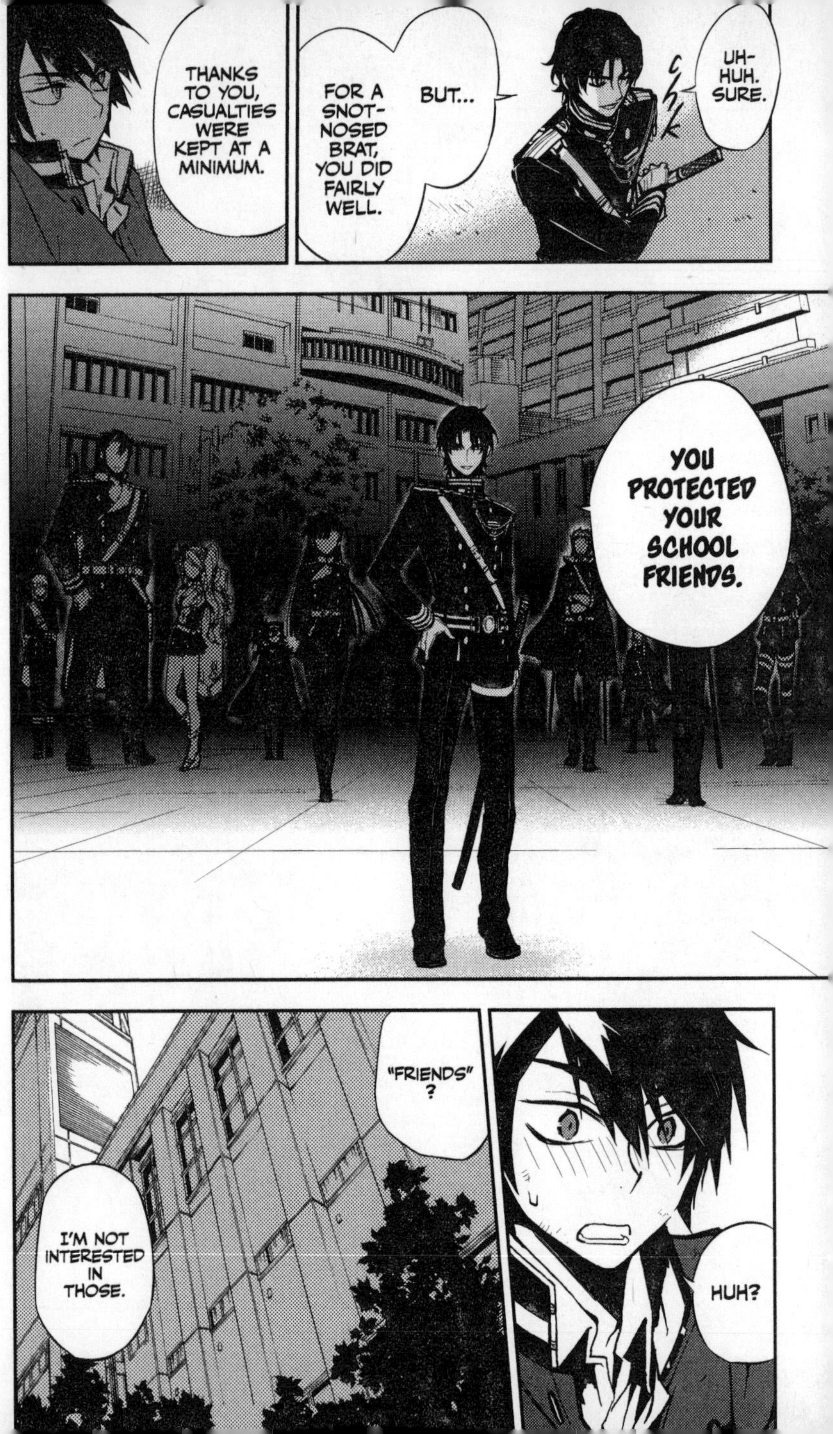
UH-HUH. SURE.
CHK
BUT...
FOR A SNOT-NOSED BRAT, YOU DID FAIRLY WELL.
THANKS TO YOU, CASUALTIES WERE KEPT AT A MINIMUM.
YOU PROTECTED YOUR SCHOOL FRIENDS.
"FRIENDS"?
HUH?
I'M NOT INTERESTED IN THOSE.

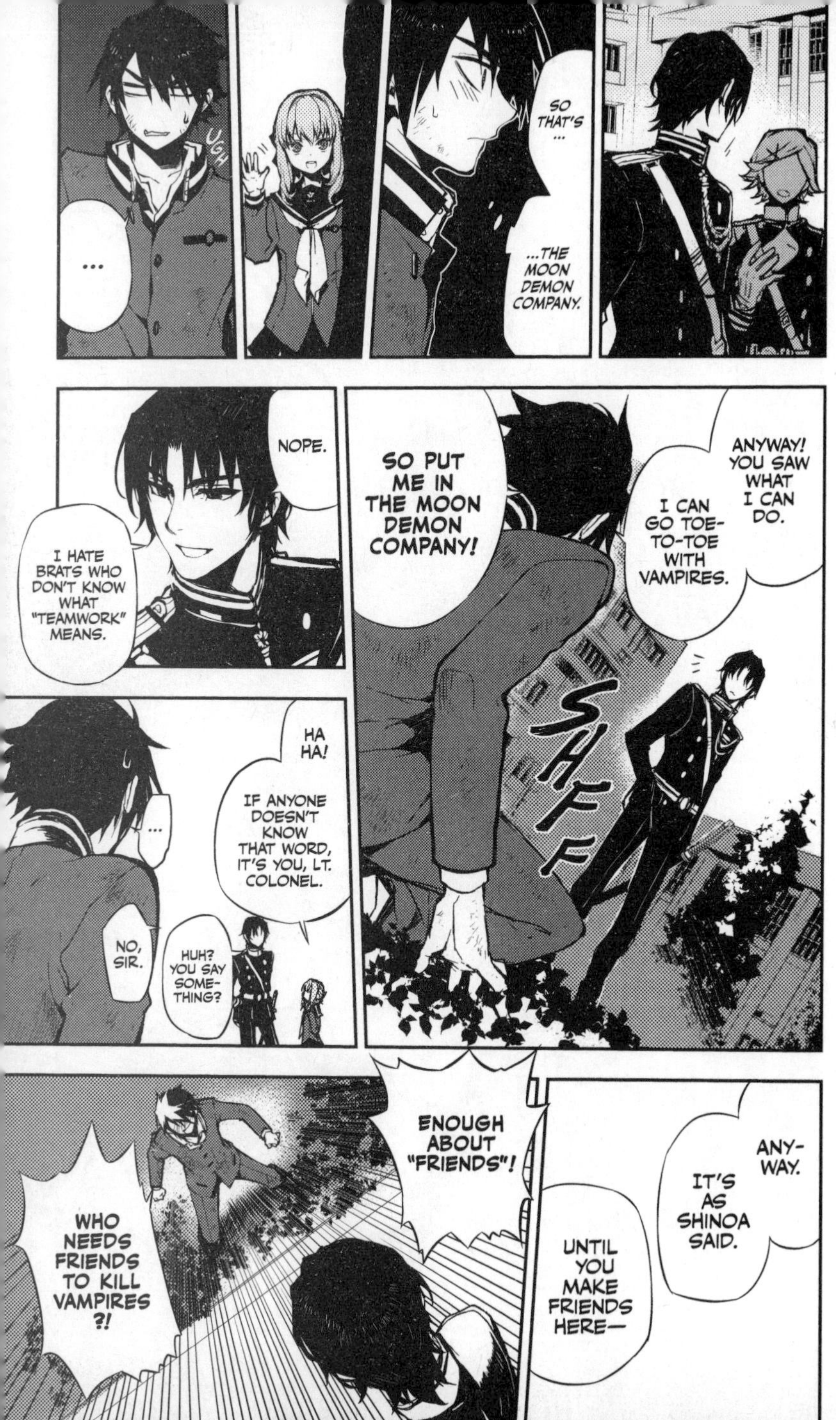
SO THAT'S ...
...THE MOON DEMON COMPANY.
UGH
...
ANYWAY! YOU SAW WHAT I CAN DO.
I CAN GO TOE-TO-TOE WITH VAMPIRES.
SO PUT ME IN THE MOON DEMON COMPANY!
SHFFF
NOPE.
I HATE BRATS WHO DON'T KNOW WHAT "TEAMWORK" MEANS.
HA HA!
IF ANYONE DOESN'T KNOW THAT WORD, IT'S YOU, LT. COLONEL.
...
HUH? YOU SAY SOMETHING?
NO, SIR.
ANY-WAY.
IT'S AS SHINOA SAID.
UNTIL YOU MAKE FRIENDS HERE—
ENOUGH ABOUT "FRIENDS"!
WHO NEEDS FRIENDS TO KILL VAMPIRES?!

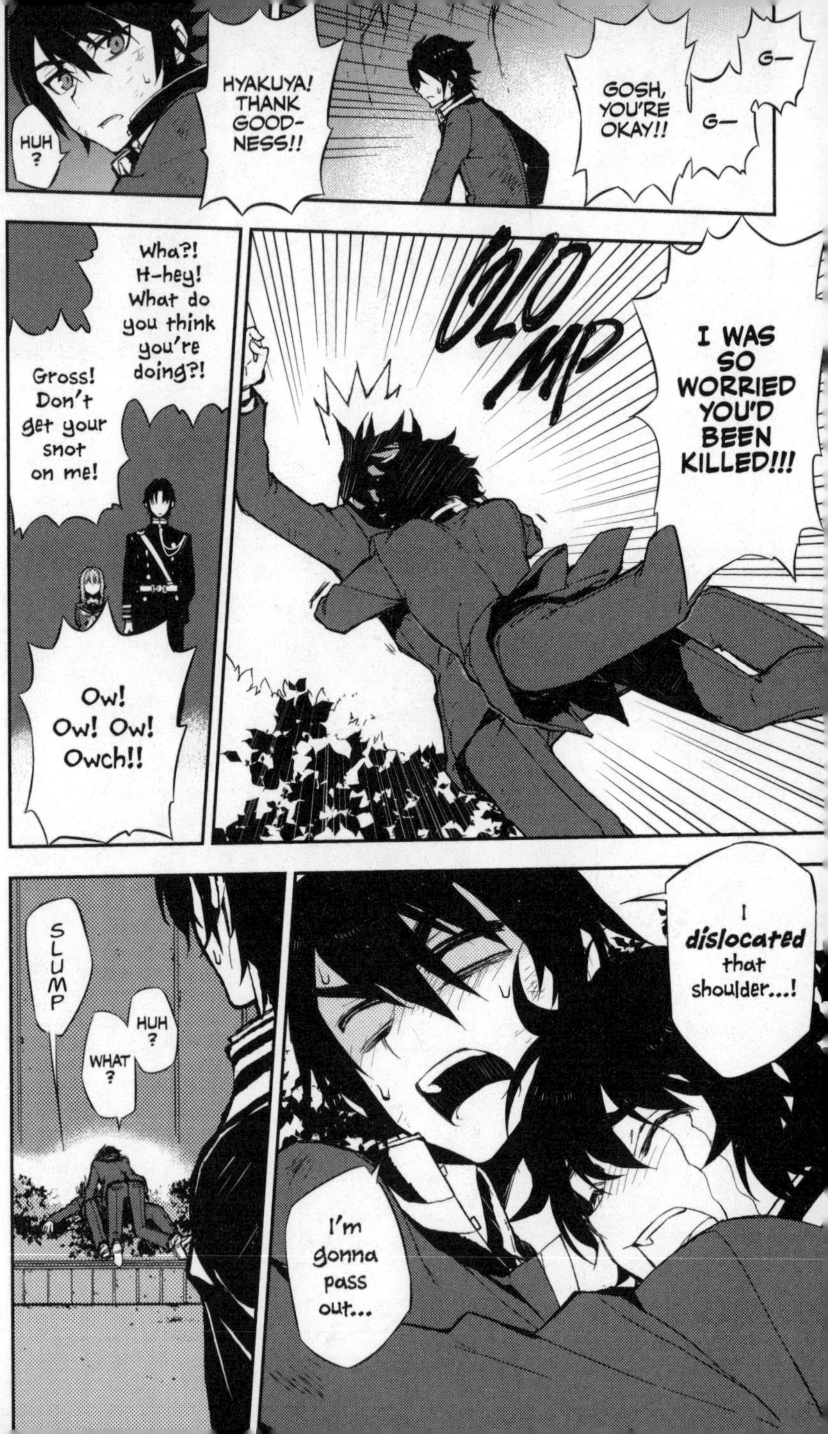
G— G—
GOSH, YOU'RE OKAY!!
HYAKUYA! THANK GOODNESS!!
HUH?
I WAS SO WORRIED YOU'D BEEN KILLED!!!
GLOMP
Wha?! H-hey! What do you think you're doing?!
Gross! Don't get your snot on me!
Ow! Ow! Ow! Owch!!
I *dislocated* that shoulder...!
I'm gonna pass out...
SLUMP
HUH?
WHAT?

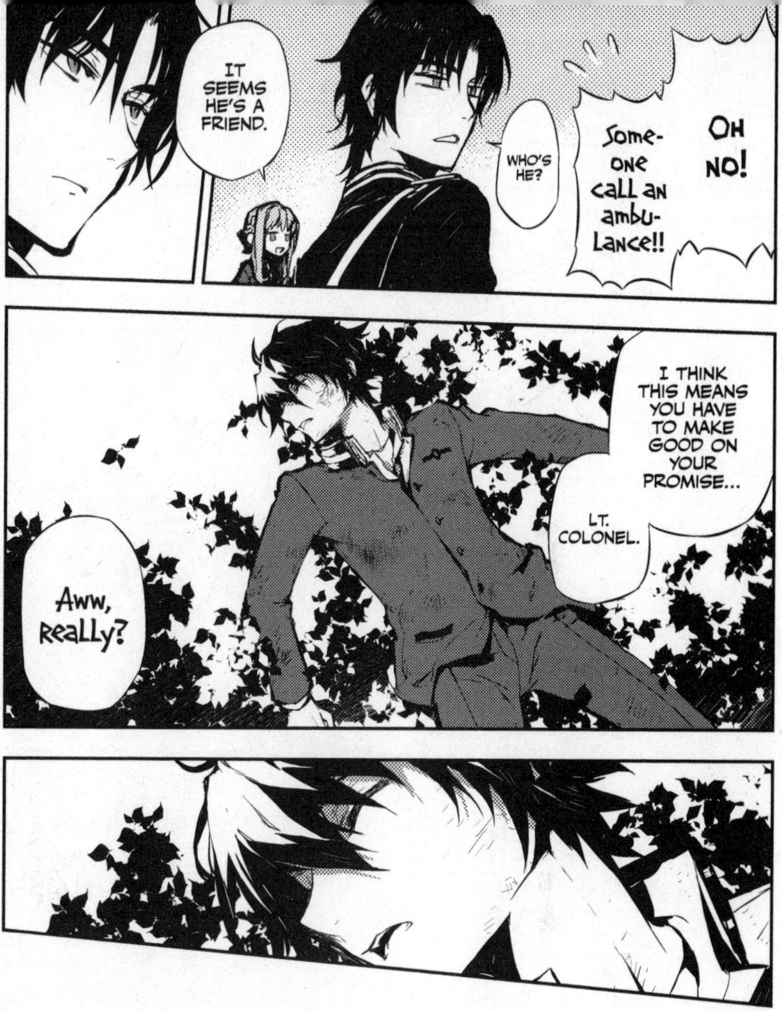
OH NO!
Some-one call an ambu-lance!!
WHO'S HE?
IT SEEMS HE'S A FRIEND.
I THINK THIS MEANS YOU HAVE TO MAKE GOOD ON YOUR PROMISE...
LT. COLONEL.
Aww, really?

I SEE THE SAME SCENE EVERY TIME I CLOSE MY EYES.

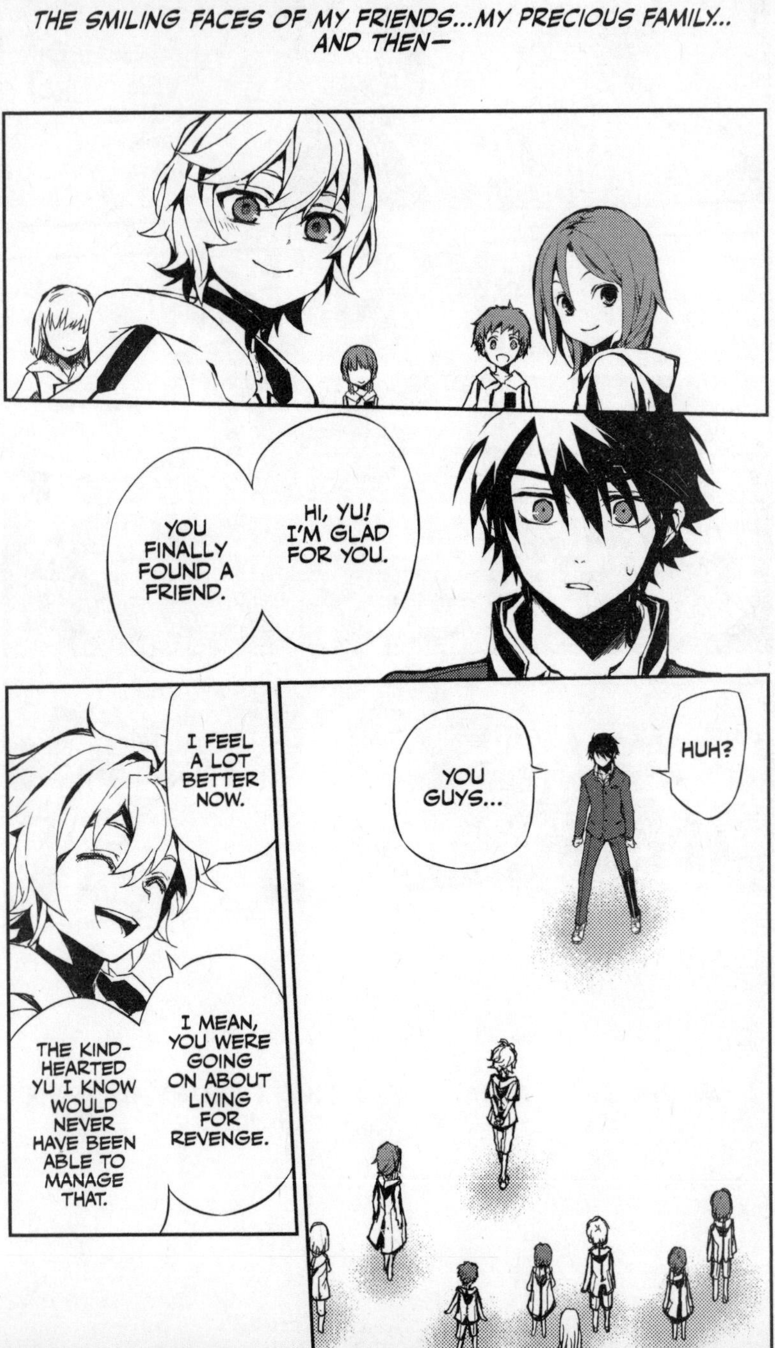
THE SMILING FACES OF MY FRIENDS...MY PRECIOUS FAMILY... AND THEN—
HI, YU! I'M GLAD FOR YOU.
YOU FINALLY FOUND A FRIEND.
HUH?
YOU GUYS...
I FEEL A LOT BETTER NOW.
I MEAN, YOU WERE GOING ON ABOUT LIVING FOR REVENGE.
THE KIND-HEARTED YU I KNOW WOULD NEVER HAVE BEEN ABLE TO MANAGE THAT.

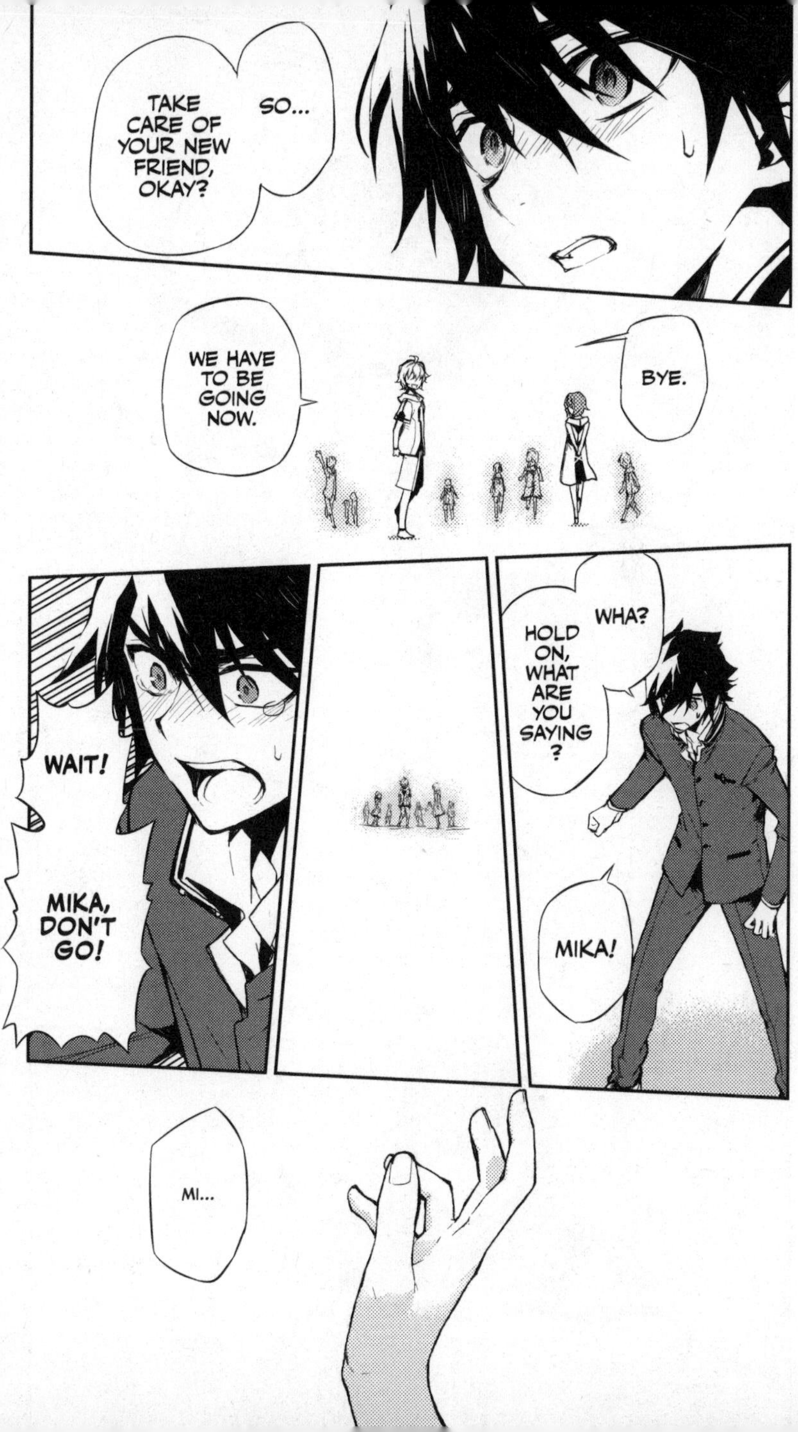
SO... TAKE CARE OF YOUR NEW FRIEND, OKAY?
BYE.
WE HAVE TO BE GOING NOW.
WHA? HOLD ON, WHAT ARE YOU SAYING?
MIKA!
WAIT!
MIKA, DON'T GO!
MI...

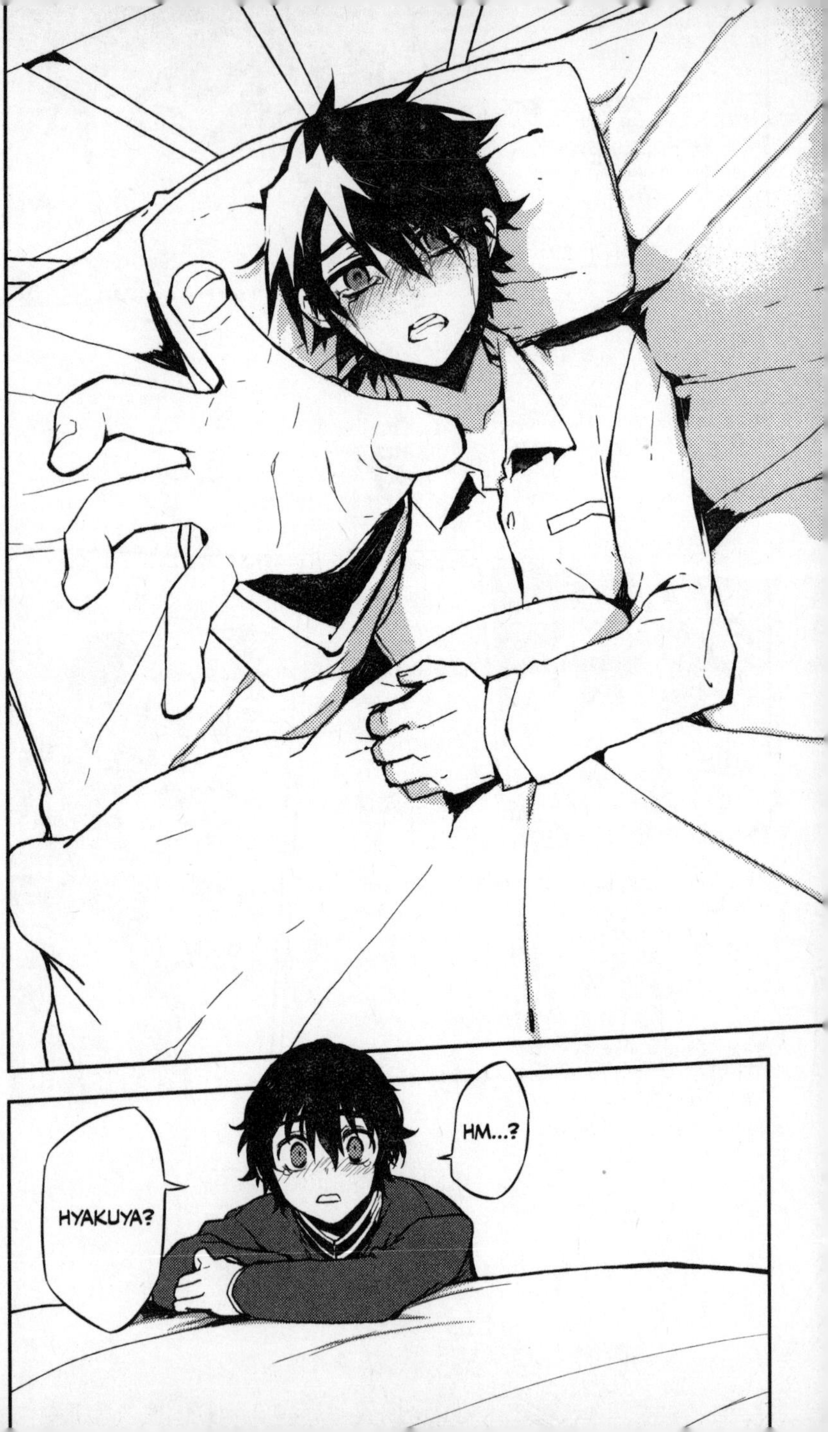
HM...?
HYAKUYA?

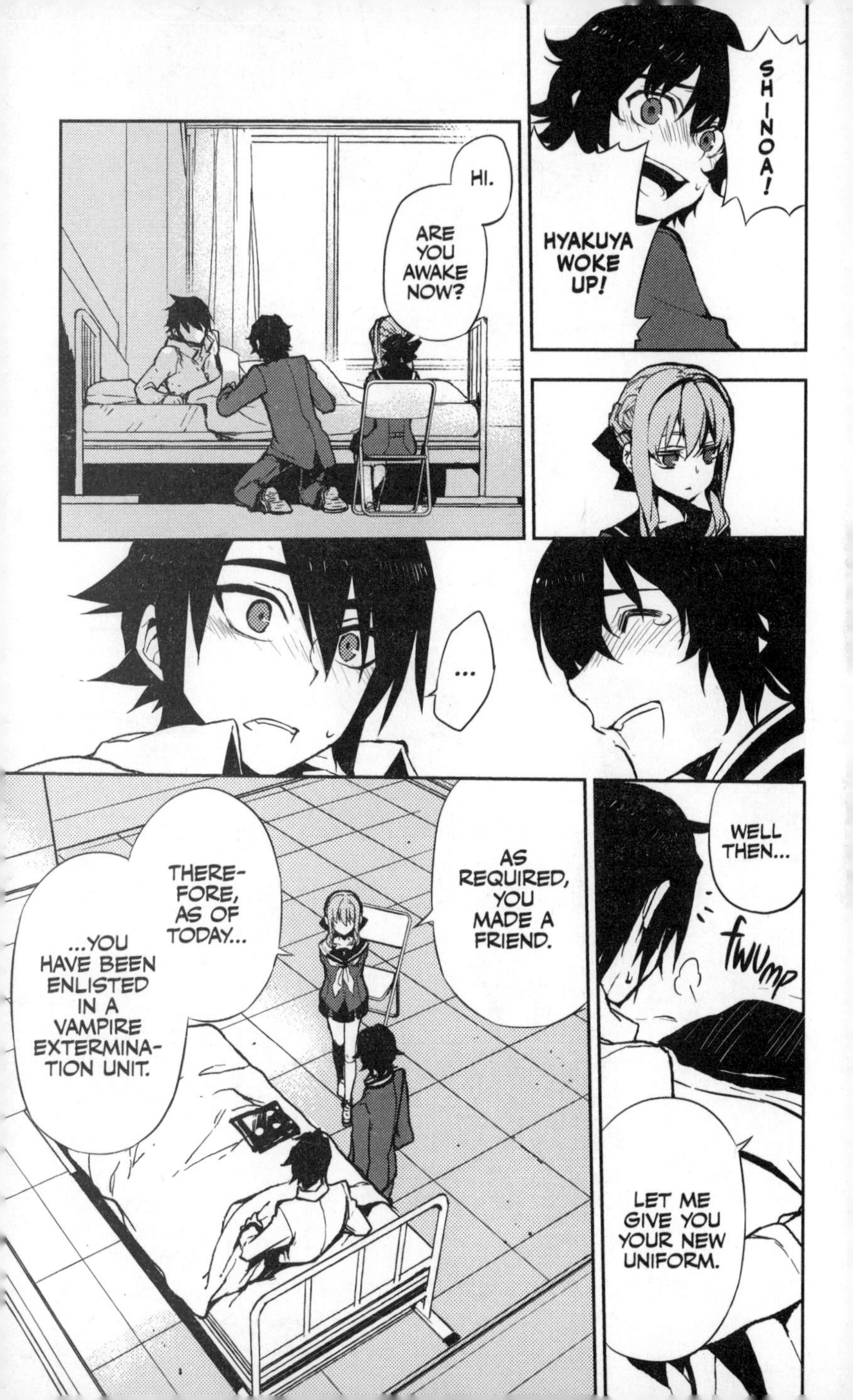
SHINOA!
HYAKUYA WOKE UP!
HI.
ARE YOU AWAKE NOW?
...
WELL THEN...
FWUMP
LET ME GIVE YOU YOUR NEW UNIFORM.
AS REQUIRED, YOU MADE A FRIEND.
THEREFORE, AS OF TODAY...
...YOU HAVE BEEN ENLISTED IN A VAMPIRE EXTERMINATION UNIT.

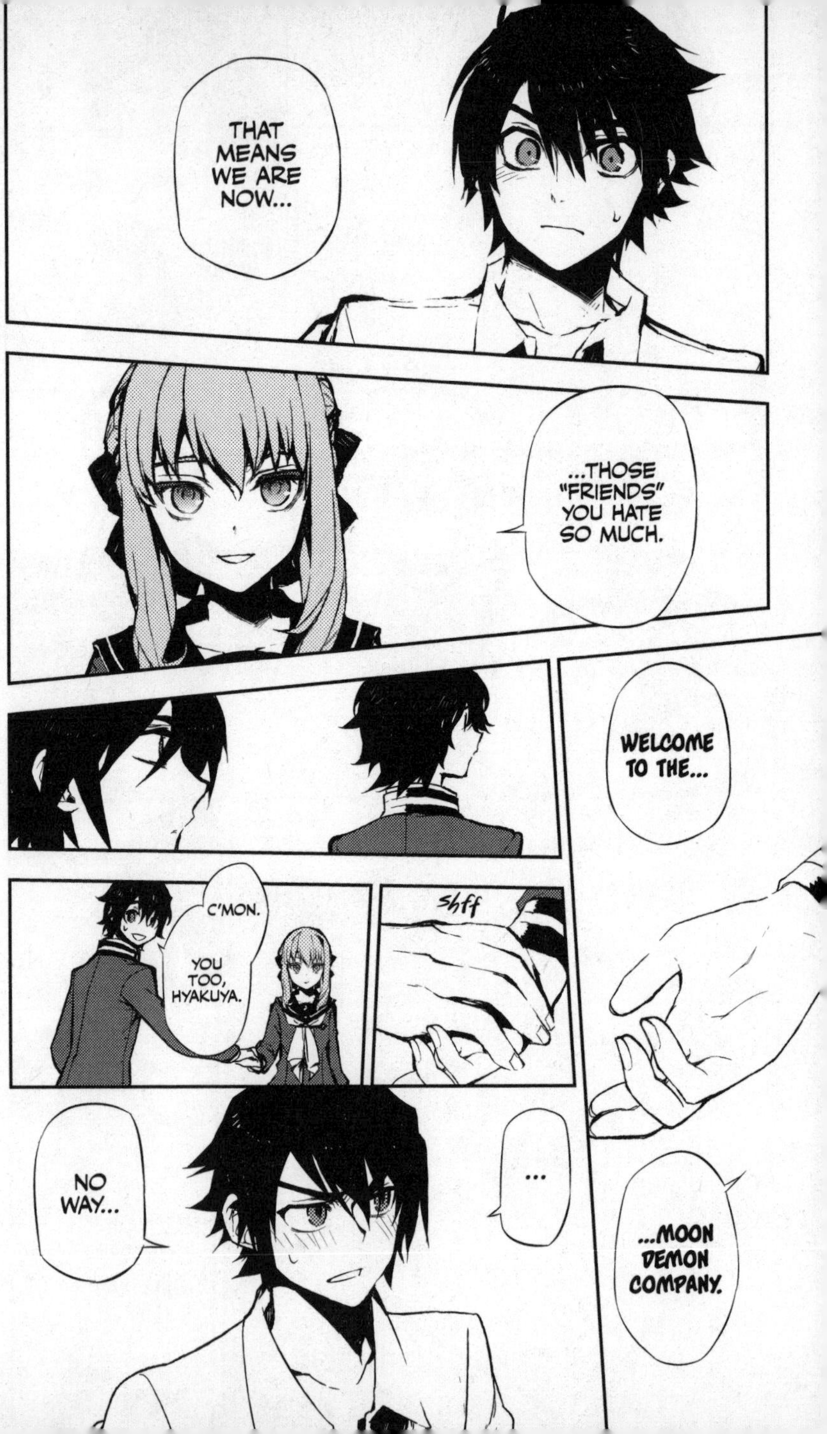
THAT MEANS WE ARE NOW...
...THOSE "FRIENDS" YOU HATE SO MUCH.
WELCOME TO THE...
...MOON DEMON COMPANY.
Shff
C'MON.
YOU TOO, HYAKUYA.
...
NO WAY...

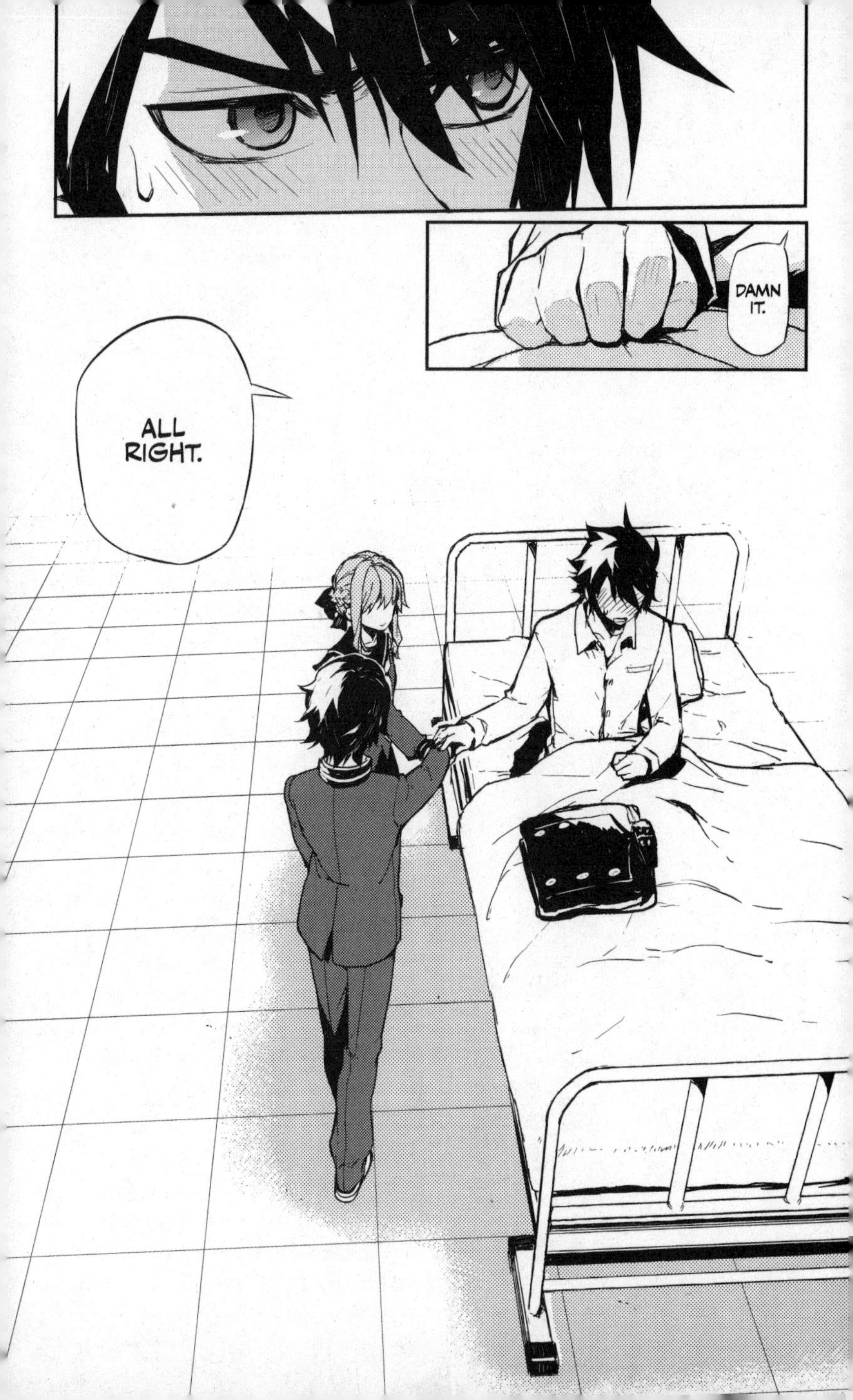
DAMN IT.
ALL RIGHT.

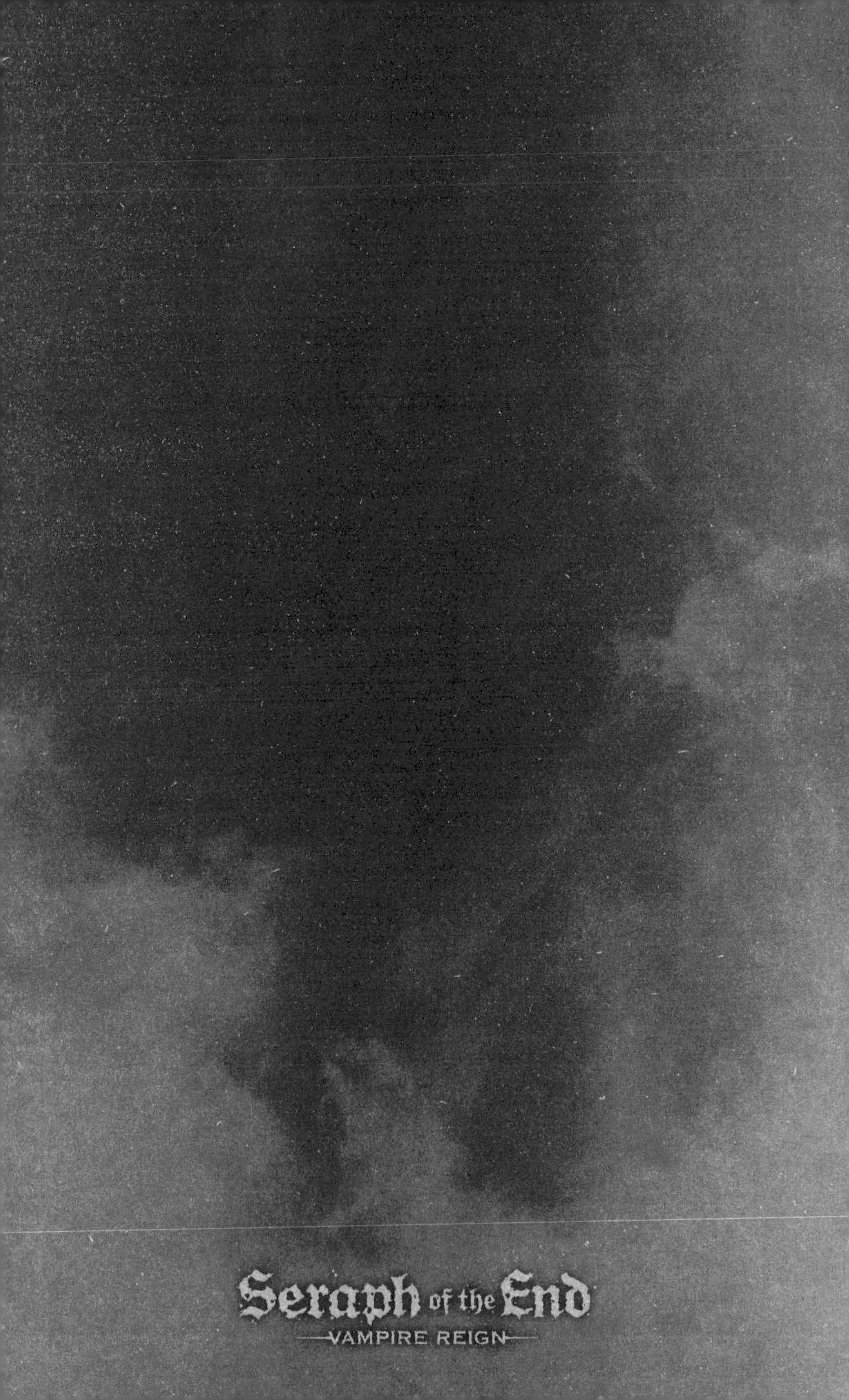
Seraph of the End
VAMPIRE REIGN

CHAPTER 3

The Demon in Your Heart

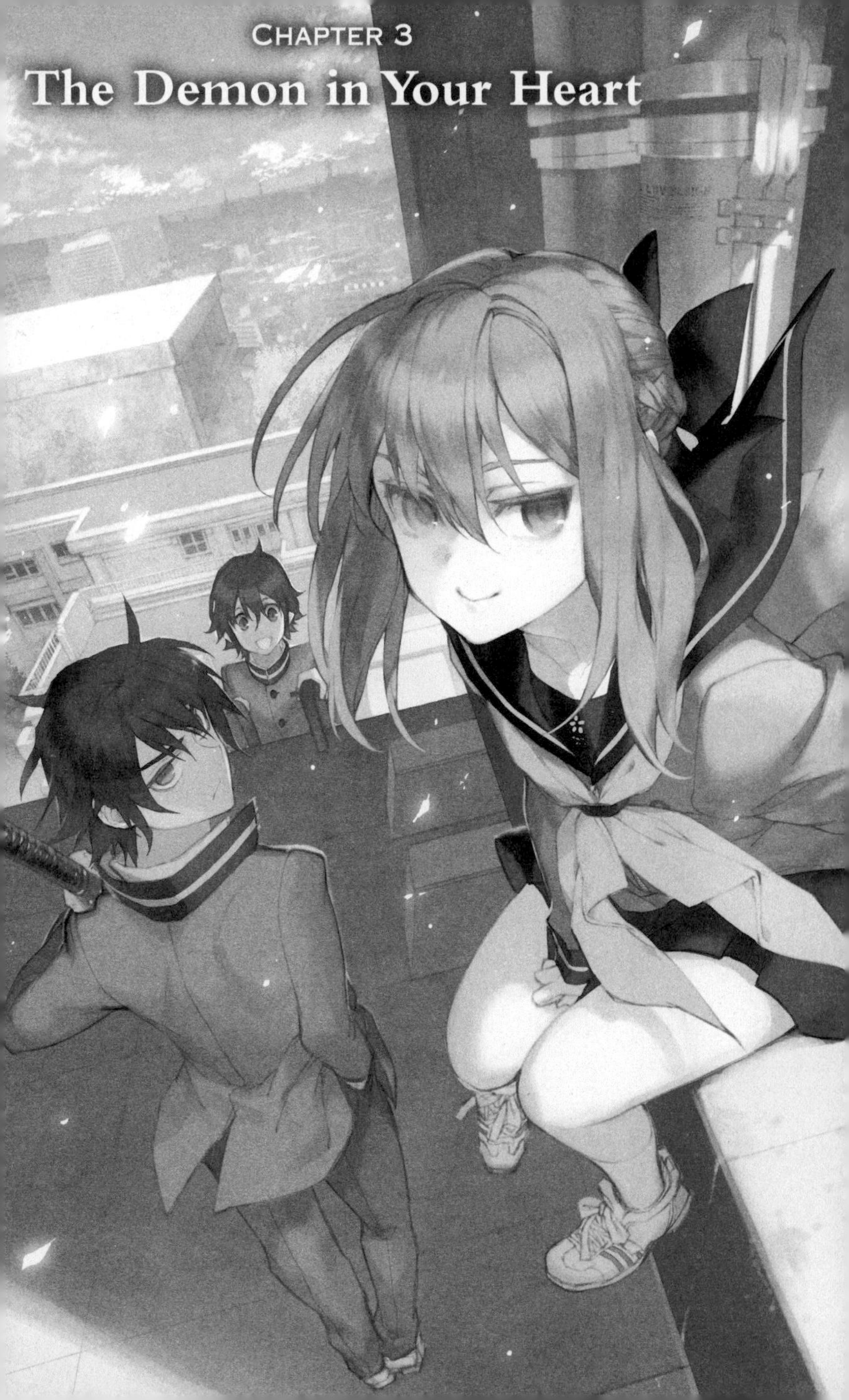

Seraph of the End
VAMPIRE REIGN

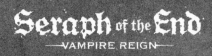

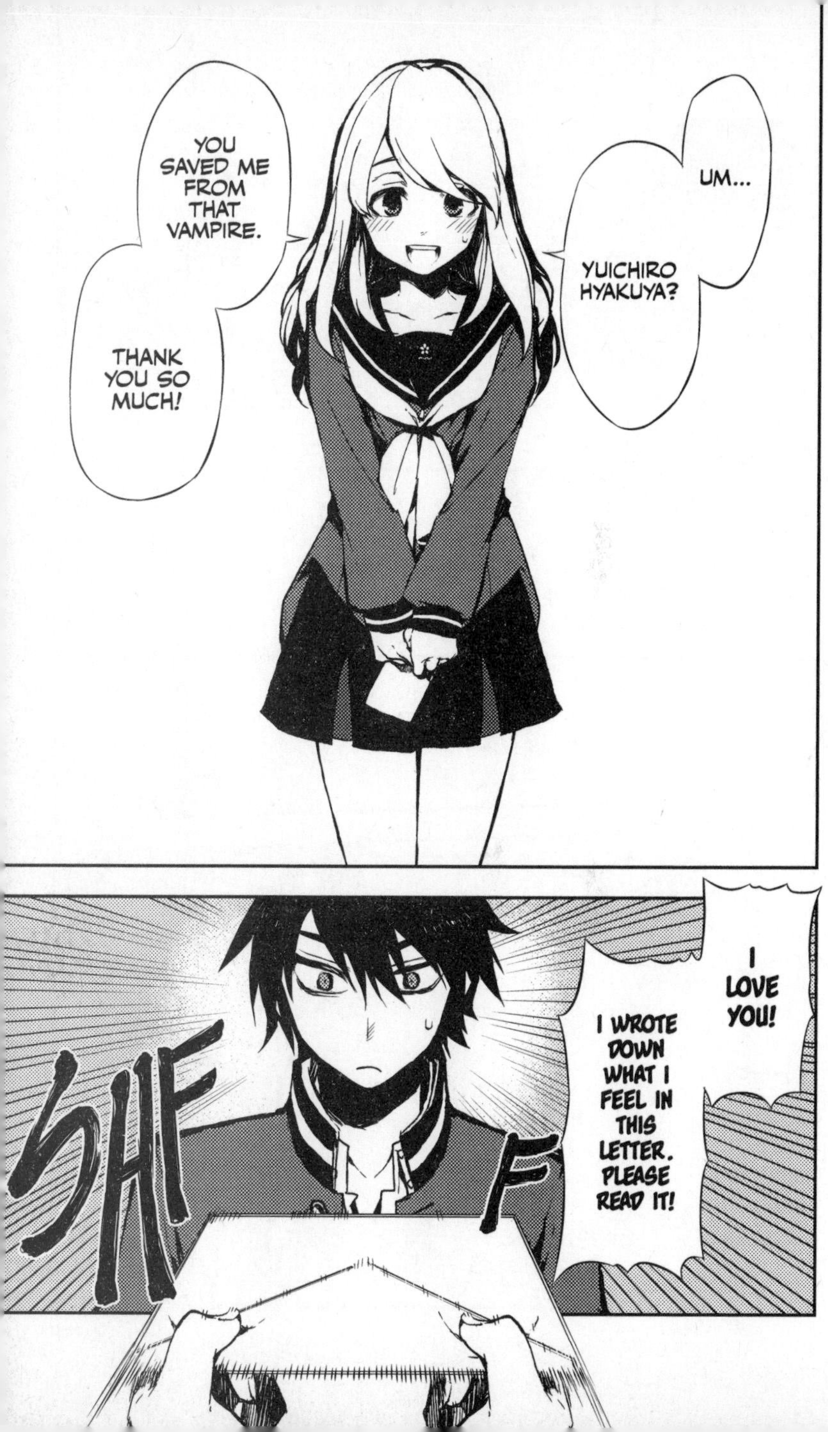
UM... YUICHIRO HYAKUYA?
YOU SAVED ME FROM THAT VAMPIRE.
THANK YOU SO MUCH!
I LOVE YOU!
I WROTE DOWN WHAT I FEEL IN THIS LETTER. PLEASE READ IT!
SHFF

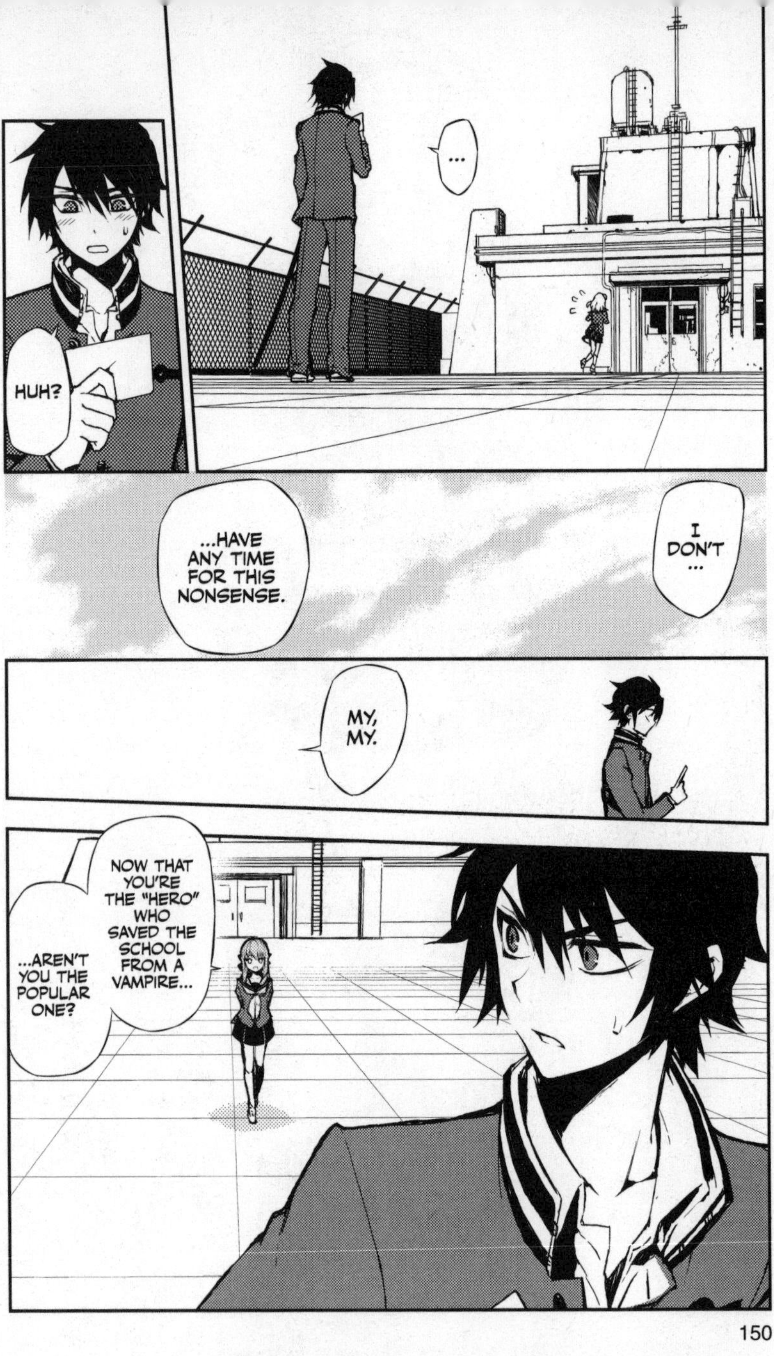
...
HUH?
I DON'T ...
...HAVE ANY TIME FOR THIS NONSENSE.
MY, MY.
NOW THAT YOU'RE THE "HERO" WHO SAVED THE SCHOOL FROM A VAMPIRE...
...AREN'T YOU THE POPULAR ONE?

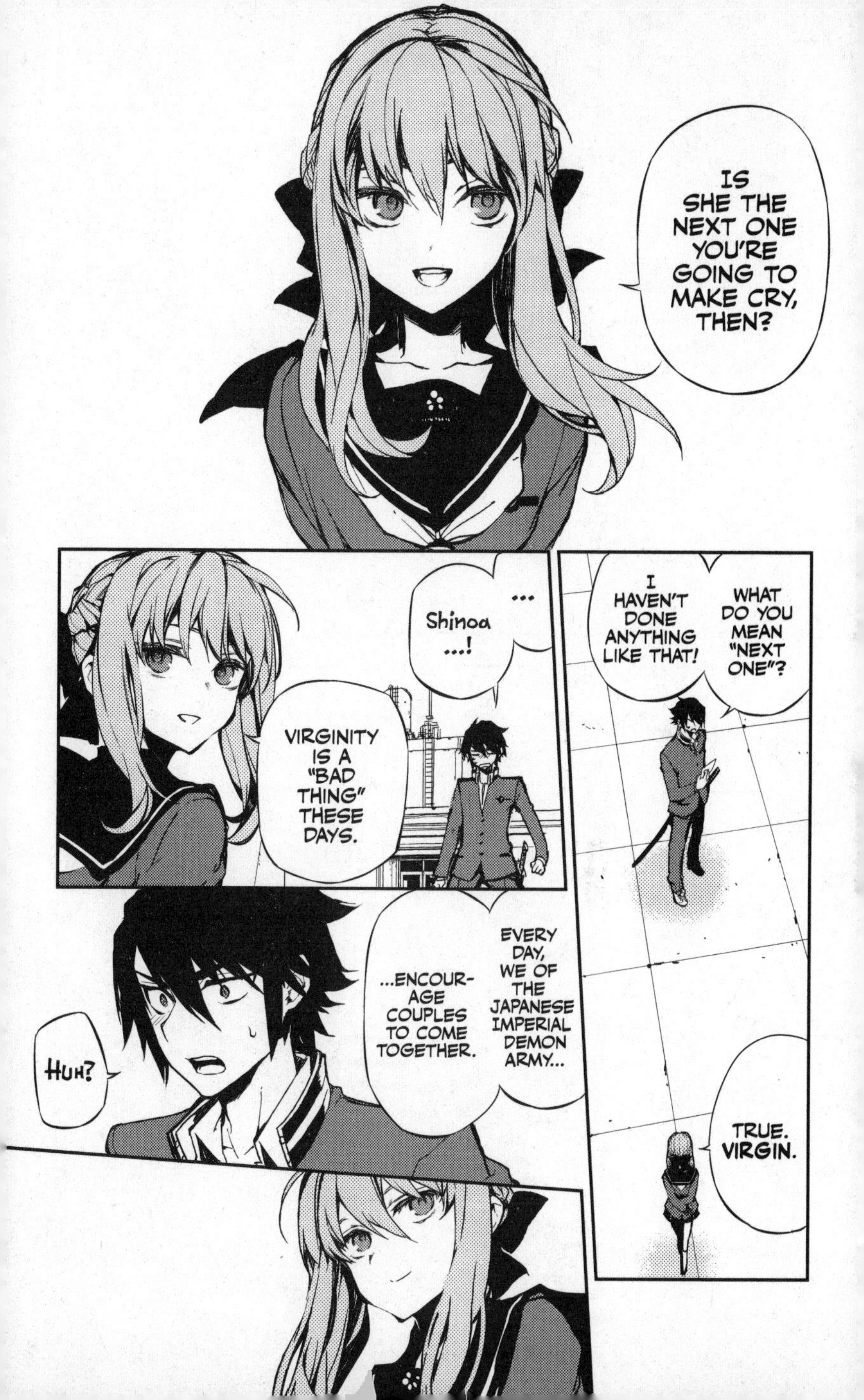
IS SHE THE NEXT ONE YOU'RE GOING TO MAKE CRY, THEN?
WHAT DO YOU MEAN "NEXT ONE"?
I HAVEN'T DONE ANYTHING LIKE THAT!
TRUE. VIRGIN.
...
Shinoa ...!
VIRGINITY IS A "BAD THING" THESE DAYS.
EVERY DAY, WE OF THE JAPANESE IMPERIAL DEMON ARMY...
...ENCOUR-AGE COUPLES TO COME TOGETHER.
HUH?

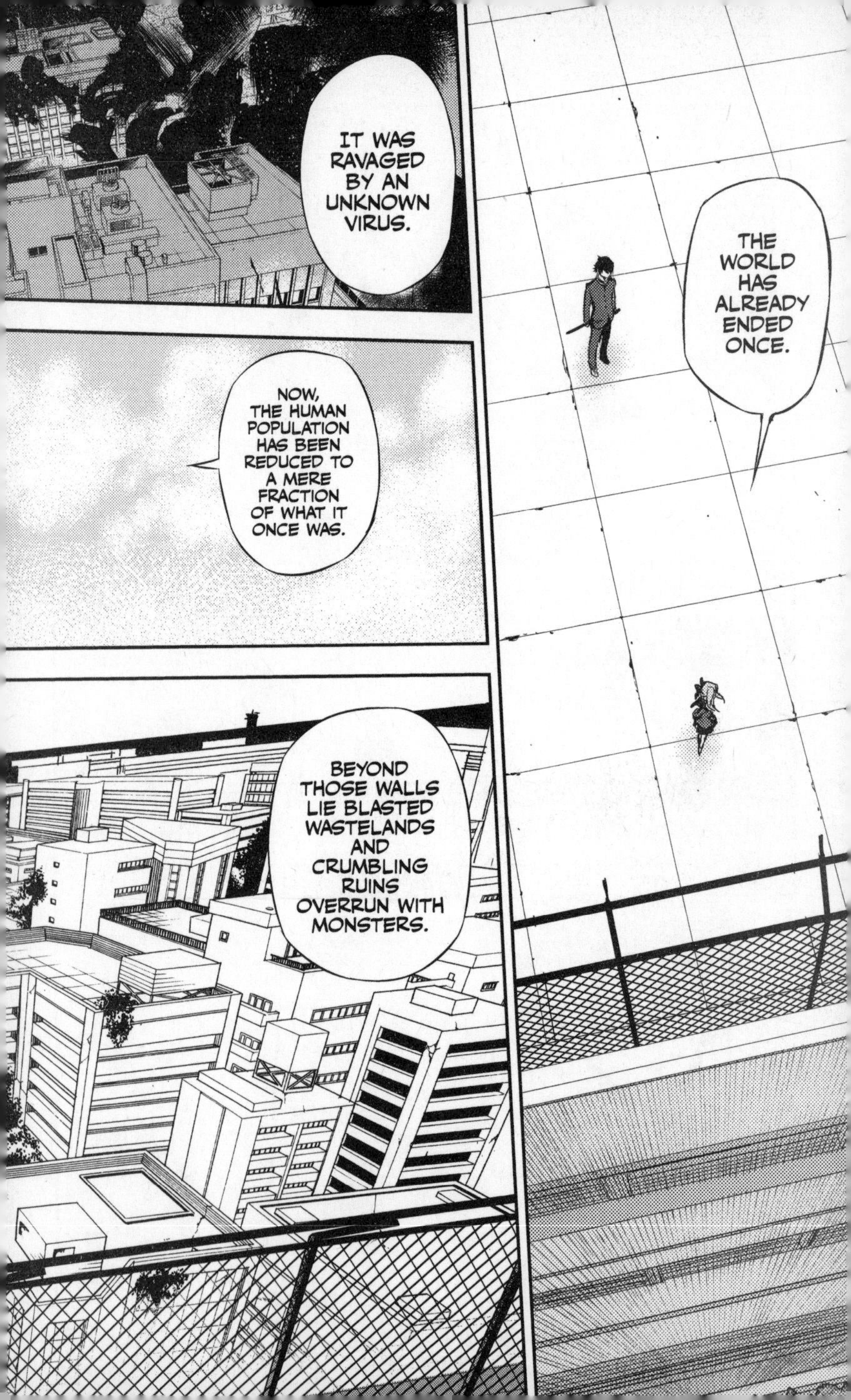
THE WORLD HAS ALREADY ENDED ONCE.
IT WAS RAVAGED BY AN UNKNOWN VIRUS.
NOW, THE HUMAN POPULATION HAS BEEN REDUCED TO A MERE FRACTION OF WHAT IT ONCE WAS.
BEYOND THOSE WALLS LIE BLASTED WASTELANDS AND CRUMBLING RUINS OVERRUN WITH MONSTERS.

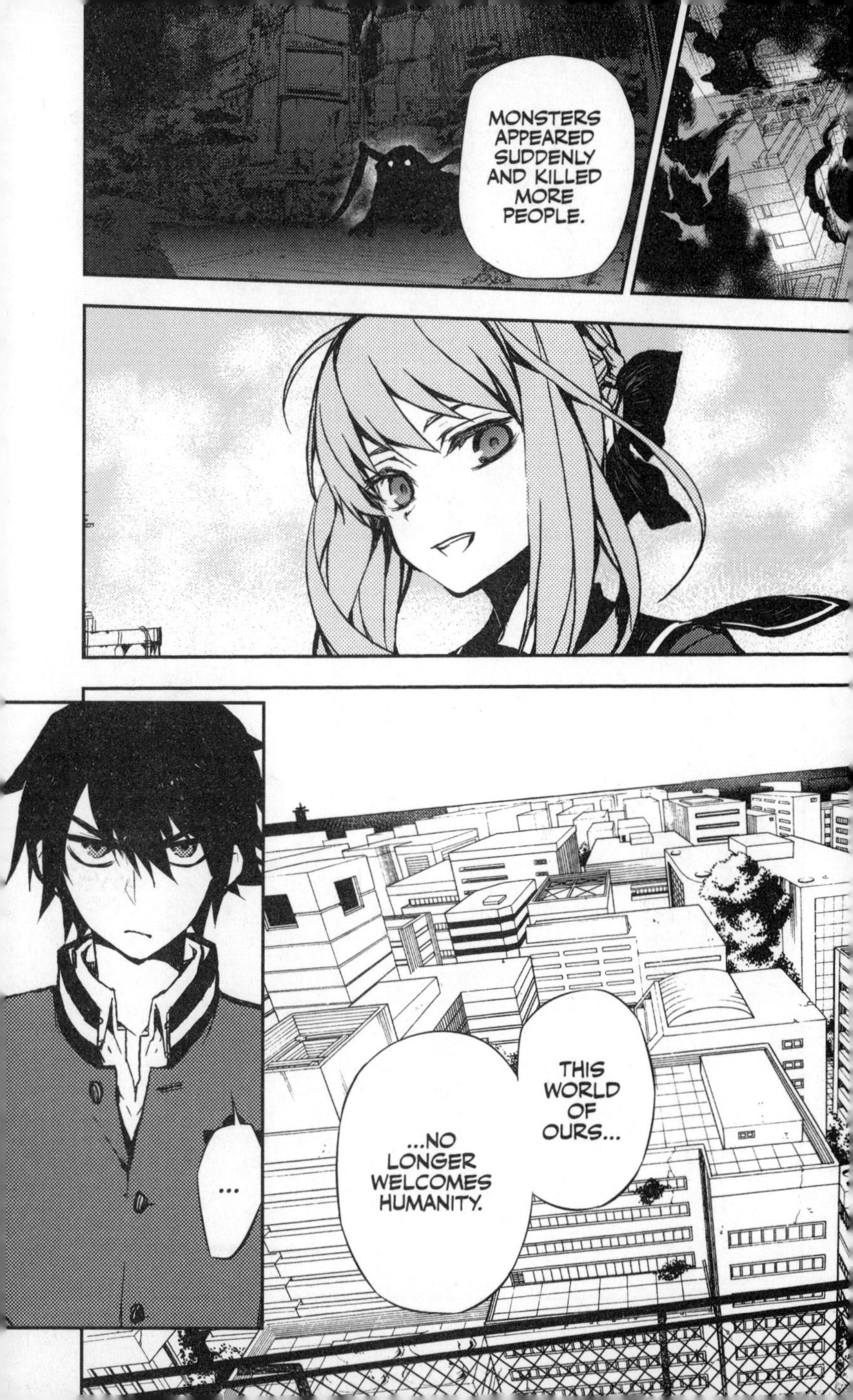
MONSTERS APPEARED SUDDENLY AND KILLED MORE PEOPLE.
THIS WORLD OF OURS...
...NO LONGER WELCOMES HUMANITY.
...

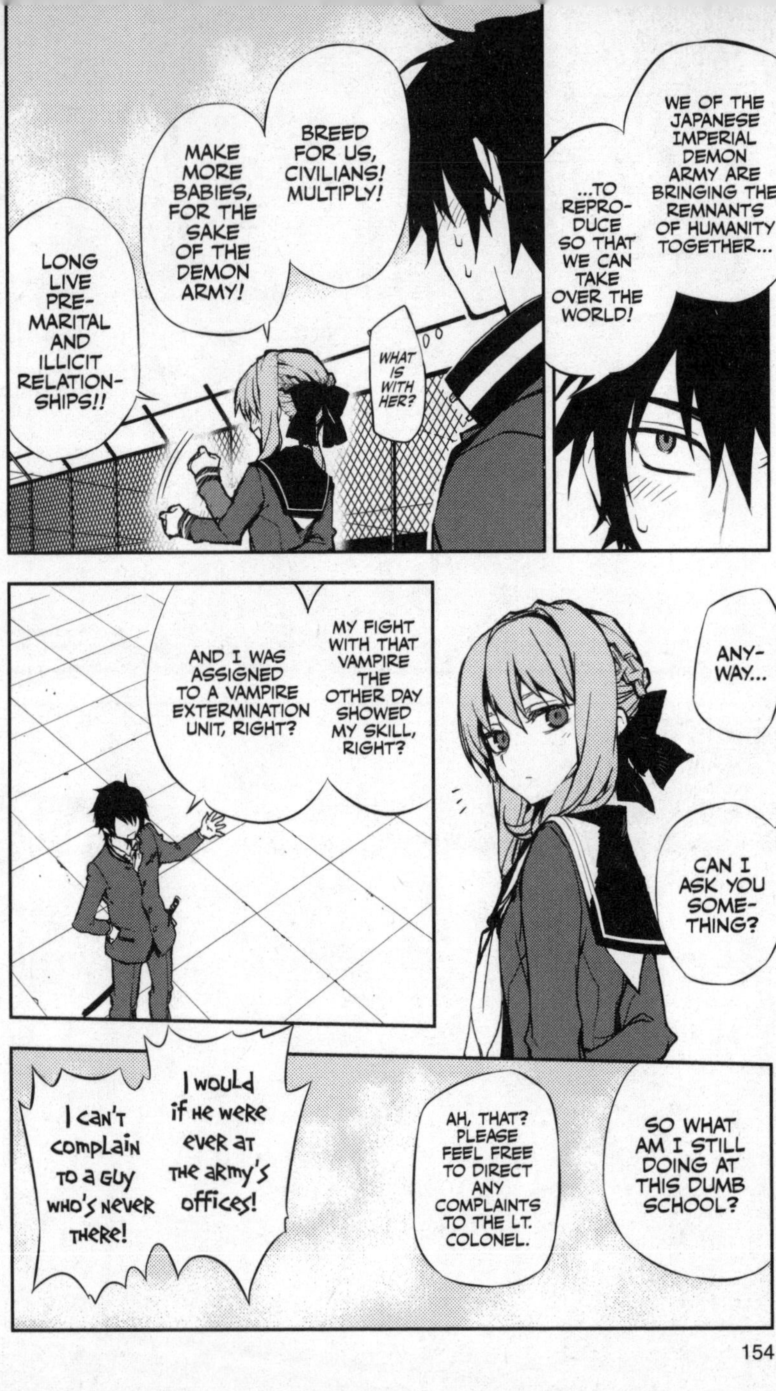
WE OF THE JAPANESE IMPERIAL DEMON ARMY ARE BRINGING THE REMNANTS OF HUMANITY TOGETHER...
...TO REPRODUCE SO THAT WE CAN TAKE OVER THE WORLD!
BREED FOR US, CIVILIANS! MULTIPLY!
MAKE MORE BABIES, FOR THE SAKE OF THE DEMON ARMY!
WHAT IS WITH HER?
LONG LIVE PRE-MARITAL AND ILLICIT RELATION-SHIPS!!
ANY-WAY...
CAN I ASK YOU SOME-THING?
MY FIGHT WITH THAT VAMPIRE THE OTHER DAY SHOWED MY SKILL, RIGHT?
AND I WAS ASSIGNED TO A VAMPIRE EXTERMINATION UNIT, RIGHT?
SO WHAT AM I STILL DOING AT THIS DUMB SCHOOL?
AH, THAT? PLEASE FEEL FREE TO DIRECT ANY COMPLAINTS TO THE LT. COLONEL.
I would if he were ever at the army's offices!
I can't complain to a guy who's never there!

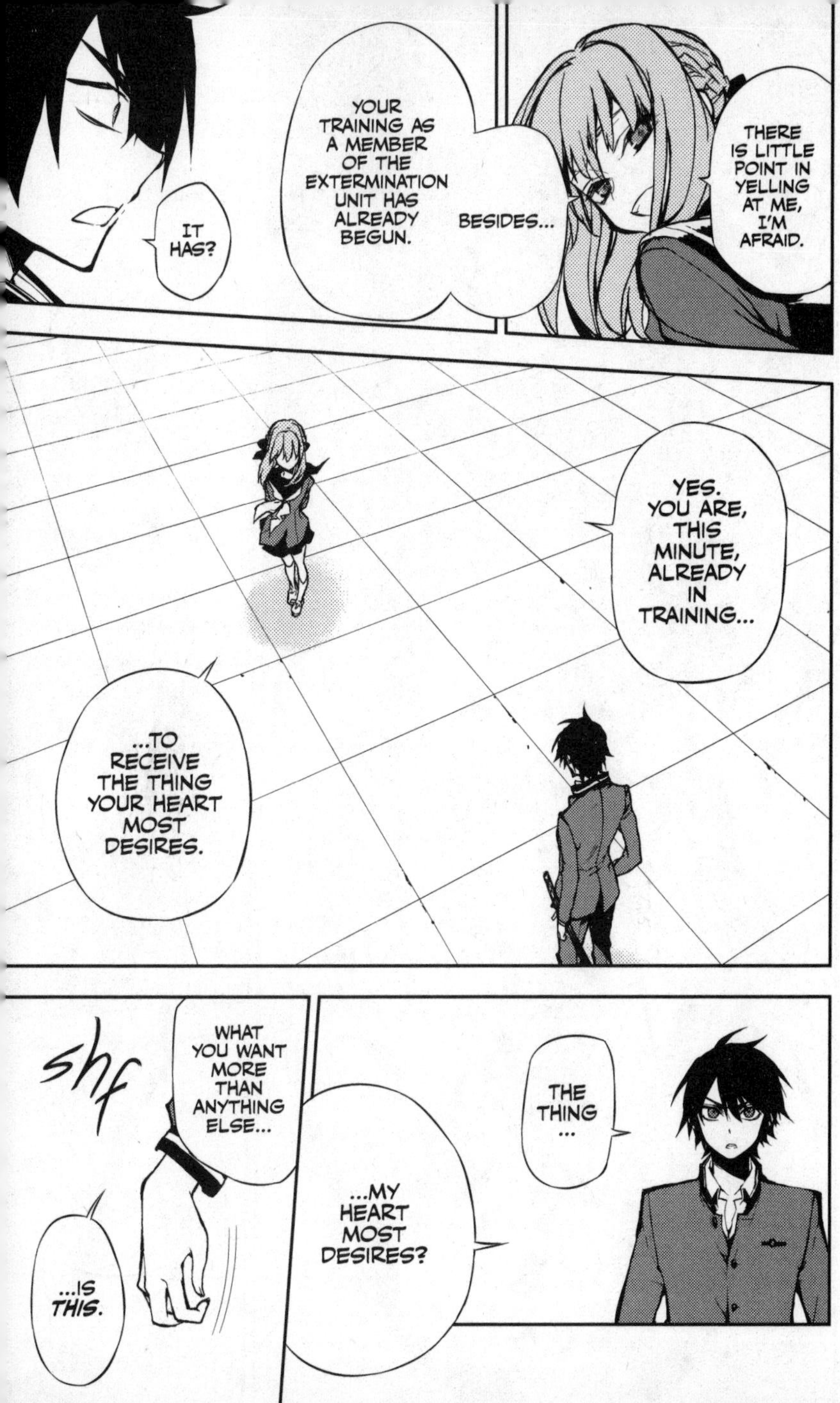
THERE IS LITTLE POINT IN YELLING AT ME, I'M AFRAID.
BESIDES...
YOUR TRAINING AS A MEMBER OF THE EXTERMINATION UNIT HAS ALREADY BEGUN.
IT HAS?
YES. YOU ARE, THIS MINUTE, ALREADY IN TRAINING...
...TO RECEIVE THE THING YOUR HEART MOST DESIRES.
THE THING...
...MY HEART MOST DESIRES?
WHAT YOU WANT MORE THAN ANYTHING ELSE...
shf
...IS *THIS*.

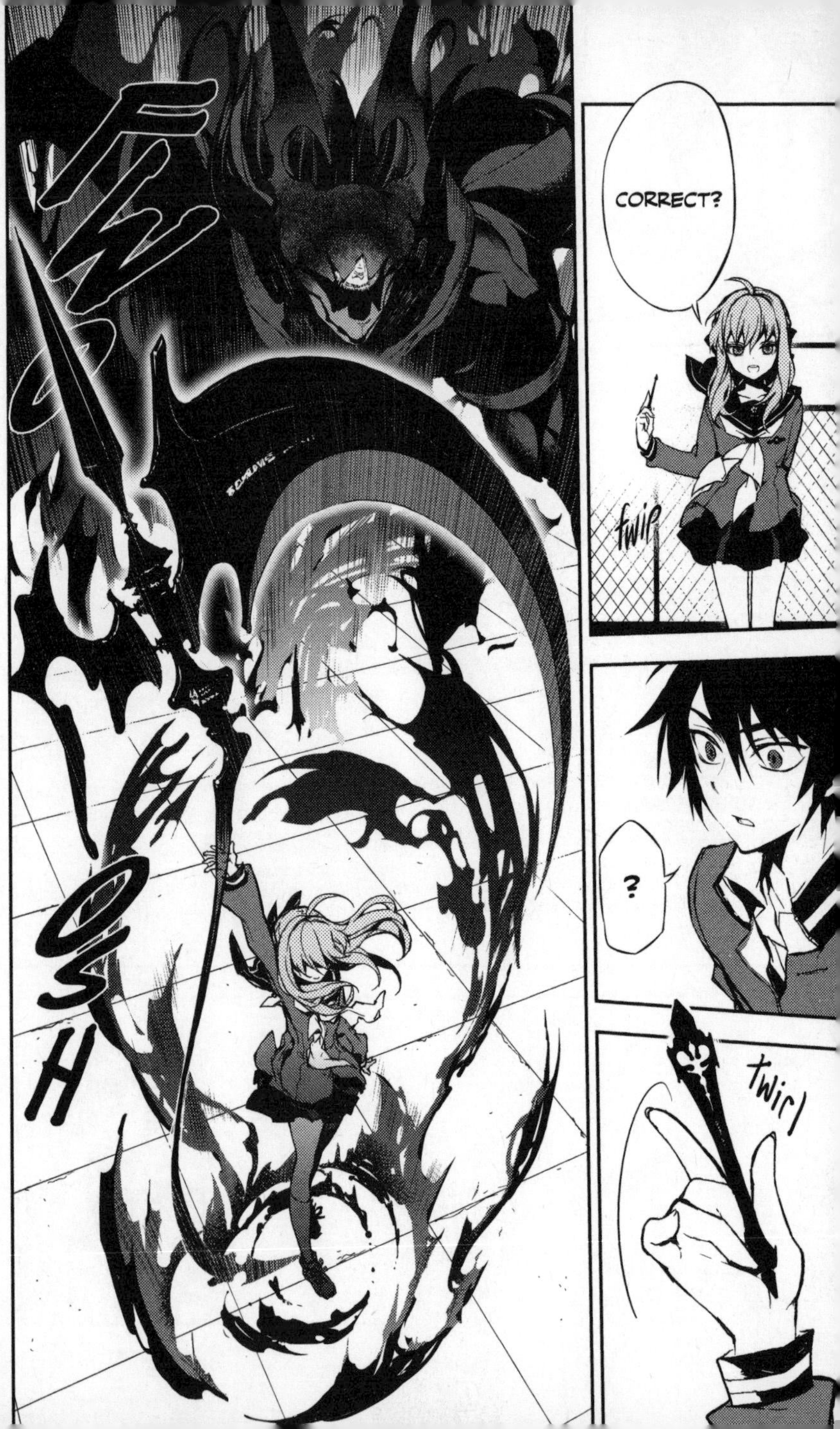
CORRECT?
twip
?
twirl
FWOOSH

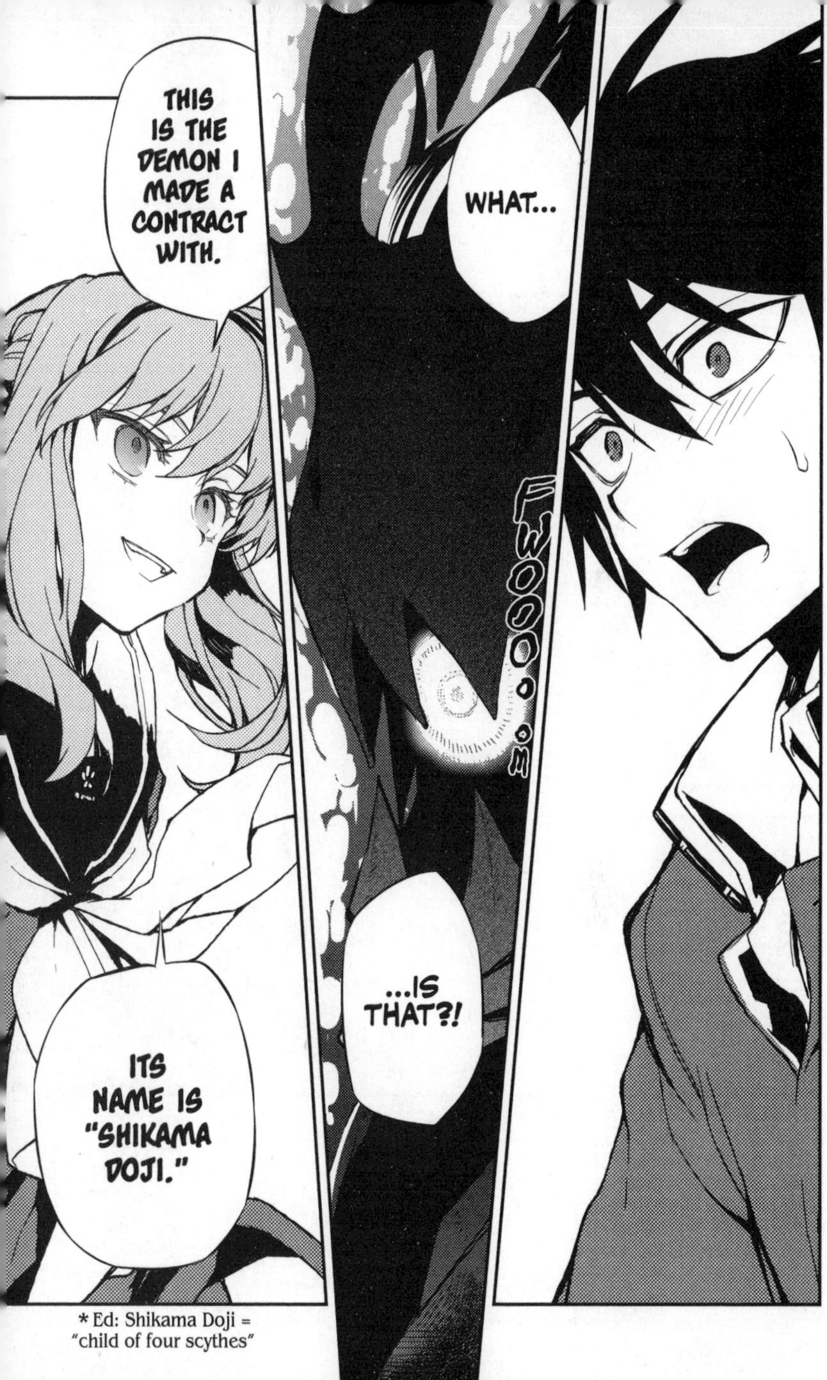
WHAT...
FWOOOOOOM
...IS THAT?!
THIS IS THE DEMON I MADE A CONTRACT WITH.
ITS NAME IS "SHIKAMA DOJI."

* Ed: Shikama Doji = "child of four scythes"

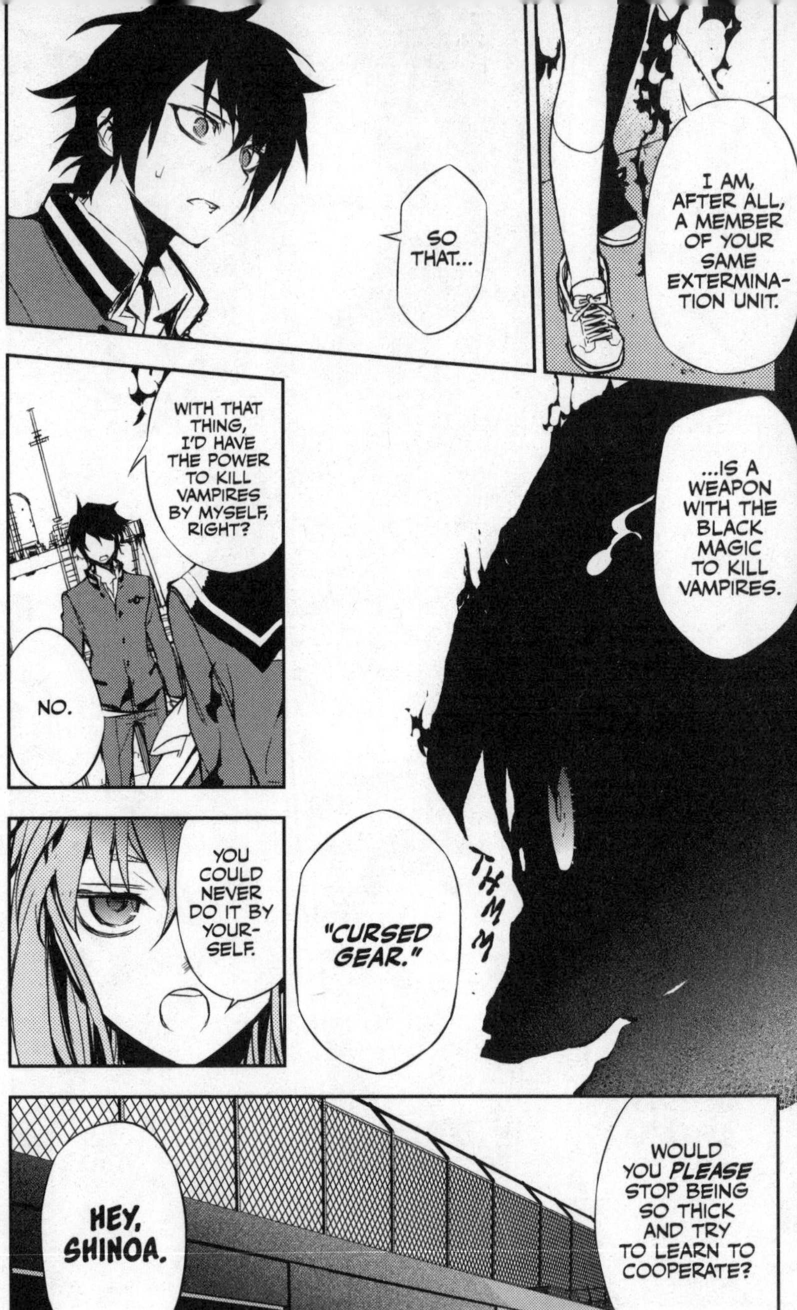

I AM, AFTER ALL, A MEMBER OF YOUR SAME EXTERMINATION UNIT.
SO THAT...
...IS A WEAPON WITH THE BLACK MAGIC TO KILL VAMPIRES.
THMM
"CURSED GEAR."
WITH THAT THING, I'D HAVE THE POWER TO KILL VAMPIRES BY MYSELF, RIGHT?
NO.
YOU COULD NEVER DO IT BY YOURSELF.
WOULD YOU *PLEASE* STOP BEING SO THICK AND TRY TO LEARN TO COOPERATE?
HEY, SHINOA.

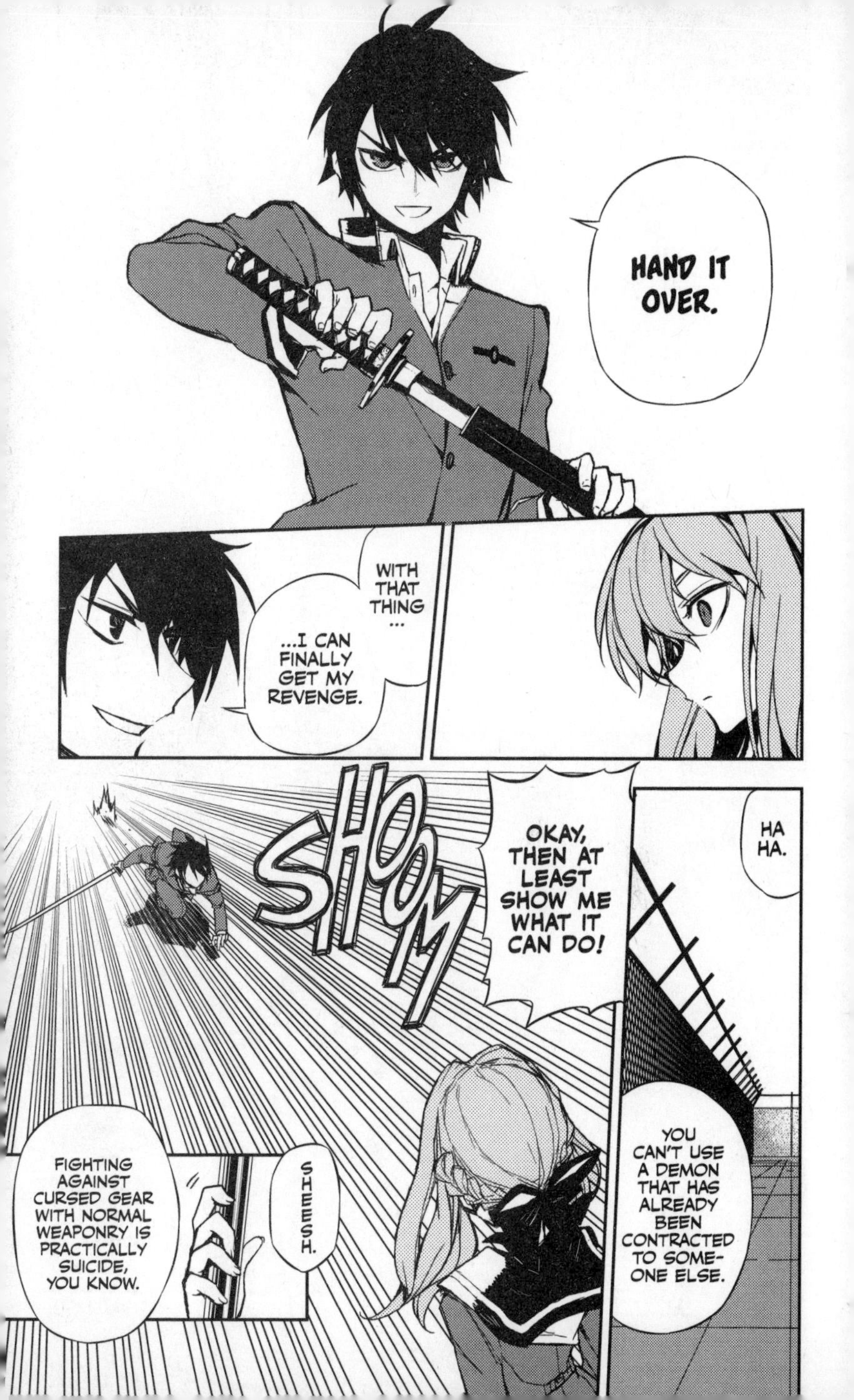
HAND IT OVER.
WITH THAT THING...
...I CAN FINALLY GET MY REVENGE.
HA HA.
YOU CAN'T USE A DEMON THAT HAS ALREADY BEEN CONTRACTED TO SOME-ONE ELSE.
SHOOM
OKAY, THEN AT LEAST SHOW ME WHAT IT CAN DO!
SHEESH.
FIGHTING AGAINST CURSED GEAR WITH NORMAL WEAPONRY IS PRACTICALLY SUICIDE, YOU KNOW.

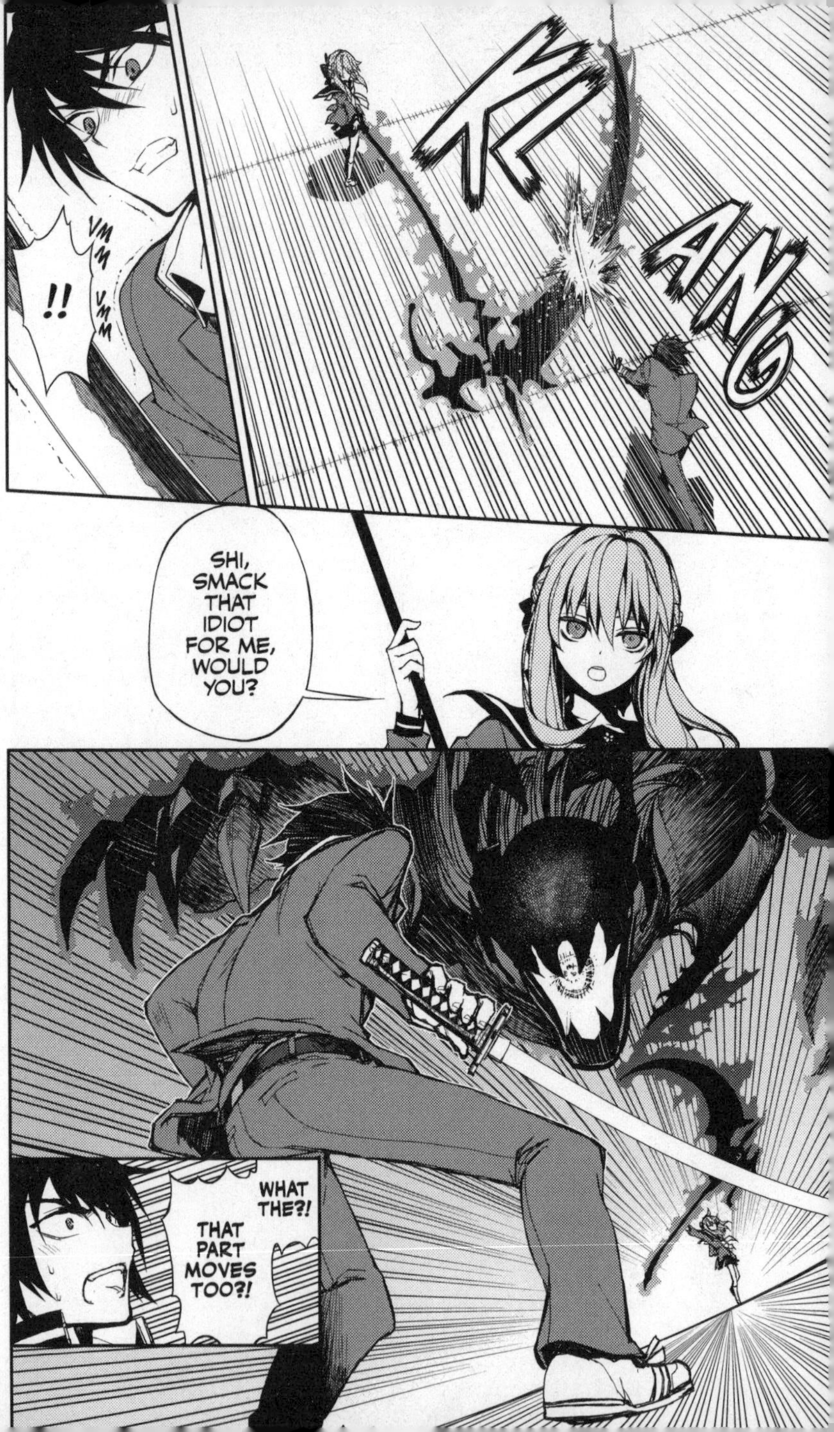
KLANG
!!
VMM VMM
SHI, SMACK THAT IDIOT FOR ME, WOULD YOU?
WHAT THE?!
THAT PART MOVES TOO?!

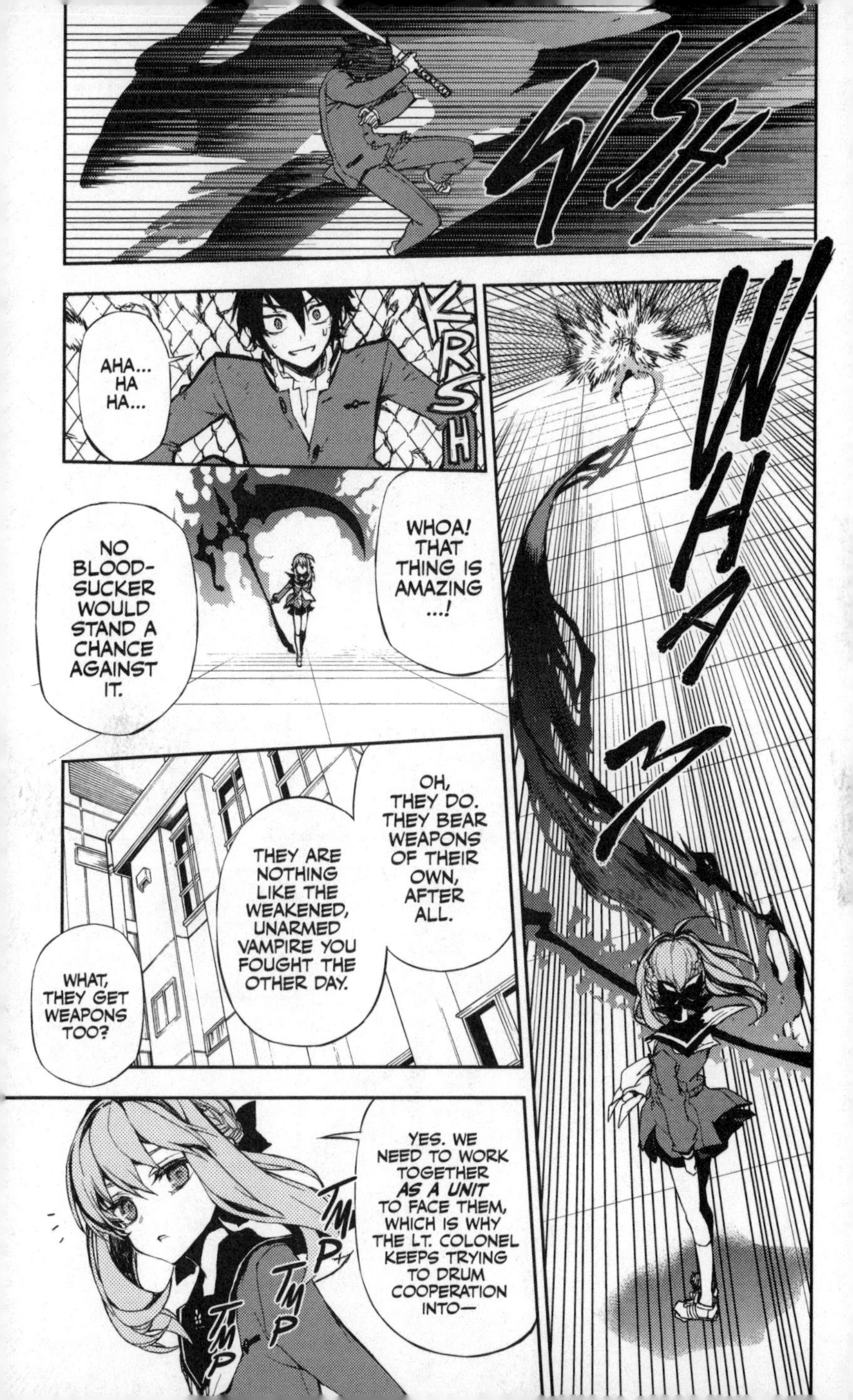

WSH
WHAMM
KRSH
AHA... HA HA...
WHOA! THAT THING IS AMAZING...!
NO BLOOD-SUCKER WOULD STAND A CHANCE AGAINST IT.
OH, THEY DO. THEY BEAR WEAPONS OF THEIR OWN, AFTER ALL.
THEY ARE NOTHING LIKE THE WEAKENED, UNARMED VAMPIRE YOU FOUGHT THE OTHER DAY.
WHAT, THEY GET WEAPONS TOO?
YES. WE NEED TO WORK TOGETHER ***AS A UNIT*** TO FACE THEM, WHICH IS WHY THE LT. COLONEL KEEPS TRYING TO DRUM COOPERATION INTO—
TMP TMP TMP TMP

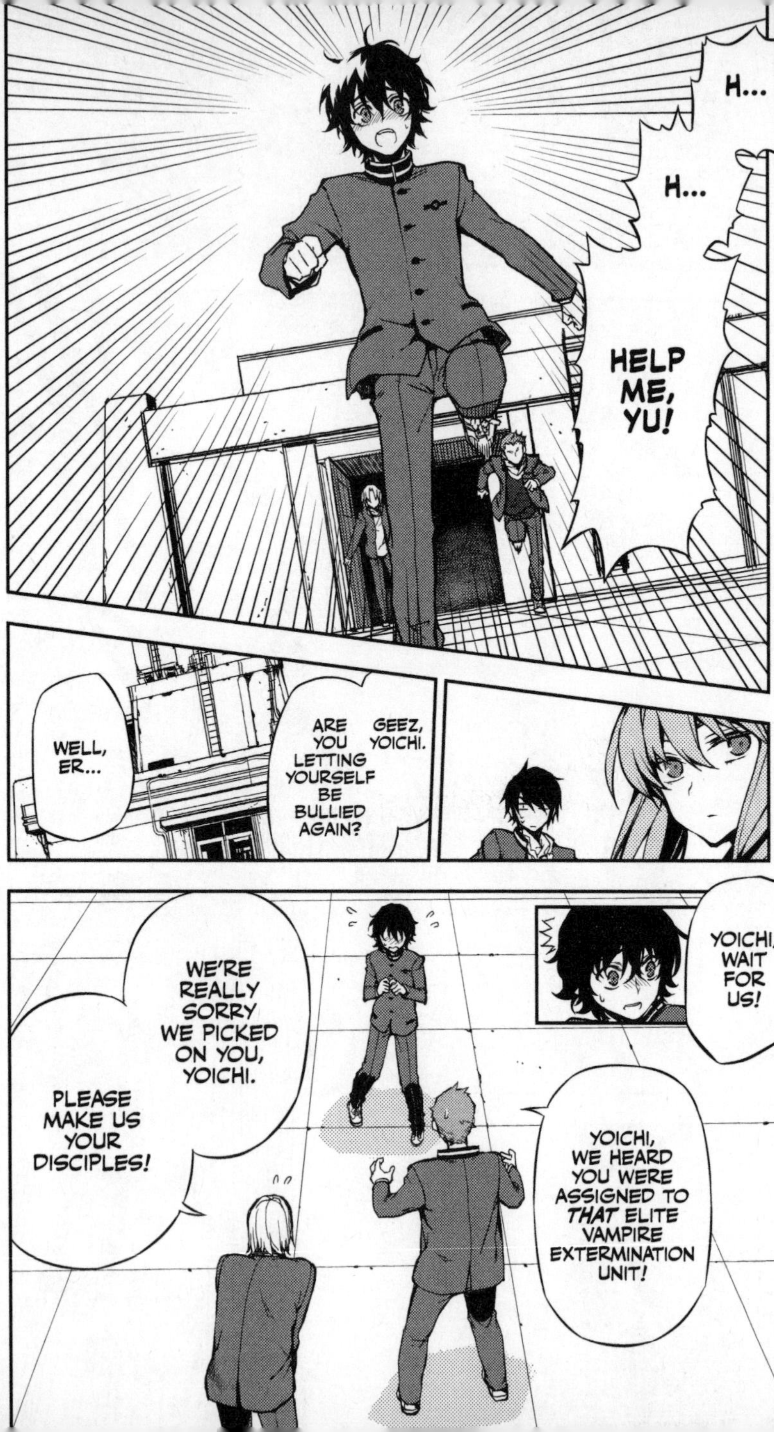
H...
H...
HELP ME, YU!
GEEZ, YOICHI.
ARE YOU LETTING YOURSELF BE BULLIED AGAIN?
WELL, ER...
YOICHI, WAIT FOR US!
YOICHI, WE HEARD YOU WERE ASSIGNED TO *THAT* ELITE VAMPIRE EXTERMINATION UNIT!
WE'RE REALLY SORRY WE PICKED ON YOU, YOICHI.
PLEASE MAKE US YOUR DISCIPLES!

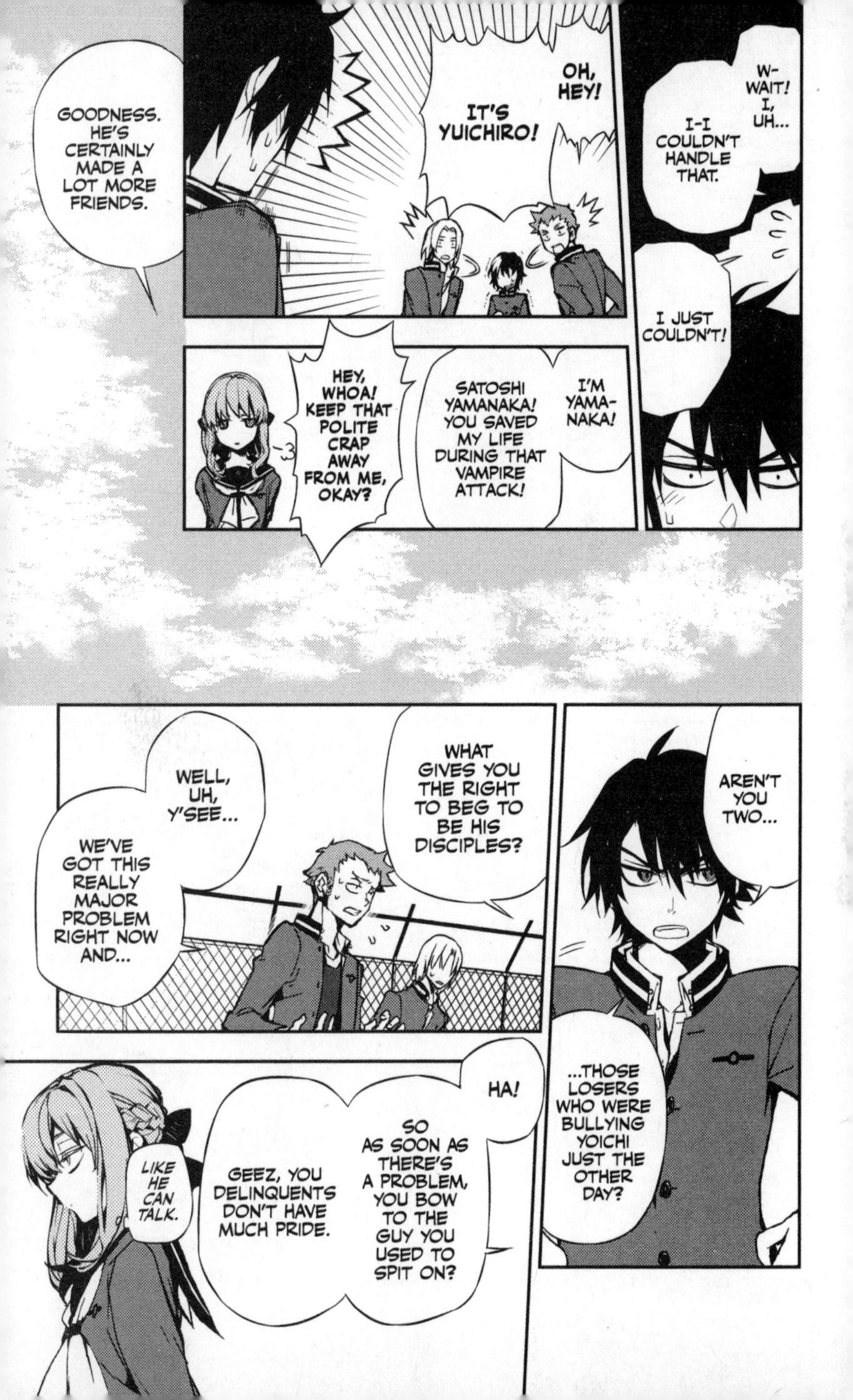
W-WAIT! I, UH...
I-I COULDN'T HANDLE THAT.
I JUST COULDN'T!
OH, HEY!
IT'S YUICHIRO!
GOODNESS. HE'S CERTAINLY MADE A LOT MORE FRIENDS.
I'M YAMANAKA!
SATOSHI YAMANAKA! YOU SAVED MY LIFE DURING THAT VAMPIRE ATTACK!
HEY, WHOA! KEEP THAT POLITE CRAP AWAY FROM ME, OKAY?
AREN'T YOU TWO...
...THOSE LOSERS WHO WERE BULLYING YOICHI JUST THE OTHER DAY?
WHAT GIVES YOU THE RIGHT TO BEG TO BE HIS DISCIPLES?
WELL, UH, Y'SEE...
WE'VE GOT THIS REALLY MAJOR PROBLEM RIGHT NOW AND...
HA!
SO AS SOON AS THERE'S A PROBLEM, YOU BOW TO THE GUY YOU USED TO SPIT ON?
GEEZ, YOU DELINQUENTS DON'T HAVE MUCH PRIDE.
LIKE HE CAN TALK.

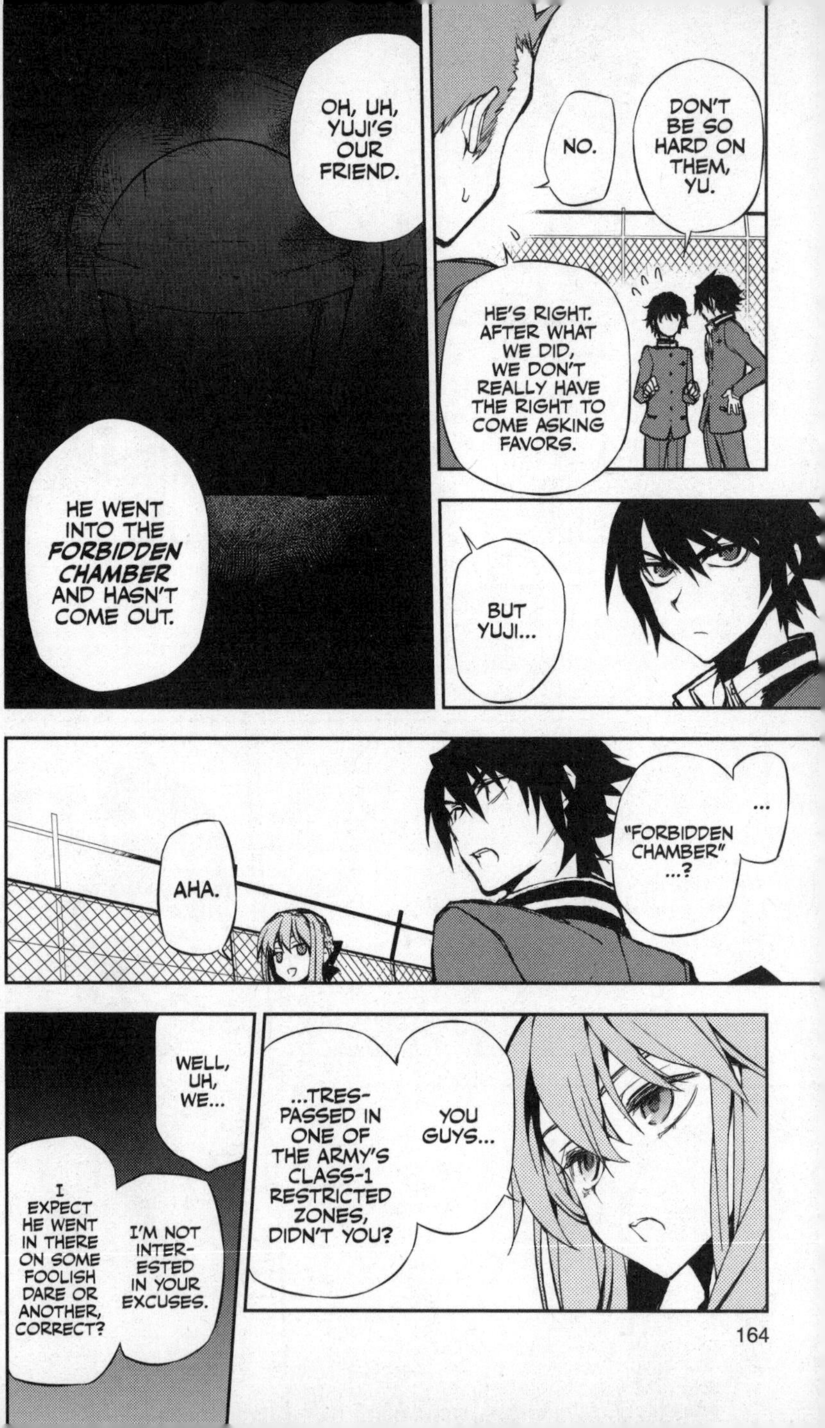
DON'T BE SO HARD ON THEM, YU.
NO.
HE'S RIGHT. AFTER WHAT WE DID, WE DON'T REALLY HAVE THE RIGHT TO COME ASKING FAVORS.
BUT YUJI...
OH, UH, YUJI'S OUR FRIEND.
HE WENT INTO THE *FORBIDDEN CHAMBER* AND HASN'T COME OUT.
... "FORBIDDEN CHAMBER" ...?
AHA.
YOU GUYS...
...TRESPASSED IN ONE OF THE ARMY'S CLASS-1 RESTRICTED ZONES, DIDN'T YOU?
WELL, UH, WE...
I'M NOT INTERESTED IN YOUR EXCUSES.
I EXPECT HE WENT IN THERE ON SOME FOOLISH DARE OR ANOTHER, CORRECT?

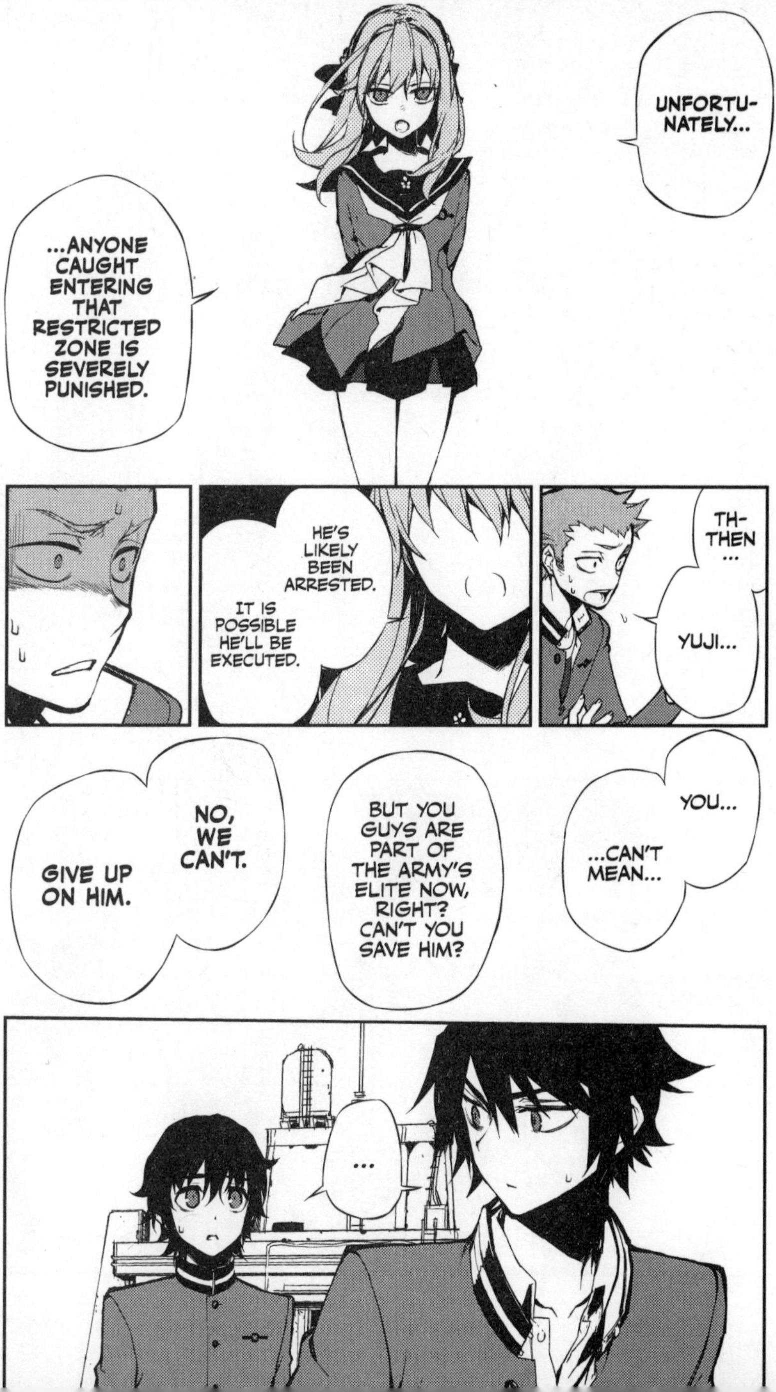
UNFORTUNATELY...
...ANYONE CAUGHT ENTERING THAT RESTRICTED ZONE IS SEVERELY PUNISHED.
TH-THEN...
YUJI...
HE'S LIKELY BEEN ARRESTED.
IT IS POSSIBLE HE'LL BE EXECUTED.
YOU...
...CAN'T MEAN...
BUT YOU GUYS ARE PART OF THE ARMY'S ELITE NOW, RIGHT? CAN'T YOU SAVE HIM?
NO, WE CAN'T.
GIVE UP ON HIM.
...

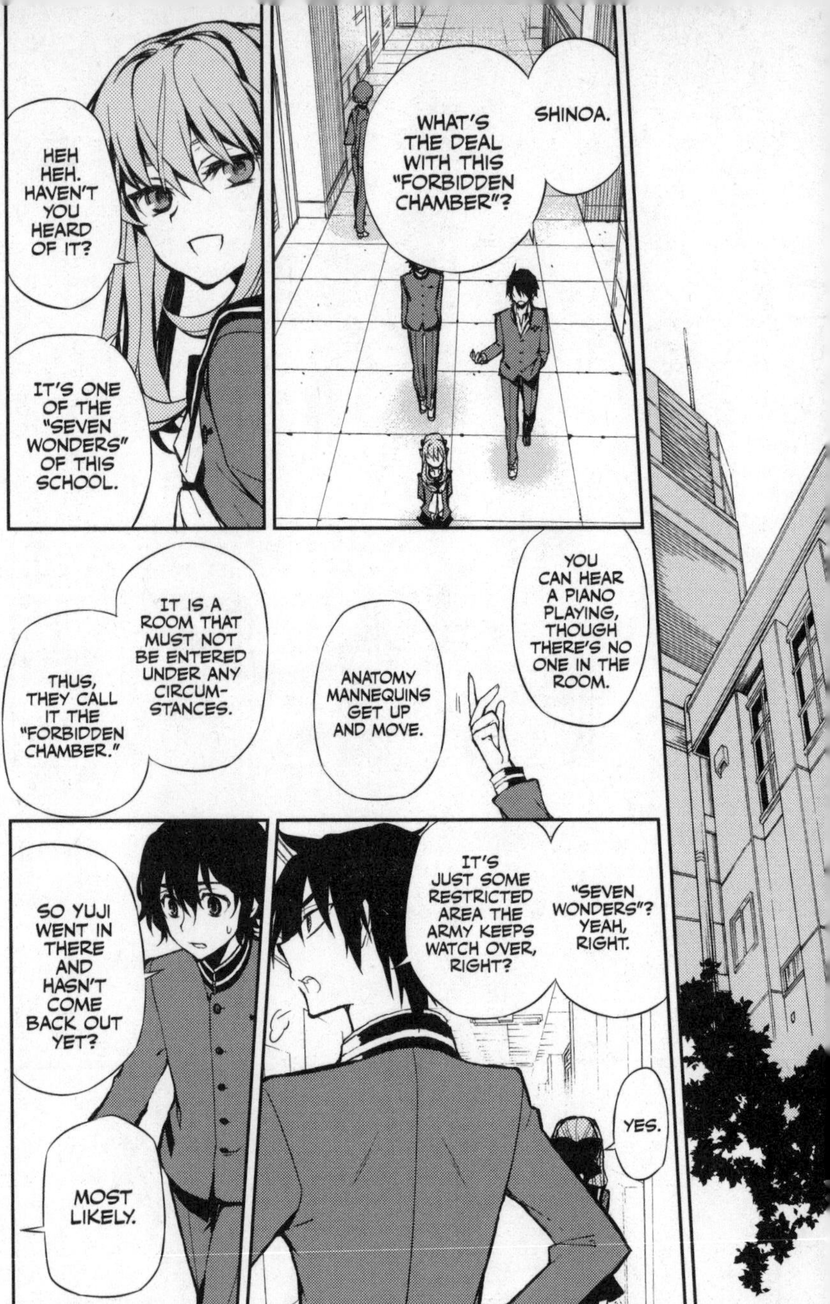
SHINOA.
WHAT'S THE DEAL WITH THIS "FORBIDDEN CHAMBER"?
HEH HEH. HAVEN'T YOU HEARD OF IT?
IT'S ONE OF THE "SEVEN WONDERS" OF THIS SCHOOL.
YOU CAN HEAR A PIANO PLAYING, THOUGH THERE'S NO ONE IN THE ROOM.
ANATOMY MANNEQUINS GET UP AND MOVE.
IT IS A ROOM THAT MUST NOT BE ENTERED UNDER ANY CIRCUM-STANCES.
THUS, THEY CALL IT THE "FORBIDDEN CHAMBER."
"SEVEN WONDERS"? YEAH, RIGHT.
IT'S JUST SOME RESTRICTED AREA THE ARMY KEEPS WATCH OVER, RIGHT?
YES.
SO YUJI WENT IN THERE AND HASN'T COME BACK OUT YET?
MOST LIKELY.

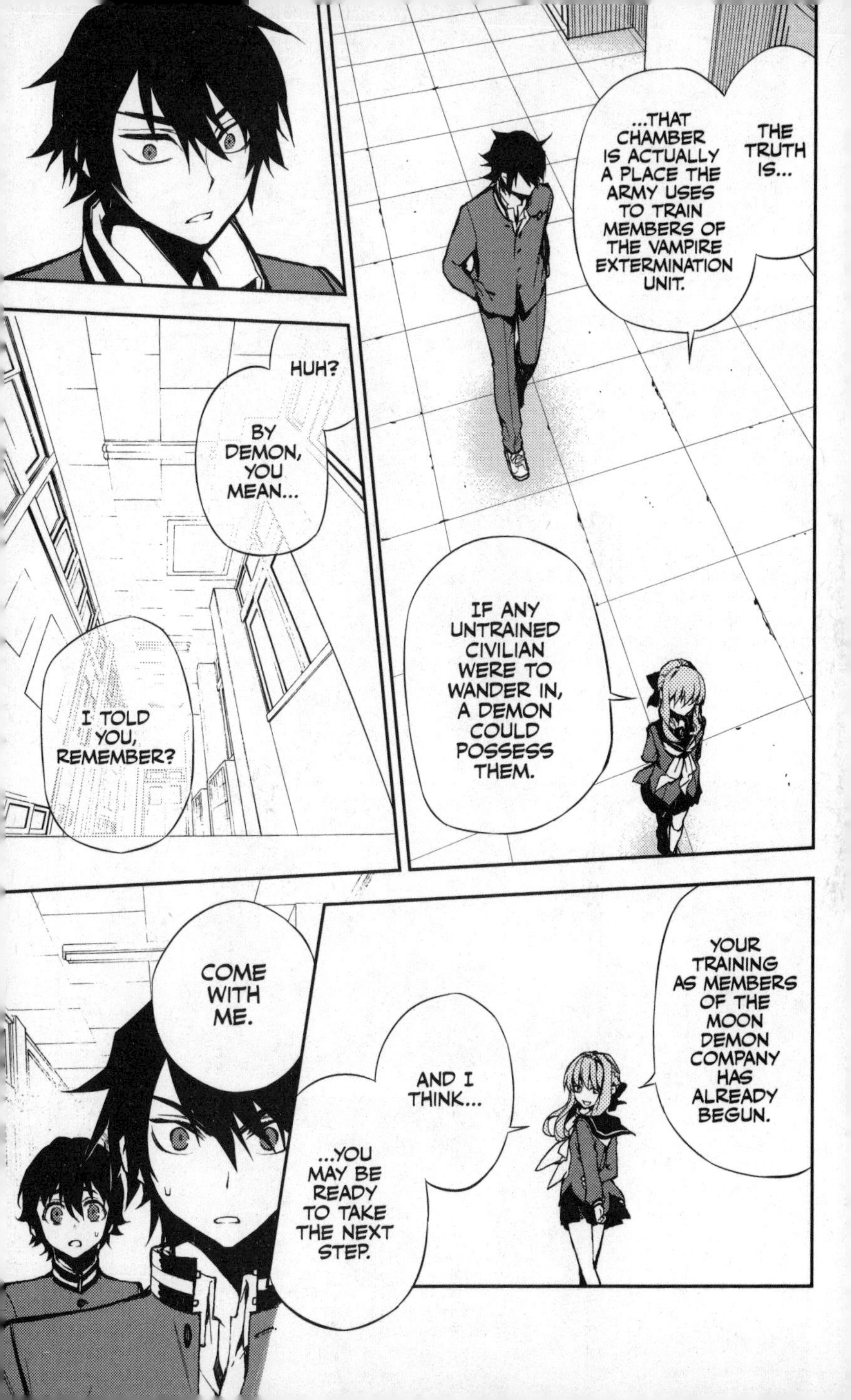
THE TRUTH IS...
...THAT CHAMBER IS ACTUALLY A PLACE THE ARMY USES TO TRAIN MEMBERS OF THE VAMPIRE EXTERMINATION UNIT.
IF ANY UNTRAINED CIVILIAN WERE TO WANDER IN, A DEMON COULD POSSESS THEM.
HUH?
BY DEMON, YOU MEAN...
I TOLD YOU, REMEMBER?
YOUR TRAINING AS MEMBERS OF THE MOON DEMON COMPANY HAS ALREADY BEGUN.
AND I THINK...
...YOU MAY BE READY TO TAKE THE NEXT STEP.
COME WITH ME.

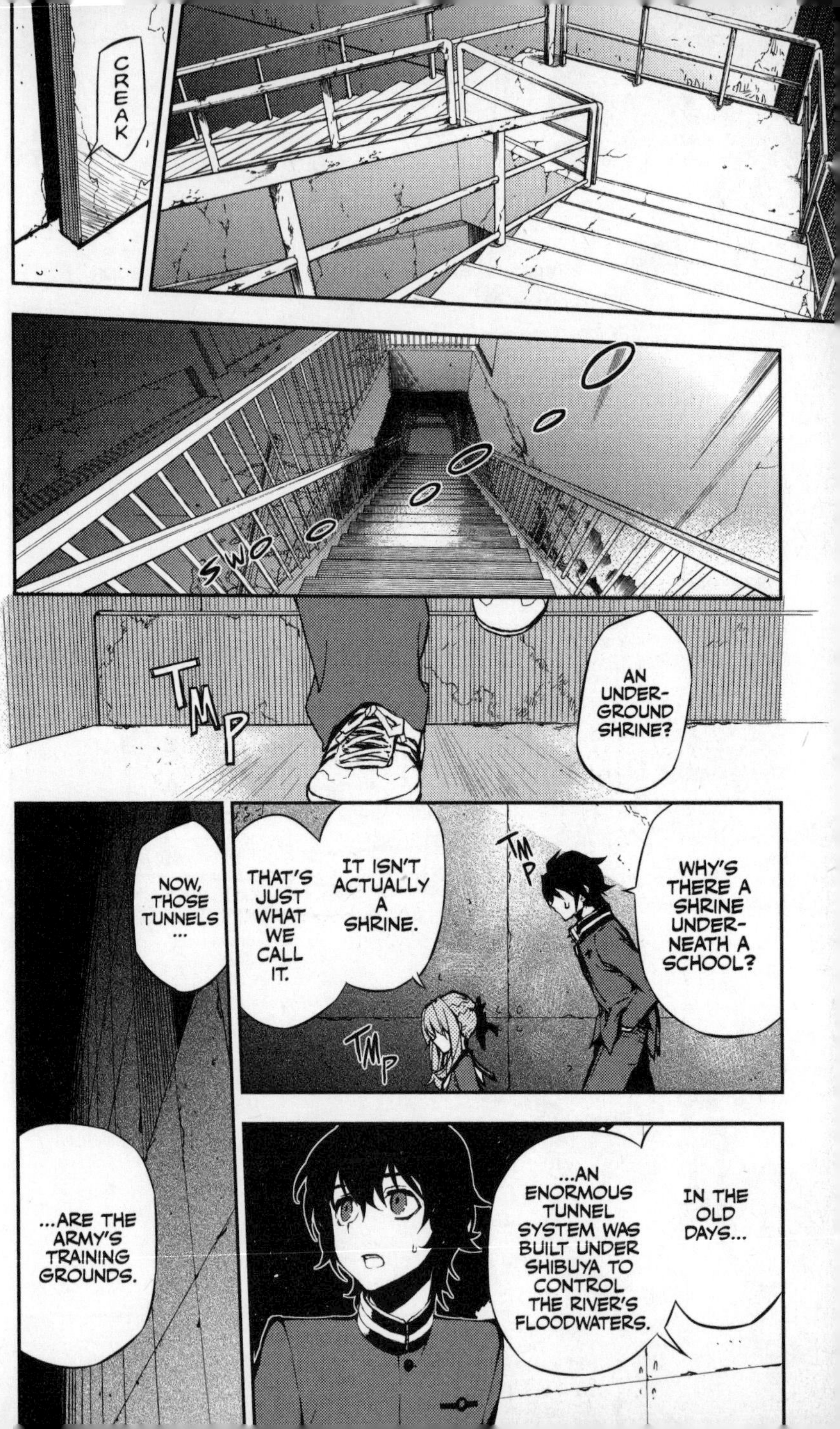
CREAK
SWOO
TMP
AN UNDER-GROUND SHRINE?
WHY'S THERE A SHRINE UNDER-NEATH A SCHOOL?
TMP
IT ISN'T ACTUALLY A SHRINE.
THAT'S JUST WHAT WE CALL IT.
TMP
IN THE OLD DAYS...
...AN ENORMOUS TUNNEL SYSTEM WAS BUILT UNDER SHIBUYA TO CONTROL THE RIVER'S FLOODWATERS.
NOW, THOSE TUNNELS...
...ARE THE ARMY'S TRAINING GROUNDS.

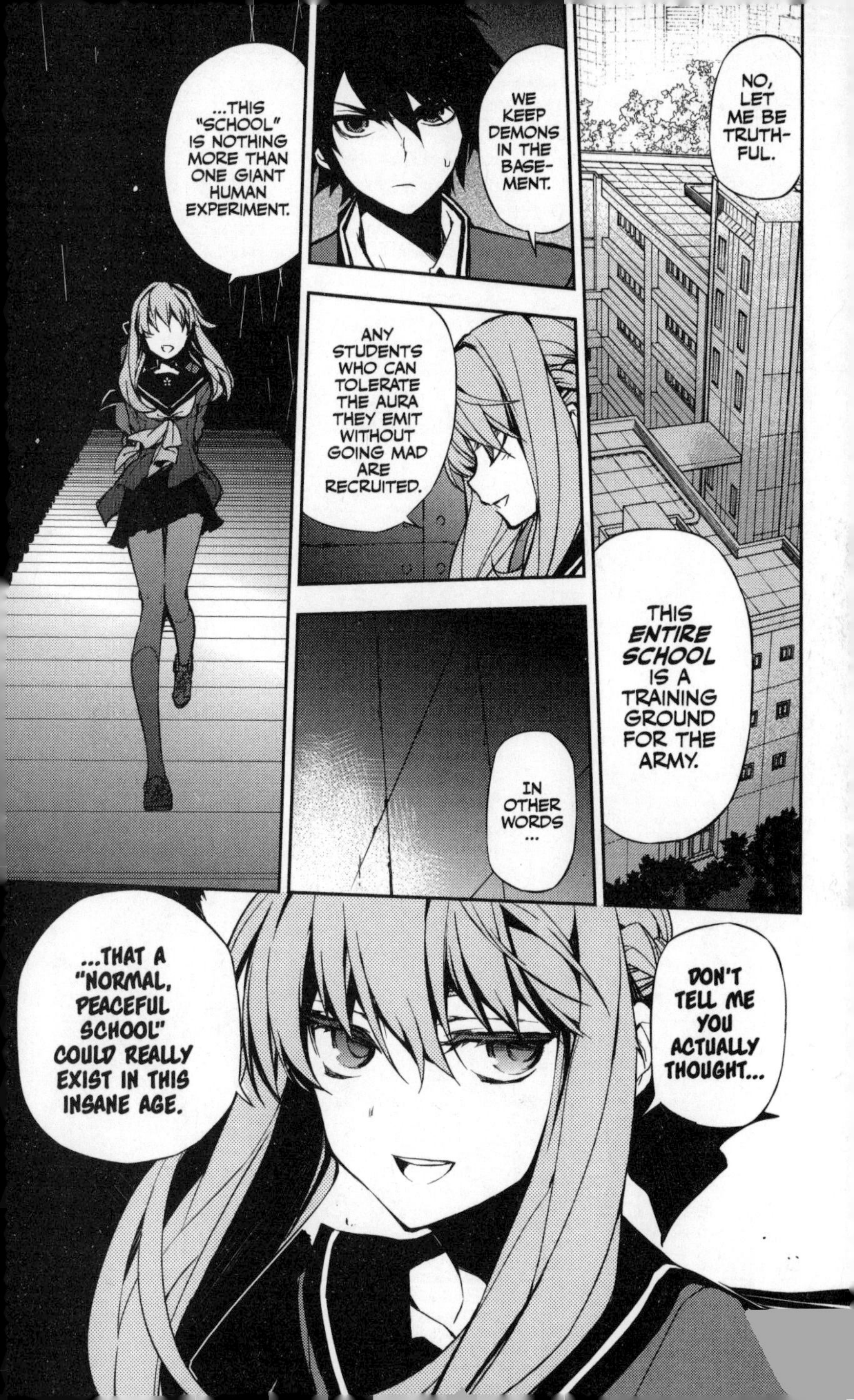
NO, LET ME BE TRUTHFUL.
THIS *ENTIRE SCHOOL* IS A TRAINING GROUND FOR THE ARMY.
WE KEEP DEMONS IN THE BASEMENT.
ANY STUDENTS WHO CAN TOLERATE THE AURA THEY EMIT WITHOUT GOING MAD ARE RECRUITED.
IN OTHER WORDS...
...THIS "SCHOOL" IS NOTHING MORE THAN ONE GIANT HUMAN EXPERIMENT.
DON'T TELL ME YOU ACTUALLY THOUGHT...
...THAT A "NORMAL, PEACEFUL SCHOOL" COULD REALLY EXIST IN THIS INSANE AGE.

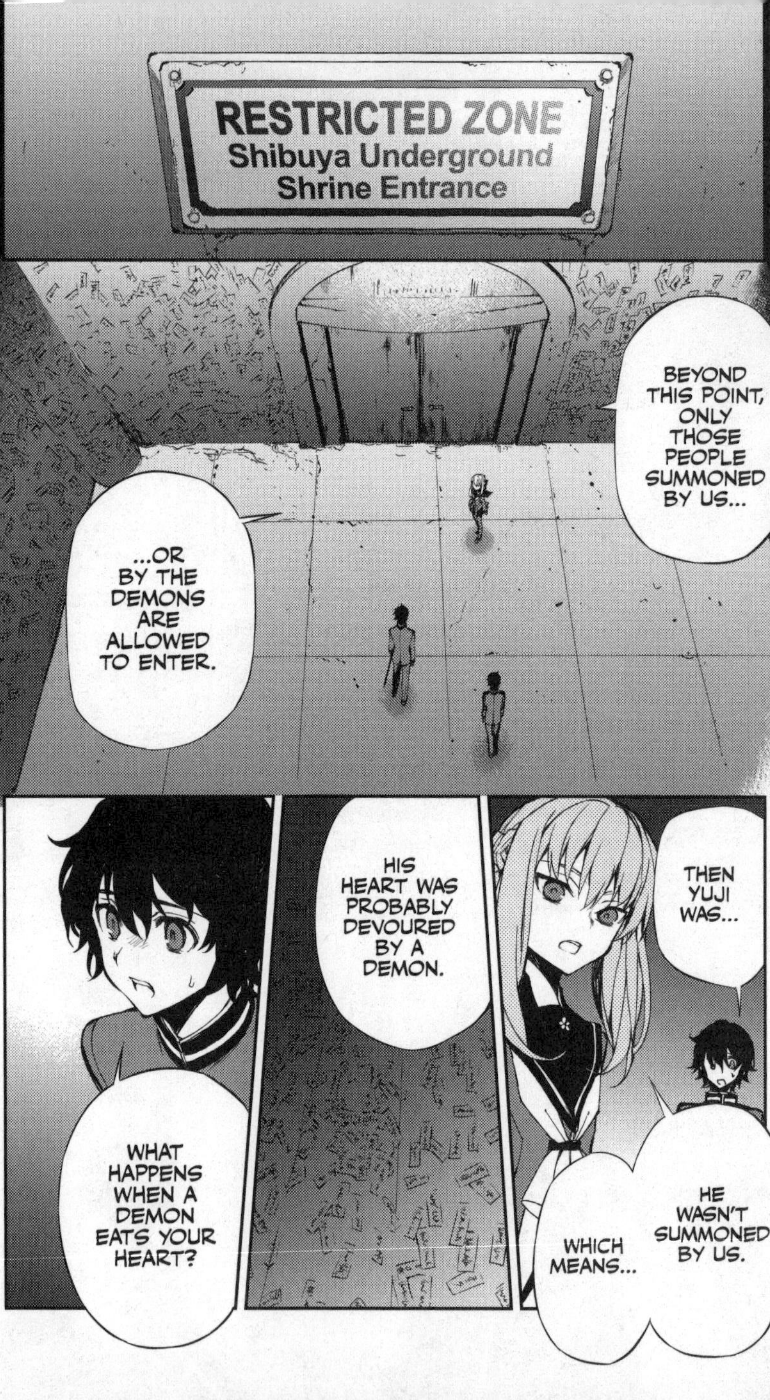
RESTRICTED ZONE
Shibuya Underground Shrine Entrance
BEYOND THIS POINT, ONLY THOSE PEOPLE SUMMONED BY US...
...OR BY THE DEMONS ARE ALLOWED TO ENTER.
THEN YUJI WAS...
HE WASN'T SUMMONED BY US.
WHICH MEANS...
HIS HEART WAS PROBABLY DEVOURED BY A DEMON.
WHAT HAPPENS WHEN A DEMON EATS YOUR HEART?

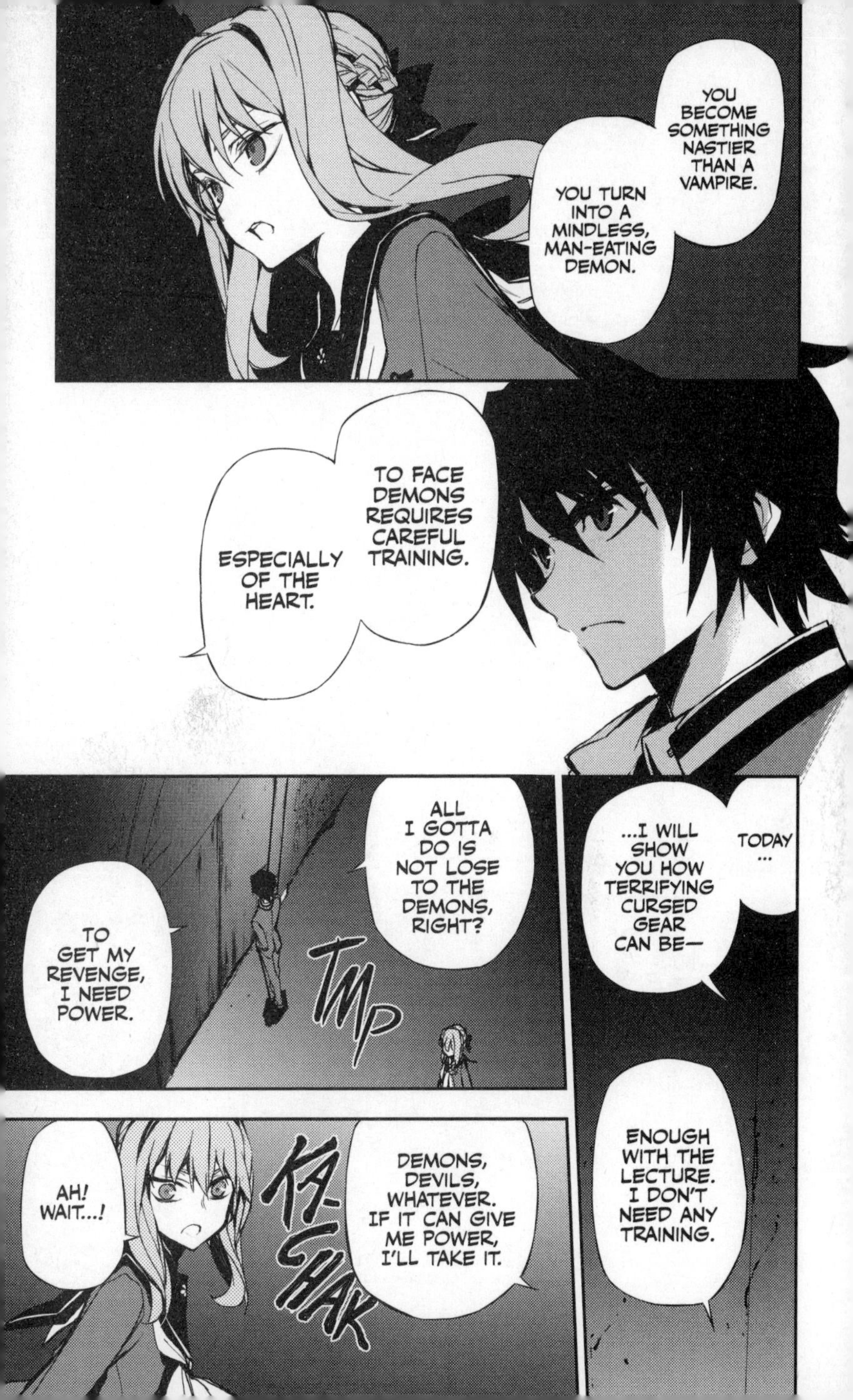
YOU BECOME SOMETHING NASTIER THAN A VAMPIRE.
YOU TURN INTO A MINDLESS, MAN-EATING DEMON.
TO FACE DEMONS REQUIRES CAREFUL TRAINING.
ESPECIALLY OF THE HEART.
TODAY...
...I WILL SHOW YOU HOW TERRIFYING CURSED GEAR CAN BE—
ENOUGH WITH THE LECTURE. I DON'T NEED ANY TRAINING.
ALL I GOTTA DO IS NOT LOSE TO THE DEMONS, RIGHT?
TMP
TO GET MY REVENGE, I NEED POWER.
DEMONS, DEVILS, WHATEVER. IF IT CAN GIVE ME POWER, I'LL TAKE IT.
KA-CHAK
AH! WAIT...!

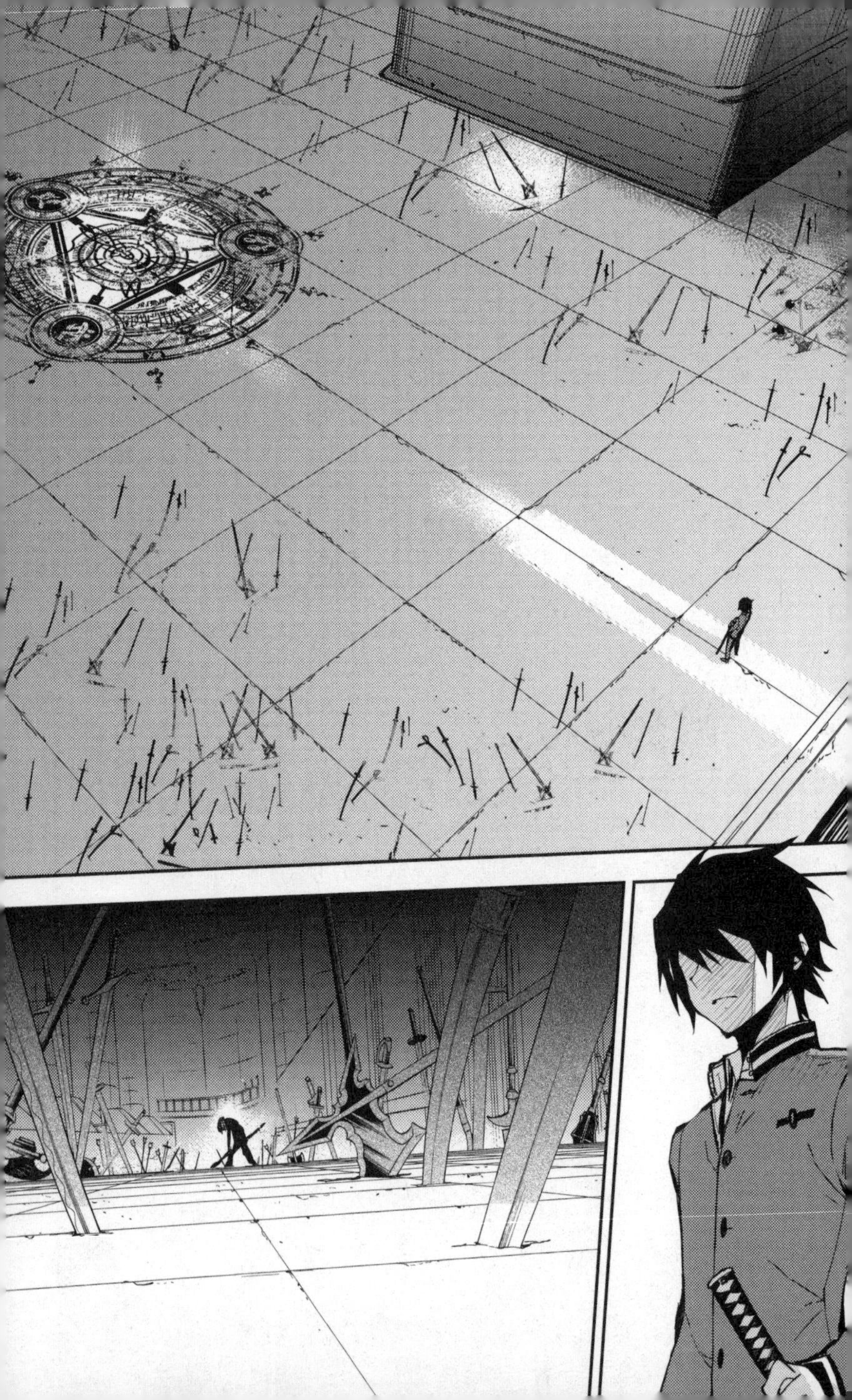

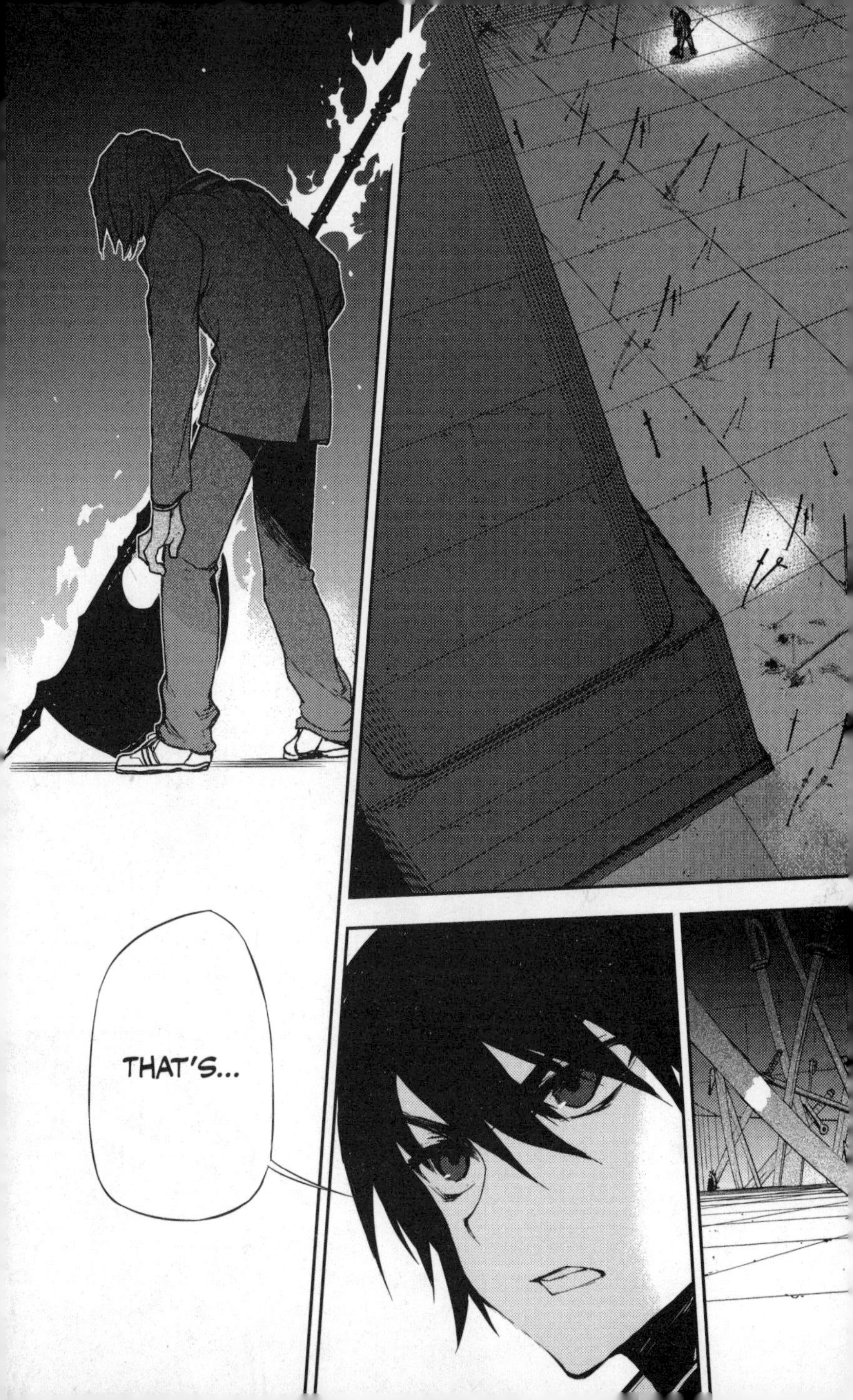
THAT'S...

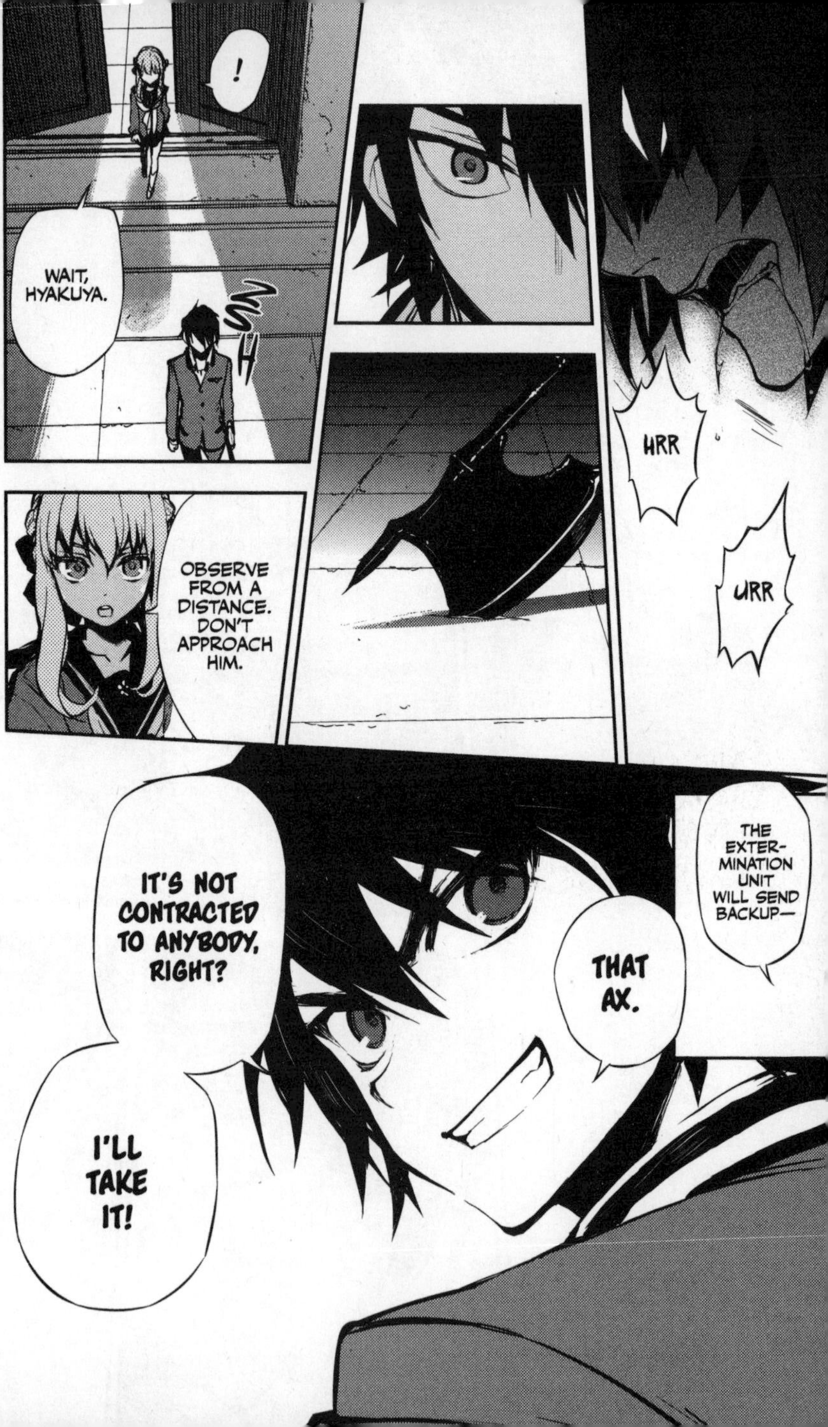
HRR
URR
!
WAIT, HYAKUYA.
SHH
OBSERVE FROM A DISTANCE. DON'T APPROACH HIM.
THE EXTER-MINATION UNIT WILL SEND BACKUP—
THAT AX.
IT'S NOT CONTRACTED TO ANYBODY, RIGHT?
I'LL TAKE IT!

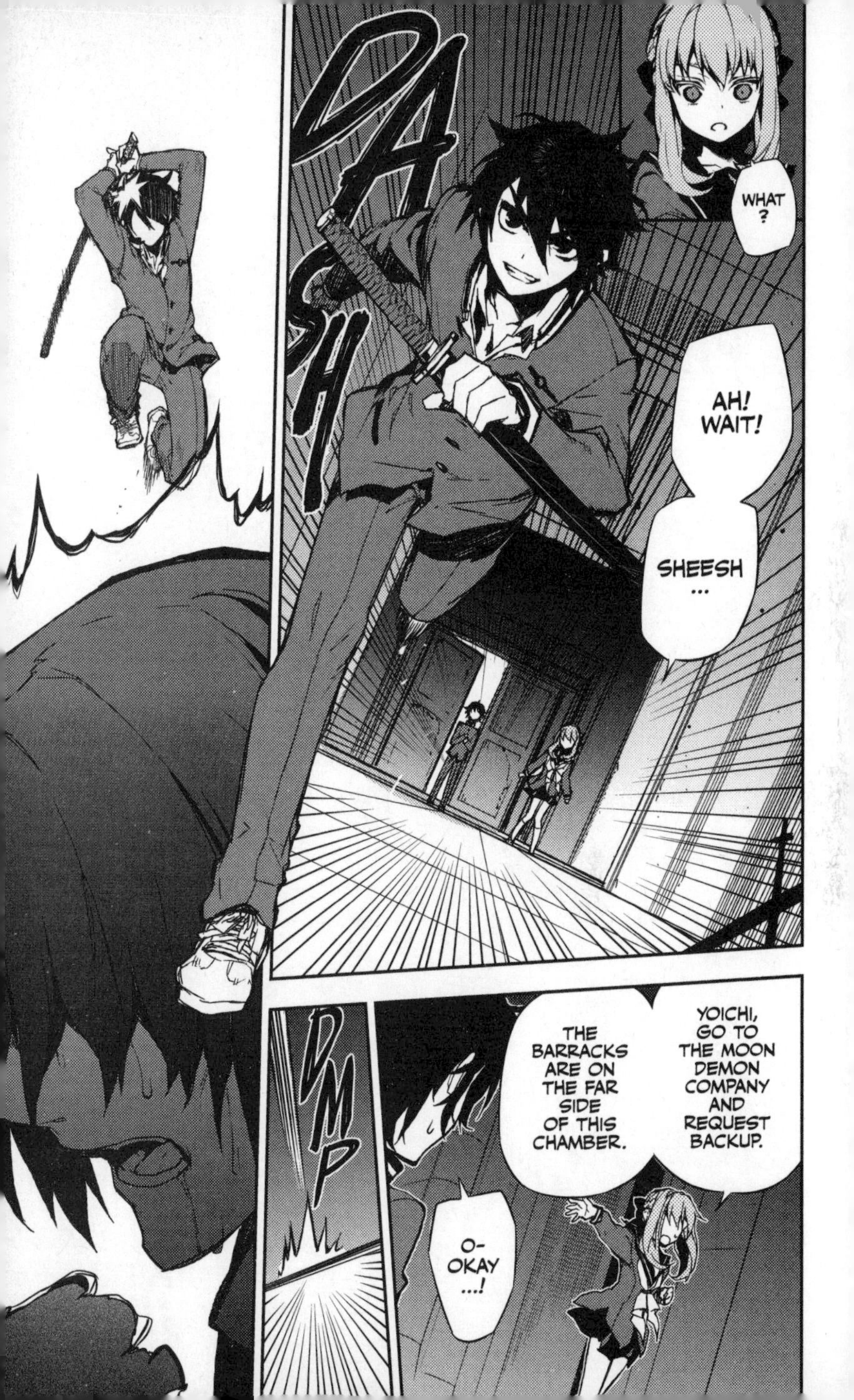
WHAT?
DASH
AH! WAIT!
SHEESH...
YOICHI, GO TO THE MOON DEMON COMPANY AND REQUEST BACKUP.
THE BARRACKS ARE ON THE FAR SIDE OF THIS CHAMBER.
O-OKAY...!
DMP

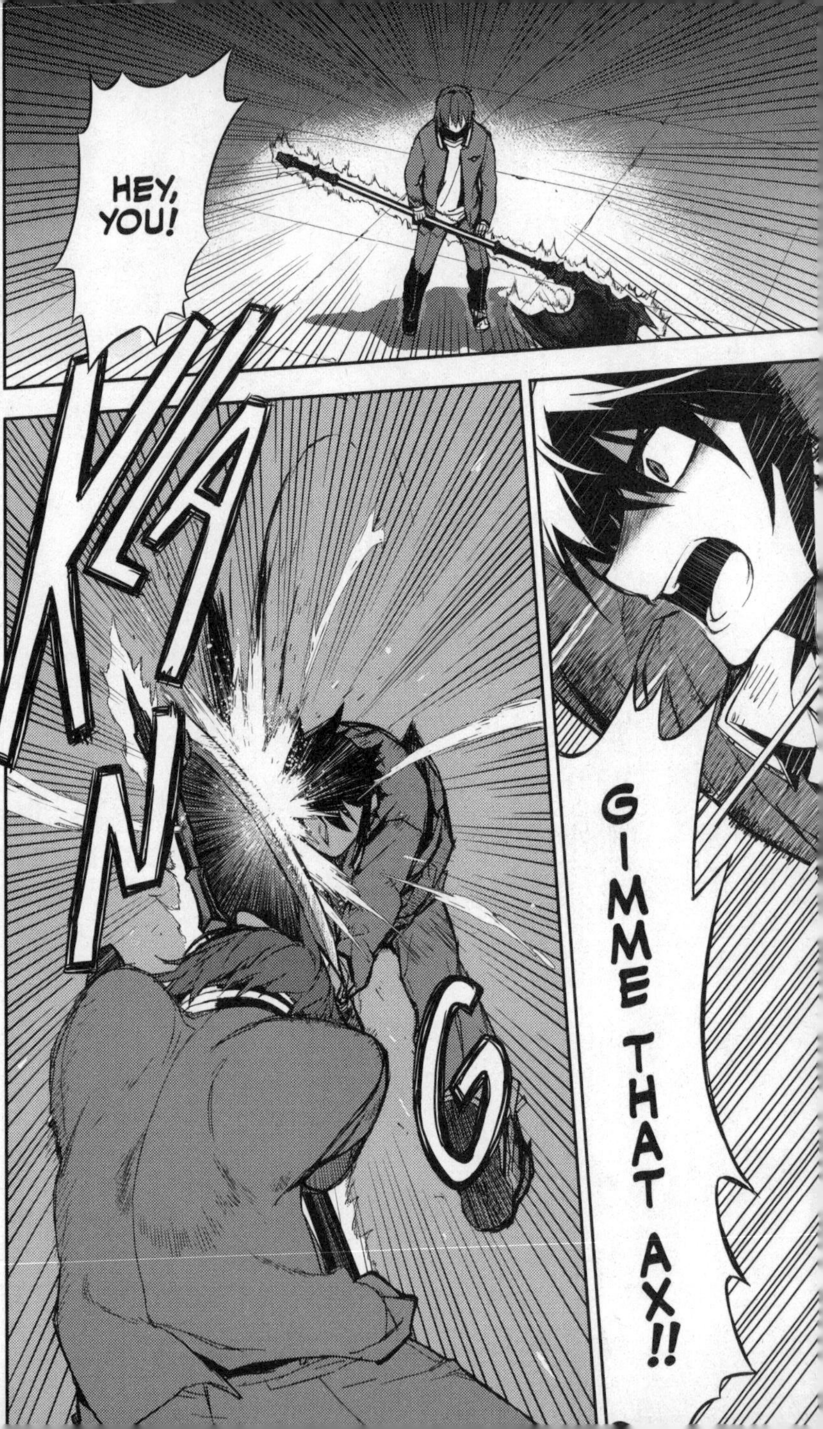
HEY, YOU!
GIMME THAT AX!!
KLANG

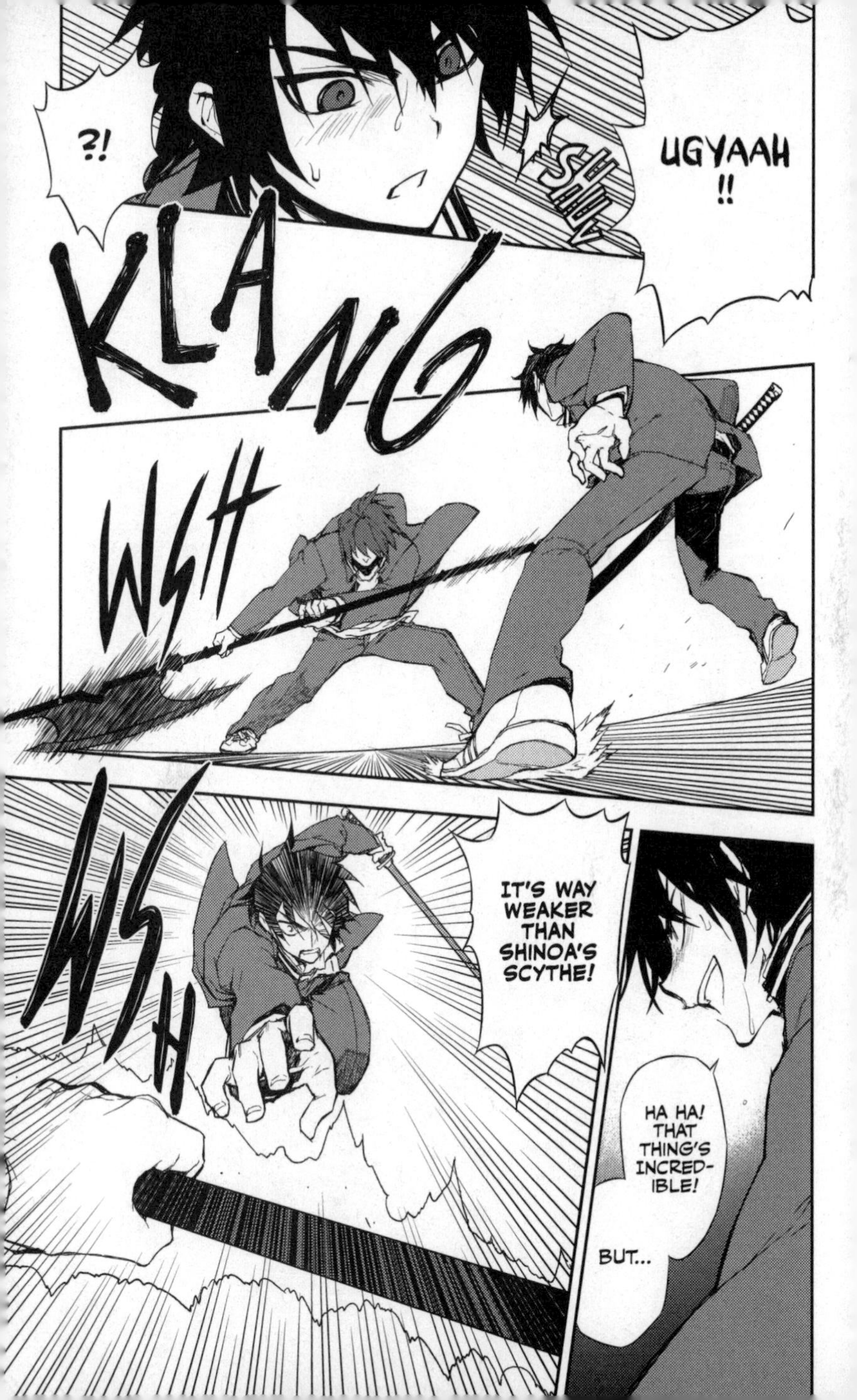
UGYAAH !!
SHUV
?!
KLANG
WSH
HA HA! THAT THING'S INCRED-IBLE!
BUT...
IT'S WAY WEAKER THAN SHINOA'S SCYTHE!
WSH

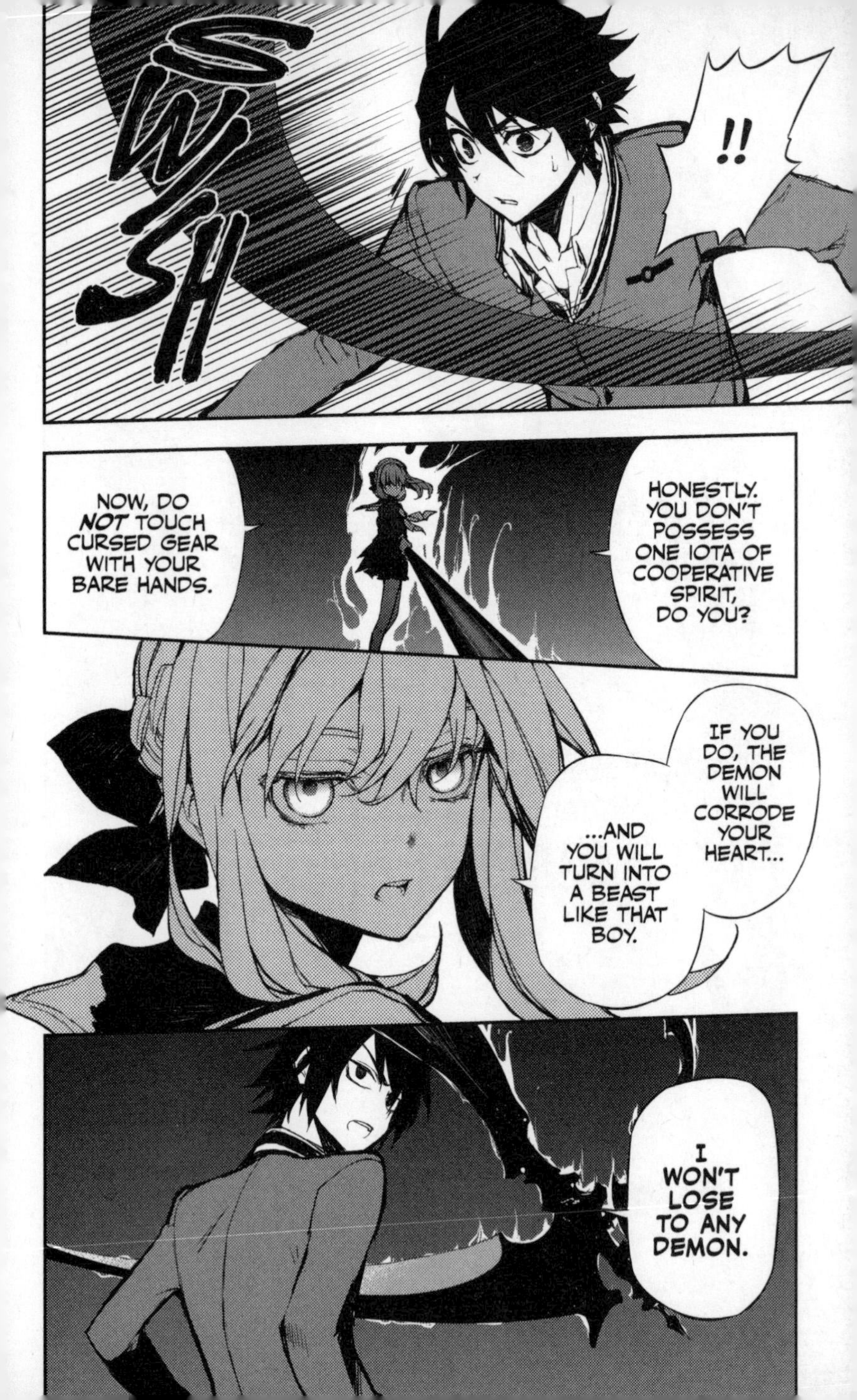
!!
SWISH
HONESTLY. YOU DON'T POSSESS ONE IOTA OF COOPERATIVE SPIRIT, DO YOU?
NOW, DO *NOT* TOUCH CURSED GEAR WITH YOUR BARE HANDS.
IF YOU DO, THE DEMON WILL CORRODE YOUR HEART...
...AND YOU WILL TURN INTO A BEAST LIKE THAT BOY.
I WON'T LOSE TO ANY DEMON.

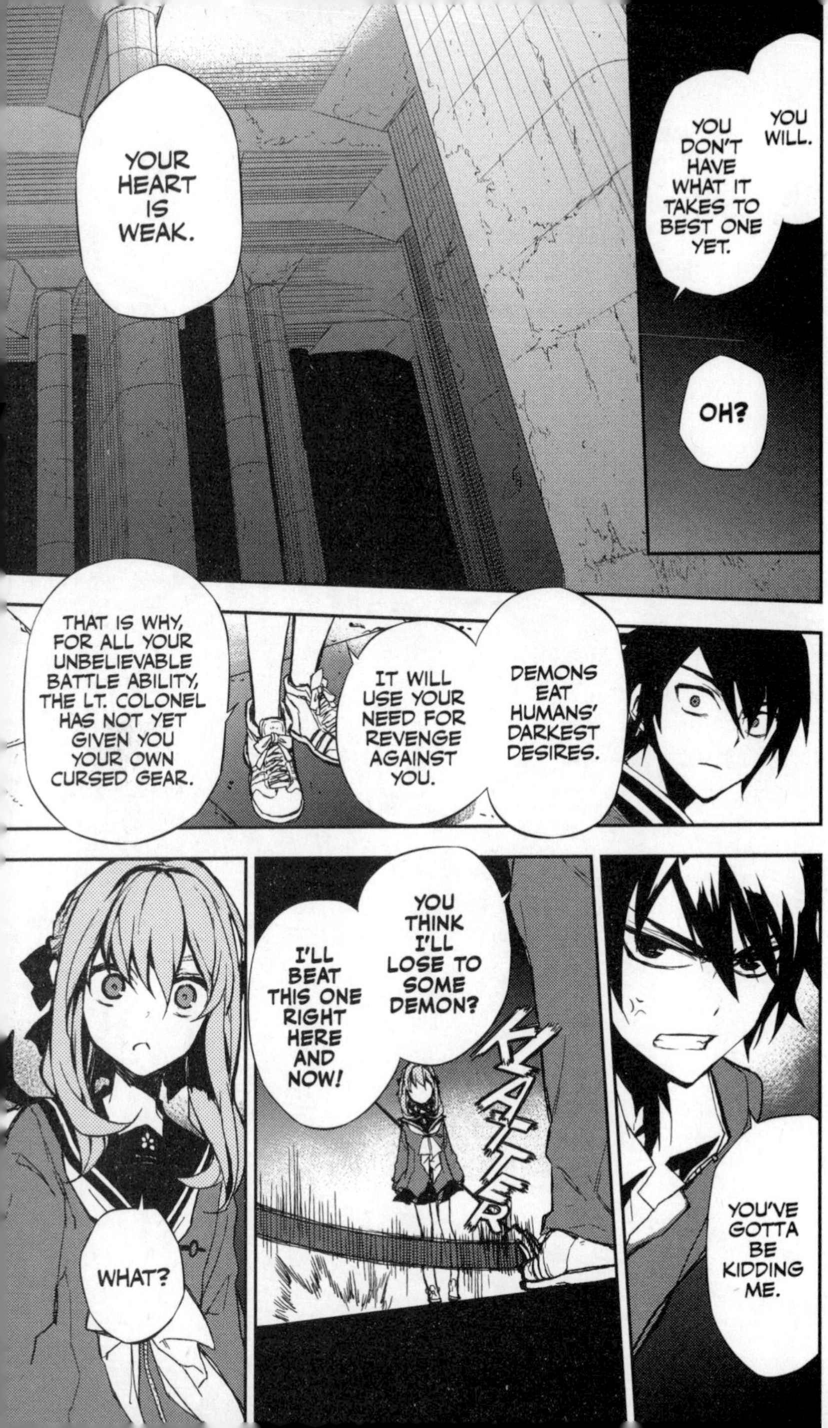
YOU WILL.
YOU DON'T HAVE WHAT IT TAKES TO BEST ONE YET.
OH?
YOUR HEART IS WEAK.
DEMONS EAT HUMANS' DARKEST DESIRES.
IT WILL USE YOUR NEED FOR REVENGE AGAINST YOU.
THAT IS WHY, FOR ALL YOUR UNBELIEVABLE BATTLE ABILITY, THE LT. COLONEL HAS NOT YET GIVEN YOU YOUR OWN CURSED GEAR.
YOU'VE GOTTA BE KIDDING ME.
YOU THINK I'LL LOSE TO SOME DEMON?
I'LL BEAT THIS ONE RIGHT HERE AND NOW!
KLATTER
WHAT?

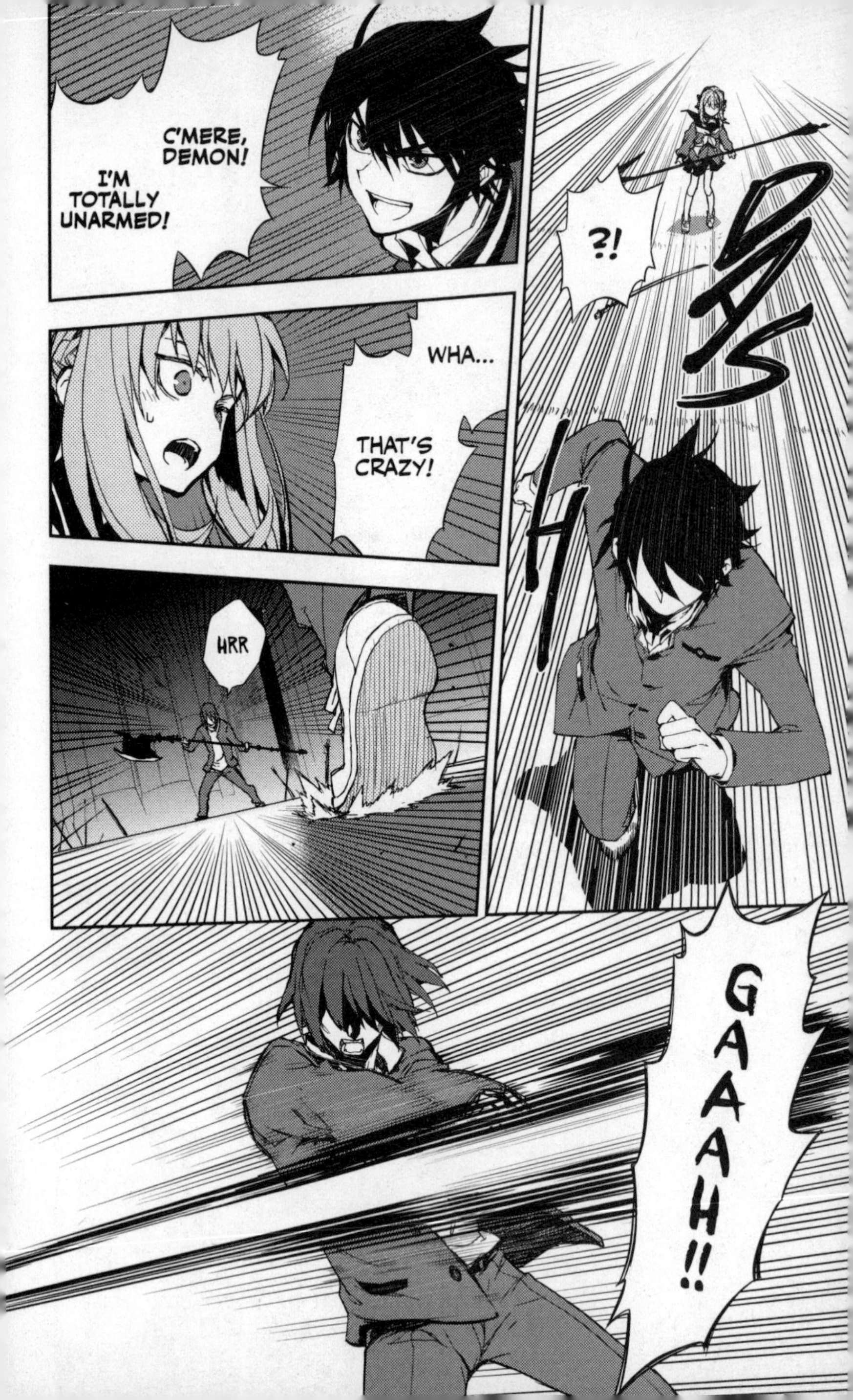
?!
DASH
C'MERE, DEMON!
I'M TOTALLY UNARMED!
WHA...
THAT'S CRAZY!
HRR
GAAAH!!

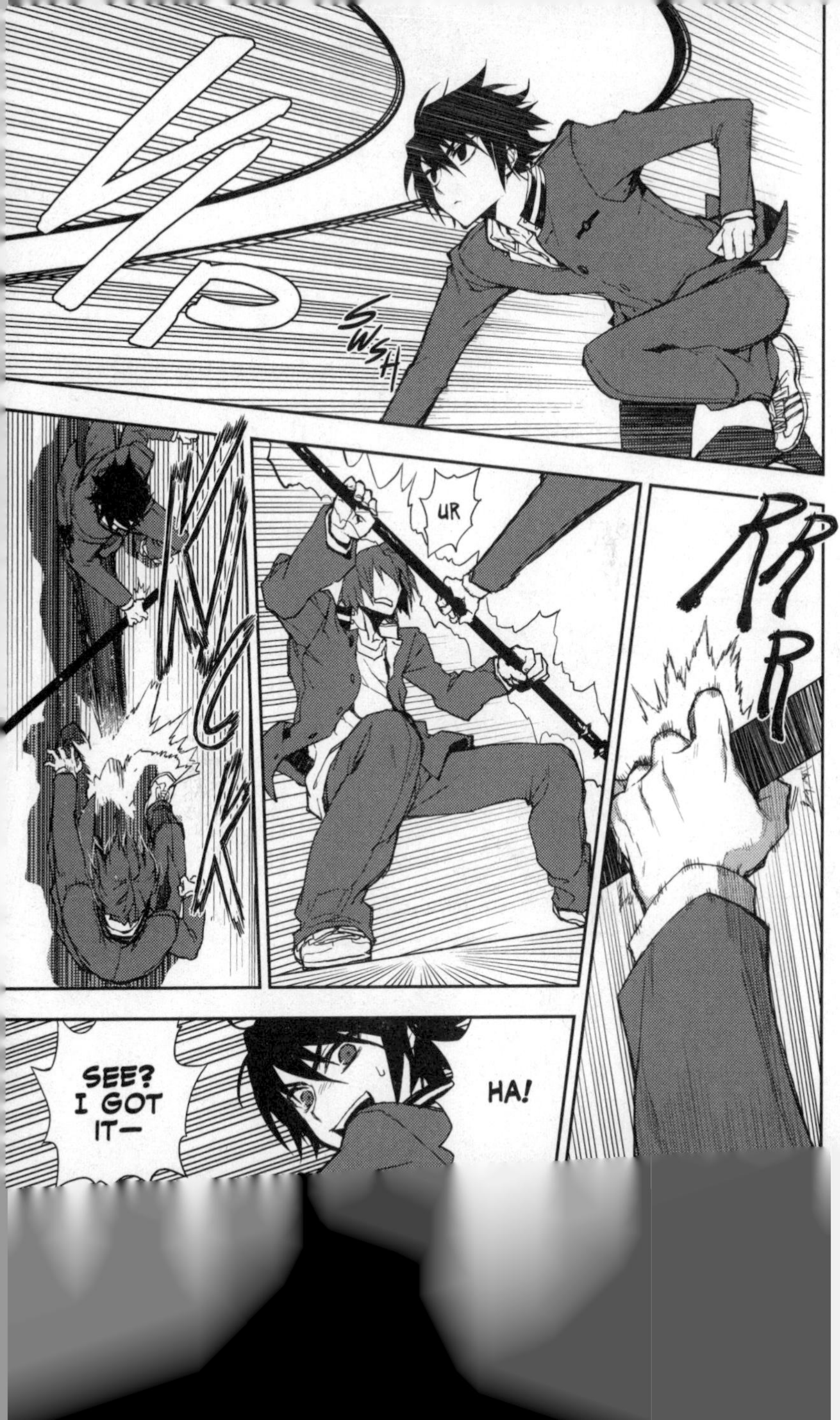
SWSH
RRR
UR
HA!
SEE? I GOT IT—

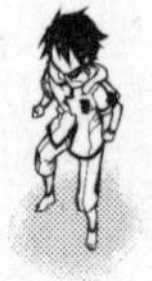

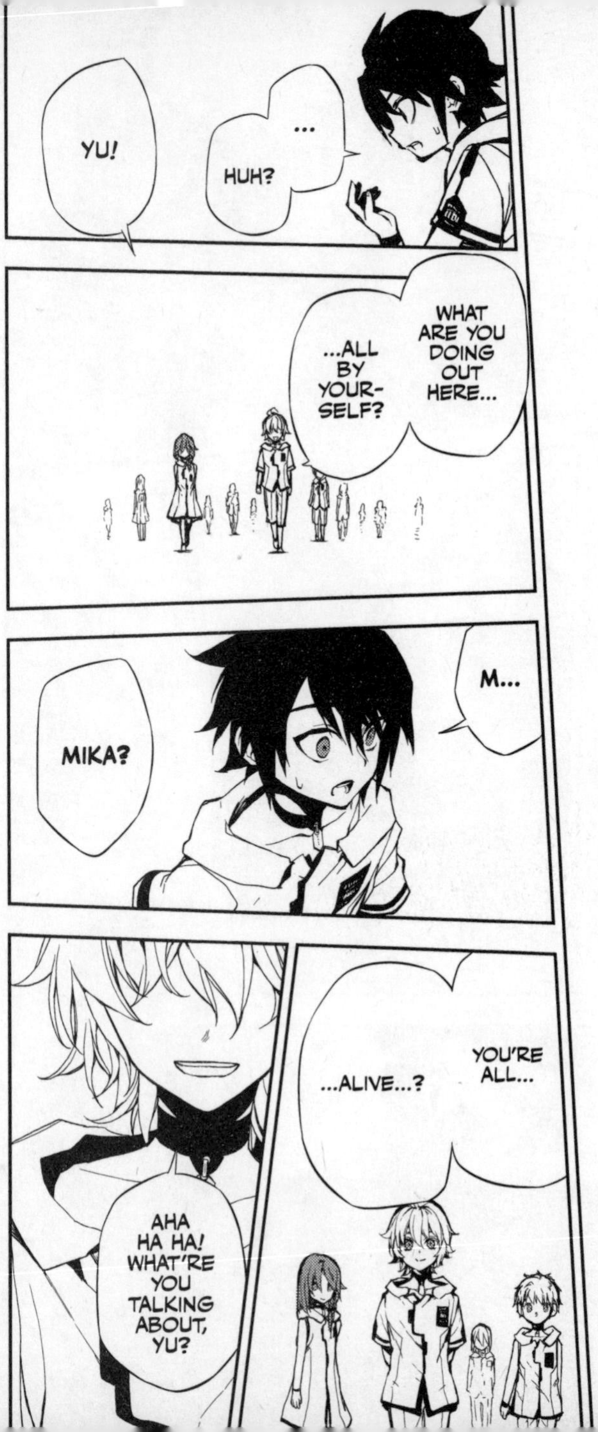
...
HUH?
YU!
WHAT ARE YOU DOING OUT HERE...
...ALL BY YOURSELF?
M...
MIKA?
YOU'RE ALL...
...ALIVE...?
AHA HA HA! WHAT'RE YOU TALKING ABOUT, YU?

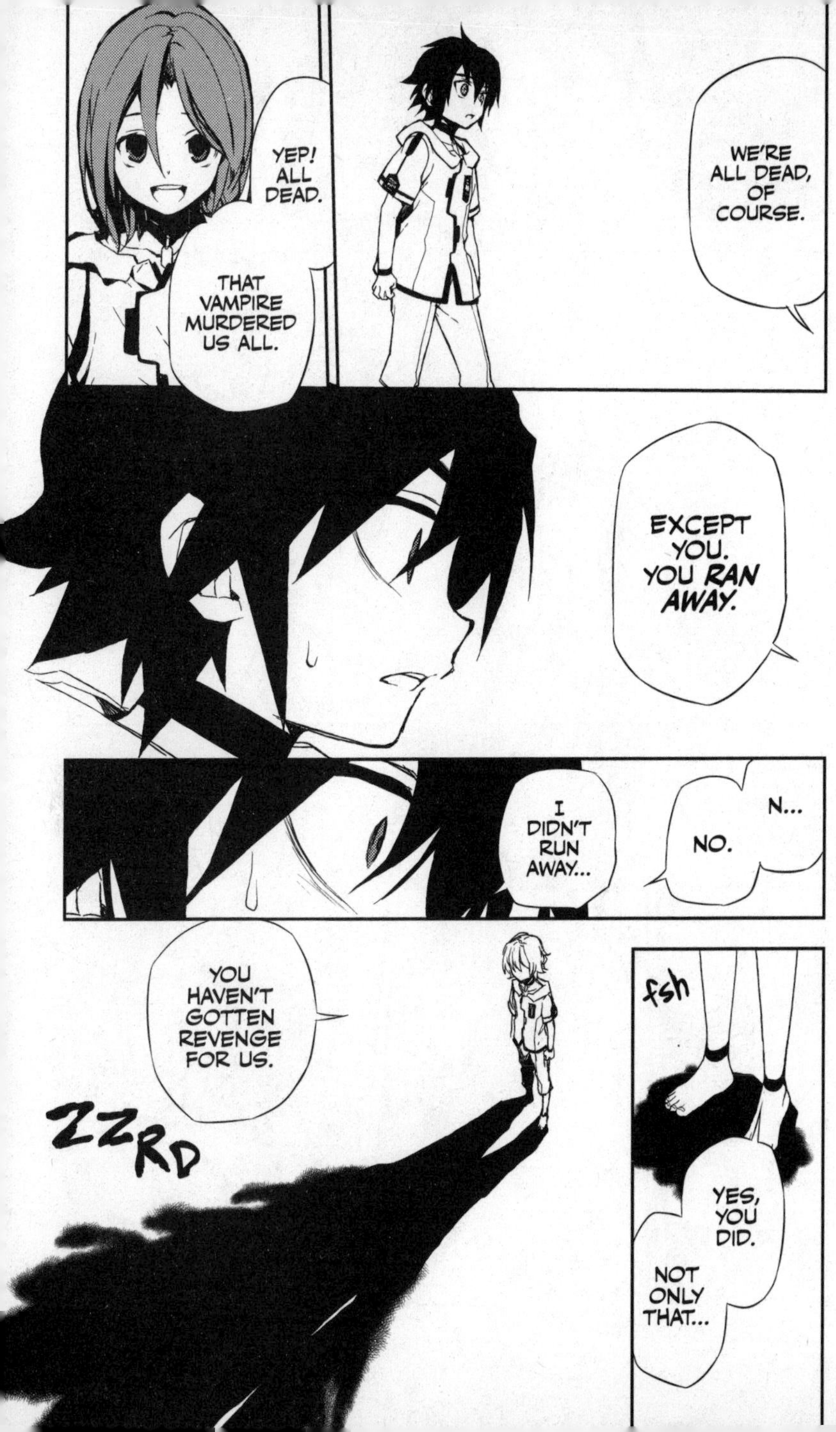
WE'RE ALL DEAD, OF COURSE.
YEP! ALL DEAD.
THAT VAMPIRE MURDERED US ALL.
EXCEPT YOU. YOU *RAN AWAY.*
N...
NO.
I DIDN'T RUN AWAY...
fsh
YES, YOU DID.
NOT ONLY THAT...
YOU HAVEN'T GOTTEN REVENGE FOR US.
ZZRD

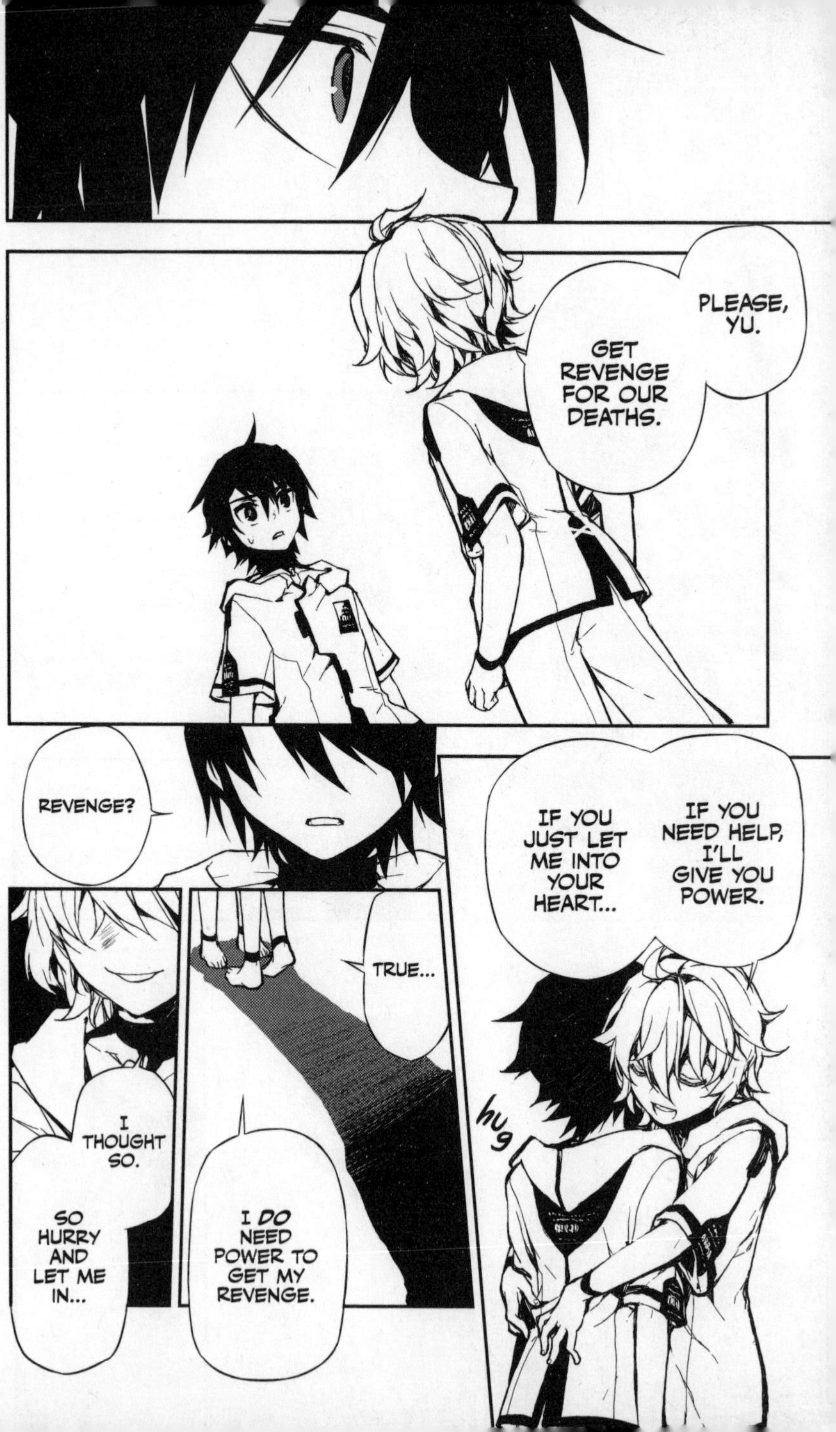
PLEASE, YU.
GET REVENGE FOR OUR DEATHS.
IF YOU NEED HELP, I'LL GIVE YOU POWER.
IF YOU JUST LET ME INTO YOUR HEART...
hug
REVENGE?
TRUE...
I *DO* NEED POWER TO GET MY REVENGE.
I THOUGHT SO.
SO HURRY AND LET ME IN...

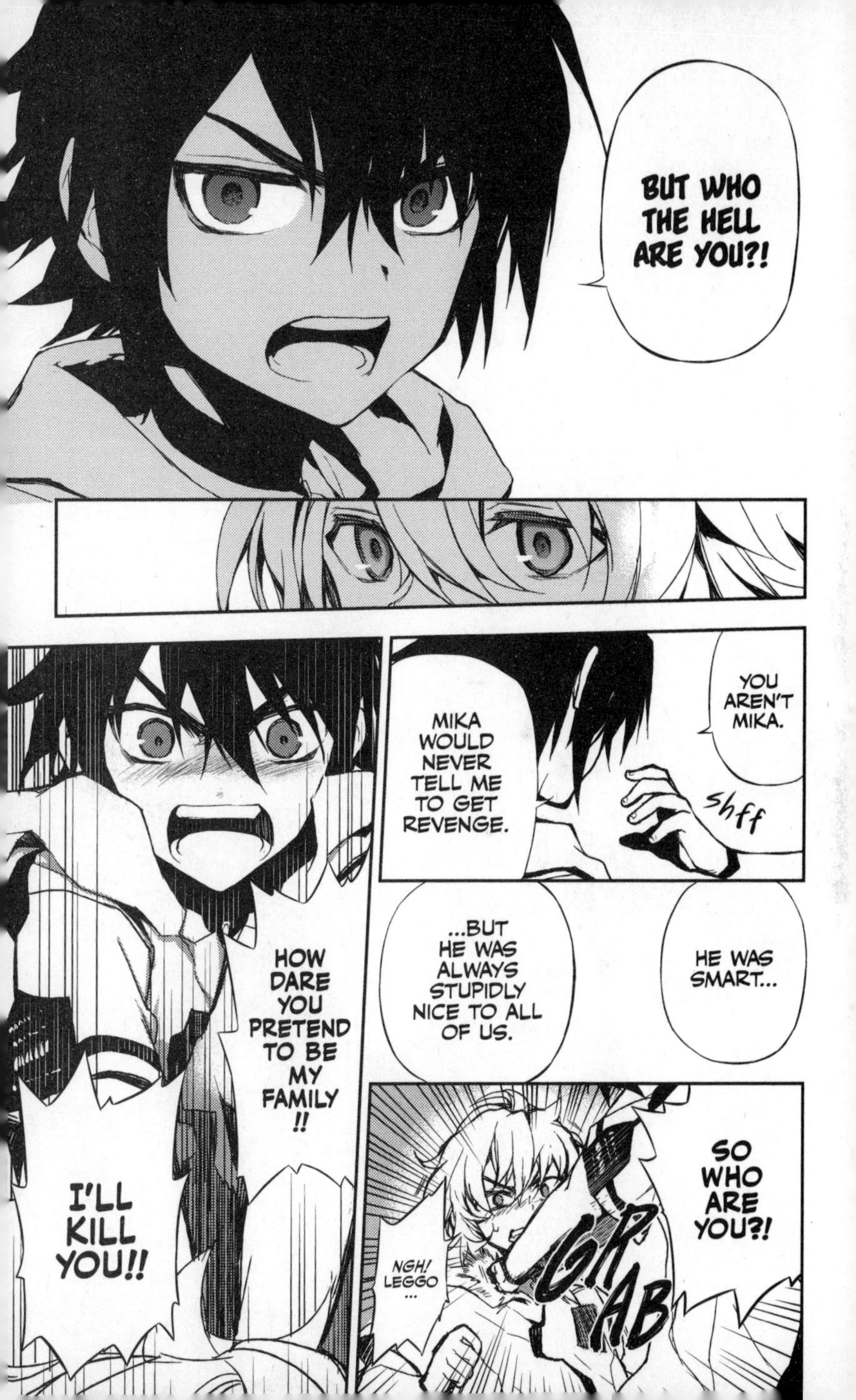
BUT WHO THE HELL ARE YOU?!
YOU AREN'T MIKA.
MIKA WOULD NEVER TELL ME TO GET REVENGE.
shff
HE WAS SMART...
...BUT HE WAS ALWAYS STUPIDLY NICE TO ALL OF US.
SO WHO ARE YOU?!
GRAB
NGH! LEGGO...
HOW DARE YOU PRETEND TO BE MY FAMILY!!
I'LL KILL YOU!!

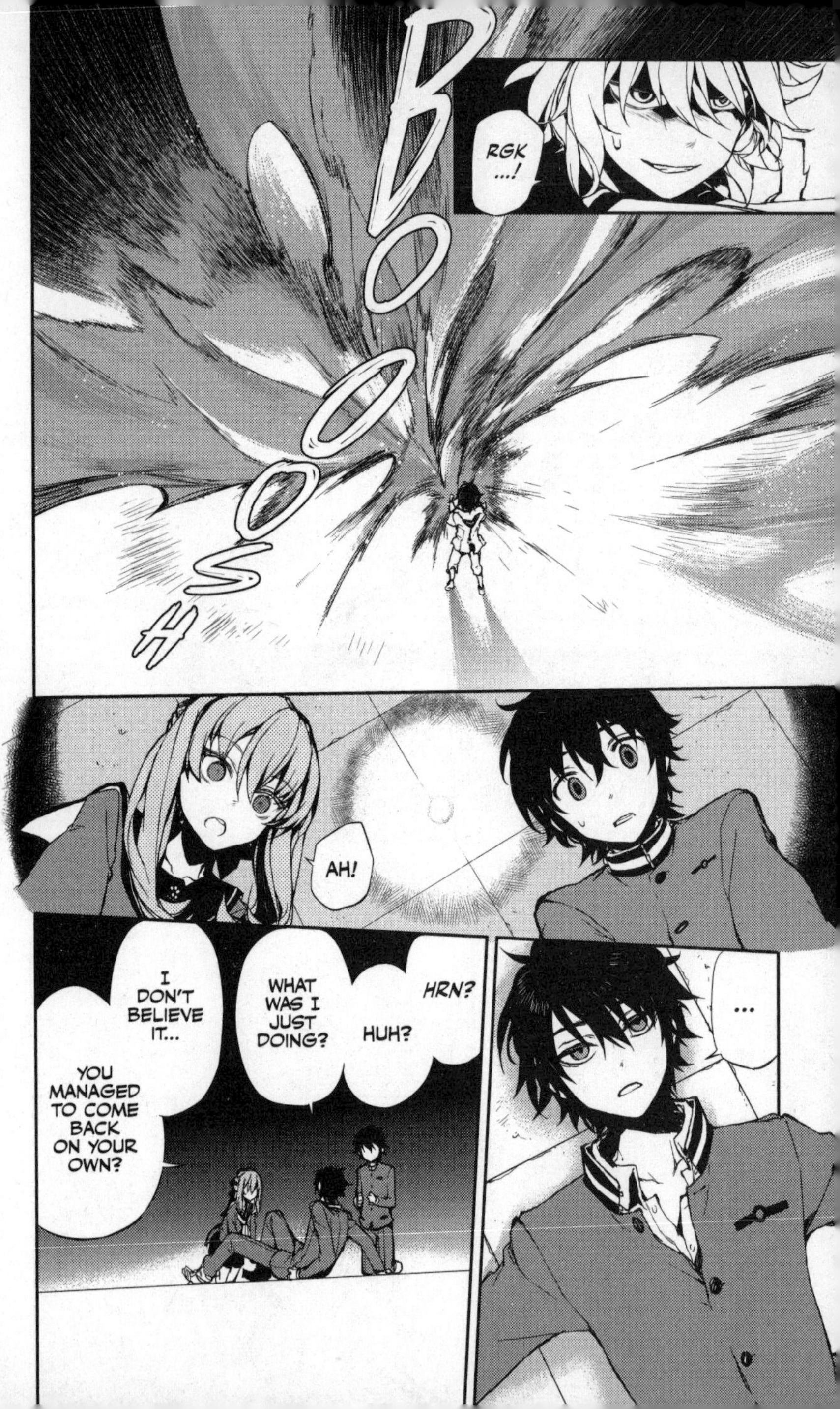
RGK ...!
BOOOSH
AH!
...
HRN?
HUH?
WHAT WAS I JUST DOING?
I DON'T BELIEVE IT...
YOU MANAGED TO COME BACK ON YOUR OWN?

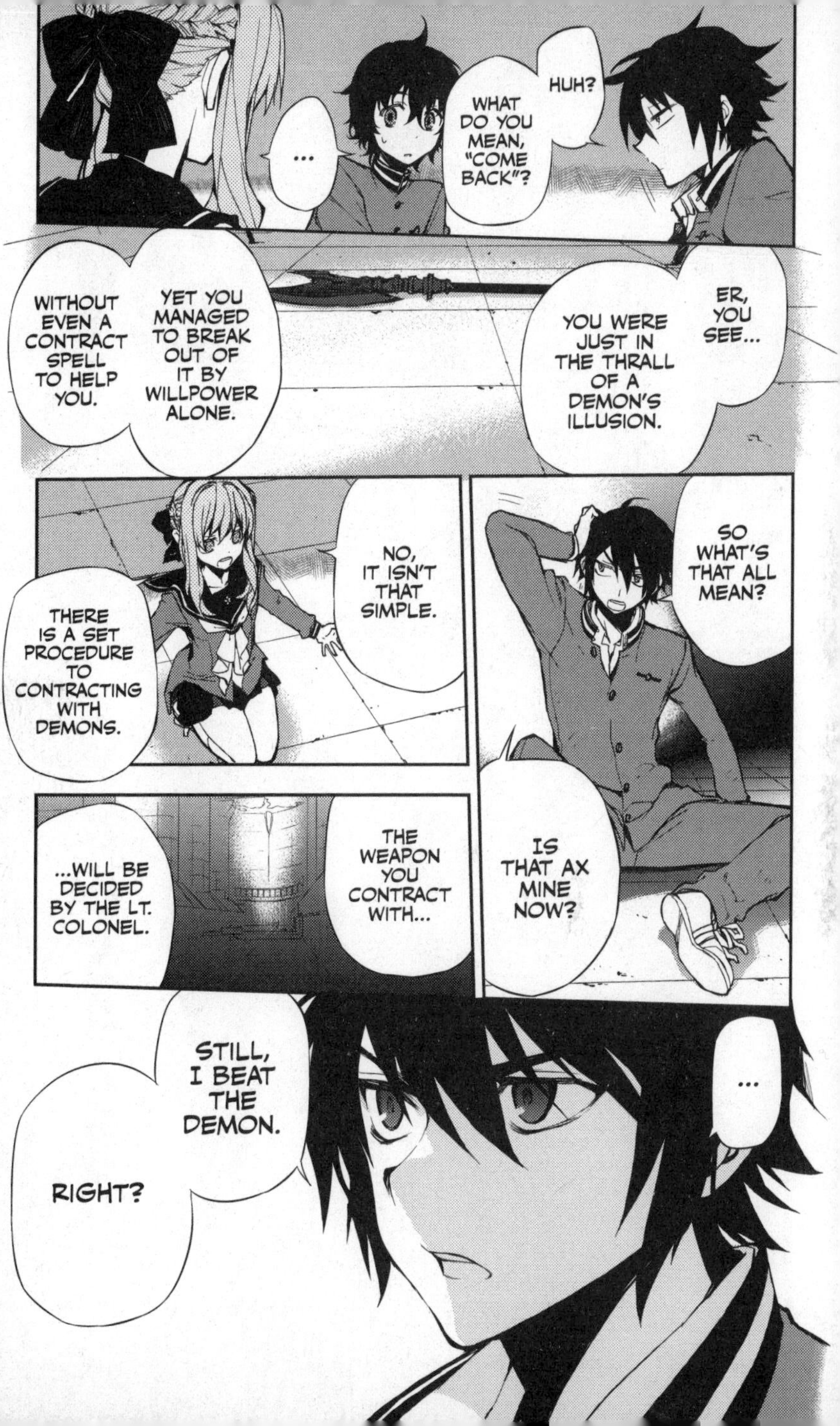
HUH?
WHAT DO YOU MEAN, "COME BACK"?
...
ER, YOU SEE...
YOU WERE JUST IN THE THRALL OF A DEMON'S ILLUSION.
YET YOU MANAGED TO BREAK OUT OF IT BY WILLPOWER ALONE.
WITHOUT EVEN A CONTRACT SPELL TO HELP YOU.
SO WHAT'S THAT ALL MEAN?
IS THAT AX MINE NOW?
NO, IT ISN'T THAT SIMPLE.
THERE IS A SET PROCEDURE TO CONTRACTING WITH DEMONS.
THE WEAPON YOU CONTRACT WITH...
...WILL BE DECIDED BY THE LT. COLONEL.
...
STILL, I BEAT THE DEMON.
RIGHT?

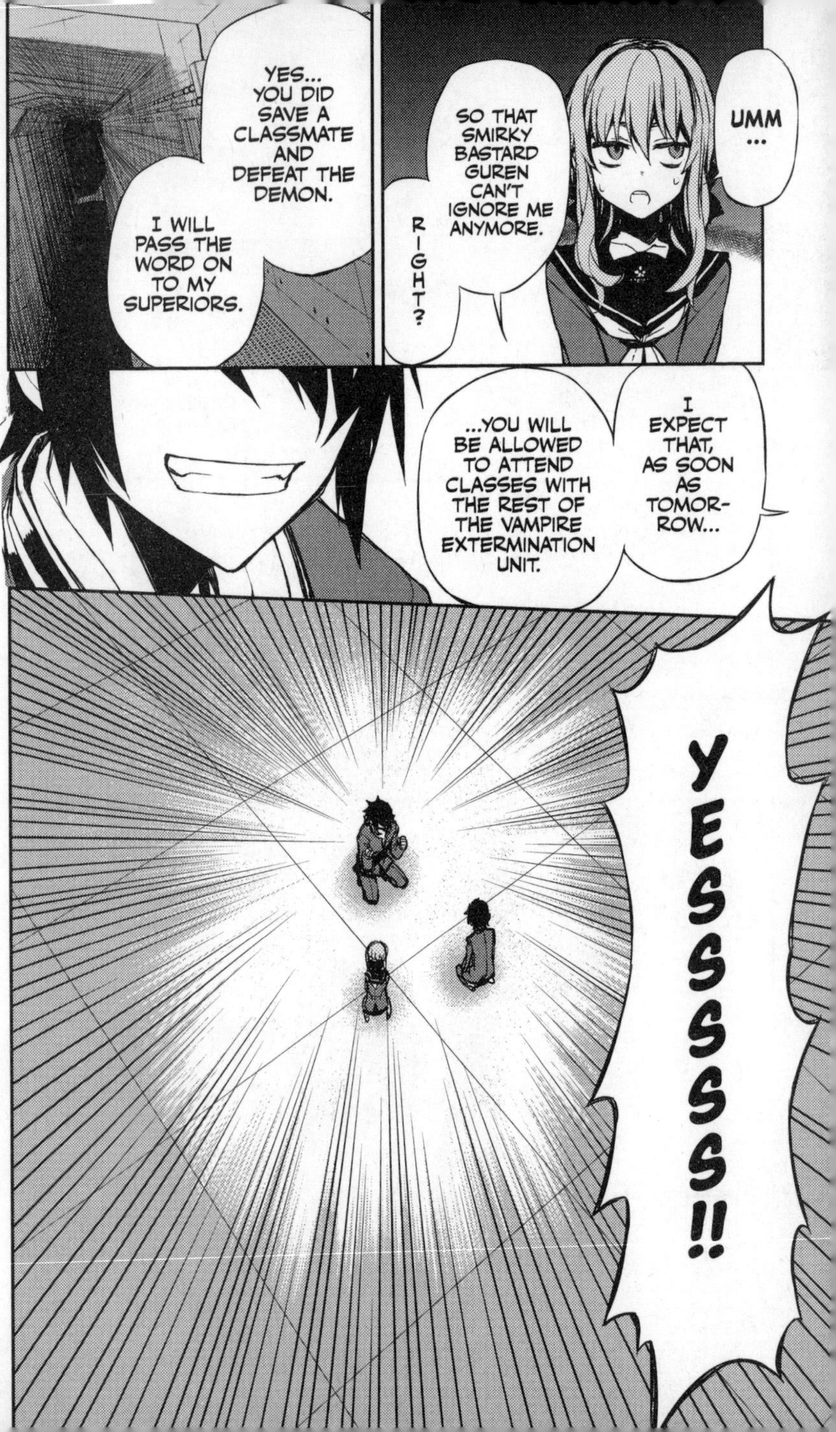
UMM...
SO THAT SMIRKY BASTARD GUREN CAN'T IGNORE ME ANYMORE.
RIGHT?
YES... YOU DID SAVE A CLASSMATE AND DEFEAT THE DEMON.
I WILL PASS THE WORD ON TO MY SUPERIORS.
I EXPECT THAT, AS SOON AS TOMOR-ROW...
...YOU WILL BE ALLOWED TO ATTEND CLASSES WITH THE REST OF THE VAMPIRE EXTERMINATION UNIT.
YESSSSSS!!

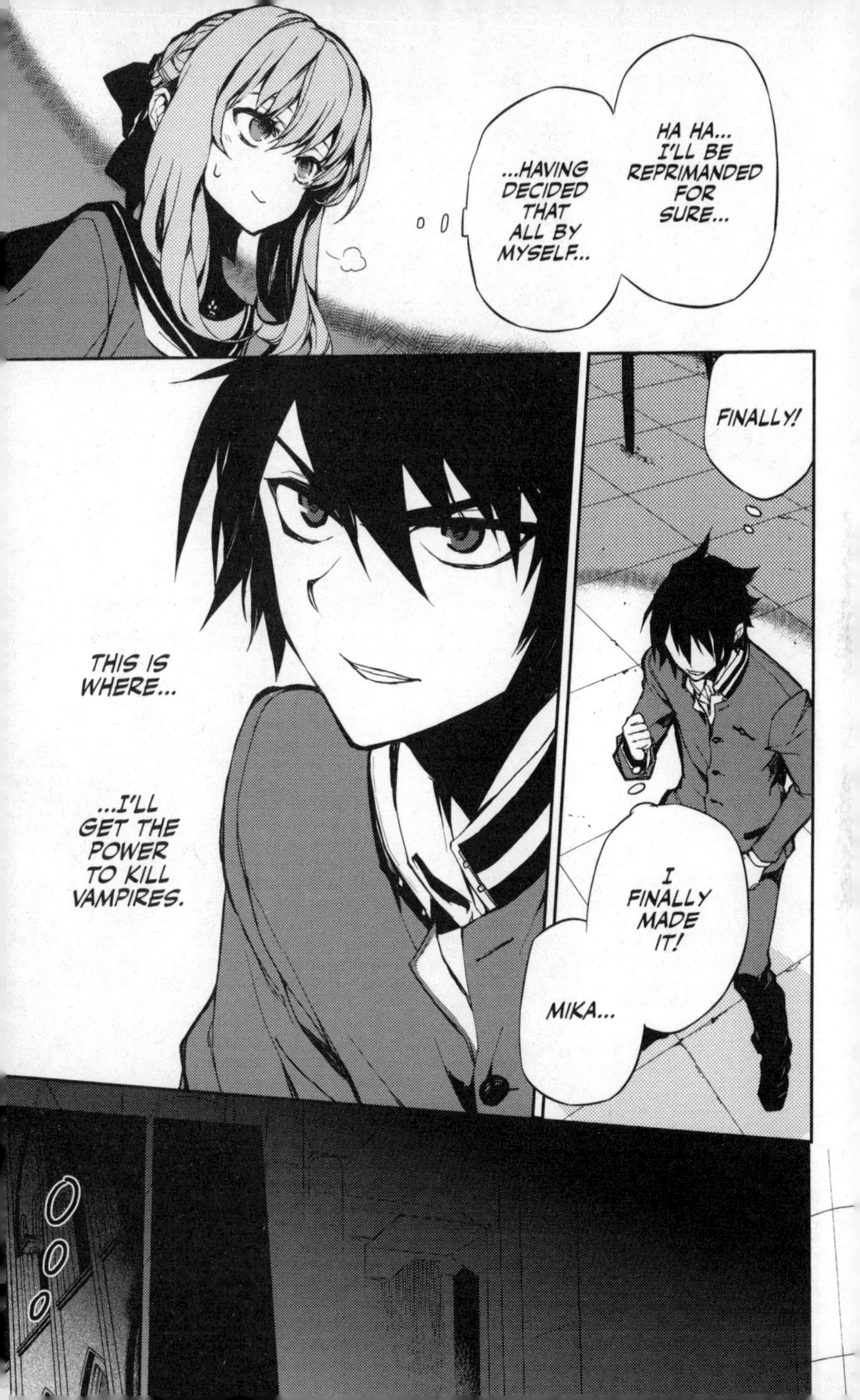
HA HA... I'LL BE REPRIMANDED FOR SURE...
...HAVING DECIDED THAT ALL BY MYSELF...
FINALLY!
I FINALLY MADE IT!
MIKA...
THIS IS WHERE...
...I'LL GET THE POWER TO KILL VAMPIRES.

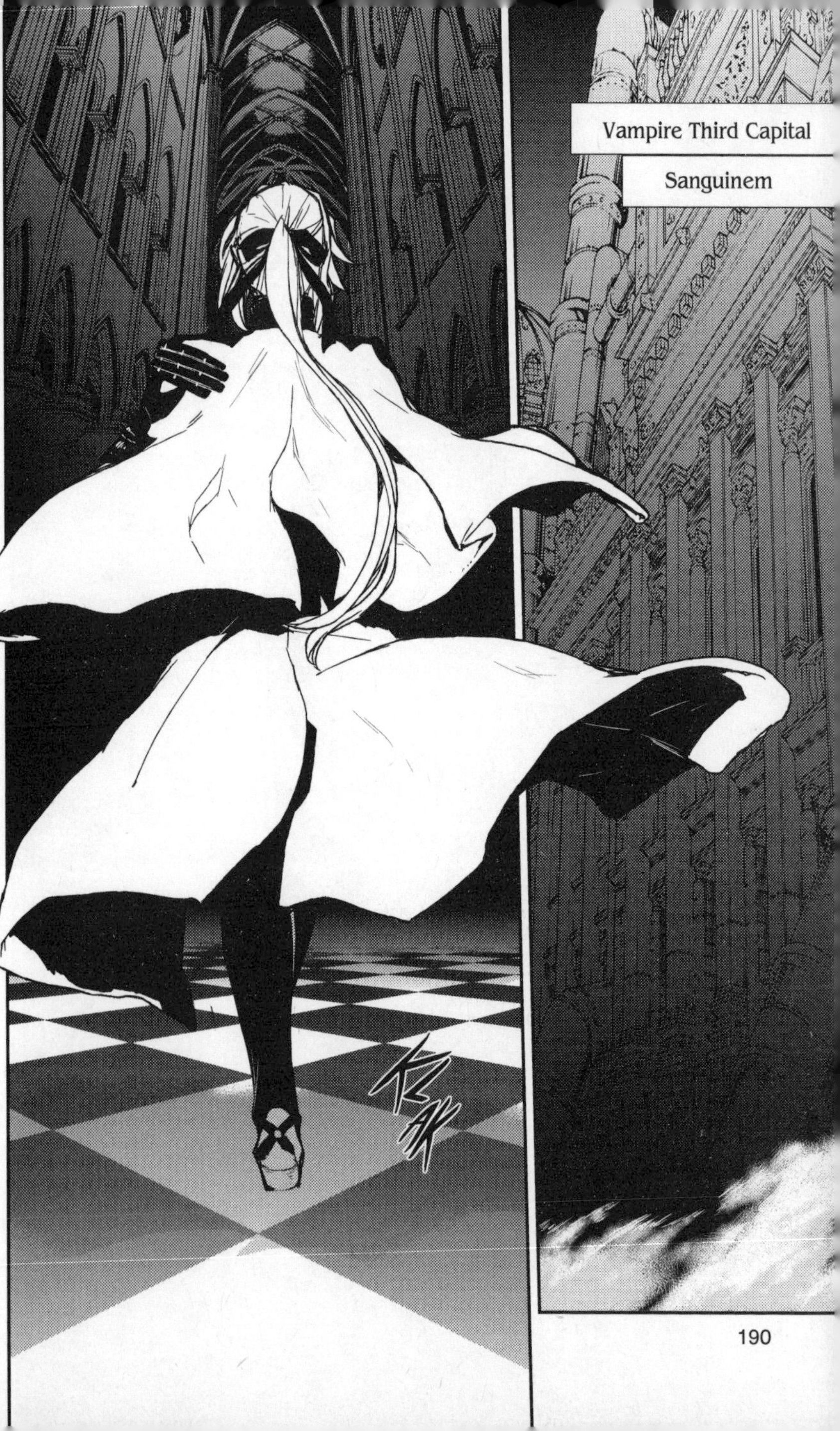
Vampire Third Capital
Sanguinem
KLAK

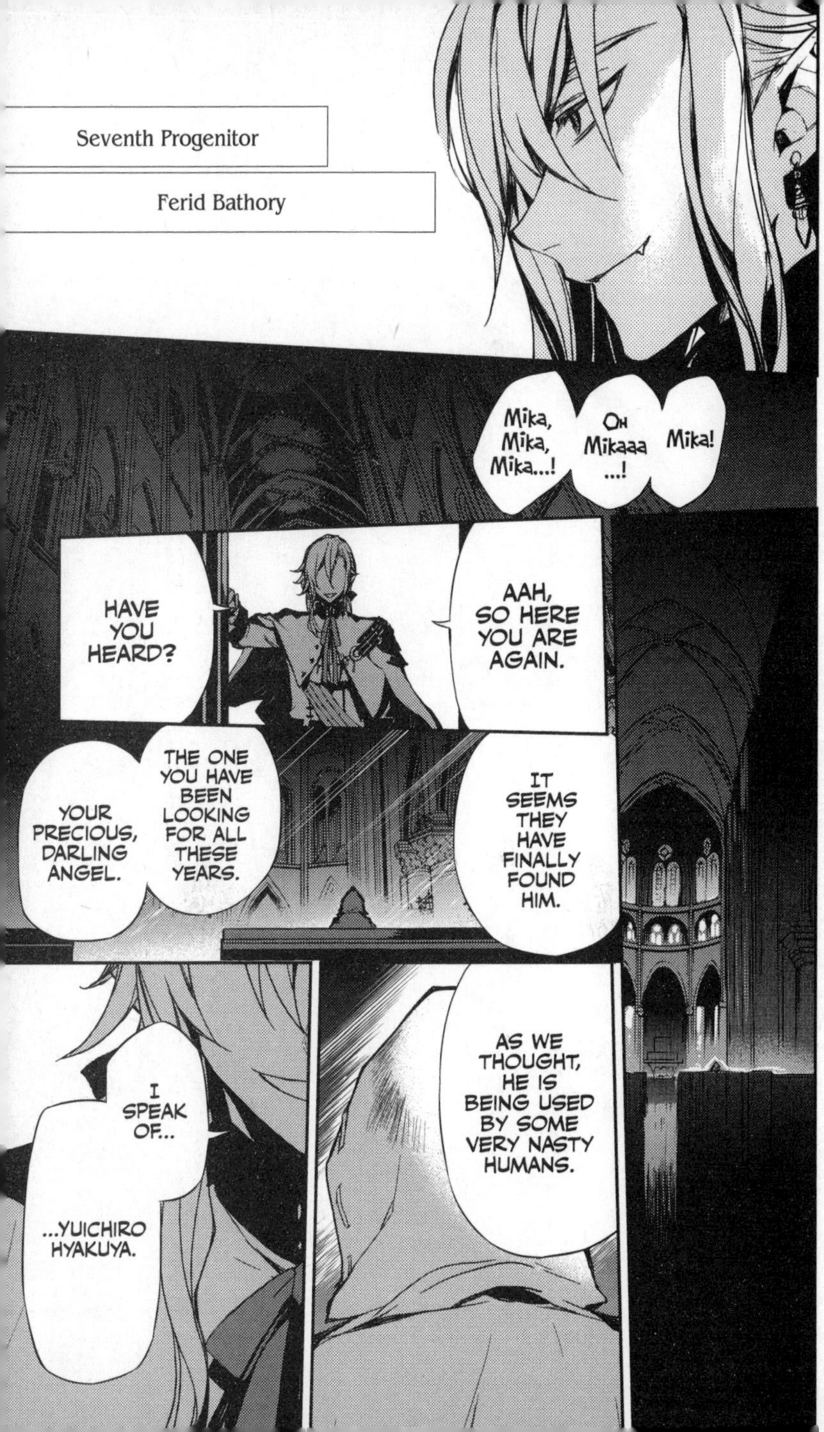
Seventh Progenitor
Ferid Bathory
Mika!
Oh Mikaaa ...!
Mika, Mika, Mika...!
AAH, SO HERE YOU ARE AGAIN.
HAVE YOU HEARD?
IT SEEMS THEY HAVE FINALLY FOUND HIM.
THE ONE YOU HAVE BEEN LOOKING FOR ALL THESE YEARS.
YOUR PRECIOUS, DARLING ANGEL.
AS WE THOUGHT, HE IS BEING USED BY SOME VERY NASTY HUMANS.
I SPEAK OF...
...YUICHIRO HYAKUYA.

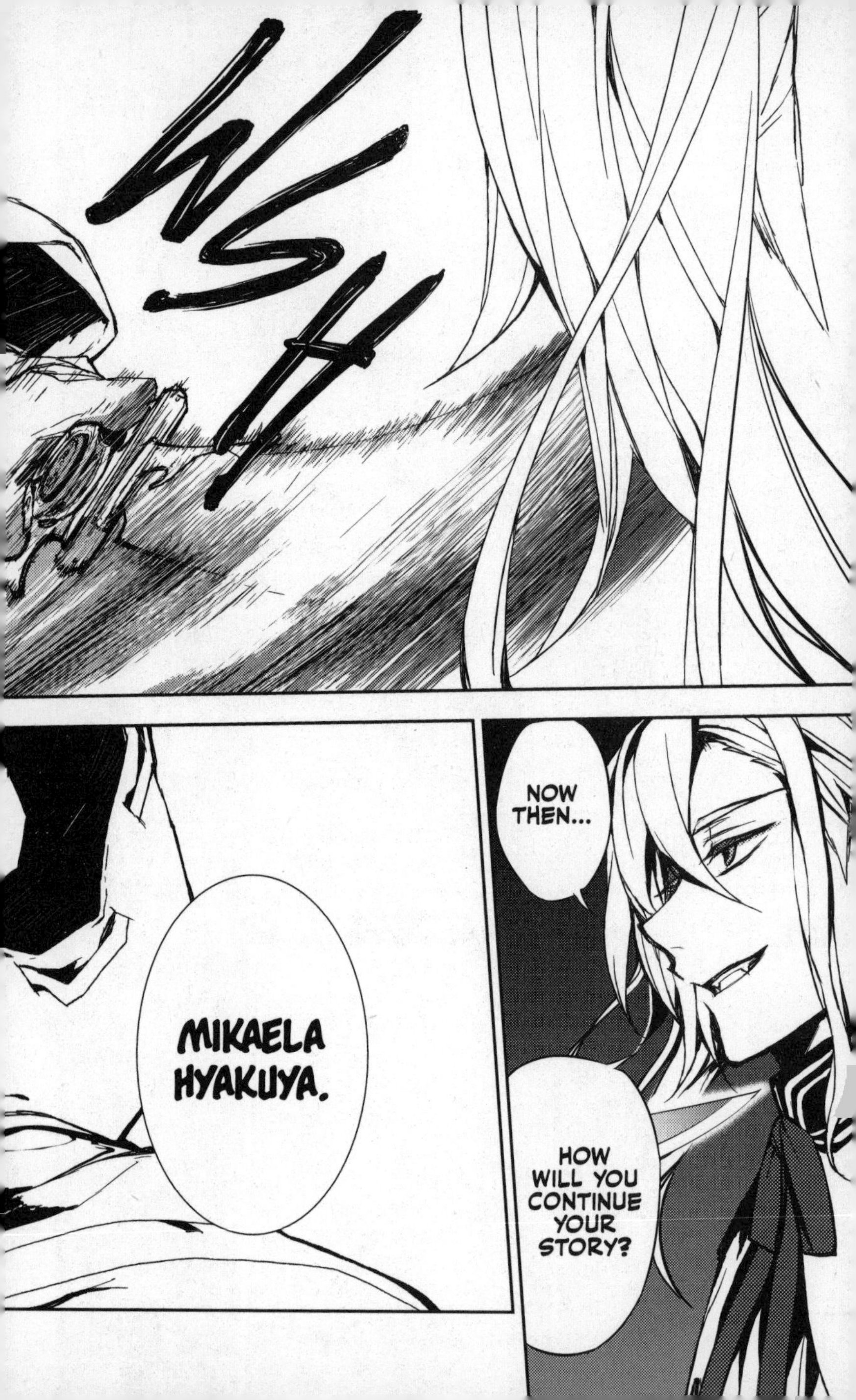
WSH
NOW THEN...
HOW WILL YOU CONTINUE YOUR STORY?
MIKAELA HYAKUYA.

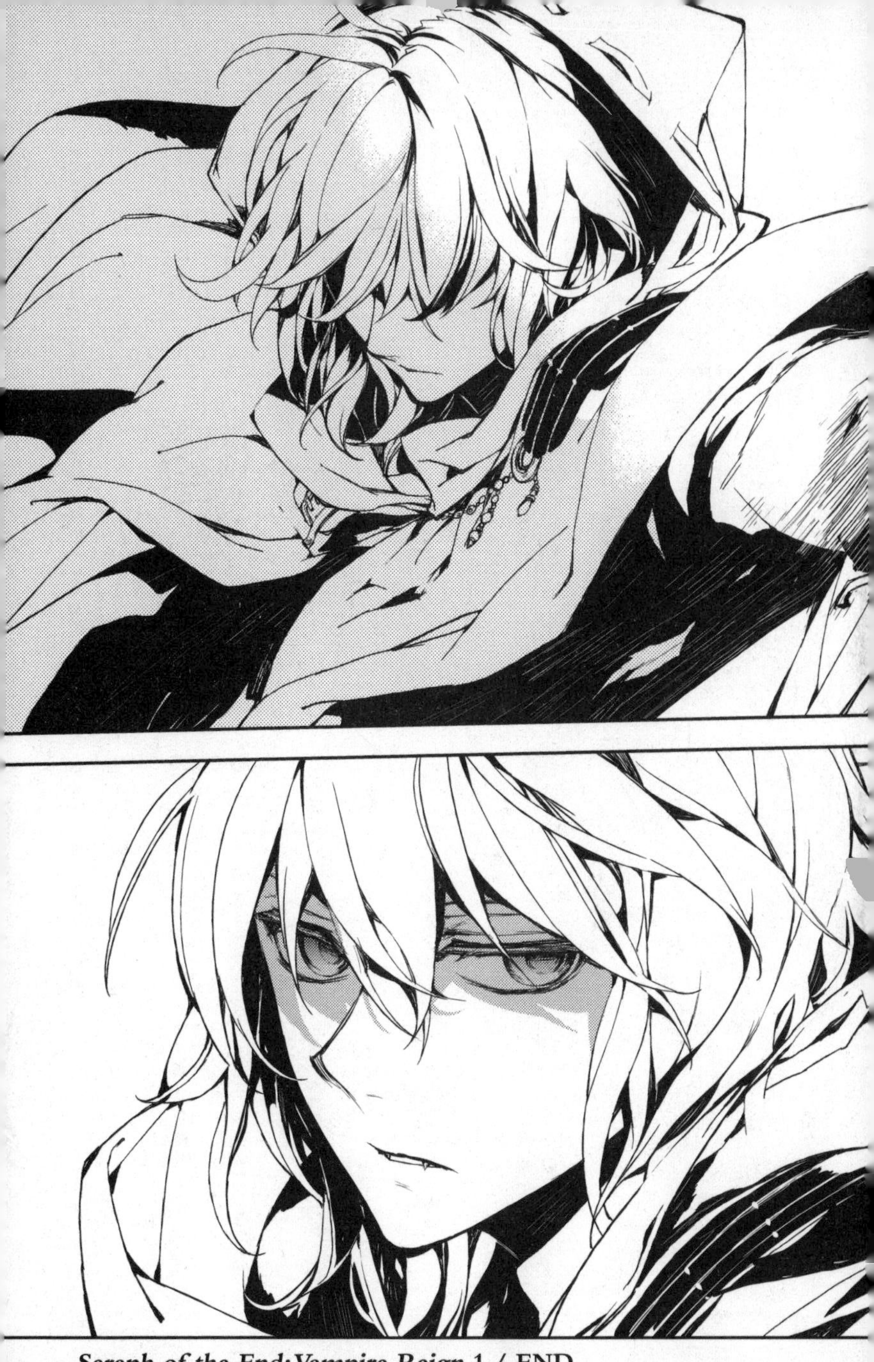

Seraph of the End: Vampire Reign 1 / END

Character Materials Collection by Takaya Kagami

KAGAMI: "WELL, THEY LEFT ME IN CHARGE OF THE BONUS CONTENT, BUT IT'S ONLY VOLUME 1, SO THERE ISN'T ANYTHING I CAN SAY WITHOUT GIVING AWAY SPOILERS!"

MAIN CHARACTER
YUICHIRO HYAKUYA

He gets lonely easily.

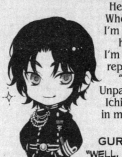

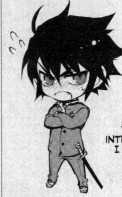

YU: "H-HEY! THAT'S MY INTRODUCTION?! I DON'T GET LONELY EASILY!"

LIEUTENANT COLONEL GUREN ICHINOSE

He's 24. Whenever I'm writing him, I'm always repeating "The Unparalleled Ichinose!" in my head.

GUREN: "WELL, I *WAS* BORN WITH UNPARALLELED GOOD LOOKS."

YU: "HUH? WHAT'S THAT SUPPOSED TO MEAN?"

MIKAELA HYAKUYA

Look Ma, I'm dead!

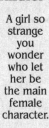

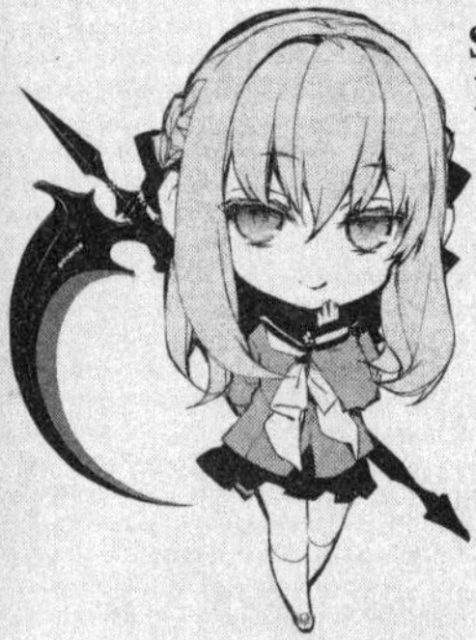

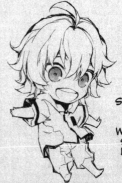

MIKA: "MA? 'MA' WHO? ARE YOU SURE THEY'LL LET YOU GET AWAY WITH WRITING SOMETHING LIKE THAT?"

SHINOA HIRAGI

A girl so strange you wonder who let her be the main female character.

SHINOA: "HOWEVER, I'M STILL BEAUTIFUL."

GUREN: "AND I AM HANDSOME."

SHINOA: "BEAUTIFUL."

GUREN: "HANDSOME."

MIKA: "I THINK WE ALL ARE. PARENTHESIS, EXCEPT YU, END PARENTHESIS."

YU: "CAN I PLEASE KILL THESE IDIOTS?! PLEASE?!"

THAT'S GENERALLY HOW IT GOES WHILE I'M WRITING THE SCRIPT. YES, IT'S SILLY. BUT BEFORE YOU THROW THE BOOK AGAINST THE WALL IN ANGER, LET ME GIVE YOU A GLIMPSE OF SOME PROPER MATERIALS INFORMATION. HERE YOU GO.

The World After the Fall— Eight years after the great disaster, the world's human population has been reduced by nine tenths. In Japan, the population is around 10 million.

Hyakuya Orphanage— The orphanage where Mika and Yu were raised before the end of the world. It was run by the Hyakuya Sect, an organization that was once a large religious group in Japan.

Hyakuya Sect— Once the largest and most influential religious group in Japan. It is shrouded in mystery and has yet to make an appearance in the main story...

Japanese Imperial Demon Army— Most of the details of this organization remain unknown. It appears to be a human faction centered around "The Emperor's Demons," a group of spellcasters headed by the illustrious Hiragi Family. After the end of the world, they began plotting the resurgence of human society.

Four Horsemen of John— Monsters that appeared at the same time as the virus that killed most humans over the age of 13. Little is known about them.

Vampires— Their goals, position in regards to the world, and even their very existence are still a mystery.

Cursed Gear— Weapons with the power to kill vampires, they're acquired by making contracts with demons. The truth behind them is still a mystery. They seem to be a new power, completely unrelated to previously understood types of spellcraft.

Seraph of the End— A being which is still entirely a mystery. Considered one of the greatest taboo subjects before the end of the world, it was researched alongside another taboo subject, "curses."

AFTERWORD

HELLO. NICE TO MEET YOU. I'M TAKAYA KAGAMI, AUTHOR OF NOVELS SUCH AS *THE LEGEND OF THE LEGENDARY HEROES* AND *A DARK RABBIT HAS SEVEN LIVES* FOR THE *FANTASIA BUNKO* LABEL. *JUMP SQUARE* ASKED ME TO PEN THE ORIGINAL SCRIPT FOR THIS STORY. I HOPE YOU ENJOY IT.

I THINK MY EDITOR AND I GOT A LITTLE TOO EXCITED ABOUT THIS PROJECT. FOR JUST THE FIRST CHAPTER, THERE WERE FOUR DIFFERENT VERSIONS AND FIFTEEN DIFFERENT DRAFTS. IT WAS SO RIDICULOUS THAT IT TOOK A YEAR AND A HALF TO COMPLETE. WE HAD MR. FURUYA, WHO WAS STORYBOARDING *KURE-NAI* AT THE TIME, DRAW CONTENT FOR THIS OVER AND OVER. WE ASKED MR. YAMAMOTO FOR FEEDBACK MULTIPLE TIMES. I BLEW DEADLINES FOR *LEGEND* AND *DARK RABBIT* AGAIN AND AGAIN, THINKING THE WHOLE TIME "OH NO, I'VE ANNOUNCED SOMETHING EVERYONE'S GOING TO GET REALLY MAD AT ME FOR" BUT SOMEHOW, HERE WE ARE. I PRAY IT IS SOMETHING READERS WILL LOVE FOR A LONG TIME TO COME.

BY THE WAY, TO THOSE OF YOU THINKING "WHO CARES ABOUT THIS KAGAMI GUY, GIVE US MORE ART BY YAMATO YAMAMOTO!"— I UNDERSTAND. HOWEVER, MR. YAMAMOTO IS CURRENTLY BUSY ENOUGH TO EXPLODE, ILLUSTRATING BOTH *SERAPH OF THE END: VAMPIRE REIGN* AND THE NOVEL *SERAPH OF THE END: GUREN ICHINOSE'S CATASTROPHE AT 16* AT THE SAME TIME. ACCORDINGLY, I DECIDED TO WRITE THE AFTERWORD. STILL, I OFF-HANDEDLY MENTIONED THAT I HAD COME UP WITH A FEW IDEAS, AND IT WOULD BE GREAT IF HE COULD FLESH THEM OUT IN FOUR-PANEL COMICS. HE AGREED! SO THERE WILL BE TWO FOUR-PANEL COMICS ON THE NEXT PAGE.

SO ANYWAY, WE ALL PLAN ON GIVING IT OUR BEST, SO I HOPE YOU KEEP READING!

OH! AND WE'RE RELEASING THE NOVEL SERIES SIMULTANEOUSLY WITH THE MANGA. IT FEATURES FIFTEEN-YEAR-OLD GUREN AS THE MAIN CHARACTER AND CHRONICLES THE LAST EIGHT MONTHS BEFORE THE END OF THE WORLD. CHECK IT OUT!

TAKAYA KAGAMI

Flair

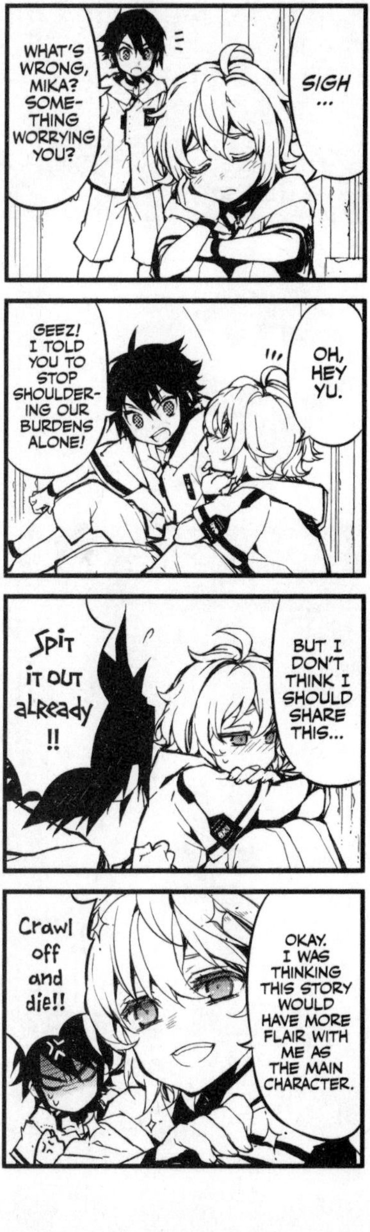
SIGH ...
WHAT'S WRONG, MIKA? SOME-THING WORRYING YOU?
OH, HEY YU.
GEEZ! I TOLD YOU TO STOP SHOULDER-ING OUR BURDENS ALONE!
BUT I DON'T THINK I SHOULD SHARE THIS...
Spit it out already!!
OKAY. I WAS THINKING THIS STORY WOULD HAVE MORE FLAIR WITH ME AS THE MAIN CHARACTER.
Crawl off and die!!

Who's the Main Character?!

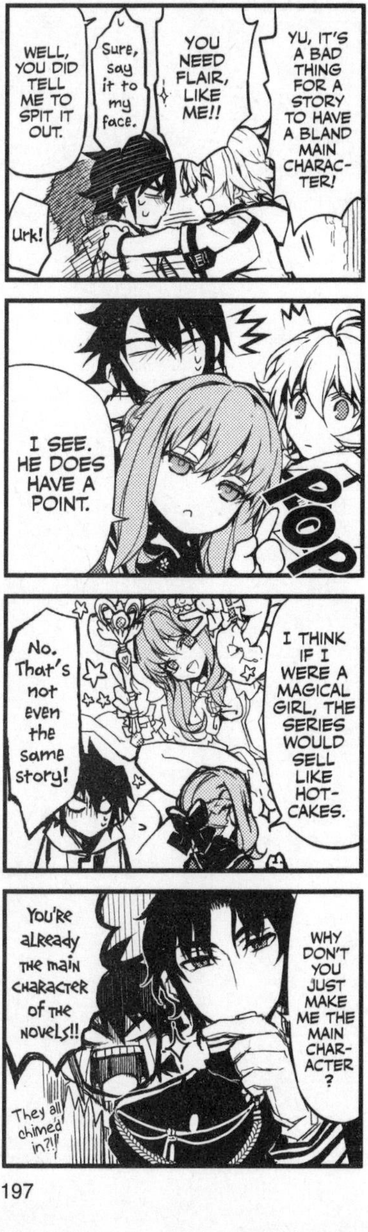
YU, IT'S A BAD THING FOR A STORY TO HAVE A BLAND MAIN CHARAC-TER!
YOU NEED FLAIR, LIKE ME!!
Sure, say it to my face.
WELL, YOU DID TELL ME TO SPIT IT OUT.
Urk!
POP
I SEE. HE DOES HAVE A POINT.
I THINK IF I WERE A MAGICAL GIRL, THE SERIES WOULD SELL LIKE HOT-CAKES.
No. That's not even the same story!
WHY DON'T YOU JUST MAKE ME THE MAIN CHAR-ACTER?
You're already the main character of the novels!!
They all chimed in?!

A brilliant sketch of Yuichiro by the author!

TAKAYA KAGAMI is a prolific light novelist whose works include the action and fantasy series *The Legend of the Legendary Heroes*, which has been adapted into manga, anime and a video game. His previous series, *A Dark Rabbit Has Seven Lives*, also spawned a manga and anime series.

66 Allow me to introduce myself. I wrote *The Legend of the Legendary Heroes* and *A Dark Rabbit Has Seven Lives*. I like curry. I hate deadlines. Pleased to meet you. 99

YAMATO YAMAMOTO, born 1983, is an artist and illustrator whose works include the *Kure-nai* manga and the light novels *Kure-nai*, *9S -Nine S-* and *Denpa Teki na Kanojo*. Both *Denpa Teki na Kanojo* and *Kure-nai* have been adapted into anime.

66 Volume 1 is finally here. I hope you're all looking forward to Yuichiro's adventures. 99

DAISUKE FURUYA previously assisted Yamato Yamamoto with storyboards for *Kure-nai*.

Seraph of the End

—VAMPIRE REIGN—

VOLUME 1
SHONEN JUMP MANGA EDITION

STORY BY **TAKAYA KAGAMI**

ART BY **YAMATO YAMAMOTO**

STORYBOARDS BY **DAISUKE FURUYA**

TRANSLATION **Adrienne Beck**
TOUCH-UP ART & LETTERING **Sabrina Heep**
DESIGN **Shawn Carrico**
EDITOR **Hope Donovan**

OWARI NO SERAPH © 2012 by Takaya Kagami,
Yamato Yamamoto, Daisuke Furuya
All rights reserved. First published in Japan in 2012 by SHUEISHA Inc., Tokyo.
English translation rights arranged by SHUEISHA Inc.

Printed in the U.S.A.

Published by VIZ Media, LLC
P.O. Box 77010
San Francisco, CA 94107

10 9
First printing, June 2014
Ninth printing, April 2021

viz.com

YOU'RE READING THE

WRONG WAY!

SERAPH OF THE END reads from right to left, starting in the upper-right corner. Japanese is read from right to left, meaning that action, sound effects, and word-balloon order are completely reversed from English order.

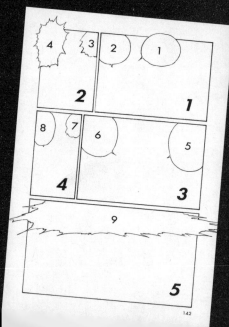